In northern mists; Arctic exploration in early times Volume v.1

Nansen, Fridtjof, 1861-1930

Nabu Public Domain Reprints:

You are holding a reproduction of an original work published before 1923 that is in the public domain in the United States of America, and possibly other countries. You may freely copy and distribute this work as no entity (individual or corporate) has a copyright on the body of the work. This book may contain prior copyright references, and library stamps (as most of these works were scanned from library copies). These have been scanned and retained as part of the historical artifact.

This book may have occasional imperfections such as missing or blurred pages, poor pictures, errant marks, etc. that were either part of the original artifact, or were introduced by the scanning process. We believe this work is culturally important, and despite the imperfections, have elected to bring it back into print as part of our continuing commitment to the preservation of printed works worldwide. We appreciate your understanding of the imperfections in the preservation process, and hope you enjoy this valuable book.

IN NORTHERN MISTS

"THE GOLDEN CLOUDS CURTAINED THE DEEP WHERE IT LAY,
AND IT LOOKED LIKE AN EDEN AWAY, FAR AWAY"

IN NORTHERN MISTS
ARCTIC EXPLORATION IN EARLY TIMES
BY FRIDTJOF NANSEN
G.C.V.O., D.Sc., D.C.L., Ph.D., PROFESSOR OF OCEANO-
GRAPHY IN THE UNIVERSITY OF CHRISTIANIA, ETC.
TRANSLATED BY ARTHUR G. CHATER
ILLUSTRATED

VOLUME ONE

LONDON : WILLIAM HEINEMANN : MCMXI

PRINTED BY
BALLANTYNE & COMPANY LTD
AT THE BALLANTYNE PRESS
TAVISTOCK STREET COVENT GARDEN
LONDON

PREFACE

THIS book owes its existence in the first instance to a rash promise made some years ago to my friend Dr. J. Scott Keltie, of London, that I would try, when time permitted, to contribute a volume on the history of arctic voyages to his series of books on geographical exploration. The subject was an attractive one; I thought I was fairly familiar with it, and did not expect the book to take a very long time when once I made a start with it. On account of other studies it was a long while before I could do this; but when at last I seriously took the work in hand, the subject in return monopolised my whole powers.

It appeared to me that the natural foundation for a history of arctic voyages was in the first place to make clear the main features in the development of knowledge of the North in early times. By tracing how ideas of the Northern World, appearing first in a dim twilight, change from age to age, how the old myths and creations of the imagination are constantly recurring, sometimes in new shapes, and how new ones are added to them, we have a curious insight into the working of the human mind in its endeavour to subject to itself the world and the universe.

But as I went deeper into the subject I became aware that the task was far greater than I had supposed: I found that much that had previously been written about it was not to be depended upon; that frequently one author had copied another, and that errors and opinions which had once gained admission remained embedded in the literary tradition. What had to be done was to confine one's self to the actual sources, and as far as possible to build up independently the best possible structure from the very foundation. But the more

PREFACE

extensive my studies became, the more riddles I perceived—riddle after riddle led to new riddles, and this drew me on farther and farther.

On many points I arrived at views which to some extent conflicted with those previously held. This made it necessary to give, not merely the bare results, but also a great part of the investigations themselves. I have followed the words of Niebuhr, which P. A. Munch took as a motto for " Det norske Folks Historie " :

" Ich werde suchen die Kritik der Geschichte nicht nach dunkeln Gefühlen, sondern forschend, auszuführen, nicht ihre Resultate, welche nur blinde Meinungen stiften, sondern die Untersuchungen selbst in ihrem ganzen Umfange vortragen."

But in this way my book has become something quite different from what was intended, and far larger. I have not reached the history of arctic voyages proper.

Many may think that too much has been included here, and yet what it has been possible to mention here is but an infinitesimal part of the mighty labour in vanished times that makes up our knowledge of the North. The majority of the voyages, and those the most important, on which the first knowledge was based, have left no certain record ; the greatest steps have been taken by unknown pioneers, and if a halo has settled upon a name here and there, it is the halo of legend.

My investigations have made it necessary to go through a great mass of literature, for which I lacked, in part, the linguistic qualifications. For the study of classical, and of mediæval Latin literature, I found in Mr. Amund Sommerfeldt a most able assistant, and most of the translations of Greek and Latin authors are due to him. By his sound and sober criticism of the often difficult original texts he was of great help to me.

In the study of Arabic literature Professor Alexander Seippel has afforded me excellent help, combined with interest in the subject, and he has translated for me the statements of Arab authors about the North.

In the preparation of this work, as so often before, I owe a

PREFACE

deep debt of gratitude to my old friend, Professor Moltke Moe. He has followed my studies from the very beginning with an interest that was highly stimulating; with his extensive knowledge in many fields bordering on those studies he has helped me by word and deed, even more often than appears in the course of the book. His intimate acquaintance with the whole world of myth has been of great importance to the work in many ways; I will mention in particular his large share in the attempt at unravelling the difficult question of Wineland and the Wineland voyages. Here his concurrence was the more valuable to me since at first he disagreed with the conclusions and views at which I had arrived; but the constantly increasing mass of evidence, which he himself helped in great measure to collect, convinced him of their justice, and I have the hope that the inquiry, particularly as regards this subject, will prove to be of value to future historical research.

With his masterly knowledge and insight Professor Alf Torp has given me sound support and advice, especially in difficult linguistic and etymological questions. Many others, whose names are mentioned in the course of the book, have also given me valuable assistance.

I owe special thanks to Dr. Axel Anthon Björnbo, Librarian of the Royal Library of Copenhagen, for his willing collaboration, which has been of great value to me. While these investigations of mine were in progress, he has been occupied in the preparation of his exhaustive and excellent work on the older cartography of Greenland. At his suggestion we have exchanged our manuscripts, and have mutually criticised each other's views according to our best ability; the book will show that this has been productive in many ways. Dr. Björnbo has also assisted me in another way: I have, for instance, obtained copies of several old maps through him. He has, besides, sent me photographs of vignettes and marginal drawings from ancient Icelandic and Norwegian MSS. in the Library of Copenhagen.

Mr. K. Eriksen has drawn the greater part of the reproduc-

PREFACE

tions of the vignettes and the old maps; other illustrations are drawn by me. In the reproduction of the maps it has been sought rather to bring before the reader in a clear form the results to which my studies have led than to produce detailed facsimiles of the originals.

In conclusion I wish to thank Mr. Arthur G. Chater for the careful and intelligent way in which he has executed the English translation. In reading the English proofs I have taken the opportunity of making a number of corrections and additions to the original text.

FRIDTJOF NANSEN

Lysaker, August 1911

CONTENTS

CHAP		PAGE
	INTRODUCTION	1
I.	ANTIQUITY, BEFORE PYTHEAS	7
II.	PYTHEAS OF MASSALIA: THE VOYAGE TO THULE	43
III.	ANTIQUITY, AFTER PYTHEAS	74
IV.	THE EARLY MIDDLE AGES	125
V.	THE AWAKENING OF MEDIÆVAL KNOWLEDGE OF THE NORTH	168
VI.	FINNS, SKRIDFINNS [LAPPS], AND THE FIRST SETTLEMENT OF SCANDINAVIA	203
VII.	THE VOYAGES OF THE NORSEMEN: DISCOVERY OF ICELAND AND GREENLAND	233
VIII.	VOYAGES TO THE UNINHABITED PARTS OF GREENLAND IN THE MIDDLE AGES	279
IX.	WINELAND THE GOOD, THE FORTUNATE ISLES, AND THE DISCOVERY OF AMERICA	312

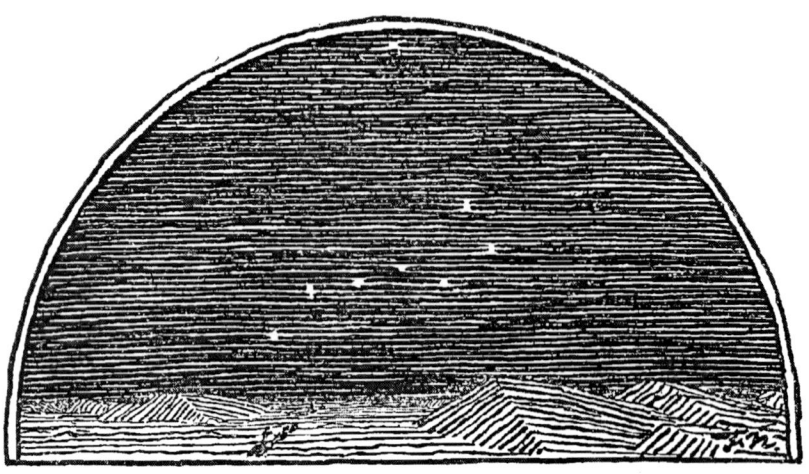

INTRODUCTION

> "For my purpose holds
> To sail beyond the sunset and the baths
> Of all the Western stars until I die."
> Tennyson, "Ulysses."

IN the beginning the world appeared to mankind like a fairy tale; everything that lay beyond the circle of familiar experience was a shifting cloudland of the fancy, a playground for all the fabled beings of mythology; but in the farthest distance, towards the west and north, was the region of darkness and mists, where sea, land and sky were merged into a congealed mass—and at the end of all gaped the immeasurable mouth of the abyss, the awful void of space.

Out of this fairy world, in course of time, the calm and sober lines of the northern landscape appeared. With unspeakable labour the eye of man has forced its way gradually towards the north, over mountains and forests, and tundra, onward through the mists along the vacant shores of the polar sea—the vast stillness, where so much struggle and suffering, so many bitter failures, so many proud victories, have vanished without a trace, muffled beneath the mantle of snow.

When our thoughts go back through the ages in a waking dream, an endless procession passes before us—like a single

INTRO-
DUCTION

mighty epic of the human mind's power of devotion to an idea, right or wrong—a procession of struggling, frost-covered figures in heavy clothes, some erect and powerful, others weak and bent so that they can scarcely drag themselves along before the sledges, many of them emaciated and dying of hunger, cold and scurvy ; but all looking out before them towards the unknown, beyond the sunset, where the goal of their struggle is to be found.

We see a Pytheas, intelligent and courageous, steering northward from the Pillars of Hercules for the discovery of Britain and Northern Europe ; we see hardy Vikings, with an Ottar, a Leif Ericson at their head, sailing in undecked boats across the ocean into ice and tempest and clearing the mists from an unseen world ; we see a Davis, a Baffin forcing their way to the north-west and opening up new routes, while a Hudson, unconquered by ice and winter, finds a lonely grave on a deserted shore, a victim of shabby pilfering. We see the bright form of a Parry surpassing all as he forces himself on ; a Nordenskiöld, broad-shouldered and confident, leading the way to new visions ; a Toll mysteriously disappearing in the drifting ice. We see men driven to despair, shooting and eating each other ; but at the same time we see noble figures, like a De Long, trying to save their journals from destruction, until they sink and die.

Midway in the procession comes a long file of a hundred and thirty men hauling heavy boats and sledges back to the south, but they are falling in their tracks ; one after another they lie there, marking the line of route with their corpses—they are Franklin's men.

And now we come to the latest drama, the Greenlander Brönlund dragging himself forward over the ice-fields through cold and winter darkness, after the leader Mylius-Erichsen and his comrade, Hagen, have both stiffened in the snow during the long and desperate journey. He reaches the depot only to wait for death, knowing that the maps and observations he has faithfully brought with him will be found and saved. He quietly

INTRODUCTION

prepares himself for the silent guest, and writes in his journal in his imperfect Danish:

> Perished,—79 Fjord, after attempt return over the inland ice, in November. I come here in waning moon and could not get farther for frost-bitten feet and darkness.
>
> The bodies of the others are in the middle of the fjord opposite the glacier (about $2\frac{1}{2}$ leagues).
>
> Hagen died November 15 and Mylius about 10 days after.
>
> JÖRGEN BRÖNLUND.

What a story in these few lines! Civilisation bows its head by the grave of this Eskimo.

What were they seeking in the ice and cold? The Norseman who wrote the "King's Mirror" gave the answer six hundred years ago: "If you wish to know what men seek in this land, or why men journey thither in so great danger of their lives, then it is the threefold nature of man which draws him thither. One part of him is emulation and desire of fame, for it is man's nature to go where there is likelihood of great danger, and to make himself famous thereby. Another part is the desire of knowledge, for it is man's nature to wish to know and see those parts of which he has heard, and to find out whether they are as it was told him or not. The third part is the desire of gain, seeing that men seek after riches in every place where they learn that profit is to be had, even though there be great danger in it."

The history of arctic discovery shows how the development of the human race has always been borne along by great illusions. Just as Columbus's discovery of the West Indies was due to a gross error of calculation, so it was the fabled isle of Brazil that drew Cabot out on his voyage, when he found North America. It was fantastic illusions of open polar seas and of passages to the riches of Cathay beyond the ice that drove men back there in spite of one failure after another; and little by little the polar regions were explored. Every complete devotion to an idea yields some profit, even though it be different from that which was expected.

IN NORTHERN MISTS

INTRODUCTION

But from first to last the history of polar exploration is a single mighty manifestation of the power of the unknown over the mind of man, perhaps greater and more evident here than in any other phase of human life. Nowhere else have we won our way more slowly, nowhere else has every new step cost so much trouble, so many privations and sufferings, and certainly nowhere have the resulting discoveries promised fewer material advantages—and nevertheless, new forces have always been found ready to carry the attack farther, to stretch once more the limits of the world.

But if it has cost a struggle, it is not without its joys. Who can describe his emotion when the last difficult ice-floe has been passed, and the sea lies open before him, leading to new realms? Or when the mist clears and mountain-summits shoot up, one behind another farther and farther away, on which the eye of man has never rested, and in the farthest distance peaks appear on the sea-horizon—on the sky above them a yellowish white reflection of the snow-fields—where the imagination pictures new continents? . . .

Ever since the Norsemen's earliest voyages arctic expeditions have certainly brought material advantages to the human race, such as rich fisheries, whaling and sealing, and so on; they have produced scientific results in the knowledge of hitherto unknown regions and conditions; but they have given us far more than this: they have tempered the human will for the conquest of difficulties; they have furnished a school of manliness and self-conquest in the midst of the slackness of varying ages, and have held up noble ideals before the rising generation; they have fed the imagination, have given fairy-tales to the child, and raised the thoughts of its elders above their daily toil. Take arctic travel out of our history, and will it not be poorer? Perhaps we have here the greatest service it has done humanity.

We speak of the first discovery of the North—but how do we know when the first man arrived in the northern regions of the earth? We know nothing but the very last steps in the

INTRODUCTION

migrations of humanity. What a stretch of time there must have been between the period of the Neanderthal man in Europe and the first Pelasgians, or Iberians, or Celts, that we find there in the neolithic age, in the earliest dawn of history. How infinitesimal in comparison with this the whole of the recent period which we call history becomes.

What took place in those long ages is still hidden from us. We only know that ice-age followed ice-age, covering Northern Europe, and to some extent Asia and North America as well, with vast glaciers which obliterated all traces of early human habitation of those regions. Between these ice-ages occurred warmer periods, when men once more made their way northward, to be again driven out by the next advance of the ice-sheet. There are many signs that the human northward migration after the last ice-age, in any case in large districts of Europe, followed fairly close upon the gradual shrinking of the boundary of the inland ice towards the interior of Scandinavia, where the ice-sheath held out longest.

The primitive state—when men wandered about the forests and plains of the warmer parts of the earth, living on what they found by chance—developed by slow gradations in the direction of the first beginnings of culture; on one side to roving hunters and fishers, on the other to agricultural people with a more fixed habitation. The nomad with his herds forms a later stage of civilisation.

The hunting stage of culture was imposed by necessity on the first pioneers and inhabitants of the northernmost and least hospitable regions of the earth. The northern lands must therefore have been first discovered by roving fishermen who came northwards following the rivers and seashores in their search for new fishing-grounds. It was the scouting eye of a hunter that first saw a sea-beach in the dreamy light of a summer night, and sought to penetrate the heavy gloom of the polar sea. And that far-travelled hunter fell asleep in the snowdrift while the northern lights played over him as a funeral fire, the first victim of the polar night's iron grasp.

IN NORTHERN MISTS

INTRO-
DUCTION

Long afterwards came the nomad and the agriculturist and established themselves in the track of the hunter.

This was thousands of years before any written history, and of these earliest colonisations we know nothing but what the chance remains we find in the ground can tell us, and these are very few and very uncertain.

It is not until we come far down into the full daylight of history that we find men setting out with the conscious purpose of exploring the unknown for its own sake. With those early hunters, it was doubtless new ground and new game that drew them on, but they too were attracted, consciously or unconsciously, by the spirit of adventure and the unknown—so deep in the soul of man does this divine force lie, the mainspring, perhaps, of the greatest of our actions. In every part of the world and in every age it has driven man forward on the path of evolution, and as long as the human ear can hear the breaking of waves over deep seas, as long as the human eye can follow the track of the northern lights over silent snow-fields, as long as human thought seeks distant worlds in infinite space, so long will the fascination of the unknown carry the human mind forward and upward.

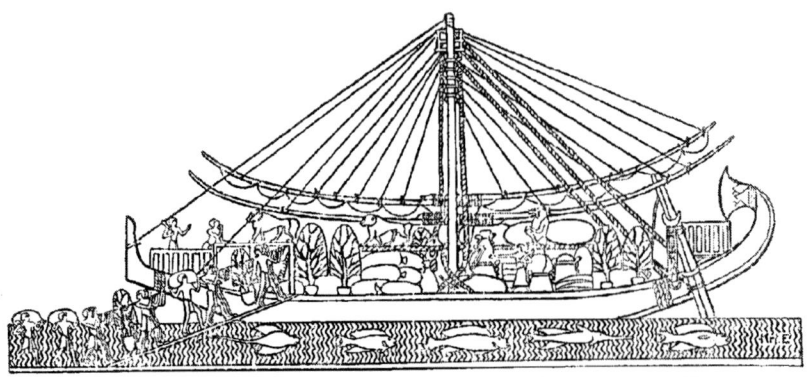

Ship of the Egyptian Punt expedition, 17th century B.C. (J. DÜMICHEN)

CHAPTER I

ANTIQUITY, BEFORE PYTHEAS

THE learned world of early antiquity had nothing but a vague premonition of the North. Along the routes of traffic commercial relations were established at a very early time with the northern lands. At first these ran perhaps along the rivers of Russia and Eastern Germany to the Baltic, afterwards along the rivers of Central Europe as well. But the information which reached the Mediterranean peoples by these routes had to go through many intermediaries with various languages, and for this reason it long remained vague and uncertain.

What the people of antiquity did not know, they supplied by poetical and mythical conceptions; and in time there grew up about the outer limits of the world, especially on the north, a whole cycle of legend which was to lay the foundation of ideas of the polar regions for thousands of years, far into the Middle Ages, and long after trustworthy knowledge had been won, even by the voyages of the Norsemen themselves.

Long before people knew whether there were lands and seas far in the north, those who studied the stars had observed that there were some bodies in the northern sky which never set, and that there was a point in the vault of heaven which

CHAPTER I

Origin of the word Arctic

never changed its place. In time, they also found that, as they moved northwards, the circle surrounding the stars that were always visible became larger, and they saw that these in their daily movements described orbits about the fixed point or pole of the heavens. The ancient Chaldeans had already found this out. From this observation it was but a short step to the deduction that the earth could not be flat, as the popular idea made it, but must in one way or another be spherical, and that if one went far enough to the north, these stars would be right over one's head. To the Greeks a circle drawn through the constellation of the Great Bear, which they called "Arktos," formed the limit of the stars that were always visible. This limit was therefore called the Bear's circle, or the "Arctic Circle," and thus this designation for the northernmost regions of the earth is derived from the sky.

The world according to Hecatæus (BUNBURY)

According to the common Greek idea it was the countries of the Mediterranean and of the East that formed the disc of the earth, or "œcumene" (the habitable world). Around this disc, according to the Homeric songs (the Iliad was put into writing about 900 B.C.), flowed the all-embracing river "Oceanus," the end of the earth and the limit of heaven. This deep, tireless, quietly flowing river, whose stream turned back upon itself, was the origin and the end of all things; it

ANTIQUITY, BEFORE PYTHEAS

was not only the father of the Oceanides and of the rivers, but also the source whence came gods and men. Nothing definite is said of this river's farther boundary; perhaps unknown lands belonging to another world whereon the sky rested were there; in any case we meet later, as in Hesiod, with ideas of lands beyond the Ocean, the Hesperides, Erythea, and the

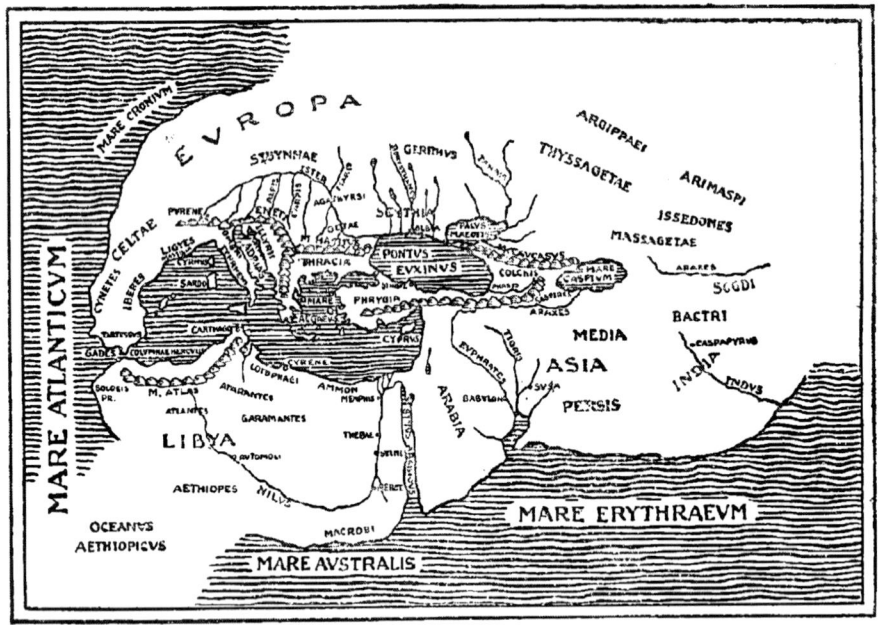

The world according to the ideas of Herodotus (J. MURRAY)

Isles of the Blest, which were probably derived from Phœnician tales. Originally conceived as a deep-flowing river, Oceanus became later the all-embracing empty ocean, which was different from the known sea (the Mediterranean) with its known coasts, even though connected with it. Herodotus (484-424 B.C.) is perhaps the first who used the name in this sense; he definitely rejects the idea of Oceanus as a river and denies that the "œcumene" should be drawn round, as though with a pair of compasses, as the Ionian geographers (Hecatæus, for example) thought. He considered it proved that the earth's disc on the western side, and probably also on the south, was surrounded by the ocean, but said that no one could know

Herodotus on the ocean

IN NORTHERN MISTS

CHAPTER I

whether this was also the case on the north and north-east. In opposition to Hecatæus[1] and the Ionian geographers (the school of Miletus) he asserted that the Caspian Sea was not a bay of the northern Oceanus, but an independent inland sea. Thus the "œcumene" became extended into the unknown on the north-east. He mentions several peoples as dwelling farthest north; but to the north of them were desert regions and inaccessible mountains; how far they reached he does not say.

He thus left the question undetermined, because, with the sound cool-headedness of the inquirer, which made him in a sense the founder of physical geography, he trusted to certain observations rather than to uncertain speculations; and therefore he maintained that the geographers of the Ionian school had not provided adequate proofs that the world was really surrounded by sea on all sides. But nevertheless, it was, perhaps, his final opinion that the earth's disc swam like an island in Oceanus.

Division of the ocean

This common name for the ocean was soon dropped, and men spoke instead of the Outer Sea beyond the Pillars of Hercules in contradistinction to the Inner Sea (i.e., the Mediterranean). The Outer Sea was also called the Atlantic Sea after Atlas. This name is first found in Herodotus. South of Asia was the Southern Ocean or the Erythræan Sea (the Red Sea and Indian Ocean). North of Europe and Asia was the Northern Ocean; and the Caspian Sea was a bay of this, in the opinion of the majority. Doubtless, most people thought that these various oceans were connected; but the common name Oceanus does not reappear as applied to them until the second century B.C.[2]

Homeric ideas of the universe

According to the Homeric conception the universe was to be imagined somewhat as a hollow globe, divided in two by the disc of the earth and its encircling Oceanus; the upper

[1] Hecatæus of Miletus (549–after 486 B.C.) was the best-known geographer of the Ionian school. He made a map of the world, and summarised the contemporary Greek ideas of geography.

[2] Cf. Kretschmer, 1892, pp. 41-42.

ANTIQUITY, BEFORE PYTHEAS

hemisphere was that of light, or the heaven; the lower one Tartarus, hidden in eternal darkness. Hades lay beneath the earth, and Tartarus was as far below Hades as the sky was above the earth. The solid vault of heaven was borne by Atlas, but its extremities certainly rested upon Oceanus (or its outer boundary), or at least were contained thereby. According to Hesiod (about 800 B.C.) an anvil falling from heaven would not reach earth till the tenth day, and from the earth it would fall for nine days and nine nights and not reach the bottom of Tartarus until the tenth. This underworld is filled to the brim with triple darkness, and the Titans have been hurled into it and cannot come out. On the brink the limits of the earth, the waste Oceanus, black Tartarus, and the starry heaven all coincide. Tartarus is a deep gulf at which even the gods shudder; in a whole year it would be impossible to search through it.[1]

So early do we find three conceptions which two thousand years later still formed the foundation of the doctrine of the earth's outer limits, especially on the north: (1) the all-embracing Oceanus or empty ocean; (2) the coincidence of sky, sea, land and underworld at the uttermost edge; and lastly (3) the dismal gulf into which even the gods were afraid of falling.

These or similar ideas still obtained long after the mathematical geographers had conceived the earth as a sphere. Pythagoras (568–about 494 B.C.) was probably the first to proclaim the doctrine of the spherical form of the earth. He relied less upon observation than upon the speculative idea that the sphere was the most perfect form. Before him Anaximander of Miletus (611–after 547 B.C.), to whom are attributed the invention of the gnomon or sun-dial, and the first representation of the earth's disc on a map, had maintained that the earth was a cylinder floating in space; the inhabited part was the upper flat end. His pupil Anaximenes (second half of the sixth century B.C.) thought that the earth had the form of a trapezium, supported by the air beneath, which it

CHAPTER I

Spherical form of the earth

[1] Berger, 1894, p. 13.

IN NORTHERN MISTS

CHAPTER I

compressed like the lid of a vase; while before him Thales of Miletus (640–about 548 B.C.) was inclined to hold that the earth's disc swam on the surface of the ocean, in the middle of the hollow sphere of heaven, and that earthquakes were caused by movements of the waters.[1]

Doctrine of zones

Parmenides of Elea (about 460 B.C.) divided the earth's sphere into five zones or belts, of which three were uninhabitable: the zone of heat, or the scorched belt round the equator, and the two zones of cold at the poles. Between the warmth and the cold there were on either side of the hot zone two temperate zones where men might live. This division was originally derived from the five zones of the heavens, where the Arctic Circle formed the boundary of the northern stars that are always visible, and the tropics that of the zone dominated by the sun. Pythagoras seems to have been the first to transfer it to the globe, the centre of the universe.[2] This idea of the earth's five habitable and uninhabitable zones was current till nearly the end of the Middle Ages; but at the same time one finds, often far on in the Middle Ages, the former conceptions of the empty ocean encircling all, and of the "œcumene" swimming in it as an island. Occasionally we meet with a vast unknown continent beyond this ocean, belonging to another world, which no one can reach.[3] Together

The abyss

with these theories, though not very conspicuously, the belief in the immeasurable gulf at the edge of the world also persisted; and this became the "Ginnungagap" of our forefathers.

The conception of the earth's form and of its uttermost limits was thus by no means consistent, and on some points it was contradictory. We must always, and especially in dealing with past times, distinguish between the views of the scientific world and those of ordinary people, two aspects which were often hopelessly mixed together. And again in the scientific

---

[1] Men like Empedocles, Leucippus, Heraclitus, Anaxagoras, and even Herodotus entertained the naive view that the earth was a disc.

[2] Cf. Kretschmer, 1892, p. 99; Berger ii., 1889, p. 36.

[3] Cf. Theopompus (about 340 B.C.) in Ælian, "Varia," iii. c. 18.

ANTIQUITY, BEFORE PYTHEAS

world we must distinguish between the mathematical-physical geographers and the historical, since the latter dealt more with descriptions and were apt to follow accounts and legends rather than what was taught by physical observations.

The world which the Greeks really knew was bounded in the earlier period on the north by the Balkans. These again gave rise to the mythical Rhipæan Mountains, which were soon moved farther to the north or north-east[1] as knowledge increased, and so they and the Alps were made the northern boundary of the known world. As to what lay farther off, the Greeks had very vague ideas; they seem to have thought that the frozen polar countries began there, where it was so cold that people had to wear breeches like the Scythians; or else it was a good climate, since it lay north of the north wind which came from the Rhipæan Mountains. But that some genuine information about the North had reached them as early as the time of the Odyssey seems to be shown by the tale of the Læstrygons—who had the long day, and whose shepherds, driving their flocks in at evening, could call to those who were setting out in the morning, since the paths of day and night were with them so close to one another—and of the Cimmerians at the gates of the underworld, who lived in a land of fog, on the shores of Oceanus, in eternal cheerless night. It is true that the poet seems to have imagined these countries somewhere in the east or north-east, probably by the Black Sea; for Odysseus came from the Læstrygons to the isle of Æa "by the mansions and dancing-places of the Dawn and by the place where the sun rises." And from Æa the Greek hero steered right out into the night and the mist

---

[1] The celebrated physician Hippocrates (470-364 B.C.) makes Scythia extend on the north to the Rhipæan Mountains, which stretch far enough to be just below the Great Bear. From them comes the north wind, which therefore does not blow farther north, so that there must be a milder climate where the Hyperboreans dwell. The Rhipæan Mountains had become altogether mythical, but seem often to have been connected with the Ural and placed north of Scythia; sometimes also they were connected with the Alps, or with the mountains farther east.

IN NORTHERN MISTS

CHAPTER I

on the dangerous waters of Oceanus and came to the Cimmerians,[1] who must therefore have dwelt beyond the sunrise, shrouded in cloud and fogs. It might be supposed that it was natural to the poet to believe that there must be night beyond the sunrise and on the way to the descent to the nether regions; but it is, perhaps, more probable that both the long day and the darkness and fog are an echo of tales about the northern summer and the long winter night, and that these tales reached the Greeks by the trade-routes along the Russian rivers and across the Black Sea, for which reason the districts where these marvels were to be found were reported to lie in that direction. A find in the passage-graves of Mycenæ (fourteenth to twelfth century B.C.) of beads made of amber from the Baltic,[2] besides many pieces of amber from the period of the Dorian migration (before the tenth century) found during the recent English excavations of the temple of Artemis at Sparta,[3] furnish certain evidence that the Greek world had intercourse with the Baltic countries long before the Odyssey was put into writing in the

---

[1] The Cimmerians of the Odyssey (xi. 14) are undoubtedly the same as the historical Cimmerians of the districts north of the Black Sea, who made several inroads into Asia Minor in the eighth century, and whose name was long preserved in the Cimmerian Bosphorus. Cf. Niese, 1882, p. 224, and K. Kretschmer, 1892, p. 7. W. Christ [1866, pp. 131-132] connects the name with the Cimbri of Jutland, whose name is alleged to have been somewhat modified under the influence of the Phœnician "kamar," dark, which may be doubtful; but Posidonius seems to have been the first to take Cimmerii and Cimbri for the same name [cf. Strabo, vii. 293], and there is nothing improbable in the supposition that the wandering Cimbri may have reached the Black Sea and been the same people as the Cimmerians, who were remarkable just in the same way for their migrations. Similarly, we find the Goths both on the shores of the Baltic and by the Black Sea, where we first meet with them in literature.

[2] O. Helm of Danzig has shown by chemical analysis that the amber of the Mycenæ beads contains 8 per cent. of succinic acid, and is thus similar to that found on the Baltic and the North Sea, and unlike all known amber from districts farther south, Sicily, Upper Italy or elsewhere. Cf. Schuchhardt, 1890, p. 223, f., and Kretschmer, 1892, p. 10.

[3] "The Times" of Sept. 28, 1909, pp. 9-10. A. W. Brogger [1909, p. 239] mentions a find from a grave at Corinth of six necklaces of amber, of the neolithic period, which is preserved in the Museum für Völkerkunde at Berlin. Brogger informs me that nothing has been published about this find, which was

ANTIQUITY, BEFORE PYTHEAS

eighth century, even though the northern lands of this poem seem to have been limited by a communication by sea between the Black Sea and the Adriatic, running north of the Balkan peninsula. Perhaps this imaginary communication may have been conceived as going by the Ister (Danube), which, at any rate later, was thought to have another outlet in the Adriatic. We may also find echoes of tales about the dark winter and light summer of the North in Sophocles's tragedy, where we are told that Orithyia was carried off by Boreas and borne over

> . . the whole mirror of the sea, to the edge of the earth,
> To the source of primæval night, where the vault of heaven ends,
> Where lies the ancient garden of Phœbus[1]

—though images of this sort may also be due to an idea that the sun remained during the night beyond the northern regions.

According to a comparatively late Greek conception there was in the far North a happy people called the Hyperboreans. They dwelt "under the shining way" (the clear northern sky) north of the roaring Boreas, so far that this cold north wind could not reach them, and therefore enjoyed a splendid climate. They did not live in houses, but in woods and groves. With them injustice and war were unknown, they were untouched by age or sickness; at joyous sacrificial feasts, with golden laurel-wreaths in their hair, and amid song and the sound of the cithara and the dancing of maidens, they led a careless existence in undisturbed gladness, and reached an immense age. When they were tired of life they threw themselves, after having eaten and drunk, joyfully and with wreaths in their hair, into the sea from a particular cliff (according to Mela and Pliny, following Hecatæus of Abdera). Among other qualities they had the power of flying, and one of them, Abaris, flew round the world on an arrow. While some geographers, especially

bought in 1877 from Prof. Aus'm Weerth of Kessenich, near Bonn. Prof. Schaafhausen briefly mentioned it at the congress at Stockholm in 1874 [Congrès internat. d'anthrop. et d'archéol. de Stockholm, Compte rendu, 1874, ii. p. 816]. Assuming that this is Baltic or North Sea amber, it points to an intercourse of even far greater antiquity, which is also probable.

[1] Strabo, vii. 295.

CHAPTER I

the Ionians, placed them in the northern regions, beyond the Rhipæan Mountains,[1] Hecatæus of Abdera (first half of the third century B.C.), who wrote a work about the Hyperboreans, collected from various sources, and more like a novel than anything else, declares that they dwelt far beyond the accessible regions, on the island of Elixœa in the farthest northern Oceanus, where the tired stars sink to rest, and where the moon is so near that one can easily distinguish the inequalities of its surface. Leto was born there, and therefore Apollo is more honoured with them than other gods. There is a marvellous temple, round like a sphere,[2] which floats freely in the air borne by wings, and which is rich in offerings. To this holy island Apollo came every ninth year; according to some authorities he came through the air in a car drawn by swans. During his visit the god himself played the cithara and danced without ceasing from the spring equinox to the rising of the Pleiades. The Boreads were hereditary kings of the island, and were likewise keepers of the sanctuary; they were descendants of Boreas and Chione. Three giant brothers, twelve feet high, performed the service of priests. When they offered the sacrifice and sang the sacred hymns to the sound of the cithara, whole clouds of swans came from the Rhipæan Mountains, surrounded the temple and settled upon it, joining in the sacred song.

Theopompus (Philip of Macedon's time) has given us, if we may trust Ælian's account ["Varia," iii. c. 18; about 200 A.D.], a remarkable variation of the Hyperborean legend in combination with others:

Europe, Asia, and Africa were islands surrounded by Oceanus; only that land which lay outside this world was a continent; its size was immense. The animals there were huge, the men were not only double our size, but lived twice

---

[1] Damastes of Sigeum (about 450 B.C., and contemporary with Herodotus) says that "beyond the Scythians dwell the Issedonians, beyond these again the Arimaspians, and beyond them are the Rhipæan Mountains, from which the north wind blows, and which are never free from snow. On the other side of the mountains are the Hyperboreans who spread down to the sea."

[2] Since the form of the sphere was the most perfect according to the opinion of the Pythagoreans.

ANTIQUITY, BEFORE PYTHEAS

as long as we. Among many great towns there were two in particular greater than the rest, and with no resemblance to one another ; they were called Machimos (the warlike) and Eusebes (the pious). The description of the latter's peaceful inhabitants has most features in common with the Hyperborean legend. The warlike inhabitants of Machimos, on the other hand, are born armed, wage war continually, and oppress their neighbours, so that this one city rules over many peoples, but its inhabitants are no less than two millions. It is true that they sometimes die of disease, but that happens seldom, since for the most part they are killed in war, by stones, or wood [that is, clubs], for they are invulnerable to iron. They have such superfluity of gold and silver that with them gold is of less value than iron is with us. Once indeed they made an expedition to our island [that is, Europe], came over the Ocean ten millions strong and arrived at the land of the Hyperboreans. But when they learned that these were the happy ones of our earth, and found their mode of life bad, poverty-stricken and despicable, they did not think it worth while to proceed farther.

Among them dwell men called Meropians, in many great cities. On the border of their country is a place which bears the significant name Anostos (without return), and resembles a gulf (" chiasma "). There reigns there neither darkness nor light, but a veil of mist of a dirty red colour lies over it. Two streams flow about this place, of which one is called Hedone (the stream of gladness), the other Lype (the stream of sorrow), and by the banks of each stand trees of the size of a great plane-tree. The fruit of the trees by the river of sorrow has the effect that any one who eats of it sheds so many tears that for the rest of his life he melts away in tears and so dies. The other trees that grow by the river of gladness bear fruit of a quite different kind. With him who tastes it all former desires come to rest; even what he has passionately loved passes into oblivion, he becomes gradually younger and goes once more through the previous stages of his existence in reverse order. From an old man he passes to the prime of life, becomes a youth, a boy, and then a child, and with that he is used up. Ælian adds : " And if the Chionian's [that is, Theopompus of Chios] tale appears credible to any one, then he may be believed, but to me he seems to be a mythologist, both in this and in other things."

There can be no doubt that the regions which we hear of in this story, with the Hyperboreans, the enormous quantities of gold, the gulf without return, and so on, were imagined as situated beyond the sea in the North ; and in the description of the warlike people of Machimos who came in great hordes southward over the sea, one might almost be tempted to think of warlike northerners, who were slain with stones and clubs, but not with iron, perhaps because they had not yet discovered the use of iron.[1]

[1] It was, moreover, a common belief in mediæval times that people who were connected with the other world could not be killed by iron.

IN NORTHERN MISTS

CHAPTER I

The legend of the happy Hyperboreans in the North has arisen from an error of popular etymology, and it has here been treated at some length as an example of how geographical myths may originate and develop.[1] The name in its original form was certainly the designation of those who brought offerings to the shrine of Apollo at Delphi (perhaps also in Delos). They were designated as " perpheroi " or " hyper-pheroi " (bringers over), which again in certain northern Greek dialects took the forms of " hyper-phoroi " or " hyper-boroi; " this, by an error, became connected in later times with " Boreas," and their home was consequently transferred to the North, many customs of the worship of Apollo being transferred with it [see O. Crusius, 1890, col. 2830]. This gives at the same time a natural explanation of their many peculiarities, their sanctity, their power of flight and the arrow (Apollo's arrow), their ceremonial feasts, and their throwing themselves from a certain cliff,[2] and so on, all of which is

---

[1] " Hyperboreans " are first mentioned in certain poems doubtfully attributed to Hesiod, but which can scarcely be later than the 7th century B.C. The full development of the myth is first found in Pindar (about 470 B.C.); but his Hyperboreans cannot be considered as dwelling especially in the north; their home, to which " the strange path could be found neither by sea nor by land," lay rather beyond the sea in the far west, and thither came Perseus borne by wings on his way to Medusa

[2] This idea can be traced back to Delphi, where any one who had incurred the god's displeasure was thrown from a cliff. Something similar happened at the annual festivals of Apollo at Leucas, where he who was chosen as a victim to ward off evil threw himself from the Leucadian rock into the sea It is true that all sorts of feathers and birds were fastened to the victims to act as a parachute, and after their fall they were rescued by boats and taken beyond the frontier, as bearers of a curse. According to some it was the priests themselves who made this leap

Among the Germanic peoples, if we may believe " Gautrek's Saga " [cf J. Grimm, 1854, p. 486; Ranisch, 1900, p. lxxvii. f.], there existed the custom that the elders of the tribe, when tired of life, used to cast themselves down from a high crag, called " ætternis stapi " (the tribal cliff), so as to die without sickness and go to Odin. As a reward for faithful service the head of the house took his thrall with him in the leap, so that he too might come thither. After Skapnartungr had divided the inheritance, he and his wife were conducted to the cliff by their children, and they went joyfully to Odin. This reminds one strongly of the happy

ANTIQUITY, BEFORE PYTHEAS

derived from the worship of Apollo. Apollonius of Rhodes (about 200 B.C.) relates that according to the legends of the Celts (in North Italy?) amber originated from the tears of Apollo, which he shed by thousands when he came to the holy people of the Hyperboreans and forsook the shining heaven.

When, after the conquests of Alexander, the Greeks became acquainted with the mythical world of India, they naturally connected the Indians' legendary country, "Uttara Kuru," beyond the Himalayas, with the country of the Hyperboreans. "This land is not too cold, not too warm, free from disease; care and sorrow are unknown there; the earth is without dust and sweetly perfumed; the rivers run in beds of gold, and instead of pebbles they roll down pearls and precious stones."

The mythical singer Aristeas of Proconnesus (sixth century?)—to whom was attributed the poem "Arimaspeia"—is said (according to Herodotus) to have penetrated into the country of the Scythians as far as the northernmost people, the Issedonians. The latter told him of the one-eyed, long-haired Arimaspians, who lived still farther north, at the uttermost end of the world, before the cave from which Boreas rushes forth. On their northern border dwelt the Griffins, lion-like monsters with the wings and beaks of eagles;[1] they were the guardians of the gold which the earth sends forth of

Hyperboreans. Thietmar of Merseburg (about A.D. 1000) has a similar legend about the tribal cliff. It is probable that the Germanic peoples in very early times, like other peoples—the Eskimo, for example—may have had the custom of taking the lives of the old and useless, or that these may have taken their own lives, by throwing themselves into the sea, for instance, as occurs among the Eskimo. On the other hand, it seems very doubtful that there should have been such tribal cliffs, and it is more probable that this legend is of literary origin and derived from the cliffs of Delphi and Leucas, which through the Hyperborean legend came down to the Roman authors Mela and Pliny, and from them was handed on to the writers of the Middle Ages and to the scribe of the "Gautrek Saga." It has been thought that many such "atte-stupar" can be pointed out in southern Sweden, but they seem all to be of recent date, and may have been suggested by this saga.

[1] These may be the architectonical figures on the roof of the temple of Delphi, transferred to the North together with the Hyperboreans At Delphi they were no doubt regarded as guardians of the temple's treasures.

IN NORTHERN MISTS

itself. But still farther north, as far as the sea, were the Hyperboreans.

But the learned Herodotus (about 450 B.C.) doubted that the Hyperboreans dwelt to the north of Boreas; for, said he, if there are people north of the north wind, then there must also be people south of the south wind. Neither did he credit the Scythians' tales about goat-footed people [1] and Sleepers far in the North. Just as little did this sceptic believe that the air of Scythia was full of feathers which prevented all seeing and moving; it was, he thought, continuous snowfall that the Scythians described thus. On the other hand, he certainly believed in the Amazons, though whether they dwelt in the North, as later authors considered, he does not say.

The idea of the Sleepers, who slept for six months, may very probably be due to legendary tales of the long northern winter-night, the length of which was fixed at six months by theoretical speculations, these tales being confused with reports that the people of Scythia slept a great part of the winter, as even to-day the peasants are said to do in certain parts of Russia, where they almost hibernate. Nor must the possibility be overlooked of stories about the winter's sleep of animals, bears, for example, being transferred to men.

Later learned geographers, in spite of the scepticism of Herodotus, occupied themselves in assigning to the Hyperboreans a dwelling-place in the unknown. The founder of scientific geography, Eratosthenes of Cyrene (275-195 B.C.), declared that Herodotus's method of disproving the existence of the Hyperboreans was ridiculous. [Cf. Strabo, i. 61.]

Even so long as five hundred years after Herodotus, Pliny declared the Hyperboreans to be a historical people, whose existence could not be doubted; and on the maps of the Middle Ages we always find them in the most northern inhabited regions, together with the Amazons and other peoples; we even find the Hyperborean Mountains (" Hyperborei Montes ")

---

[1] This idea has been explained as being derived from stories of people dressed in breeches of goats' skin.

ANTIQUITY, BEFORE PYTHEAS

in Northern Europe and the Hyperborean Sea ("Oceanus Hyperboreus") to the north of them. Adam of Bremen (eleventh century) thought that the Scandinavians were the Hyperboreans.

Archæological finds show that as long ago as the Scandinavian Bronze Age, or before, there must have been some sort of communication between the Mediterranean and the northern lands. One of the earliest trade-routes between the Mediterranean and the Baltic certainly went from the Black Sea up the navigable river Borysthenes (Dnieper), of which early mention is made by the Greeks, thence along its tributary the Bug to the Vistula, and down the latter to the coast. We also find this route in common use in later antiquity. When we first meet with the Goths in history they are established at both ends of it, by the mouths of the Vistula and of the Borysthenes. The Eruli, who came from the North, are also mentioned by the side of the Goths on the Black Sea. What the wandering nation of the Cimmerians was we do not know, but, as before remarked (p. 14), they may have been Cimbri who in those early times had migrated to the northern shore of the Black Sea by this very route. This trade-route was well known in its details to our forefathers in Scandinavia, which likewise points to an ancient communication. Somewhat later it is probable that men travelled from the Baltic up the Vistula and across to the March, a tributary of the Danube, and so either down this river to the Black Sea or overland to the Adriatic. A similar line of communication certainly ran between the North Sea and the

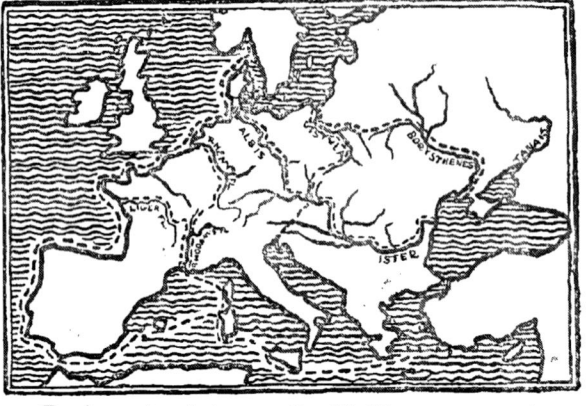

Trade-routes between the Mediterranean and the North

Trade-routes between the Mediterranean and the North

Mediterranean along the Elbe to the Adriatic, and up the Rhine across to the Rhone and down this to the coast, or across the Alps to the Po.

But very early there was also communication by sea along the coasts of western Europe between the Mediterranean and the North. This is shown amongst other things by the distribution, about 2000 B.C., of cromlechs over Sicily, Corsica, Portugal and the north of Spain, Brittany, the British Isles,

Cromlechs : on the right, in Portugal (after Cartailhac) ; on the left, in Denmark (after S. Müller)

the North Sea coast of Germany, Denmark and southern Scandinavia as far as Bohuslen [cf. S. Müller, 1909, p. 24 f.], and perhaps farther. Somewhat later, in the middle of the second millennium B.C., the passage-graves or chambered barrows followed the same route northward from the Mediterranean. That this sea-communication was comparatively active in those far-off times is proved by the fact that cromlechs, which originated in the grave-chambers of the beginning of the Mycenæan period in the eastern Mediterranean, reached Denmark, by this much longer route round the coast, before the single graves, which were an older form in the Mediterranean countries, but which spread by the slower route overland, through Central Europe.

That as far back as the Stone Age there was communication by one way or another, perhaps along the coast between Spain and the shore of the North Sea or the Baltic, appears probable from the fact that amber beads have been found in the Iberian peninsula containing 2 per cent. of succinic acid, a proportion which is taken to indicate its northern (Baltic) origin [cf. L. Siret, 1909, p. 138].

ANTIQUITY, BEFORE PYTHEAS

On account of the many intermediaries, speaking different languages, through which it passed, the information which reached the Mediterranean by these various routes was very defective. According to Herodotus [iv. 24] the Scythians on their trading journeys to the bald-headed Agrippæans required no fewer than seven different interpreters to enable them to barter with the peoples on the way. Their first more direct knowledge of northern and western Europe must certainly have reached the Mediterranean peoples through the tin trade and the amber trade. It is worth remarking that it was precisely these two articles, representing two powerful sides of human nature, utility and the love of ornament, that were to be of such great importance also as regards knowledge of the North.

Ancient Egyptian ship; from a grave in western Thebes (after R. Lepsius)

We do not know when, where, or how tin first came into use, the metal which, together with copper, was as important in the Bronze Age as iron is in our time. In Egypt it is found in the oldest pyramid-graves, and in the third millennium B.C. bronze was in general use there, though we know not whence the tin came to make it. Tin-ore occurs in comparatively few places on the earth, and if China, which formed a world by itself, be excluded, the only places where we know that the metal was obtained in ancient times are north-west Spain, the Cassiterides (probably in Brittany) and Cornwall,[1] which still possesses rich deposits; and as far as we can trace history back, the civilised peoples of the Mediterranean and the Orient obtained their tin from western Europe.[2] If

---

[1] Strabo [iii. 147] and Diodorus [v. 38], following Posidonius, mention these three districts as the places where tin was found.

[2] In the three districts named tin oxide (SnO_2) occurs in lodes in the solid rock,

CHAPTER I

IN NORTHERN MISTS

the first tin in Egypt and in the valley of the Euphrates also came from there, the civilisation of western Europe, implied by regular working of mines, would be given a venerable age which could almost rival the oldest civilisations of the Mediterranean. But this is difficult to believe, as we should expect to find traces of this early connection with Egypt along the trade-routes between that country and the place of origin of the tin; and no archæological evidence to prove this is at present forthcoming.[1]

This possibility is nevertheless not wholly excluded: finds of beads of northern (?) amber in Egyptian graves of the Fifth Dynasty (about 3500 B.C.) may point to ancient unknown communication with the farthest parts of Europe. In Spain, too, neolithic objects have been found, of ivory and other substances, which may have come from Egypt [cf. L. Siret, 1909]. It is certain that the earliest notices of tin in literature mention it as coming from the uttermost limits of Europe. In his lament over Tyre the prophet Ezekiel says [xxvii. 12]: "Tarshish was thy merchant by reason of the multitude of all kind of riches; with silver, iron, tin, and lead, they traded in thy fairs." Herodotus [iii. 115] says that it came from the Cassiterides. As Tarsis was the starting-point of the tin-trade with the Cassiterides,[2] these two statements are in agreement.

Figures and thin rods of tin have been found in association with stone implements on the sites of pile-dwellings in Switzerland. Tin rings have also been found at Hallstatt. In barrows (of the Bronze Age?) in the island of Anrum, on

---

as well as (sometimes in conjunction with gold and silver) in the gravel or sand of streams, and it was certainly in the latter form that tin was first extracted, after its discovery by some accident or other.

[1] It is possible, of course, that the first bronze, like silk, may have reached the people of the Orient and Egypt from China, without their knowing from whence it was originally derived. Bronze articles have been found at Troy which may indicate a connection with China, and it has even been asserted that Chinese characters have been found there [cf. Schliemann, 1881, p. 519]. Tin is also known to occur in Persia, but it has not been ascertained that it was worked there in ancient times. Strabo [xv. 724] says, however, that the Drangæ in Drangiana, near the Indus, "suffer from want of wine, but tin occurs with them." Tin is found in the Fichtelgebirge, and it has been thought possible to identify prehistoric tin-mines there [cf. O. Schrader, 1901, article "Zinn"].

[2] The Phœnicians' "Tarsis" (or Tarshish), rich in silver, called by the Greeks "Tartessos," was on the south-west coast of Spain between the Pillars of Hercules and the Guadiana. About 1100 B.C. Tyre established there the colony "Gadir" (i.e., "fortress"), called by the Greeks "Gadeira," and by the Romans "Gades" (now Cadiz).

ANTIQUITY, BEFORE PYTHEAS

the west coast of Sleswick, there were found a dagger or arrowhead and several other objects of tin, besides a lump of the metal, and in Denmark it is known that tin was used for ornament on oak chests of the earliest Bronze Age, which again points to coastal traffic with the south-west.

In the Iliad tin is spoken of as a rare and costly metal, used for the decoration of weapons, and it appears that arms were then made of copper, bronze not being yet in general use, as was the case in the later time of the Odyssey. But in the excavations at Troy, curiously enough, bronze objects were found immediately above the neolithic strata, which would seem to show that the Bronze Age reached the Greeks from Egypt without any intervening copper age.

The Homeric songs do not allude to tin as a Phœnician commodity, like amber. This may mean that the Greeks even in the earliest times obtained it through their own commercial relations with Gaul, without employing the Phœnicians as middlemen.

Possibly the Greek word for tin, "kassiteros," and the name of the tin-islands, "Kassiterides," themselves point to this direct connection. The same word is also found in Sanscrit, "kastîra," and in Arabic, "qazdir." Professor Alf Torp thinks that the word both in Greek and in Sanscrit "must be borrowed from somewhere, but whence or when is not known. 'Kassiteros,' of course, occurs as early as Homer, 'kastîra' is in Indian literature much later, but as far as that goes it may well be old in Sanscrit. I do not know of any Celtic word one could think of; a 'cassitír' (woodland) is hardly to the point; it is true that 'tír' means 'land,' but no other 'cass' is known to me except one that means 'hair'" (in a letter of November 9, 1909). We may therefore look upon it as certain that "kassiteros" is not an original Greek word; it must in all probability have come from the country whence the Greeks first obtained tin (analogous cases are the name of copper from the island of Cyprus, that of bronze from Brundisium, etc.). That this country was India, as some have thought, is improbable, since it is stated in the "Periplus Maris Erythræi" [xlix.], confirmed by Pliny [xxxiv. 163], that tin was imported into India from Alexandria in exchange for ivory, precious stones and perfumes; we must therefore suppose that the name reached India with the tin from the Greeks, and not vice versâ. It is very possible that the word consists of two parts, of which the second "-teros" may be connected with the Celtic word "tír" for land (Latin "terra"). The first part, "kassi," occurs in many Celtic words and names. Ptolemy [ii. 8] mentions in Gaul, in or near Brittany: "Bidu-kasioi," "Uenelio-kasioi," "Tri-kasioi," and "Uadi-kasioi." As mentioned by Reinach [1892, p. 278], there was a people in Brittany called "Cassi" (a British king, "Cassi-vellaunos," an Arvernian chief, "Ver-cassi-vellaunos," etc.). It may be supposed that the country was named after these people, or was in some other way referred to by such a word and called "Kassi-tír." In this case the Cassiterides might be sought for in Brittany, and this agrees with what we have arrived at in another way. But this would entail the assumption that the Celts were already in Gaul at the time of the Iliad.

Professor Alf Torp has called attention to the remarkable circumstance that "the Cymric word for tin, 'ystaen,' resembles 'stannum,' which cannot be genuine Latin. I am inclined to think that both words are derived from an Iberian word; the Romans would in that case have got it from Galicia, and the Cymri doubtless from a primitive Iberian population in the British Isles. In some way or other our word 'tin' must be connected with this word, though the 'i' is curious in the face of the Cymric 'a'" (letter of November 9, 1909). In connection with this hypothesis of Professor Torp, it may be of interest to notice that in the tin district of Morbihan in Brittany, by the mouth of the Vilaine, is "Penestin," where the deposits still contain much tin, and the name of which must come

ANTIQUITY, BEFORE PYTHEAS

from the Celtic "pen" (= head, cape) and "estein" (= tin).[1] It is conceivable that the Latin "stannum" was derived from Brittany rather than from Galicia.

In ancient Egyptian there is no word for tin; as in early Latin, it is described as white lead (dhti hs), which may point to a common western origin for these two metals.

There has been great diversity of opinion as to where the Cassiterides of the Greeks were to be found. Herodotus [iii. 115] did not know where they were: "in spite of all his trouble, he had not been able to learn from any eye-witness what the sea is like in that region [that is, on the north side] of Europe. But it is certain that tin comes from the uttermost end, as also amber." Posidonius mentioned the islands as lying between Spain and Britain (see above, p. 23). Strabo says [iii. 175]:

"The Cassiterides are ten, and lie near to one another, in the midst of the sea northwards from the harbour of the Artabri [Galicia]. One of them is unoccupied, while the others are inhabited by people in black cloaks, with the robe fastened on the breast and reaching down to their feet, who wander about with staves in their hands like the Furies in tragedy. They live for the most part as herdsmen on their cattle; but as they also have mines of tin and lead they barter these metals and hides for pottery, salt, and articles of copper with the merchants. Formerly the Phœnicians alone carried on this trade from Gadir and kept the sea-route secret from every one else; but as the Romans once sailed in pursuit of one of their vessels with the object of finding out the position of their markets, the captain intentionally allowed his ship to be stranded on a sandbank and brought the same destruction upon his pursuers; but he saved himself from the wreck, and was compensated by the State for the value of his loss. Nevertheless the Romans discovered the sea-route after repeated attempts, and when Publius Crassus [under Cæsar] had also traversed it he saw the metals dug out from near the surface and that the inhabitants were peaceful, and he proved this sea-passage to be practicable, if one wished to make it, although it is longer[2] than that which divides Britain [from the continent]"

---

[1] Cf. S Reinach, 1892, p. 277. In Breton tin is called "sten," a name which is certainly not borrowed from the Latin "stannum," as Reinach thinks; according to the above-quoted opinion of Professor Torp we must believe that the borrowing has been in the opposite direction.

[2] The explanation of this statement may be that Crassus sailed to the Cassiterides from the mouth of the Garonne, up which river the route ran to Narbo. What is alluded to here would then be the sea-passage from the Garonne.

CHAPTER I

It is unlikely that the Cassiterides were Cornwall, as has been commonly supposed, since this peninsula can with difficulty be regarded as a group of islands ; moreover this would not agree with the descriptions which always mention them as separate from Britain, and usually farther south. The Scilly Isles, lying far out in the sea, where tin has never been worked to any great extent, and whose waters are dangerous to navigate, are out of the question. On the other hand, it may almost be regarded as certain that the Cassiterides are the same as the "Œstrymnides" (see below), and these must be looked for on the coast of Gaul. Furthermore tin is mentioned as "Celtic" by several Greek authorities ; in the "Mirabiles auscultationes" of Aristotle or Pseudo-Aristotle [i. 834, A. 6] it is so called, and Ephorus (about 340 B.C.) speaks [in Scymnus of Chios] of Tartessus [i.e., Gadir], "the famous city," as "rich in alluvial tin from Celtica [Gaul], in gold, as also in copper."[1] It may further be mentioned that Mela referred to the Cassiterides[2] as "Celtican,"

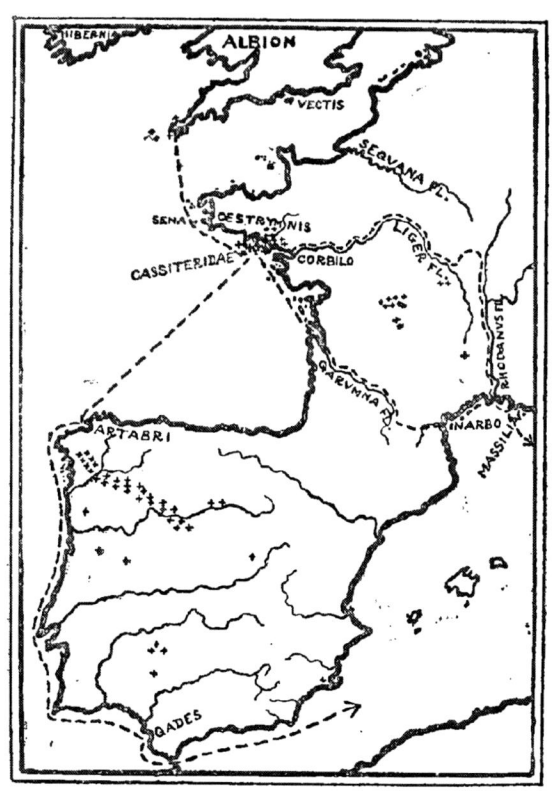

Places where tin is found in western Europe (marked with crosses), and routes of the tin-trade in ancient times (after L. Siret, 1908)

---

[1] Pliny [xxxiv. 162] mentions the tinning of copper objects as a Gaulish invention.

[2] Strabo's repeated statement [ii. 120 and 175] that the Cassiterides lay north

ANTIQUITY, BEFORE PYTHEAS

which would mean that they belonged to the north-west coast of Spain, unless it is confused with Celtic; and in his description of the islands of Europe, going from south to north, he puts them immediately before "Sena," or the Île de Seine at the western extremity of Brittany, which means in any case that they would be to the south of that island. Everything points to the islands being situated on the south coast of Brittany, and there is much in favour of Louis Siret's assumption [1908] that they are the islands of Morbihan ("Les Îles du Morbraz"), west of the mouth of the Loire, exactly where "Penestin" is situated. This agrees very well, as we shall see later, with the description of Himilco's voyage to the Œstrymnides. The free alluvial deposits along the shore in this district, near the mouth of the Vilaine, still contain a good deal of tin, together with gold and other precious metals; but in those distant times they may have been very rich in tin, and as they lie on the very seashore they were naturally discovered early and became the most important source of tin until they were partly exhausted. In the meantime the rich tin deposits of Cornwall had begun to be utilised, and they became in turn the most important, while the Cassiterides were gradually forgotten.

CHAPTER I

Diodorus [v. 22] alludes to the tin trade in the following terms: "On that promontory of Prettanike [Britain] which is called 'Belerion,' the inhabitants are very hospitable, and they have become civilised by intercourse with foreign merchants. They produce tin, by actively working the land which contains it. This is rocky and contains veins of earth, and by working and smelting the products they obtain pure metal This they make into the form of knuckle-bones and bring it to an island which lies off the coast of Britain and is called 'Ictis.' For when the intervening space becomes dry at ebb-tide they bring a quantity of tin to the island in waggons. A curious thing happens with the islands near the coast between Europe and Britain; for when the dividing strait is filled at high

---

of the land of the Artabri [north-west Spain] also points decisively to Brittany. The idea must be derived from Eratosthenes, who borrowed from Pytheas, and the latter placed Cabæum, the promontory of Brittany, farther west than Cape Finisterre. Diodorus [v. 38] says that the islands lay opposite Iberia in the Ocean. That they are always mentioned in connection with the Artabri or north-west Spain shows that the voyage to them was made from that country.

CHAPTER I

water they appear as islands, but when the sea recedes at the ebb and leaves a great space of dry land, they look like part of the mainland. Here the merchants buy it from the natives and bring it across to Gaul; but finally they journey on foot through Gaul, and bring the goods on horses to the mouth of the river Rhone." In another place [v. 38] he says that the tin is conveyed on horseback to Massalia and to the Roman commercial town of Narbo.

Bunbury [1883, ii. p. 197] thinks that "this characteristic account leaves no reasonable doubt that Ictis was St. Michael's Mount in Cornwall (Belerion), to which the description precisely answers, and which contains a small port such as would have been well suited to ancient traders." The description decidedly does not fit, as some have thought, the island of Vectis (Wight); moreover the tin would in any case have had to be brought to the latter by sea from Cornwall, and not in waggons. It is, however, also possible that we have here some confusion with the original tin district in Brittany, where such places as Ictis, with the change between flood and ebb tide, are well known, from Cæsar's description among others. But as Diodorus did not know the tin-mines of Brittany, which in his time had lost their importance, and had heard of tin-mines in Belerion, he transferred to the latter the whole description which he found in earlier writers. This supposition may be confirmed by Pliny's statement [Hist. Nat. iv. 16, 104]: "The historian Timæus says that in six days' sailing inwards from Britain the island of 'Mictis' is reached, in which white lead (tin) occurs. Thither the Britons sail in vessels of wicker-work, covered with hides." Originally the passage doubtless read "insulam Ictis," which by transference of the "m" became "insula Mictis," and this again has been amended to "insulam Mictis." It is impossible to identify the description with Vectis, which moreover has just been mentioned by Pliny, and it is also difficult to understand how it could be a place in Cornwall, but it is consistent with the tin district of Brittany.

We do not know how or at what period this tin industry first developed. Perhaps it was as early as the end of the neolithic period; but it is improbable that it should have been independently developed by the Iberian aborigines who lived in the tin districts of Iberia, and doubtless also of Brittany; it is far more likely to be due to communication with the Mediterranean through a seafaring, commercial people, and we know of none other than the Phœnicians. How early they began their widespread commerce and industry is unknown; but they must have reached this part of the world long before Gadir was founded by the Tyrians about 1100 B.C. It is conceivable that in their search for gold and silver they discovered these deposits of tin and knew how to take advantage of them. As already remarked, there was as early as 2000 B.C. a

ANTIQUITY, BEFORE PYTHEAS

continuous communication by sea along the coasts of western Europe, and it is probable that there arose at a very early time efficient navigators on the coasts of northern Spain and Brittany, just those districts which are rich in tin, where there are many good harbours. For a long time the tin trade was carried on by sea, southward along the coast to Tarsis in southern Spain ; but by degrees an overland trade-route also came into use, going up the Loire and down the Rhone to the Mediterranean. This route became known to the Greeks, and the Phocæan colony Massalia was founded upon it about 600 B.C. ; later the Greek colony of Corbilo was possibly founded at its other extremity, by the mouth of the Loire (?). Later still another trade-route ran along the Garonne overland to the Roman Narbo (Narbonne). On the development of the Cornish tin industry, the same routes by sea and land continued to be used. Thus it was that the tin trade furnished one of the first and most important steps in the path of the exploration of the North.

When Phaethon one day had persuaded his father Helios to let him drive the chariot of the sun across the sky, the horses ran away with him and he first came too near the vault of heaven and set fire to it, so that the Milky Way was formed ; then he approached too near the earth, set the mountains on fire, dried up rivers and lakes, burned up the Sahara, scorched the negroes black, until, to avoid greater disasters in his wild career, Zeus struck him down with his thunderbolt into the river Eridanus. His sisters, the daughters of the sun, wept so much over him that the gods in pity changed them into poplars, and their tears then flowed every year as amber on the river's banks. "For this reason amber came to be called 'electron,' because the sun has the name of 'Elector.'" In this way the Greeks, in their poetry, thought that amber was formed. The mythical river Eridanus, which no doubt was originally in the north (cf. Herodotus), was later identified sometimes with the Rhone, sometimes with the Po. Herodotus [iii. 115] says of northern Europe : " I do not suppose

CHAPTER I that there is a river which the barbarians call Eridanus, and which flows into the sea to the northward, from whence amber may come. . . . For in the first place the name Eridanus itself shows that it is Hellenic and not barbarian, and that it has been invented by some poet or other "; and in the second, he was not able to find any eye-witness who could tell him about it (cf. p. 27); but in any case he thought that amber as well as tin came from the uttermost limits of Europe.

The most important sources of amber in Europe are the southern coast of the Baltic, especially Samland, and the west coast of Jutland with the North Frisian islands. It is also found in small quantities in many places in western and central Europe, on the Adriatic, in Sicily, in South Africa, Burmah, the west coast of America, etc. Northern amber, from the Baltic and the North Sea, is distinguished from other kinds that have been investigated, by the comparatively large proportion of succinic acid it contains, and it seems as though almost all that was used in early antiquity in the Mediterranean countries and in Egypt was derived from the north. Along the coasts of the Baltic and North Sea the amber is washed by the waves from the loose strata of the sea-bottom and thrown up on the beach. When these washed-up lumps were found by the fishers and hunters of early times they naturally attracted them by their brilliance and colour and by the facility with which they could be cut. It is no wonder, therefore, that amber was used as early as the Stone Age for amulets and

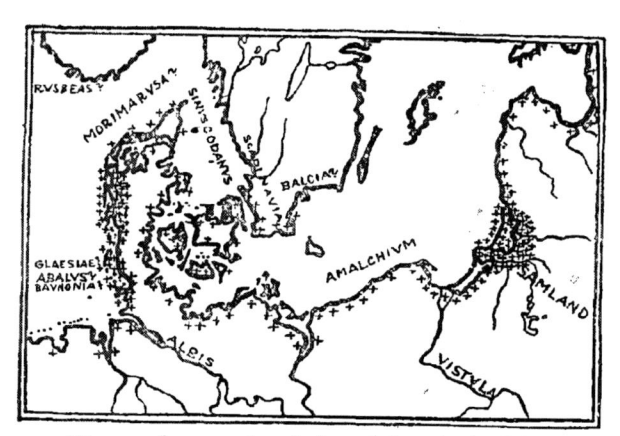

Places where amber is found (marked with crosses)

ornaments by the people on the Baltic and North Seas, and spread from thence over the whole of the North. In those distant times articles of amber were still rare in the South; but in the Bronze Age, in proportion as gold and bronze reach the north, they become rarer there, but more numerous farther south. In the passage-graves of Mycenæ (fourteenth to twelfth centuries B.C.) there are many of them, as also in Sparta at the time of the Dorian migration (twelfth to tenth centuries B.C.; cf. p. 14). It is evident that amber was the medium of exchange wherewith the people of the North bought the precious metals from the South, and in this way it comes that the two classes of archæological finds have changed their localities. The neolithic ornaments of amber at Corinth, already referred to, the amber beads of the Fifth Dynasty in Egypt, and those of the neolithic period in Spain, show, however, if they are northern, that this connection between South and North goes back a very long way. But the Greek tribes among whom the Iliad originated do not appear to have known amber, as it is not mentioned in the poem, and it is first named in the more recent portions of the Odyssey (put into writing in the eighth century B.C.). Among the jewels which the Phœnician merchant offered to the Queen of Syria was "the golden necklace hung with pieces of amber" [Od. xv. 460]. We must therefore believe that the Phœnicians were the middlemen from whom the Greeks obtained it at that time. But it was not so much esteemed by the Greeks of the classical period as it became later, and they rejected it in their art industries, for which reason it is seldom mentioned by Greek authors. Thales of Miletus (600 B.C.) discovered that when rubbed it attracted other bodies, and from this important discovery made so long ago has sprung the knowledge of that force which dominates our time, and which has been named from the Greek word for amber, "electron."

Among the Romans of the Empire this substance was so highly prized that Pliny tells us [xxxvii., chap. 12] that "a human likeness made of it, however small, exceeds the price

CHAPTER I

of a healthy living person." This was both on account of its beauty and of its occult properties ; when worn as an amulet it was able to ward off secret poisons, sorcery and other evils. It therefore naturally became an article that was in great demand, and for which merchants made long voyages.

It has been thought that the North Sea amber came into the southern market before that of the Baltic, and as the Eridanus of the myth was sometimes taken for the Rhone and sometimes for the Po, it was believed that in early times amber was carried up the Rhine and across to both these rivers, later also up the Elbe to the Adriatic [cf. Schrader, 1901, " Bernstein "]. It was thought that the archæological finds also favoured this theory ; but it must still be regarded as doubtful, and it is scarcely probable that the Phœnicians obtained it from the mouths of the Rhone and the Po, while they may have brought it by sea at an early period. By what routes amber was distributed in the earliest times is still unknown.

Voyages of the Phœnicians

Even though the Phœnicians were for the most part a commercial and industrial people, who were not specially interested in scientific research, there can be no doubt that by their distant voyages they contributed much geographical knowledge to their age, and in many ways they influenced Greek geography, especially through Miletus, which from the beginning was partly a Phœnician colony, and where the first Greek school of geographers, the Ionian school, developed. Thales of Miletus was himself probably a Semite. How far they attained on their voyages is unknown. Hitherto no certain relics of Phœnician colonies have been found along the coasts of western Europe farther north than south-west Spain (Tarsis), and there is no historically certain foundation for the supposition that these seafaring merchants of antiquity, the Phœnicians, Carthaginians and Gaditanians, on their voyages beyond the Pillars of Hercules and northwards along the coasts of western Europe, should have penetrated beyond the tin country and as far as the waters of northern Europe, even to Scandinavia and the Baltic, whence they themselves might have brought amber.[1] But a hypothesis of this sort cannot be disproved, and is by no means improbable. Everything points to the Phœnicians having been uncommonly capable seamen with good and swift-sailing ships; and a seafaring people who achieved the far more difficult enterprise of circumnavigating Africa, and of sailing southwards along its west coast with whole fleets to found colonies, cannot have found it impossible to sail along the west and north coast of Europe, where there are plenty of natural harbours. It would then be natural for them to try to reach the North Sea and the Baltic, if they expected to find the precious amber there, and on this point they certainly had information from the merchants who brought it either by land or by sea. It has already been remarked that it is first mentioned in history as a Phœnician article of commerce.[2] It may be supposed that the Phœnicians at an

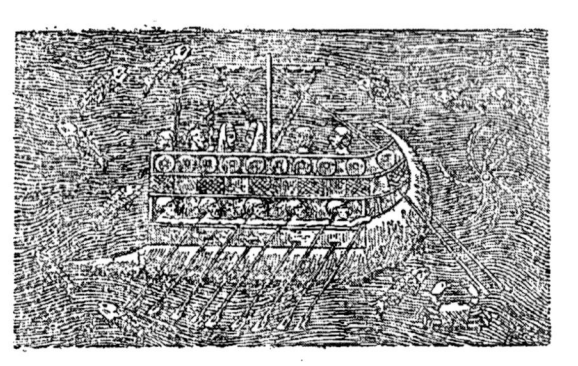

Phœnician warship, according to an Assyrian representation

---

[1] Georg Mair [1899, p. 20, f.] has allowed himself to be led astray by Sven Nilsson's fanciful pictures [1862, 1865] into regarding it as a historical fact that the Phœnicians had permanent colonies in Skane and regular communication with Scandinavia, even so far north as the Lofoten isles, whose rich fisheries are supposed to have attracted them.

[2] In a translation of the cuneiform inscription on the obelisk of the Assyrian king Asurnasirabal (885-860 B.C.) the Assyriologist J. Oppert has the following remarkable passage, which is taken as referring to this king's great predecessor Tiglath Pileser I., of about 1100 B.C.: "In the seas of the trade-winds his fleets fished for pearls, in the seas where the pole-star stands in the zenith they fished for the saffron which attracts." [Cf. Schweiger-Lerchenfeld, 1898, p. 141.] Oppert has since altered the latter part of his translation to "fished for that which looks like copper." Both interpretations might mean amber, and if the translation were correct this inscription would furnish a remarkable piece of evidence for direct communication between Assyria and the Baltic as early as the ninth century B.C., and in that case we might suppose it established by

CHAPTER I

early period obtained amber from their harbours on the Black Sea;[1] but after having pursued this prosperous carrying-trade from their harbours here and in the west, it is not improbable that they themselves tried to penetrate to the amber countries with their ships.[2] The Phœnicians, however, tried to keep their trade-routes secret from their dangerous and more warlike rivals the Greeks, and it is therefore not surprising that no mention of these routes should be extant, even if they really undertook such voyages; but it is undeniably more remarkable still that no certain trace of them has been found along the coasts of western Europe.

Himilco's voyage, 500 B.C.

The only thing we know is that about the year 500 B.C. the Carthaginians are said to have sent out an expedition under Himilco through the Pillars of Hercules and thence northwards along the coast. This is the first northern sea voyage of which mention is to be found in literature. At that time Tyre, the mother-city of Gadir, had been destroyed. Until

---

means of the Phœnicians. But unfortunately another eminent Assyriologist, Professor Schrader, has disputed the correctness of the translation given above, which he thinks is the result of a false reading of the inscription. According to Schrader there is no mention of pearls, or amber, or fleets, or pole-star, or zenith; the whole refers merely to this ancient king's hunting in the mountains of Assyria which took place "in the days when the star Sukud shone, gleaming like bronze." [Cf. Verhandl. d. Berliner Gesellsch. f. Anthrop. Ethnol. u. Urgesch. 1885, pp. 65, 66, 306, 372; and Mair, 1903, p. 47.] The last interpretation is undeniably more probable than the first, and it may well be thought that the bronze-coloured star which shone may have been Venus

[1] That amber may have followed this route in early times is made probable by the finds of ornaments of amber in graves of the Bronze Age (Halstatt period) in the Caucasus, at Koban and Samthavro.

[2] Franz Mathias [1902, p. 73] draws attention to the statement of Von Alten ["Die Bohlwege im Gebiet der Ems und Weser," p. 40 and Pl. V.; this paper has not been accessible to me] that in 1818 there was found a piece of amber with a Phœnician inscription on one of the oldest and deepest-lying bog causeways ("Moorbrucken") on the prehistoric trade-route from the district of the Weser and Ems to the Rhine. As one would expect amber to be carried from the countries in the north-east towards the south, and not in the reverse direction, this find, if properly authenticated, might show that there were Phœnicians on the coast to the north. But the piece, if it be Phœnician, may also have come from the south by chance.

ANTIQUITY, BEFORE PYTHEAS

then she had controlled the trade of the west. It was natural that Gadir in her isolated position should seek support from Carthage, which was now rising into power. To strengthen her trade communications, therefore, this flourishing city sent out Hanno's great expedition along the west coast of Africa, and Himilco to the tin country in the north. Himilco seems to have written an account of the journey; but of this all that has been preserved is a few casual pieces of information in a poem ("Ora Maritima") by the late Roman author Rufus Festus Avienus[1] (of the end of the fourth century A.D.). The only other place where Himilco's name is mentioned is in Pliny [Hist. Nat. ii. 67, 169], who merely says that he made a voyage to explore the outer coast of Europe, contemporary with Hanno's voyage to the south along the west coast of Africa, and in addition he names him in the list of his authorities. But Pliny himself probably never saw his work; it cannot be seen that he has made use of it.

It is true that Avienus makes a pretence of having used Himilco's original account, but certainly he had never seen it. He may have utilised a Greek authority of about the time of the Christian era [cf. Marx, 1895]. This again was a compound of Greek tales, of which a part may have been taken from a Punic source, but of the latter no trace is found in any other known classical writer, with the exception of Pliny. Unfortunately the information given us by Avienus shows little intelligence in the use of his authorities, and his poem is often obscure.

In the description of the coast of western Europe [vv. 90-129] we read:

"And here the projecting ridge raises its head—the older age called it 'Œstrymnis'—and all the high mass of rocky ridge turns mostly towards the warm south wind. But beneath the top of this promontory the Œstrymnian Bay opens out before the eyes of the inhabitants. In the midst of this rise the islands which are called Œstrymnides, scattered widely about, and rich in metals, in tin and in lead. Here live a multitude of men with enterprise and active industry, all

---

[1] See on this subject specially Mullenhoff, 1870, 1. pp. 73-203. Also W. Christ, 1866; Marx, 1895; G. Mair, 1899; and others.

having continually commercial interests; they plough in skilful fashion far and wide the foaming sea ['fretum,' literally, strait], and the currents of monster-bearing Ocean with their small boats. For these people do not know how to fit together [literally, weave] keels of fir or maple; they do not bend their craft with deal, in the usual way; but strange to say, they make their ships of hides sewed together, and often traverse the vast sea with the help of hides. Two days' voyage from thence lay the great island, which the ancients called 'the Holy Island,'[1] and it is inhabited by the people of Hierne [i.e., Ireland] far and wide, and near to it again extends the island of Albion. And it was the custom of the men of Tartessus to trade to the borders of the Œstrymnides, also colonists from Carthage and the many who voyage between the Pillars of Hercules visited these seas. The Carthaginian Himilco assures us that these seas can scarcely be sailed through in four months, as he has himself related of his experience on his voyage; thus no breeze drives the ship forward, so dead is the sluggish wind of this idle sea. He also adds that there is much seaweed among the waves, and that it often holds the ship back like bushes. Nevertheless he says that the sea has no great depth, and that the surface of the earth is barely covered by a little water. The monsters of the sea move continually hither and thither, and the wild beasts swim among the sluggish and slowly creeping ships."

It may be difficult to decide how much of this is really derived from Himilco. The name "Œstrymnis" is not found elsewhere in literature, and may be taken from him.[2] The supposition that it was Cape Finisterre and that the Œstrymnic Bay ("sinus Œstrymnicus") was the Bay of Biscay is improbable; a bay so open and wide could scarcely have been described in terms which a Latin author would have rendered by "sinus"; besides which there would be difficulties with the Œstrymnides which were widely spread therein. Œstrymnis is certainly in Brittany, and since it "turns chiefly towards the warm south wind," we may suppose it to be a headland

---

[1] This epithet, which constantly recurs when Ireland is mentioned, may perhaps in ancient times be due to the resemblance between the Greek words "hieros" (holy) and "Hierne" (Ireland), which latter may be derived from the native name of the island, "Erin." In later times, of course, it is due to Ireland's early conversion to Christianity and its monastic system.

[2] In spite of Mullenhoff's contrary view [1870, p. 92], it does not appear to me altogether impossible that it may have arisen through a corruption of the name of the people whom Pytheas calls "Ostimians" or "Ostimnians," and which in some manuscripts of Strabo [iv. 195] also takes the forms "Osismians" [cf. also Mela, iii. 2, 7; Pliny, iv. 32; Ptolemy, ii. 8, 5; Orosius, 6, 8] and "Ostidamnians" [i. 64], and who lived in Brittany.

ANTIQUITY, BEFORE PYTHEAS

on the south coast. That the Œstrymnic Bay opens out beneath this headland ("sub hujus") agrees with all that we know of it. As already stated, the tin-producing Œstrymnides are undoubtedly the Cassiterides, which may probably be the islands in the bay by the mouth of the Vilaine and Quiberon, on the south side of Brittany, where tin occurs.

It is just in this district, at the mouth of the Loire, that we find the Veneti as the only people famous for seamanship in ancient times in these parts. But, according to Cæsar's valuable description, they had strong, seaworthy ships, built wholly of oak and with leather sails. This seems scarcely to tally with the statement that the people of the Œstrymnides sailed the sea in boats of hide, the coracles of the Celts, which is also confirmed by Pliny's statement [xxxiv. c. 47] that "according to fabulous tales tin was brought in ships of wicker-work sewed round with hides from islands in the Atlantic Ocean." Either the Veneti must have acquired the art of shipbuilding after the voyage of Himilco—perhaps, indeed, through their intercourse with Carthaginians and Gaditanians—or else we must believe that the statement in Avienus rests upon a misinterpretation of the original authorities, and that the flowery language really means that the ships were not built of fir, maple or spruce, but of oak, the omission of which is striking.

Thus a comparison of the various statements points definitely to Brittany as the place where we must look for the tin-bearing islands. That it was two days' voyage thence to the holy island of Hierne, and that near to it lay the land of Albion, also agrees; but too much weight must not be laid upon this, as we do not know for certain whether this is really derived from Himilco.

The sea-monsters may be taken as accessories put in to make the voyage terrible; but on the other hand they may be the great whales of the Bay of Biscay, of which there were many in those days, before whaling was undertaken there. The exaggerated description of the length and difficulties of the voyage fits in badly with the information that the men of Tartessus and the Carthaginians were in the habit of trading there. How much of this is due to misunderstanding of the original, or to downright interpolation, we do not know. With the universal desire of the Carthaginians and Phœnicians to keep the monopoly of their trade-routes, Himilco may have added this to frighten others. It is also possible that he made

IN NORTHERN MISTS

a longer voyage in four months, but that Avienus's authority gave an obscure and bungled account of it.

The description of the shallow water, and of the seaweed which holds the ships back, etc., seems to correspond to the actual conditions. In another part of the poem something similar occurs, where we read [v. 375]: "Outside the Pillars of Hercules along the side of Europe the Carthaginians once had villages and towns. They were in the habit of building their fleets with flatter bottoms, since a broader ship could float upon the surface of a shallower sea."[1] One is reminded of the shallow west coast of France, where the tide lays large tracts alternately dry (covered with seaweed) and under water, so that it might well be said that "the surface of the earth is barely covered by a little water." Ebb and flood were, of course, an unknown phenomenon in the Mediterranean. In this respect also the description suits the voyage to Brittany, where the sea is shallow. It has been asserted that the expression "seaweed among the waves" might show that Himilco had been near to or in the Sargasso Sea; but there is no reason whatever for supposing this; the explanation given above is more natural, besides which the Sargasso Sea could hardly be described as shallow and as lying on the way to Œstrymnis.[2]

On the Atlantic Ocean Avienus has the following [vv. 380-389]:

"Farther to the west from these Pillars there is boundless sea. Himilco relates that the ocean extends far, none has visited these seas; none has sailed ships over these waters, because propelling winds are lacking on these deeps, and no breeze from heaven helps the ship. Likewise because darkness ['caligo' = darkness, usually owing to fog] screens the light of day with a sort of clothing,

---

[1] In Cæsar's description [B.G., iii. 13] of the ships of the Veneti it is also stated that "the keels were somewhat flatter than in our ships, whereby they were better able to cope with the shallows and the falling tides."

[2] It has been alleged as a proof that the Phœnicians really knew of the Sargasso Sea that Sargasso weed is mentioned by Theophrastus ["Historia Plantarum," iv. 6, 4], but I have not been able to find anything of the sort in this author; nor can I find any statement in Aristotle [Miral. Auscult.] which can be thus interpreted, as some have thought.

ANTIQUITY, BEFORE PYTHEAS

and because a fog always conceals the sea, and because the weather is perpetually cloudy with thick atmosphere."

If we may believe Avienus that this description is derived from Himilco, it possesses great interest, since here and in the description (above) of the voyage to Œstrymnis we find the same ideas of the western sea and of the uttermost sea which appear later, after Pytheas's time, in the accounts of the thick and sluggish sea without wind round Thule, and in this case it shows that already at that early period ideas of this sort had developed. Müllenhoff [1870, pp. 78, 93 f.], it is true, takes it for granted that these descriptions in Avienus cannot be derived from Himilco, but his reasons for so doing do not appear convincing. Aristotle says ["Meteorologica," ii. 1, 14] that the sea beyond the Pillars of Hercules was muddy and shallow, and little stirred by the winds. This shows clearly enough that ideas of that kind were current among the Greeks even before Pytheas, and they must doubtless have got them from the Phœnicians.

That some very ancient authority is really the basis of the description of the west coast of Europe as far as the Œstrymnides, which we find in Avienus, is proved again by the fact that the regions farther to the north or north-east are clearly enough represented as entirely unknown, when we read [vv. 129-145]:

"If any one dares to steer his boat from the Œstrymnic Islands in the direction where the air is cold at the axis of Lycaon,[1] he will arrive at the country of the Ligurians, which is void of inhabitants. For by the host of the Celts and by numerous battles it has lately been rendered void. And the expelled Ligurians came, as fate often drives people away, to the districts where there is hardly anything but bush. Many sharp stones are there in those parts, and cold rocks, and the mountains rise threateningly to heaven. And the refugees lived for a long time in narrow places among rocks away from the sea. For they were afraid of waves [i.e., afraid to come near the coast] by reason of the old danger. Later, when security had given them boldness, peace and quietness persuaded them to leave their high positions, and now they descended to places by the sea."

---

[1] Lycaon was the father of Callisto, and the latter became a she-bear and was placed among the stars as the constellation of the Great Bear. At the axis of Lycaon means, therefore, in the north.

Müllenhoff thinks [1870, pp. 86 f.] that this mention of the expulsion of the Ligurians by the Celts is necessarily a late addition by a man from the district of Massalia where the Ligurians lived; but it seems more probable that the name is here used as a common designation for the pre-Celtic people who dwelt in these north-western regions; and if it is the north side of Brittany which is here spoken of, the Ligurians of southern Gaul will not be so far away after all. It is clear that in ancient times the people of west and north-west Europe were called "Ligyans." Hesiod mentioned them as the people of the west in contradistinction to the Scythians of the east [cf. Strabo, vii. 300], and in the legend of Phaëthon occurs the Ligyan king Cycnus at the mouth of the amber-producing river Eridanus, which doubtless was originally supposed to fall into the sea on the north or north-west. We may interpret it as meaning that the aborigines, Ligyans or Ligurians, were driven by the immigrant Celts up into the bush-covered mountainous parts of Brittany. In any case this passage in Avienus, which assumes that the districts farther north are unknown, is a strong proof that his information is ancient and derived from Himilco, and that the latter penetrated as far as the north coast of Brittany, or the south of Britain, but no farther.

CHAPTER II

PYTHEAS OF MASSALIA
THE VOYAGE TO THULE

AMONG all the vague and fabulous ideas about the North that prevailed in antiquity, the name of Pytheas stands out as the only one who gives us a firmer foothold. By his extraordinary voyage (or voyages?) this eminent astronomer and geographer, of the Phocæan colony of Massalia (now Marseilles), contributed a knowledge of the northern countries based upon personal experience, and set his mark more or less upon all that was known of the farthest north for the next thousand or fifteen hundred years. Even though later writers like Polybius and Strabo declared themselves unwilling to believe in his "incredible" statements, they could not neglect him.[1]

Pytheas wrote at least one work, which, if we may believe Geminus of Rhodes, was called "On the Ocean"; but all his writings have been lost for ages, and we only know him through chance quotations in much later

[1] As to Pytheas, see in particular: Müllenhoff, 1870, pp. 211 f.; Berger, iii., 1891, pp. 1 f.; Hergt, 1893; Markham, 1893; Ahlenius, 1894; Matthias, 1901; Kähler, 1903; Detlefsen, 1904; Callegari, 1904; Mair, 1906.

CHAPTER II

authors (chiefly Strabo and Pliny) who have not even read his work themselves, but quote at second hand; and several of them (especially Polybius and Strabo) tried to represent him as an impostor and laid stress upon what they thought would make him ridiculous and lessen his reputation.[1] The scraps of information we possess about him and his voyages have thus come down on the stream of time as chance wreckage, partly distorted and perverted by hostile forces. It is too much to hope that from such fragments we may be able to form a trustworthy idea of the original work, but nevertheless from the little we know there arises a figure which in strength, intelligence, and bold endurance far surpasses the discoverers of most periods.

Personal circumstances and date of the voyage

Of Pytheas's personal circumstances we have no certain information, and we do not even know when he lived. As he was unknown to Aristotle, but was known to his pupil Dicæarchus (who died about 285 B.C.), he was probably a contemporary of Aristotle and Alexander, and his voyage may have been undertaken about 330-325 B.C. So little do we know about the voyage that doubts have been raised as to whether it was really a sea-voyage, or whether a great part of it did not lie overland. Nor do we know whether

---

[1] The principal authorities on Pytheas are · Strabo (1st century A.D.), who did not know his original works, but quotes for the most part from Polybius (2nd century B.C.), who was very hostile to Pytheas, and from Erastosthenes, Hipparchus, and Timæus. Pliny has derived much information from Pytheas, though he does not know him directly, but chiefly through Timæus, Isidorus of Charax, who again knew him through Erastosthenes, &c. Diodorus Siculus (1st century B.C.) knows him chiefly through Timæus. Geminus of Rhodes (1st century B.C.), who has a quotation from him, possibly knew his original work, "On the Ocean," but he may have quoted from Crates of Mallus. Solinus (3rd century A.D.), who has much information about Pytheas, knows him chiefly through Pliny and Timæus. Further second-hand quotations and pieces of information derived from Pytheas occur in Pomponius Mela (1st century A.D), Cleomedes (2nd century A.D.), Ptolemy (3rd century A.D), Agathemerus (3rd century A.D.), scholiasts on Apollonius of Rhodes, Ammianus Marcellinus (4th century A.D.), Orosius (5th century A.D.), Isidorus Hispaliensis (7th century A.D.), and others.

PYTHEAS OF MASSALIA

Pytheas made one or several long journeys to the North. According to a statement of Polybius, Pytheas was a poor man: for he finds it (according to Strabo, ii. 104) "incredible that it should be possible for a private individual without means to accomplish journeys of such wide extent." If it be true that he was poor, which is uncertain, we must doubtless suppose that Pytheas either had command of a public expedition, fitted out by the merchants of the enterprising city of Massalia, or that he accompanied such an expedition as an astronomer and explorer. At that time the city was at the height of its prosperity, after it had expelled the Carthaginians, as the result of the successful war with them, from the rich fisheries of the Iberian coast, and had also succeeded in establishing commercial relations there, whereby its ships were able to sail out beyond the Pillars of Hercules; a thing which cannot have been so easy for them during the former sea-supremacy of Carthage in the western Mediterranean, which was re-established in 306 B.C., whereby the western ocean again became more or less closed to the Massalians. It is very probable that the flourishing city of Massalia desired to send out an expedition to find the sea-route to the outer coasts of the continent, from whence it was known that the two important articles of commerce, tin and amber, were obtained. But it is evident that Pytheas had more than this business motive for his journey. From all that we know it appears that with him too the object was to reach the most northern point possible, in order to find out how far the "œcumene" extended, to determine the position of the Arctic Circle and the Pole, and to see the light northern nights and the midnight sun, which to the Greeks of that time was so remarkable a phenomenon.

We know that Pytheas was an eminent astronomer. He was the first in history to introduce astronomical measurements for ascertaining the geographical situation of a place; and this by itself is enough to give him a prominent position among the geographers of all times.

By means of a great gnomon he determined, with surprising accuracy, the latitude of his own city, Massalia,[1] which formed the starting-point of his journey, and in relation to which he laid down the latitude of more northerly places.

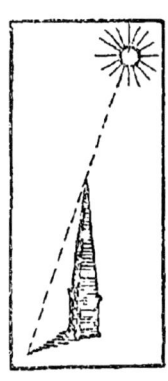

Pytheas also made other astronomical measurements which show him to have been a remarkably good observer. He found that the pole of the heavens did not coincide, as the earlier astronomer Eudoxus had supposed, with any star; but that it made an almost regular rectangle with three stars lying near it.[2] The pole of the heavens was naturally of consequence to Pytheas, who steered by the stars; but it is nevertheless striking that he should have considered it necessary to measure it with such accuracy, if he had not some other object in doing so. He may have required the pole for the adjustment of the equinoctial sun-dial ("polus"), whose pointers had to be parallel with the axis of the heavens;[3] but it is also possible that he had discovered

Gnomon

---

[1] A "gnomon" was the pillar or projection which cast the shadow on the various Greek forms of sun-dial. In the case mentioned above the gnomon was a vertical column raised on a plane. By measuring the length of the shadow at the solstice, Pytheas found that it was $41\frac{4}{5}$: 120 or $\frac{209}{600}$ of the height of the column. According to that the altitude of the sun was 70° 47′ 50″. From this must be deducted the obliquity of the ecliptic, which was at that time 23° 44′ 40″, and the semi-diameter of the sun (16′), as the shadow is not determined by the sun's centre but by its upper edge, besides the refraction, which however is unimportant. When the equatorial altitude thus arrived at is deducted from 90°, we get the latitude of Massalia as 43° 13′ N. The new observatory of Marseilles is at 43° 18′ 19″; but it lies some distance to the north of the ancient city, where Pytheas's gnomon probably stood in the market-place. It will be seen that this is an accuracy of measurement which was not surpassed until very much later times.

[2] It has been supposed that these three stars were β of the Little Bear, a and κ of Draco. The pole was at that time far from the present pole-star, and nearer to β of the Little Bear.

[3] Both "gnomon" and "polus" are mentioned as early as Herodotus; and Athenæus [v. 42] describes the polus in the library on board the ship "Hiero" which was built by Archimedes.

PYTHEAS OF MASSALIA

that by measuring the altitude of the pole above the horizon he obtained directly the latitude of the spot on the earth, and that this was a simpler method of determining the latitude than by measuring the altitude of the sun by a gnomon. Nor is it likely that he possessed the requisite knowledge for calculating gnomon measurements unless they were taken either at the solstice or the equinox. To judge by quotations in various authors he must have given the latitude of several places in numbers of parts of a circle north of Massalia.[1] These results of his may perhaps be partly based on measurements of the polar altitude. Whether Pytheas was acquainted with any instrument for the measurement of angles we do not know; but it is not unlikely, since even the Chaldeans appear to have invented a kind of parallactic rule, which was improved upon by the Alexandrians, and was called by the Romans "triquetrum" (regula Ptolemaica). The instrument resembled a large pair of compasses with long straight rods for legs, and the angle was determined by measuring, in measure of length, the distance between these two legs.[2] As the pole of the heavens

Sundial

---

[1] It is not probable that Pytheas divided the earth's circumference into degrees. Even Eratosthenes (275-194 B.C.) still divided the circumference of the earth into sixty parts, each equal to 4200 stadia, and the division into degrees was first universally employed by Hipparchus. But Aristarchus of Samos, and perhaps even Thales, had already learnt that the sun's diameter was 2 × 360 or 720 times contained in the circle described by them. It is possible that they originally had this from the Chaldæans.

[2] When it is brought forward as a proof of Pytheas having made such angle-measurements [cf. Mair, 1906, p. 28], that Hipparchus is said to have given the sun's height (in cubits) above the horizon at the winter solstice for three different places in north-west Europe [cf. Strabo, ii. 75], it must be remembered that if these altitudes were direct measurements by Pytheas himself, he must have been at each of these three places at the winter solstice, that is to say, in three different winters, where he found that in one place the sun stood six cubits, in another four cubits, and in the third less than three cubits above the horizon. This is improbable, and it is more reasonable to suppose that these altitudes are the result of calculations either by Pytheas himself or by Hipparchus from his data.

did not coincide with any star, such measurements cannot have been very accurate, unless Pytheas took the trouble to measure a circumpolar star in its upper and lower culmination; or, indeed, in only one of them, for he may easily have found the distance of the star from the pole by his earlier observations to determine the position of the pole itself. It is also quite possible that by the aid of the rectangle formed

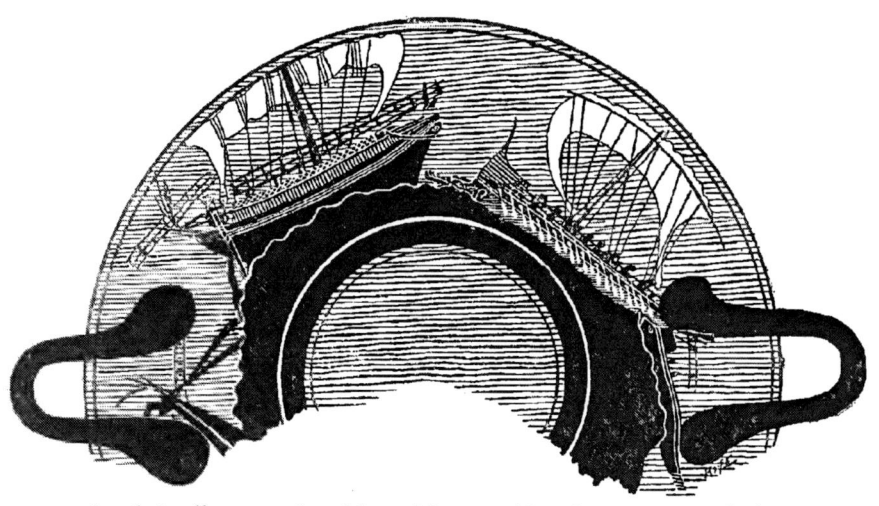

Greek trading-vessel and longship (warship), from a vase painting (about 500 B.C.)

by the pole with three stars, he was able to obtain an approximate measurement of the altitude of the pole. Another indication used by the Greeks to obtain the latitude of a place was the length of its longest day. To determine this Pytheas may have used the equinoctial dial ("polus"), or the water-clock, the "clepsydra" of the Greeks.

It is not known what kind of ship he had for his voyage; but if it was equal to the best that Massalia at that time could afford, it may well have been a good sea-craft. As it was necessary to be prepared for hostilities on the part of the Carthaginians and Gaditanians, he doubtless had a warship (longship), which sailed faster than the broader merchantmen, and which could also be rowed by one or more banks of oars.

PYTHEAS OF MASSALIA

It may have been considerably over 100 feet long, and far larger than those in which later the Norsemen crossed the Atlantic. It has been asserted that Pytheas must have gone on foot for the greater part of his journey, since, according to Strabo [ii. 104], he is said to have stated " not only that he had visited the whole of Britain on foot, but he also gives its circumference as more than 40,000 stadia." But, as Professor Alf Torp has pointed out to me, it is not stated that he " traversed " it, but " visited " it on foot. The meaning must be that he put in at many places on the coast, and made longer or shorter excursions into the country. That a man should be able to traverse such great distances alone on foot, through the roadless and forest-clad countries of that period, seems impossible.

Pytheas's probable routes

We do not know what previous knowledge Pytheas may have had about the regions visited by him; but it is probable that he had heard of the tin country through the merchants who brought the tin overland through Gaul and down the Rhone to Massalia. In a similar way he had certainly also heard of the amber country. Besides this, he may have been acquainted with the trading voyages of the Phœnicians and Carthaginians along the west coast of Europe, and with the voyage of Himilco. Although it is true that the Phœnician

CHAPTER II

sailors tried to keep the secret of their routes from their dangerous rivals the Greeks and Massalians, they cannot have been altogether successful in the long run, whether their intercourse was hostile or friendly; a few sailor prisoners would have been enough to bring the information.

The voyage northward

When Pytheas sailed out through the Pillars of Hercules he soon arrived, in passing the Sacred Promontory (Cape St. Vincent), at the limit of the world as known to the Greeks. He sailed northward along the west and north coast of Iberia (Portugal and Spain). He made observations of the tides, that remarkable phenomenon to a man from the Mediterranean, and their cause, and was the first Greek to connect them with the moon. He proceeded farther north, and found that the north-western part of Celtica (Gaul) formed a peninsula, Cabæum (Brittany), where the Ostimians lived. He supposed that it extended farther west than Cape Finisterre; but errors of that sort are easily understood at a time when no means existed of determining longitude.

Britain

Farther north he came to Brettanice (Britain), which he appears to have circumnavigated. The Sicilian historian Diodorus, an elder contemporary of Strabo, says [v. 21]: " Britain is triangular in form like Sicily; but the sides are not of equal length; the nearest promontory is Kantion [Kent], and according to what is reported it is 100 stadia distant (from the continent). The second promontory is Belerion [Cornwall], which is said to be four days' sail from the continent. The third lies towards the sea [i.e., towards the north] and is called Orkan.[1] Of the three

---

[1] In Diodorus it is called Orkan, but this may be the accusative of Orkas, as in later writers, also in Ptolemy (Mullenhoff, 1870, p. 377, thinks that Orkan is the real form), and from which the name Orcades has been formed for the group of islands immediately to the north. Orkneyar or Orkneys certainly comes from the same word, which must presumably be of Celtic origin. P. A. Munch [1852, pp. 44-46] thought that the name came from the Gaelic word " orc " for the grampus (the specific name of which in Latin was therefore " Delphinus orca," now called " Orca gladiator "). This species of whale is common on the coasts of Norway, the Shetlands and Orkneys, the Færoes and farther west.

PYTHEAS OF MASSALIA

sides the one which runs parallel to Europe is the shortest, 7500 stadia; the second, which extends from the place of crossing [Kent] to the point [i.e., Orkan], is 15,000 stadia; but the last is 20,000 stadia, so that the circumference amounts to 42,500 stadia."

These statements must originally have been due to Pytheas, even though Diodorus has taken them at second hand (perhaps from Timæus). But Pytheas cannot very well have acquired such an idea of the shape of the island without having sailed round it. It is true that the estimate attributed to him of the island's circumference is more than double the reality,[1] a discrepancy which is adduced by Strabo as a proof that Pytheas was a liar;[2] but neither Strabo nor Diodorus was acquainted with his own description, and there are many indications that the exaggeration cannot be attributed to himself, but to a later writer, probably Timæus. Pytheas in his work can only have stated how many days he took to sail along the coasts, and his day's sail in those unknown waters was certainly a short one. But the uncritical Timæus, who was moreover a historian and not a geographer, may, according to the custom of his time, have converted Pytheas's day's journeys into stadia at the usual equation of 1000 stadia (about 100 geographical miles) for one day's sailing.[3] Timæus served to a great extent as the authority for later authors who have mentioned Pytheas, and it is probably through him that the erroneous information as to the circumference of Britain

---

It usually swims in schools, and is the great whale's deadliest enemy, attacking it in numbers and cutting blubber out of its sides. The Eskimo in Greenland assert that it is sometimes dangerous to kayaks; I myself have only once seen a grampus attack a boat; but in any case it is a species which easily draws attention to itself wherever it appears.

[1] Allowing for the greater bays, and putting a degree of latitude at 700 stadia, the sides of Great Britain are about 4000, 7800 and 12,000 stadia, altogether 23,800 stadia, or about 2375 miles.

[2] Strabo erred just as much on his side in making the circumference of Britain much too small.

[3] Cf. Hergt, 1893, p. 44. This hypothesis is supported by the round numbers which answer to 7½, 15, and 20 days' sail.

CHAPTER II

Astronomical measurements in Britain

reached Polybius, Strabo, Diodorus, Pliny, and Solinus. In this way geographical explorers may easily have gross errors attributed to them, when their original observations are lost.

From statements of Hipparchus, preserved by Strabo [ii. 71, 74, 75, 115, 125, 134], we may conclude that Pytheas obtained astronomical data at various spots in Britain and Orkan. Hipparchus has made use of these in his tables of climate, and he was able from them to point out that the longest day in the most northern part of Britain was of eighteen equinoctial hours,[1] and in an inhabited country, which according to Pytheas lay farther north than Britain, the longest day was of nineteen equinoctial hours. If the length of day is fixed in round numbers of hours, a longest day of eighteen hours fits the northernmost part of Scotland,[2] while the country still farther north with a longest day of nineteen hours agrees exactly with Shetland.[3] These data are important, as they

[1] The Greeks divided the day into twelve hours at all times of the year; it was thus only at the equinoxes, when the day was really twelve hours long, that the hours were of the same length as ours. These are, therefore, called equinoctial hours.

[2] A similar statement in Cleomedes [1. 7], after Eratosthenes and Posidonius [1. 10], may also be derived from Pytheas: "the longest day in Britain has eighteen hours."

[3] If we assume that the length of the day was found by a theoretical calculation of the time between the rising and setting of the sun's centre above the horizon, without taking account of refraction, then a longest day of nineteen hours answers to 60° 52′ N. lat.; but if we suppose that the length of the day was found by direct observation and was calculated from the first appearance of the sun's limb in the morning until its final disappearance in the evening, then horizontal refraction will be of importance (besides having to take the sun's semi-diameter into account), and a longest day of nineteen hours then answers to 59° 59′ N. lat. Now the Shetland Isles lie between 59° 51′ and 60° 51′ N. lat.; while the northern point of the Orkneys lies in 59° 23′ N. lat., and has a longest day, theoretically of 18 hours 27 minutes, and actually of 18 hours 36 minutes. A longest day of 18 hours answers theoretically to 57° 59′, actually to fully 57° N. lat. Professor H. Geelmuyden has had the kindness to work out several of these calculations for me. Hipparchus said that at the winter solstice the sun attained to a height of less than three cubits above the horizon in the regions where the longest day was of nineteen hours. If we take one cubit as equal to two degrees these regions will then lie north of 60° N. lat.

show that Pytheas must have been in the most northerly parts of the British Isles, and reached Shetland.[1]

But the bold and hardy explorer does not seem to have stopped here. He continued his course northward over the ocean, and came to the uttermost region, "Thule," which was the land of the midnight sun, " where the tropic coincides with the Arctic Circle."[2]

On this section of Pytheas's voyage Geminus of Rhodes (1st century B.C.) has an important quotation in his Astronomy [vi. 9]. After mentioning that the days get longer the farther north one goes, he continues:

> To these regions [i.e., to the north] the Massalian Pytheas seems also to have come. He says at least in his treatise "On the Ocean": "the Barbarians showed us the place where the sun goes to rest. For it was the case that in these parts the nights were very short, in some places two, in others three hours long, so that the sun rose again a short time after it had set."

The name of Thule is not mentioned, but that must be the country in question. It does not appear from this whether Pytheas himself thought that the shortest night of the year

---

[1] It may be possible, as many think, that it was the Shetlands that he called Orkan (or Orkas), but the more reliable of the known quotations from him seem rather to show that it was really the northernmost point of Britain, or the neighbouring Orkneys that were thus called by him, and have thenceforward been known by that name; while it is later authors who have extended the name also to Shetland. If this supposition be correct: that the islands north of Britain mentioned by Pliny [Nat. Hist. iv. 104] are originally derived from Pytheas, which may be doubtful, and that Berricen (or Nerigon) is Mainland of Shetland, then Orkan cannot apply to these. But, as we shall see later, it it is very doubtful what Pliny's islands may have been originally.

[2] Cf. Strabo [ii. 114] and Cleomedes [i. 7]. The Arctic Circle (or Circle of the Bear) was, as already mentioned, the circle round the celestial pole which formed the limit of the continuously visible (circumpolar) stars, and it had been given this name because in Asia Minor (and Greece) it ran through the Great Bear (Arctus). Its distance in degrees from the north celestial pole is equal to the latitude of the place of observation, and consequently increases as one goes farther north. At the polar circle, as mentioned above, it coincides with the Tropic of Cancer, and at the North Pole with the Equator. Cleomedes has also the remarkable statement that the latitude for a summer day of one month in length runs through Thule.

was of two or three hours, or whether that was the length of the night at the time he happened to be at these places; but the first case is doubtless the more probable. At any rate Geminus seems to have understood him thus, since in the passage immediately preceding he is speaking of the regions where the longest day is of seventeen or eighteen hours, and he goes on to speak of those where the longest day is of twenty-three hours. If on the other hand it is the length of the night at the time Pytheas was there that is meant, then it seems strange that he should require to be shown by the barbarians where the sun rose and set, which he could just as well have seen for himself; for it is scarcely credible that after having journeyed so far his stay should have been so brief that the sky was overcast the whole time.[1]

If the longest day of the year was determined by direct observations of the points at which the sun first appeared and finally disappeared in places with a free horizon to the north, then days of twenty-one and twenty-two hours at that time will answer to 63° 39' and 64° 39' N. lat. Calculated theoretically, from the centre of the sun and without taking refraction into account, they will be 64° 32' and 65° 31' N. lat. respectively.[2]

In addition to this there are two things to be remarked in the passage quoted in Geminus. First, that the country spoken of by Pytheas was inhabited (by barbarians). Secondly, that he himself must have been there with his expedition, for he says that "the barbarians showed us," etc. Consequently he cannot, as some writers think, have reported merely what he had heard from others about this country (Thule).

[1] It may be thought that Pytheas is merely relating a legend current among the barbarians that the sun went to its resting-place during the night, a myth which is moreover almost universal. But it seems more probable that as an astronomer he had something else in his mind. If he had had the two points accurately indicated to him, where the sun set and rose on the shortest night of the year, he must easily have been able, by measuring the angle between them, to ascertain how long the sun was down.

[2] These figures are kindly supplied by Professor H. Geelmuyden.

PYTHEAS OF MASSALIA

Statements in Strabo also show clearly that Pytheas referred to Thule as inhabited.

Other pieces of information derived from Pytheas establish consistently that Thule extended northwards as far as the Arctic Circle. Eratosthenes, Strabo, Pomponius Mela, Pliny, Cleomedes, Solinus, and others, all have statements which show clearly that Pytheas described Thule as the land of the midnight sun.

If we now sum up what is known of Pytheas's voyage to the North, we shall find that it all hangs well together: he first came to the north of Scotland, where the longest day was of eighteen hours, thence to Shetland with a longest day of nineteen hours, and then to a land beyond all, Thule, where the longest day was in one place twenty-one hours and in another twenty-two, and which extended northwards as far as the midnight sun and the Arctic Circle (at that time in 66° 15′ N. lat.). There is nothing intrinsically impossible in the supposition that this remarkable explorer, who besides being an eminent astronomer must have been a capable seaman, had heard in the north of Scotland of an inhabited country still farther to the north, and then wished to visit this also. We must remember how, as an astronomer, he was specially interested in determining the extent of the " œcumene " on the north, and in seeing with his own eyes the remarkable phenomena of northern latitudes, in particular the midnight sun. It is not surprising that he was prepared to risk much to attain this end; and he had already shown by his voyage to the northernmost point of Britain that he was an explorer of more than ordinary boldness, and equal to the task.

Nevertheless it has seemed incredible to many—not only in antiquity, but in our own time as well—that Pytheas should have penetrated not only so far into the unknown as to the islands north of Scotland, but that he should have ventured yet farther into the absolutely unexplored Northern Ocean, and found an extreme country beyond this. He would thus have

CHAPTER II

pushed back the limit of the learned world's knowledge from the south coast of Britain to the Arctic Circle, or about sixteen degrees farther north. As a feat of such daring and endurance has appeared superhuman, a great deal of ingenuity has been employed, especially by Müllenhoff [1870, 1., pp. 392 f.], to prove that Thule was Shetland, that Pytheas himself did not get farther than the Orkneys or the north of Scotland, and that he heard from the natives of the country still farther north, which he never saw. But in order to do this almost all the statements that have been preserved on this part of Pytheas's voyage must be arbitrarily distorted; and to alter or explain away one's authorities so as to make them fit a preconceived opinion is an unfortunate proceeding. Unless, like Polybius and Strabo, we are willing to declare the whole to be a freely imaginative work, which however is remarkably consistent, we must try to draw our conclusions from the statements in the authorities as they stand, and in that case it must for the following reasons be regarded as impossible that Thule means Shetland:

Thule is not Shetland

(1) It is improbable that (as Müllenhoff asserts) so capable an astronomer as Pytheas should have made a mistake of several hours when he gave the length of the night as two or three hours. There is little intrinsic probability in the conjecture that he had overcast weather all the time he was in the north of Scotland and Orkney, and therefore relied on the approximate statements of the natives, which he did not fully understand, and which when translated into Greek measures of time might produce gross errors. But it is worse when we look at it in connection with Hipparchus's statements from Pytheas, that in Britain the longest day was of eighteen hours, and nineteen hours in a region (i.e., Shetland) farther north, where the sun at the winter solstice stood less than three cubits above the horizon. Unless he has given the latter region a long extension to the north, he must have made several conflicting statements about the same region. It will be seen that this leads us to a violent

PYTHEAS OF MASSALIA

and arbitrary alteration of the whole system of information, which is otherwise consistent.

(2) The assertion that Pytheas did not himself say that he had been in the country where the night was two and three hours long, conflicts with the words of Geminus. Cleomedes also tells us that Pytheas is said to have been in Thule.

(3) The definite statements in a majority of the authorities that Thule lay within the Arctic Circle and was the land of the midnight sun, also exclude the Shetland Isles. The astronomer Pytheas cannot have been so far mistaken as to the latitude of these islands.

(4) That it was six days' sail to Thule from Britain[1] will not suit Shetland, even if we make allowance for the frequently obscure statements as to the day's journeys that are attributed to Pytheas (e.g., by Strabo).

(5) That Strabo in one place [ii. 114] calls Thule "the northernmost of the British Isles" cannot be used, as Müllenhoff uses it, as a proof of its belonging to these islands and having a Celtic population. There is not a word to this effect. To Strabo, who also placed Ierne (Ireland) out in the sea north of Britain, it must have been natural to call all the islands in that part of the world British. Indeed, he says himself in the same breath that Thule, according to Pytheas, lay within the Arctic Circle. How little weight he attached to the expression British is additionally apparent from another passage [ii. 75], where he says that "Hipparchus, relying on Pytheas, placed these inhabited regions [Shetland] farther north than Britain."

(6) Pliny [Nat. Hist. iv. 104] mentions among islands north of Britain as "the greatest of all, 'Berricen,' which is

---

[1] According to existing MSS. of Solinus [c. 22] it was five days' sail to Thule from the Orcades, which must here be Shetland, and which are mentioned as the second station on the way to Thule; the Ebudes (Hebrides) were the first station. Mommsen [1895, p. 219] regards the passage as corrupt, and considers it a later interpolation of between the 7th and 9th centuries.

IN NORTHERN MISTS

CHAPTER II

the starting-place for Thule." Berricen, which in some MSS. is written "Nerigon," has been taken for Mainland of Shetland,[1] while others have seen in the form Nerigon the first appearance in literature of the name of Norway ("Noregr"),[2] though with doubtful justification, since this name was hardly in existence at that time. But whether the island be Shetland or Norway, this passage in Pliny puts Thule outside the Scottish islands. And the reference to that country makes it probable that the statements, in part at any rate, are derived from Pytheas.

(7) Finally, it may perhaps be pointed out that Thule is nowhere referred to as a group of islands; the name rather suggests the idea of a continuous land or a single island. To this it may be objected that neither is Orkan referred to as an archipelago in the oldest authorities; but it is uncertain whether in Pytheas, as in Diodorus, Orkan was not used of the northern point of Brettanice, and only later transferred to the islands lying to the north of this. Thule, on the other hand, always appears as a land far out in the ocean, and it is moreover uncertain whether Pytheas ever expressly described it as an island.

Thule is not Iceland

But if none of the statements about Thule answers to Shetland, it becomes a question where we are to look for this country.[3] The Irish monk Dicuil, who wrote about

---

[1] Cf. Brenner, 1877, pp. 32, 98.

[2] Cf. Keyser (1839), 1868, p. 92.

[3] If we were able to make out the etymological origin of the name Thule, it would perhaps give us some indication of where we ought to look for the country. But the various attempts that have been made to solve this riddle have been without success. It has been asserted by several authors that it comes from an old Gothic word "tiele," or "tiule," which is said to mean limit [cf. Forbiger, 1842, iii. p. 312], or an Old Saxon word "thyle," "thul," "tell" (or "tell," "till," "tiul"), said to mean the same [cf. Markham, 1893, p. 519, and Callegari, 1904, p. 47], but Professor Alf Torp, whom I have consulted, says that no such word can be found in either of these languages. The word has been further erroneously connected with the name Telemarken, which accordingly would mean borderland, but which in reality must be derived from the Norwegian word "tele," Old Norse "þeli," frozen earth, and it is by no means

PYTHEAS OF MASSALIA

825 A.D., regarded it as self-evident that Iceland, which had then been discovered by Irish monks, must be Thule, and called it so. After him Adam of Bremen and many others

impossible that Thule should be a Greek corruption of such a word. E. Benediksson has supposed that Thule might come from a Gallic word "houl," for sun [cf. Callegari, 1904, p. 47], which with a preposition " de " (or other prefix) might have been thus corrupted in Greek ; but Professor Torp informs me in a letter that no such Gallic word exists, though there is a Cymric "haul," " which in Gallic of that time must have sounded approximately 'hâvel,'" and it "is quite impossible that a preposition or prefix 'de' could have coalesced with initial ' h ' so as to result in anything like Thule." The Irish "temel" (Cymric " tywyll ") for dark, which has also been tried [Keyser, 1839, p. 397 ; 1868, p. 166], or "tawel" for silent, still [Mullenhoff, 1870, i. p. 408], are of no more use, according to Torp, since both words at that time had "m," which has later become "w." The only Celtic root which in his opinion might be thought of is "'tel' (=raise, raise oneself), to which the Irish 'telach' and 'tulach' (=a height, mound) ; but this does not seem very appropriate. The Germanic form of this root is 'thel' (modification 'thul') ; but in Germanic this is not applied to soil or land which rises. I cannot find anything else, either in Celtic or Germanic ; it is thus impossible for me to decide to which of the languages the word may belong ; I can only say that the Greek θ (th) rather points to Germanic. For no Celtic word begins with an aspirate, whereas Germanic, as you know, has transmutation of consonants (Indo-germanic 't' to 'th,' etc.), and it is not impossible that this sound-change goes as far back as the time of Pytheas." Professor Torp has further drawn my attention to the fact that from the above-mentioned "thel," raise oneself, is formed the Old Norse "þollr," tree (cf. "þoll" = fir-tree), which in early times was "þull" as radical form. There might be a bare possibility of Thule being connected with this word.

If it should appear, as hinted here, that the word Thule is of Germanic origin, then the probability of the country lying outside the British Isles would be greatly strengthened ; for Britain and the Scottish Islands were at that time not yet inhabited by a Germanic race, and the native Celts can only have known a Germanic name for a country from its own Germanic inhabitants. This land farther north must then be Norway.

It has been pointed out [cf. Cuno, 1871, i. p. 102 ; Mair, 1899, p. 15] that the name Thule reminds one of " Tyle," the capital of the Celtic colony which was established in Thrace in the 3rd century B.C. But we know nothing of the origin of this latter name, and here again there is the difficulty that it begins with "t" and not "th."

It may be further mentioned that C. Hofmann [1865, p. 17] has suggested that Thule may come from such a name as "Thumla," which in the Upsala Edda [ii. 492] is the name of an unknown island, but which was also the name of an island at the mouth of the Gota river (cf. Thumlaheide in Hising). He

CHAPTER II

IN NORTHERN MISTS

CHAPTER II

have looked upon Iceland as the Thule of the ancients. The objections to this hypothesis are: first, that Thule was inhabited (cf. Geminus, Strabo, and others, see pp. 54-55), while Iceland probably was not at that time. Even in Dicuil's time only a few monks seem to have lived there (see below on the discovery of Iceland). Nor is it likely that Pytheas should have continued his voyage at haphazard across the ocean, unless he had heard that he would find land in that direction. To this must be added that Iceland lies so far away that the distance of six days' sail will not suit it at all. Finally, if Pytheas had sailed northward at haphazard from Scotland or from Shetland, the least likely thing to happen was for him to be carried towards Iceland; neither the currents nor the prevailing winds bear in that direction; but, on the other hand, they would carry him towards Norway, and it would be natural for him to make the land there, perhaps just between 63° and 64° N. lat. or thereabouts.

Thule is Norway

All the statements about Thule which have been preserved answer to Norway,[1] but to no other country; and even if it may seem a bold idea that there should be communication over the North Sea between the Scottish islands and Norway 300 years before Christ, or 1000 years before the age of the Vikings, we are compelled to accept it, if we are to rely upon our authorities as they stand, without arbitrarily altering them; and Pytheas will then be the first man in history to sail over the North Sea and arrive on our coasts.[2]

thinks that a Greek could not pronounce such a combination of sounds as "ml" ($\mu\lambda$), but would pronounce it as "l" (λ). The word would therefore become "Thula," or according to the usual form of the declension "Thule." Meanwhile we know of no name resembling Thumla for any district which Pytheas could have reached from Britain.

[1] That Thule was Norway or Scandinavia was assumed as early as Procopius. In the last century this view was supported by Geijer, 1825; Sven Nilsson, 1837; R. Keyser, 1839; Petersen; H. J. Thue, 1843; and others. In recent years it has been especially maintained by Hergt, 1893.

[2] Mullenhoff's reasons for supposing that Thule cannot have been Norway are of little weight, and in part disclose an imperfect knowledge of the conditions. That Pytheas, if he came to Norway, must have found new species of animals

PYTHEAS OF MASSALIA

That Thule, according to Strabo, lies six days' sail " north of " Brettanice is no objection to its being Norway. " North of " can only mean " farther north than," in the same way that Brittany and places in Britain are described as being so many stadia north of Massalia. It also looks as though Eratosthenes, according to the latitudes and distances which he has taken from Pytheas, actually puts Thule to the northeast of Britain (see his map, p. 49), or precisely where Norway lies. Besides, Pytheas had no means of determining his course in overcast weather, or of fixing the longitude, for which reasons he supposed, for instance, that Cabæum (the extreme point of Brittany) lay farther west than Cape Finisterre.

That Thule is often referred to as an island by later authors is of little weight. In the first place we do not know whether Pytheas himself so described it; according to all the geographical ideas of the ancients about the north a land in the ocean farther north than the British Isles must necessarily have been an island, even if Pytheas did not say so. In the next place, if a traveller sails northwards, as he did, from one island to another, and then steers a course over the sea from Shetland and arrives at a country still farther north, it would be unlikely that he should believe himself back again on the continent. Besides, Pytheas made another voyage eastwards along the north coast of Germany, past the mouth of the Elbe, and then he had the sea always to the north of him in the direction of his Thule. In order to discover that this

---

and new races of men, especially the Lapps with their reindeer, which, according to Mullenhoff, he evidently did not find, is, for instance, an untenable assertion; for in the first place it is very uncertain whether the reindeer-Lapps had reached Norway so early as that time, since they appear to be a comparatively late immigration. In the second place, if they were really already living in Finmarken and the northern part of Helgeland (Hálogaland), it is unreasonable to suppose that a seafarer who went along the coast as far as to the neighbourhood of the Arctic Circle should have met with these Lapps. Finally, it is impossible to take it for granted that Pytheas did not mention all the things that are not to be found in the chance quotations of later writers.

land was connected with the continent, he would have had to sail right up into the Gulf of Bothnia. It would therefore have been illogical of Pytheas if he had not conceived Thule as a great island, as in fact it was spoken of later. It is mentioned indeed as the greatest of all islands. When the Romans first heard of Sweden or Scandinavia (Skåne) in the Baltic, they likewise called it an island, and so it was long thought to be.

According to what has been advanced above we must then believe that Pytheas had already received information in northern Brettanice or in the Scottish islands about Thule or Norway across the sea. But from this it follows that in his time, or more than a thousand years before the beginning of the Viking age, there must have been communication by sea between North Britain and Norway. It may seem that this is putting back the Norsemen's navigation of the high seas to a very remote period; but as we shall see in a later chapter on the voyages of the Norsemen, there are good reasons for thinking that their seafaring is of very ancient date.

Pytheas may have sailed from Shetland with a southwesterly wind and a favourable current towards the north-east, and have arrived off the coast of Norway in the Romsdal or Nordmore district, where the longest day of the year was of twenty-one hours, and where there is a free outlook over the sea to the north, so that the barbarians may well have shown him where the sun went to rest. From here he may then have sailed northwards along the coast of Helgeland, perhaps far enough to enable him to see the midnight sun, somewhere north of Donna or Bodo; this depends upon how early in the summer he reached there. On midsummer night he would have been able to see a little of the midnight sun even at about $65\frac{1}{2}°$ N. lat.; or south of Vega.[1]

---

[1] The Arctic Circle at that time lay in 66° 15′ 20″. If we put the horizontal refraction plus the sun's semi-diameter at 50′ in round figures, then the upper edge of the sun would be visible at midnight at the summer solstice a little north of 65° 25′.

PYTHEAS OF MASSALIA

It is nowhere expressly stated that Pytheas himself saw the midnight sun; but a passage in Pomponius Mela [iii. 6, 57] may perhaps point to this. He says of Thule: " but at the summer solstice there is no night there, since the sun then no longer shows merely a reflection, but also the greater part of itself." It is most reasonable to suppose that this statement is due to actual observation; for if it were only a theoretical conclusion it seems extraordinary that he should not rather mention that the whole of the sun is above the horizon in northern regions, which was clearly enough grasped long before his time (cf. for instance Geminus of Rhodes). Now it may, of course, be thought that such an observation was made by people who came from northernmost Europe later than Pytheas's time and before Mela wrote; but so long as we do not know of any such authority it is doubtless more reasonable to suppose that like so many other pieces of information it is derived from Pytheas.

CHAPTER II

Strabo has a statement about what Pytheas said of the peoples of the northernmost regions. In a special section wherein he is speaking of Thule, and, as usual, trying to cast suspicion on Pytheas's veracity, he says:

The inhabitants of the northern regions

"Yet as far as celestial phenomena and mathematical calculations are concerned, he seems to have handled these subjects fairly well. [Thus he says not inappropriately that] in the regions near the cold zone the finer fruits are lacking and there are few animals, and that the people live on millet [i e., oats] and other things, especially green vegetables, wild fruits and roots; but among those that have corn and honey they make a drink thereof. But because they have no clear sunshine they thresh the corn in large buildings after the ears have been brought thither; for it becomes spoilt on the open threshing-floors by reason of the want of sunshine and the heavy showers."

As Diodorus [v. 21] says something similar about the harvest in Britain, it seems possible that Strabo is here thinking rather of what Pytheas had said in a more general way about the peoples near the cold regions, than of his observations on the actual inhabitants of Thule, though, as already remarked, the passage occurs in a section devoted to the latter. The mention of honey may strengthen this view; for even though

IN NORTHERN MISTS

CHAPTER II

bee-keeping is now practised in Norway as far north as Hedemarken, and also on the west coast, it is doubtful whether such was the case at that time, though it is not impossible. That wild honey is alluded to, or honey imported from abroad, is improbable.

In the MSS. of Solinus there is a statement about the people of Thule which will be referred to later. Even if the passage were genuine it could hardly, as some have thought, be derived from Pytheas; in any case it does not agree with what he is said by Strabo to have related of the people of the North. In particular it may be pointed out that while the inhabitants of Thule according to the Solinus MSS. lived principally as herdsmen, and are not spoken of as agriculturists, Strabo says nothing about cattle, but on the contrary calls them tillers of the soil. In both accounts they also live on herbs and wild fruits; but, in spite of that, these two passages cannot be derived from the same description. It is true that Strabo was not acquainted with Pytheas's original work, in which other northern peoples may have been referred to; but this is not very likely.

Length of the voyage

Most writers have thought that Pytheas completed his voyage in comparatively few months, and that he was only some few days in Thule; while others have considered that he spent many years over it.[1] There is no cogent reason for assuming this. As regards the first hypothesis, it is by no means impossible that he should have sailed from Spain to Helgeland in Norway and back again in one summer. But as the greater part of the voyage lay through unknown regions, and as he frequently stopped to investigate the country and the people, he cannot have proceeded very rapidly. To this must probably be added that he often had to barter with the

---

[1] Cf. Markham, 1893. If the longest day of the year is given in the different authorities (Strabo, Geminus, etc.) at various places as seventeen, eighteen, nineteen hours, etc., after the statements of Pytheas, it must not, of course, be assumed that Pytheas was at each of these places precisely on Midsummer Day. It was only one of the Greek methods of indicating the latitude of places.

natives to obtain the necessary provisions, since he certainly cannot have carried stores for so long a time. It therefore seems doubtful whether he was ready to return the same summer or autumn, and it is more reasonable to suppose that he wintered at some place on the way.

Whether it be Thule or Britain that is referred to in the passage quoted above from Strabo, it seems to imply that he was in one of these countries at the harvest, and saw there the gathering in of the corn ; but, of course, there is also the possibility that the people may have told him about it (through interpreters) : and more than that we can scarcely say. It might be objected that if Pytheas had spent a winter in Norway it is probable that he would have furnished many details, remarkable at that time, about the northern winter, of which we hear nothing in any of our authors. But it must always be remembered how utterly casual and defective are the quotations from him which have been preserved, and how little we know of what he really related.

Pytheas also furnished information about the sea on the other side of Thule. This may be concluded from the following passages in particular :

Strabo says [i. 63] : "Thule, which Pytheas says lies six days' sail north of Brettanice, and is near to the congealed sea ($\pi\epsilon\pi\eta\gamma o\tilde{\iota}a$ $\theta \acute{a} \lambda a \tau \tau a$, i.e., the Polar Sea)."

Pliny [iv. 16 (30)] : "After one day's sail from Thule the frozen sea ('mare concretum') is reached, called by some 'Cronium.'"[1]

---

[1] The origin of this name for the northernmost or outer sea, which occurs in several authors, is somewhat uncertain. It is usually supposed [cf. Hergt, 1893, p. 71] that it comes from the Greek god "Cronos" (Latin "Saturn"). R. Keyser [1839, p. 396, 1868, p. 165] thought (after Toland in 1725) that it was of Celtic origin and cognate with the Welsh "croni," to collect together ; "Muir-croinn" was supposed still to be Irish for the Polar Sea, and to have some such meaning as the curdled sea ; but no such word is to be found in Irish or Old Irish [cf. Mullenhoff, 1870, p. 415].

IN NORTHERN MISTS

CHAPTER II

Solinus [22, 11]: "Beyond Thule we meet with the sluggish and congealed sea ('pigrum et concretum mare ')."

Finally we have a well-known passage in Strabo [ii. 104] which says that Pytheas asserted that in addition to having visited the whole of Britain . . .

> "He had also undertaken investigations concerning Thule and those regions, in which there was no longer any distinction of land or sea or air, but a mixture of the three like sea-lung, in which he says that land and sea and everything floats, and this [i.e., the mixture] binds all together, and can neither be traversed on foot nor by boat. The substance resembling lung he has seen himself, as he says; the rest he relates according to what he has heard. This is Pytheas's tale, and he adds that when he returned here, he visited the whole ocean coast of Europe from Gadeira to Tanais."

This much-disputed description of the sea beyond Thule has first passed through Polybius, who did not believe in Pytheas and tried to throw ridicule upon him. Whether Polybius obtained it directly, or at second hand through some older writer, we do not know. From him it came down to Strabo, who had as little belief in it, and was, moreover, liable to misunderstand and to be hasty in his quotations. The passage is evidently torn from its context and has been much abbreviated in order to accentuate its improbability. It is, therefore, impossible to decide what Pytheas himself said. As it has come down to us the passage is extremely obscure, and it does not even appear clearly how much Pytheas asserted that he had himself seen, and how much he had heard; whether he had only heard of the stiffened and congealed sea (the Polar Sea), while he had really seen the condition that he compared to a lung. As to the meaning of this word there have been many and very different guesses. Some have thought that a common jelly-fish may have been called a sea-lung in the Mediterranean countries at that time, in analogy to its German designation, "Meerlunge." It may also be thought that Pytheas merely wished to describe a

---

[1] Hergt [1893, p. 71] lays stress on the use of "ultra" here and not "trans," and thinks that this does not indicate an immediate connection with Thule, but that we must rather suppose an intervening space (?).

spongy, soft mass, like an ordinary lung.[1] In both cases the description may mean a gelatinous or pulpy mass, and what Pytheas himself saw may have been the ice sludge in the sea which is formed over a great extent along the edge of the drift ice, when this has been ground to a pulp by the action of waves. The expression " can neither be traversed on foot nor by boat " is exactly applicable to this ice-sludge. If we add to this the thick fog, which is often found near drift ice, then the description that the air is also involved in the mixture, and that land and sea and everything is merged in it, will appear very graphic. But that Pytheas should have been far enough out in the sea north of Norway to have met with drift ice is scarcely credible.[2] If, on the other hand, he wintered in Norway, he may well have seen something similar on a small scale. Along the Norwegian coast, in the Skagerak, there may be ice and ice-sludge enough in the late winter, and in the fjords as well; but in that case it is probable that he would also have seen solid ice in the fjords, and would have been able to give a clearer description of the whole, which would have left no room for such misunderstandings on the part of Polybius and Strabo. It may also appear unlikely that Pytheas should not have known ice before; he must, one would think, have seen it on pools of water in the winter even in Massalia, and from the Black Sea ice was, of course, well known to the Greeks. But then it is strange that he should have given such an obscure description of such a condition, and have said that the land was also involved in the mixture; unless we are to regard the whole passage as figurative, in which case the word land

[1] Perhaps it is worth while to remark in this connection that on its second occurrence in the quotation the word is simply " lung " and not " sea-lung." If this is not to be looked upon merely as an abbreviation, it may indicate that the writer was really thinking of a bodily lung [cf. Hergt, 1893, p. 74].

[2] It has occurred that drift-ice has been brought as far as the neighbourhood of Shetland by the East-Icelandic Polar current; but this is so entirely exceptional that it cannot be argued that Pytheas might have seen drift-ice there.

may be taken as an expression for the solid as opposed to the liquid form (the sea) and the gaseous (the air).

It appears most probable that Pytheas himself never saw the Polar Sea, but heard something about it from the natives,[1] and his description of the outer ocean has then been coloured by older Greek, or even Phœnician, ideas.[2] It may suggest the old conception, which we find even in Homer, that at the extreme limits of the world heaven, earth, ocean, and Tartarus meet. To this may possibly have been added Platonic ideas of an amalgamation of the elements, earth, sea, and air; and this may have led to a general supposition that in the outer ocean everything was merged in a primeval chaos which was neither solid, liquid, nor gaseous. It is further legitimate to suppose that Pytheas in the course of his voyage in northern waters may have thought in some way or other that he had found indications of such a state of things as pointed out by Kähler [1903], for example, when he arrived at the flat coasts of Holland and North Germany (die Wattenzone), where the sea at high water pours in over the swampy land through a network of innumerable channels, which might suggest the idea of a lung, and where the peat bogs are sometimes impossible to traverse, being neither land nor sea. If Pytheas said that this was like a lung, he can only have used the word as a figure of speech, for it is incredible that he should have really regarded this as the lung of the sea, whose breathing was the ebb and

[1] It is difficult to understand how he was able to converse with the natives; but probably he took interpreters with him. In the south of England, for instance, he may have found people who had come in contact through the tin-trade with the Mediterranean peoples and understood their languages, and who could thus act as interpreters with the Celts. It would not be so easy with the Germanic people of Thule. But in Scotland he may have found Celts who understood the speech of Thule, and who could act as interpreters through the more southern Celtic people.

[2] It has already been mentioned that Avienus ascribes even to Himilco some similar ideas of the extreme parts of the ocean; and that Aristotle thought that the sea beyond the Pillars of Hercules was muddy and shallow and little stirred by the winds.

PYTHEAS OF MASSALIA

flood, as he had discovered the connection between the tides and the moon.

Other interpretations are also possible; but as we do not know what Pytheas really said, a true solution of the riddle is unattainable, and it is vain to speculate further upon it. In any case one thing is certain: his description of the outer ocean gave rise to an idea in the minds of others that it was sluggish and stiffened, or congealed, a conception which is current with most later authors who have written on it, far down into the Middle Ages. It is the same idea which we recognise as the congealed ("geliberôt") sea in the "Meregarto" and under the name of "Lebermeer" in German mediæval poetry, "la mar betée" in French, and "la mar betada" in Provençal poetry. Seafaring peoples between the Red and the Yellow Seas have similar tales,[1] but whether they are due to Greek influence or the reverse is not easy to decide.

Since Pytheas, as mentioned above, was probably acquainted with both the east and west coasts of Britain, we must assume either that on his way back from Norway he sailed southwards along the side which he had not seen on his voyage northwards, or else that he made more than one voyage to Britain. From Strabo (see above, p. 66) we know that Pytheas also asserted that he had visited "the whole ocean coast of Europe from Gadeira to Tanais," and that he had furnished information "about the Ostiæi[2] and the countries beyond the Rhine as far as the Scythians," all of which Strabo looks upon as imaginary. As Thule is never alluded to as lying north of these regions, but always as north of Britain, we cannot believe that he went straight from Norway south or south-eastwards to Jutland or the north coast of Germany. The meaning of Strabo's words must be that he claimed to have sailed along the west and north-west coast of Europe (which

---

[1] According to a communication from Professor Moltke Moe.

[2] It has been supposed by some that this name, which may remind one of the "Æstii" (Esthonians) mentioned by Tacitus, is really a clerical error for "Ostimii."

CHAPTER II

The voyage along the coast of Germany

CHAPTER II

looks towards the ocean) as far as the borders of Asia, since Tanais (the Don) was generally used as defining the frontier of the two continents.

We do not know when Pytheas undertook this voyage; but the passage quoted from Strabo [ii. 104] points to some time after the journey to Thule. There is no sufficient reason for believing that it was all accomplished at one time, or even in one year, as some will have it. It is more probable that a discoverer and explorer like Pytheas made several voyages, according as he had opportunity; and the rich commercial city of Massalia was greatly interested in the communications with the tin and amber countries, and in hearing about them.

Abalus and Balcia

On his voyage along the coast beyond the Rhine, Pytheas must have come to an island where there was amber, for according to Pliny [Nat. Hist., xxxvii. 2, 11]: "Pytheas relates that the 'Gutones,' a Germanic people, dwelt on a bay of the sea ('æstuarium') called 'Metuonidis,'[1] the extent of which was 6000 stadia. From thence it was one day's sail to the island of 'Abalus.' Here in the spring the waves cast up amber, which is washed out of the congealed sea ['mare concretum,' the Polar Sea]. The natives use it instead of wood for fire, and sell it to the neighbouring Teutons. This was also believed by Timæus, but he calls the island 'Basilia.'"

It is possible that this island, Abalus, is the same as the amber island mentioned in another passage of Pliny [iv. 13, 27], where he says of the Scythian coast that there are reports of "many islands without a name, and Timæus relates that among them is one off Scythia, a day's sail away, which is called 'Baunonia,' and on which the waves cast up amber in

---

[1] The more usual spelling "Mentonomon" (after some MSS.) can hardly be right [cf. Detlefsen, 1904, p. 9]. The name may be connected with the Frisian "meden" (Old Frisian "mede" or "medu," English "meadow") for low-lying, swampy pasture, and in that case would suit the German North Sea coast well, between the Rhine and Sleswick-Holstein.

PYTHEAS OF MASSALIA

the springtime." In any case they are both mentioned in very similar terms [cf. Hergt, 1893, pp. 31 f.]. In the same place we read that "Xenophon, of Lampsacus [about 100 B.C.], mentions that three days' sail from the Scythian coast there is an island called 'Balcia,' of immense size. Pythias calls it 'Basilia.'" This conflicts with the passage quoted above from Pliny, and here there must be a misunderstanding or confusion of some kind, either on the part of Pliny or of his authority. A possible explanation may be that Pytheas referred to his island of Abalus as a $\beta\alpha\sigma\iota\lambda\epsilon\iota\alpha$ $\nu\tilde{\eta}\sigma\sigma$, i.e., an island with a king [cf. Detlefsen, 1904, p. 18]. This would agree with the statement of Diodorus Siculus (1st century B.C.) [v. 23], which he gives without quoting any authority: "Just opposite Scythia, above Galatia [Gaul], an island lies in the ocean called 'Basilia'; upon it amber is cast up by the waves, which is otherwise not found in any place on the earth." It is probable that this is taken from Timæus and originally derived from Pytheas, and that the island is the same as Abalus. It is to be noticed that in Pytheas's time the name Germania was not yet used; northern Europe, east of the Rhine, was counted as Scythia, whereas the name Germania was well known in the time of Diodorus.

Pytheas may also have heard of, or visited, a country or a large island (Jutland?), which lay three days' sail from the coast he was sailing along, and he may likewise have referred to it as a king's island ($\beta\alpha\sigma\iota\lambda\epsilon\iota\alpha$). Timæus, or others, may have taken this for a name, both for Abalus and for this larger and more distant island, which has later been assumed to be the same as Balcia, a name that may be derived either from Pytheas or from some later writer.

As the Gutones resemble the Gytoni (Goths) of Tacitus, who lived on the Vistula, and as further Basilia and Balcia were the same country, the name of which was connected with that of the Baltic Sea, and as this country was identified with the south of Sweden, it was thought that Pytheas must have been in the amber country on the south coast of the Baltic, and even in Skåne. This view may appear to be supported by the fact that Strabo says he lied about the "Ostiæi," who might then be the Esthonians. But as already remarked this word may be an error for "Ostimians"; and Gutones may further be an error for Teutones, since a carelessly written Τευ may easily be read as Γου [cf. Hergt, 1893, p. 33], and immediately afterwards it is stated that the Teutones (not Gutones) lived near Abalus. Whether Pytheas really mentioned "Balcia" or "Baltia" is, as already remarked, extremely doubtful; but even if he did so, and even if it lay in the Baltic, it is not certain that he was there, and he may only have been told about it. We need not therefore believe that he went farther than the coast of the North Sea. "Abalus" may have been Heligoland [cf. Hergt], or perhaps rather one of the islands of Sleswick,[1] where beach-washed amber is common, as along the whole west coast of Jutland. The statement that the natives used amber as fuel is a misunderstanding, which may be due to a discovery of Pytheas that amber was combustible. If he had really sailed past the Skaw and through the Belts into the Baltic, it is unlikely that he should only have mentioned one amber island Abalus, and another immense island farther off. We should expect him to have changed the ideas of his time about these regions to a greater extent than this. It is true that he might have travelled overland to the south coast of the Baltic; but neither is this very probable. It must nevertheless be borne in mind, as will be pointed out later, that until Strabo's time no other voyages in these regions were known in literature, and it is, therefore, possible that much of what we find in Mela and Pliny on the subject was originally derived from

[1] The name may have some connection with those of Habel and Appeland among the Halligen Islands on the west coast of Sleswick [cf. Detlefsen, 1904, p. 60]. It also has some resemblance to "Sabalingu," which is given by Ptolemy as the name of a tribe in Jutland. The name Abalus (Greek, Abalos) has a remarkable likeness to Avalon (the apple-island) of Welsh folk-lore, and it is possibly originally the same word (?).

PYTHEAS OF MASSALIA

Pytheas. If we did not possess this one chance passage in Pliny about Abalus and the amber, we should not know that Pytheas had said anything about it. But of how much more are we ignorant for want of similar casual quotations?

Little as we know of Pytheas himself, he yet appears to us as one of the most capable and undaunted explorers the world has seen. Besides being the first, of whom we have certain record, to sail along the coasts of northern Gaul and Germany, he was the discoverer of Great Britain, of the Scottish isles and Shetland, and last, but not least, of Thule or Norway, as far north as to the Arctic Circle. No other single traveller known to history has made such far-reaching and important discoveries.

But Pytheas was too far in advance of his time; his description of the new lands in the North was so pronouncedly antagonistic to current ideas that it won little acceptance throughout the whole succeeding period of antiquity. His younger contemporary, Dicæarchus, doubted him, and Polybius and Strabo, who came two hundred and three hundred years later, endeavoured, as we have seen, to throw suspicion upon Pytheas and to stamp him as an impostor. The two eminent geographers and astronomers, Eratosthenes and Hipparchus, seem to have valued him more according to his deserts. Polybius's desire to lessen the fame of Pytheas may perhaps be explained by the fact that the former, a friend of Scipio, had taken part in many Roman campaigns, and claimed to be more widely travelled than any other geographer. But as his farthest north was the south of Gaul, he did not like the idea that an earlier traveller, who enjoyed great renown, should have penetrated so much farther into regions which were entirely unknown to himself. Men are not always above such littleness.

The World according to Strabo (K. Kretschmer, 1892)

CHAPTER III

ANTIQUITY, AFTER PYTHEAS

THERE was a long interval after the time of Pytheas before the world's knowledge of the North was again added to, so far as we can judge from the literature that has come down to us. The mist in which for a moment he showed a ray of light settled down again. That no other known traveller can have penetrated into these northern regions during the next two or three centuries appears from the unwillingness of Polybius and Strabo to believe in Pytheas, and from the fact that Strabo pronounces him a liar [i. 63], because "all who have seen Britain and Ierne say nothing about Thule, though they mention other small islands near Britain"; furthermore, he says expressly [vii. 294] that "the region along the ocean beyond Albis [the Elbe] is entirely unknown to us. For neither do we know of any one among the ancients who made this voyage along the coast in the eastern regions to the opening of the Caspian Sea, nor have the Romans ever penetrated into the countries beyond Albis, nor has any one yet traversed them by land." If any other traveller had been currently mentioned in literature it is incredible that the well-read Strabo should not have known it. He therefore ascribed all that he found about these regions to Pytheas.

There are nevertheless indications that the Greeks had commercial relations with the coasts of the Baltic and North Sea, and fresh obscure statements, which may be derived from such a connection, appear later in Pliny, and to some extent also in Mela. It may be supposed that enterprising Greek traders and seamen, enticed by Pytheas's accounts of the amber country, attempted to follow in his track, and succeeded in reaching the land of promise whence this costly commodity came. And if they had once found out the way, they would certainly not have relinquished it except upon compulsion. But it must be remembered that the voyage was long, and that they had first to pass through the western Mediterranean and the Pillars of Hercules, where the Carthaginians had regained their power and obtained the command of the sea. The overland route was easier and safer; it ran through the country of tribes which in those distant times may have been comparatively peaceful. The trade communication between the Black Sea and the Baltic countries seems, as mentioned above, to have developed early, and it may be thought that the active Greek traders would try it in order to reach a district where so much profit was to be expected; but no certain indication of this communication can be produced from any older author of note after Pytheas's time, so far as we know them, and even so late an author as Ptolemy has little to tell us of the regions east of the Vistula.

The founder of scientific geography, Eratosthenes (275–circa 194 B.C.),[1] librarian of the Museum of Alexandria, based what he says of the North chiefly on Pytheas. He divided

[1] As to what we know of the work of this important geographer see in particular Berger [1880].

CHAPTER III the surface of the earth into climates (zones) and constructed the first map of the world, whereon an attempt was made to fix the position of the various places by lines of latitude and meridians. He started with seven known points, along the old meridian of Rhodes. They were: Thule, the Borysthenes, the Hellespont, Rhodes, Alexandria, Syene, and Meroe. Through these points he laid down lines of latitude (see the map). He also made an attempt to calculate the circumference of the globe by measurement, and found it 250,000 stadia (=25,000 geographical miles), which is 34,000 stadia (= 3400 geographical miles) too much. He placed the island of Thule under the Arctic Circle,[1] far out in the sea to the north of Brettanice. This was to him the uttermost land and the northern limit of the " œcumene," which he calculated to be 38,000 stadia (= 3800 geographical miles) broad,[2] which according to his measurement of the circumference of the earth is about 54° 17′, since each of his degrees of latitude will be about 700 stadia. His " œcumene " thus extended from the latitude of the Cinnamon Coast (Somaliland) and Taprobane (Ceylon), 8800 stadia north of the equator, to the Arctic Circle. South of it was uninhabitable on account of the heat, and north of it all was frozen.

Eratosthenes was especially an advocate of the island-form of the " œcumene," and thought that it was entirely surrounded by the ocean, which had been encountered in every quarter where the utmost limits of the world had been reached. By a perversion of the journey of Patrocles to a voyage round India and the east coast of the continent into the Caspian Sea, he again represented the latter as an open bay of the northern ocean, in spite of the fact that Herodotus, and also Aristotle, had asserted that it was closed. The view that the Caspian Sea was a bay remained current until the time of Ptolemy. Eratosthenes also held that the occurrence of tides on all

---

[1] According to Eratosthenes' accurate calculation the Arctic Circle lay in 66° 9′ N. lat.

[2] Cf. Strabo, 1. 63, ii. 114. More accurately it should be 37,400 stadia.

ANTIQUITY, AFTER PYTHEAS

the outer coasts was a proof of the continuity of the ocean. He said that "if the great extent of the Atlantic Ocean did not make it impossible, we should be able to make the voyage from Iberia to India along the same latitude." This was 1700 years before Columbus.

With the scientific investigator's lack of respect for authorities, he had the audacity to doubt Homer's geographical

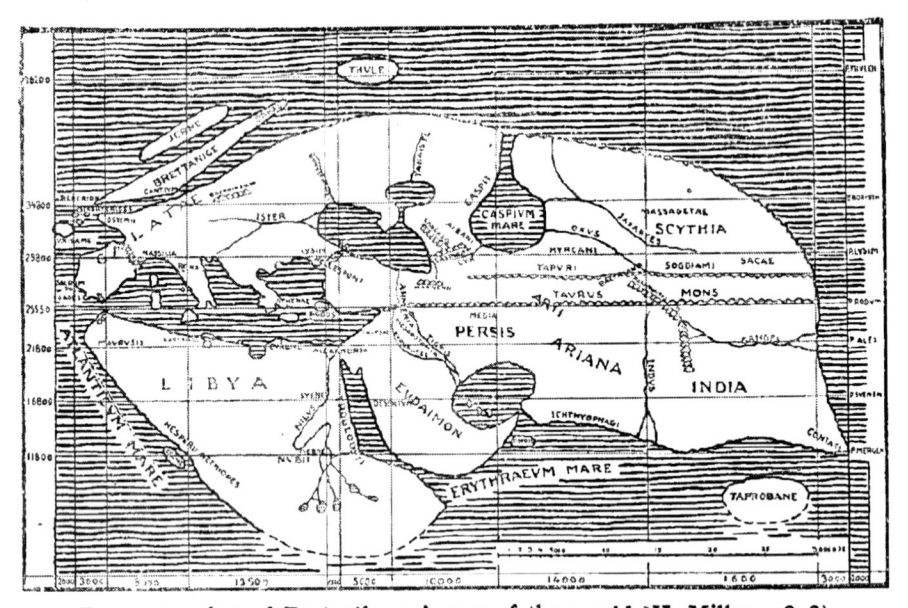

Reconstruction of Eratosthenes' map of the world (K. Miller, 1898)

knowledge, and gave offence to many by saying that people would never discover where the islands of Æolus, Circe, and Calypso, described in the Odyssey, really were, until they had found the tailor who had made the bag of the winds for Æolus.

Hipparchus (circa 190–125 B.C.) also relies upon Pytheas, and has nothing new to tell us of the northern regions. Against Eratosthenes' proof of the continuity of the ocean, to which allusion has just been made, he objected that the tides are by no means uniform on all coasts, and in support of this assertion he referred to the Babylonian Seleucus.[1]

[1] Cf. Strabo, i. 5-6. Seleucus of Selucia on the Tigris lived in the middle of the 2nd century B.C., and was one of the few who (like Aristarchus of Samos,

IN NORTHERN MISTS

CHAPTER III

But it is not clear whether Hipparchus was an opponent of the doctrine of the island-form of the "œcumene," as has been generally supposed; probably he merely wished to point out that the evidence adduced by Eratosthenes was insufficient. Hipparchus calculated a continuous table of latitude, or climate-table, for the various known localities, as far north as Thule. He introduced the division into degrees. It is also probable that he was the first to use a kind of map-projection with the aid of converging meridians, which he drew in straight lines; but as he was more an astronomer than a geographer it is unlikely that he constructed any complete map of the world.

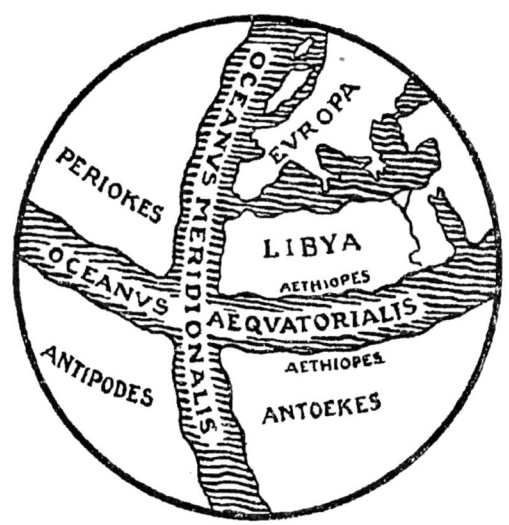

Polybius, 204-127 B.C.

Polybius (circa 204–127 B.C.), as we have seen, pronounced against the trustworthiness of Pytheas, and declared that all the country north of Narbo, the Alps, and the Tanais was

Terrestrial globe, according to Crates of Mallus (K. Kretschmer)

unknown. Like Herodotus, he left the question open whether there was a continuous ocean on the north side; but he appears to have inclined to the old notion of the "œcumene" as circular.

Crates of Mallus, 150 B.C.

The Stoic and grammarian Crates of Mallus (about 150 B.C.), who was not a geographer, constructed the first terrestrial globe, in which he made the Atlantic Ocean extend like a belt round the world through both the poles, and with the Stoic's worship of Homer he thought he could follow in this ocean Odysseus's voyage to the regions of the Læstrygons'

c. 260 B.C.) held the doctrine of the earth's rotation and movement round the sun.

ANTIQUITY, AFTER PYTHEAS

long day and the Cimmerians' polar night. Since the school of the Stoics considered it necessary that there should be ocean in the torrid zone, so that the sun might easily keep up its warmth by the aid of vapours from the sea—for warmth was supported by moisture—Crates placed a belt of ocean round the earth between the tropics, which formed the limits of the sun's path. These two belts of water left four masses of land of which only one was known to men.

The physical geographer Posidonius of Apamea in Syria (135-51 B.C.), who lived for a long time at Rhodes, took the Rhipæan Mountains for the Alps, and speaks of the Hyperboreans to the north of them. He thought that the Ocean surrounded the " œcumene " continuously :

"for its waves were not confined by any fetters of land, but it stretched to infinity and nothing made its waters turbid."

A ship sailing with an east wind from the Pillars of Hercules must reach India after traversing 70,000 stadia, which he thought was the half-circumference of the earth along the latitude of Rhodes. The greatest circumference he calculated at 180,000 stadia. These erroneous calculations were adopted by Ptolemy, and were afterwards of great significance to Columbus.

He made a journey as far as Gadir in order to see the outer Ocean for himself, to measure the tides and to examine the correctness of the generally accepted idea that the sun, on its setting in the western ocean, gave out a hissing sound like a red-hot body being dipped into water. He rightly connected the tides with the moon, finding that their monthly period corresponded with the full moon ; whereas others had thought, for instance, that they were due to changes in the rivers of Gaul.

Cæsar's Gallic War and his invasion of Britain (55-45 B.C.) contributed fresh information about these portions of Western Europe ; but it cannot be seen that they gave anything new about the North. Cæsar describes Britain as a triangle. This is undoubtedly the same idea that we find in his contemporary Diodorus Siculus, and is derived from Pytheas. Cæsar merely gives different proportions between the sides from those of Diodorus. He puts Hibernia to the west of Britain, not to the north like Strabo, and makes its size about two-thirds of the latter, from which it is separated by a strait of about the same breadth as that between Gaul and Britain. Between Ireland (Hibernia) and Britain is an island, " Mona " (Anglesey), and scattered about it many other islands. In some of them there was said to be a month of unbroken night at the winter solstice ; but of this Cæsar was unable to obtain certain information. This must be an echo of the tales about Thule, which he had got from older Greek or Roman authors.

Cæsar is a good example of the Romans' views of and sense for geography. In spite of this military nation having extended their empire to the bounds of the unknown in every direction, they never produced a scientific geographer, nor did they send out anything that we should call a voyage of exploration, as the Phœnicians, Carthaginians, and Greeks had done. They were above all a practical people, with more sense for organisation than for research and science, and in addition they lacked commercial interests as compared with those other peoples. But during their long campaigns under the Empire, and by their extensive communications with the most distant regions, they brought together an abundance of geographical information hitherto unknown to the classical world. It is natural that it should have been a Greek who, in one of the most important geographical works that have come down to us from ancient times, endeavoured to collect a part of this information, together with the knowledge already acquired by the Greeks, into a systematic statement.

This man was the famous geographer Strabo, a native of Asia Minor (about 63 B.C.–25 A.D.). But unfortunately this critic has nothing to tell us about the North, and in his anxiety to avoid exaggeration he has, like Polybius, been at great pains to discredit Pytheas, of whose statements he will take no account ; nor has he made use of the knowledge of

ANTIQUITY, AFTER PYTHEAS

the northernmost regions which we see, from Pliny among others, that other Greek authors possessed. He has not even made use of the geographical knowledge which was gained in his own time during the Roman campaign in Northern Germania under Augustus, if indeed he knew of it. To him the Ister (Danube), the mountainous districts of the Hercynian Forest, and the country as far as the Tyregetæ formed, roughly, the northern boundary of the known world. He thinks it is only ignorance of the more distant regions that has made people believe the fables " of the Rhipæan Mountains and the Hyperboreans, as well as all that Pytheas of Massalia has invented about the coast of the ocean, making use of his astronomical and mathematical knowledge as a cloak." " Ierne " (Ireland) was placed by Strabo out in the ocean to the north of Britain. He took it for the most northern land, and thought that its latitude (which would have to be about 54° N.) formed the boundary of the " œcumene."

"For," he says [II. 115], "living writers tell us of nothing beyond Ierne, which lies near to Britain on the north, and is inhabited by savages who live miserably on account of the cold." He says further [IV. 201] of this island at the end of the world: "of this we have nothing certain to relate, except that its inhabitants are even more savage than the Britons, as they are both cannibals and omnivorous [or grass-eaters?], and consider it commendable to devour their deceased parents,[1] as well as openly to have commerce not only with other women, but also with their own mothers and sisters But this we relate perhaps without sufficient authority; although cannibalism at least is said to be a Scythian custom, and the Celts, the Iberians, and other peoples are reported to have practised it under the stress of a siege."

---

[1] Herodotus [IV. 26] says of the Issedonians in Scythia that " when a man's father dies, all the relatives bring cattle ; and when they have slain them as a sacrifice and cut the flesh in pieces, they also cut up their host's deceased father , then they mix all the flesh together and serve it for the meal ; but the head they decorate with gold, after having taken the hair off and washed it ; and afterwards they treat it as an idol and bring offerings to it every year." Such a cannibal custom, if it really existed, may have been connected with religious ideas. But Herodotus [i, 216] attributes to the Massagetæ the following still more horrible custom : " when a man grows very old, all his relatives assemble and slay him, and together with him several kinds of cattle ; then they boil the flesh and hold a banquet. This is accounted among them the happiest end."

IN NORTHERN MISTS

CHAPTER III

Strabo evidently attributes to a cold climate a remarkable capacity for brutalising people, and he considers that the reports of the still more distant Thule must be even more uncertain.

The breadth of the "œcumene," from north to south, he made only 30,000 stadia, and thought that Eratosthenes, deceived by the fables of Pytheas, had put the limit 8000 stadia (= 11° 26′) too far north. Of the countries beyond the Albis (Elbe), he says, nothing is known. Nevertheless he mentions the Cimbri as dwelling on a peninsula by the northern ocean; but he has no very clear idea of where this peninsula is.

> No one can believe, he thinks [vii. 292], that the reason for their wandering and piratical life was that they were driven out of their peninsula [which must be Jutland] by a great inundation, for they still have the same country as before, and it is ridiculous to suppose that they left it in anger at a natural and constant phenomenon, which occurs twice daily [i.e., the tides], etc. But it appears from Strabo's statements that there had been many reports of a great storm-flood in Denmark, which the Cimbri escaped from with difficulty.
>
> Of the customs of these people Strabo relates among other things that they were accompanied on their expeditions by priestesses with gray hair, white clothes, and bare feet. "They went with drawn swords to meet the captives in the camp, crowned them with garlands and led them to a sacrificial vessel of metal, holding twenty amphoræ [Roman cubic feet]. Here they had a ladder, upon which one of them mounted and, bent over the vessel, they cut the throat of the prisoner, who was held up. They made auguries from the blood running into the vessel; while others opened the corpse and inspected the entrails, prophesying victory for their army. And in battle they beat skins stretched upon the wicker-work of their chariots, making a hideous noise." This is one of the first descriptions of the customs of the warrior-hordes roving about Europe, who came in contact with the classical world from the unknown north, and who in later centuries were to come more frequently. But the description is certainly influenced by Greek ideas.

Strabo thought that besides the world known to the Greeks and Romans, other continents or worlds, where other races of men dwelt, might be discovered.

Albinovanus Pedo — In a work called "Suasoriæ" (circa 37 A.D.) of the Spanish-born rhetorician Seneca there are preserved fragments of a poem, written by Albinovanus Pedo (in the time of Augustus), which described an expedition of Germanicus

ANTIQUITY, AFTER PYTHEAS

in the North Sea. It has been thought that this may have been the younger Germanicus's unfortunate campaign in 16 A.D., when he sailed out from the Ems with a fleet of a thousand ships. This supposition is strengthened by the fact that Tacitus mentions a cavalry leader, Albinovanus Pedo, under the same commander in 15 A.D., and it is easy to believe that he was the poet.[1] But as this unhappy fleet did not get far from the coast, and the poem describes a voyage into unknown regions, others have thought that it might be an expedition undertaken by Drusus, the elder Germanicus, in some year between 12 and 9 B.C.[2] How this may be is of less importance to us, as the poem does not mention any fresh discoveries. It is interesting because it gives us a picture of the ideas current at that time about the northern limits of the world. Where the fragments commence, the travellers have long ago left daylight and the sun behind them, and, having passed beyond the limits of the known world, plunge boldly into the forbidden darkness towards the end of the western world. There they believe that the sea, which beneath its sluggish ("pigris") waves is full of hideous monsters, savage whales ("pistris"), and sea-hounds ("æquoreosque canes = seals?), rises and takes hold of the ship—the noise itself increases the horror—and now they think the ships will stick in the mud, and the fleet will remain there, deserted by the winds[3] of the ocean—now that they themselves will be left there helpless and be torn to pieces by the monsters of the deep. And the man who stands high in the prow strives

[1] Cf. M. Schanz: "Geschichte der Romischen Literatur," ii. p. 241, 1899; in I. Muller: "Handb. Klass. Altert.-Wiss.," bd. viii. See also Mullenhoff, iv., 1900, p. 47.

[2] Cf. Detlefsen, 1897, p. 197; 1904, p. 45. By his voyage in 12 B.C. with his fleet along the coast of the North Sea from the mouth of the Rhine and the Zuyder Zee to the mouth of the Ems, Drusus won fame as the first general who had sailed in the North Sea. The Romans, of course, were not great seafarers.

[3] The MSS. have "flamine" (winds); but it has been thought that "flumine" (streams) gives a better meaning [cf. Detlefsen, 1897, p. 198]. "Flamine" (winds) might, however, suit the ideas of the earth's limits (cf. the description of Himilco's voyage in Avienus, see above, p. 37].

CHAPTER III

with his eyes to break through the impenetrable air, but can see nothing, and relieves his oppression in the following words: "Whither are we being carried? The day itself flees from us, and uttermost nature closes in the deserted world with continual darkness. Or are we sailing towards people on the other side, who dwell under another heaven, and towards another unknown world?[1] The gods call us back and forbid the eyes of mortals to see the boundary of things. Why do we violate strange seas and sacred waters with our oars, disturbing the peaceful habitations of the gods?"

This last conception is clearly derived from the "Isles of the Blest" of the Greeks (originally of the Phœnicians), which were situated in the deep currents of Oceanus and are already referred to in Hesiod.

Seneca, on the other hand, says of the outer limits of the world: "Thus is nature, beyond all things is the ocean, beyond the ocean nothing" ("ita est rerum natura, post omnia oceanus, post oceanum nihil"), and Pliny speaks of the empty space ("inane") that puts an end to the voyage beyond the ocean.

---

[1] The text has here "alium liberis (or 'libris') intactum quærimus orbem," which might be: "towards another world untouched by books," that is, of which no book has said anything. As such an expression is quite at variance with the generally pompous style of the poem, Detlefsen [1897, p. 200, 1904, p. 47] has thought that "libris" here was "libra" = "libella," that is, the level used by builders, with two legs and a plumb hanging in the middle, and the meaning would then be that this part of the earth's circumference was not touched by the plumb of the level, but that the latter was obliquely inclined over the abyss at the end of the world. This explanation seems to make Pedo's poem even more artificial than it is, and Detlefsen appears to think [1897, p. 200] that the builder's level is used to find perpendicular lines, instead of horizontal. It is probable, however, that such an idea of a gulf or abyss at the end of the world was current at that time, as it was much later (cf. Adam of Bremen, and also the Ginnungagap of the Norsemen), even if it does not appear in this poem. It might be thought that "libris" was here used in the sense of sounding-lead, so that the meaning would be, "untouched by soundings," in other words, a sea where no soundings had been made; but this meaning of "libris" would be unusual, and besides one would then expect some word for sea, and not "orbem."

ANTIQUITY, AFTER PYTHEAS

In the year 5 A.D. the emperor Augustus, in connection with Tiberius's expedition to the Elbe, sent a Roman fleet from the Rhine along the coast of Germania; it sailed northward by the land of the Cimbri (Jutland), past its northern extremity (the Skaw), probably into the Cattegat, and perhaps to the Danish islands. Augustus himself, in the Ancyra inscription, tells us of the voyage of this fleet, and says that it came "even to the people of the Cimbri, whither before that time no Roman had penetrated either by land or sea,[1] and the Cimbri and the Charydes (Harudes, Horder), and the Semnones, and other Germanic peoples in those districts sent ambassadors to ask for my friendship and that of the Roman people."[2] Velleius [ii. 106] also gives an account of this voyage, and Pliny [ii. 167] gives the following description of it : " The Northern Ocean has also been in great part traversed; by the orders of the divine Augustus a fleet sailed round Germania to the Cimbrian Cape, and saw therefrom a sea that was immeasurable, or heard that it was so, and came to the Scythian region and to places that were stiff [with cold] from too much moisture. It is therefore very improbable that the seas can run short where there is such superfluity of moisture." Müllenhoff thinks [iv., 1900, p. 45] that on this voyage they saw the Norwegian mountains, the immense " Mons Sævo " (see later under Pliny), rising out of the sea. This is not impossible, but we read nothing about it; nor indeed is it very probable. On the other hand, it is likely that the voyage resulted in fresh knowledge about the North, and that at any rate some of the statements in Mela and Pliny may be derived from this source.

The oldest known Latin geography, "De Chorographia," was written about 43 A.D. by an otherwise unknown

CHAPTER III
Augustus, 5 A.D.

Mela, c. 43 A.D.

---

[1] I cannot, with Detlefsen [1904, p. 48], find anything in this expression to show that Augustus gives the Greeks the credit for having penetrated beyond the Cimbrian Cape earlier.

[2] Cf. Mullenhoff, ii., 1887, p. 285, and iv., 1900, p. 45; Holz, 1894, p. 23; Detlefsen, 1904, p. 47.

CHAPTER III Pomponius Mela, of Tingentera, in Spain. With the strange mental poverty of Roman literature, Mela bases his work chiefly on older Greek sources (e.g., Herodotus and Eratosthenes) which are several centuries before his time; but in addition he gives much information not found elsewhere. Whether this is also for the most part taken from older writers it is impossible to say, as he nowhere gives his authorities. His descriptions, especially those of more distant regions, are sometimes made obscure and contradictory by his evidently having drawn upon different sources without combining them into a whole.

The world according to Mela

He begins with these words of wisdom: "All this, whatever it is, to which we give the name of universe and heaven, is one and includes itself and everything in a circle ('ambitu'). In the middle of the universe floats the earth, which is surrounded on all sides by sea, and is divided by it from west to east [that is, by the equatorial sea, as in Crates of Mallus] into two parts, which are called hemispheres." Whether one is to conclude from this that the earth in his opinion was a sphere or a round disc, he seems to leave the reader to determine. He divides the earth into the five zones of Parmenides. The two temperate or habitable zones seem, according to Mela, to coincide with the two masses of land, while the uninhabitable ones, the torrid and the two frigid zones, are continuous sea. On the southern continent dwell the Antichthons, who are unknown, on account of the heat of the intervening region. On the northern one we dwell, and this is what he proposes to describe.

ANTIQUITY, AFTER PYTHEAS

Europe is bounded on the west by the Atlantic, and on the north by the British Ocean. Asia has on the north the Scythian Ocean.

CHAPTER III

[iii. c. 5.] In proof of the continuity of these oceans he appeals not only to the physicists and Homer, but also to Cornelius Nepos, "who is more modern and trustworthy," and who confirms it and "cites Quintus Metellus Celer as witness thereto, and says that he has narrated the following: When he was governing Gaul as proconsul the king of the Boti [1] gave him some Indians," who "by stress of storm had been carried away from Indian waters, and after having traversed all the space between, had finally reached the shores of Germania."

Mela has many ancient fables to tell of the peoples in the northern districts of Germania, Sarmatia and Scythia, which last was his name for what is now Russia and for the north of Asia. It appears that he too was of the opinion that a cold climate develops savagery and cruelty.

He says of Germania [iii. c. 3]: "The inhabitants are immense in soul and body; and besides their natural savagery they exercise both, their souls in warfare, their bodies by accustoming them to constant hardship, especially cold." "Might is right to such an extent that they are not even ashamed of robbery; only to their guests are they kind, and merciful towards suppliants." The people of Sarmatia were nomads. [iii. c. 4.] "They are alike warlike, free, unconstrained, and so savage and cruel that the women go to war together with the men. In order that they may be fitted thereto the right breast is burned off immediately after birth, whereby the hand which is drawn out [in drawing a bow] becomes adapted for shooting [by the breast not coming in the way or because the arm grew stronger] and the breast becomes manly.[2] To draw the

---

[1] K. Miller [vi., 1898, p. 105] proposes to read "Gotorum rex" (the king of the Goths) instead of the "Botorum rex" of the MSS. The last name is otherwise unknown, and has also been read "Boiorum." Pliny, who has the same story almost word for word [Nat. Hist., ii. c. 67, 170] says that the same Celer had the Indians from the king of the Suevi.

[2] This was a common idea among the Greeks about the Amazons [cf. Hippocrates, Περι ἀερων, etc., c. 17; Strabo, xi. 504; Diodorus, ii. 45]; it has even been sought to derive the name itself from this, since "mazos" (μαζός) means breast, and "a" (α) is the negative particle, this would therefore be "without breasts." But other explanations of the origin of the name have been given, e.g., that they were not suckled at the breast. It is possible that the name meant something quite different, but that owing to its resemblance to the Greek word for breast it gave rise to the legend, and not vice versa. In Latin the Amazons were sometimes called "Unimammia" (one-breasted), but in Greek

CHAPTER III

bow, to ride and to hunt are employments for the young girls ; when grown up it is their duty to fight the foe, so that it is held to be a shame not to have killed some one, and the punishment is that they are not allowed to marry." [1] It would appear that the northern countries, according to the view of Mela, had a tendency to "emancipate" women, even though he always regards it as a severe punishment for them to have to live as virgins.[1] Among the Xamati in his western Asia, at the mouth of the Tanais [i. c 19], "the women engage in the same occupations as the men" "The men fight on foot and with arrows, the women on horseback, not using swords, but catching men in snares and killing them by dragging them along." Those who have not killed an enemy must live unmarried. Amongst other peoples the women do not confine themselves to this snaring of men ; the Mæotides who dwell in the country of the Amazons are governed by women ; and farthest north live the Amazons ; but he does not tell us whether the latter could dispense with men altogether, and reproduce themselves like the women he tells us of on an island off the coast of Africa, who were hairy all over the body. "This is related by Hanno, and it seems worthy of credit, because he brought back the skin of some he had killed." [iii c. 9]

But this increasing savagery towards the north had a limit, as in the early Greek idea, after which things became better again ; for beyond the country of the Amazons [i. c. 19] and other wild races, like the Thyssagetæ and Turcæ who inhabited immense forests and lived by hunting,[2] there extended, apparently towards the north-east (?), a " great desert and rugged tract, full of mountains, as far as the Aremphæans, who had very just customs and were looked upon as holy."[3] "Beyond them rise the Rhipæan Mountains and behind them lies the region that borders on the Ocean." In addition, the happy "Hyperboreans" dwelt in the north. In his description of Scythia he says of them [iii. c. 5] : " Then [i.e., after Sarmatia]

art they were always represented with well-developed breasts. Hippocrates says that the right breasts of the Scythian women were burned off by the mother with a special bronze instrument, while the girls were quite small, because " then the breast ceased to grow, and all force and development were transmitted to the right shoulder and the arm."

[1] Cf. Herodotus, iv. cc. 116, 117.

[2] Cf. Herodotus, iv. c. 22.

[3] These are Herodotus's "Argippæi" or "Argimpæi" [iv. c. 23], who lived in tents of felt in winter. They were bald, whereas those of Mela go bareheaded.

ANTIQUITY, AFTER PYTHEAS

come the neighbouring parts of Asia [or the parts bordering on Asia?]. Except where continual winter and unbearable cold reigns, the Scythian people dwell there, almost all known by the name of 'Belcæ' (?). On the shore of Asia come first the Hyperboreans, beyond the north wind and the Rhipæan

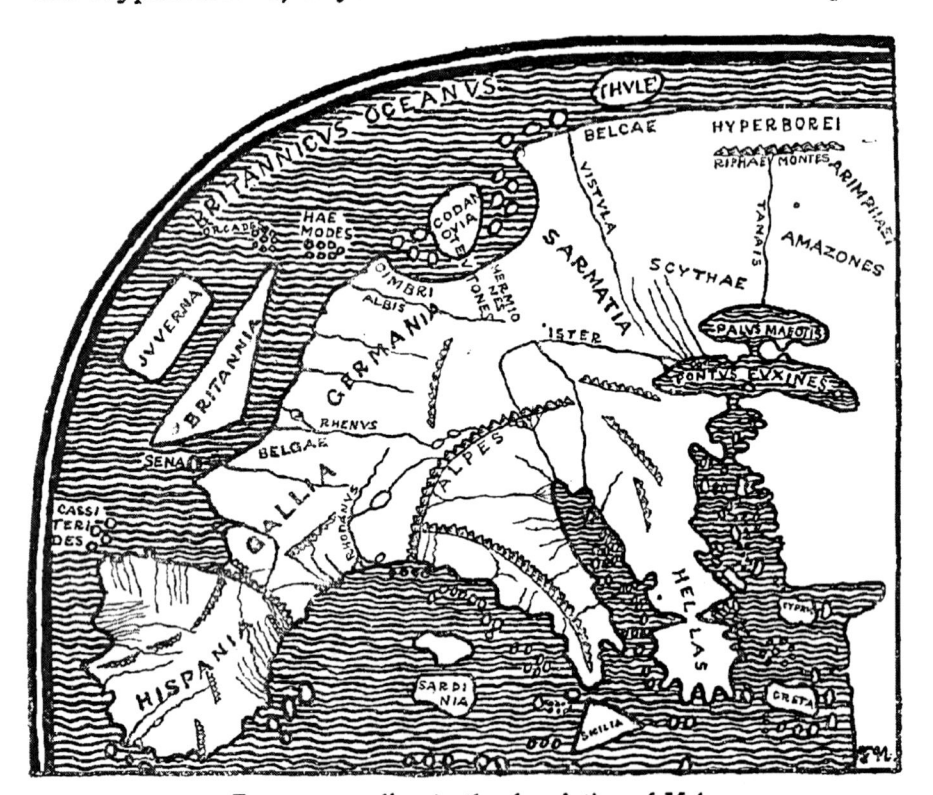

Europe according to the description of Mela

Mountains under the very pivot of the stars" [i.e., the pole]. In their country the sun rose at the vernal equinox and set at the autumnal equinox, so that they had six months day and six months night. "This narrow [or holy?] sunny land is in itself fertile." He goes on to give a description of the happy life of the Hyperboreans, taken from Greek sources.

On north-western Europe Mela has much information which is not met with in earlier authors. The tin-islands, the Cassiterides, lay off the north-west of Spain, where the

CHAPTER III "Celtici" lived [iii. c. 6]. "Beyond ('super') Britain is Juverna [Ireland], nearly as large, with a climate unfavourable to the ripening of corn, but with such excellent pastures that if the cattle are allowed to graze for more than a small part of the day, they burst in pieces. The inhabitants are rude and more ignorant than other peoples of all kinds of virtue. Religion is altogether unknown to them."

"The Orcades are thirty in number, divided from each other by narrow straits; the Hæmodæ seven, drawn towards Germany" ("septem Hæmodæ contra Germaniam vectæ"). This is the first time, so far as is known, that these two groups of islands are mentioned in literature. Diodorus, it is true, had already spoken of "Orkan" or "Orkas," but not as a group of islands. As this name is probably derived from Pytheas, it is likely that the other, "Hæmodæ," is also his. Possibly the groups were re-discovered under the emperor Claudius (about 43 A.D.) or more definite information may have been received about them; but on the other hand, Mela says that the knowledge of Britain that was acquired during this campaign would be brought back by Claudius himself in his triumph. It will be most reasonable to suppose that Mela's thirty Orcades are the Orkneys—the number is approximately correct—and not the Orkneys and Shetlands together. The seven Hæmodæ, on the other hand, must be the latter, and can hardly be the Hebrides, as many would believe, since Mela mentions the islands off the west coast of Europe in a definite order, and he names first "Juverna," then the "Orcades," and next the "Hæmodæ," which are "carried ('vectæ') towards Germany"[1] (cf. also Pliny later).

In his description of Germania [iii. c. 3] Mela says:

"Beyond ('super') Albis is an immense bay, Codanus, full of many great and small islands. Here the sea which is received in the bosom of the

---

[1] To understand [like K. Müller, vi., 1898, p. 105] "vectæ" as the name of an island ("Vectis" = the Isle of Wight) seems in itself somewhat improbable, and is moreover excluded by Mela's rhetorical style, which demands a clause following Hæmodæ to balance that attached to Orcades just before.

shore is nowhere broad and nowhere like a sea, but as the waters everywhere flow between and often go over [i.e., over the tongues of land or shallows which connect the islands] it is split up into the appearance of rivers, which are undefined and widely separated ; where the sea touches the shores [of the mainland], since it is held in by the shores of the islands which are not far from each other, and since nearly everywhere it is not large [i.e., broad], it runs in a narrow channel and like a strait ('fretum'), and turning with the shore it is curved like a long eyebrow. In this [sea] dwell the Cimbri and the Teutons, and beyond [the sea, or the Cimbri and Teutons?] the extreme people of Germania, namely the Hermiones."

The meaning of this description, which seems to be as involved as the many sounds he is talking about, must probably be that in the immense bay of Codanus there are a number of islands with many narrow straits between them, like rivers. Along the shore of the mainland there is formed, by the almost continuous line of islands lying outside, a long curving strait, which is nearly everywhere of the same narrowness. In this sea—that is to say, on the peninsulas and islands in this bay—dwell the Cimbri and Teutons, and farther away in Germania the Hermiones.

In his account of the islands along the coast of Europe, Mela says further [iii. c. 6] :

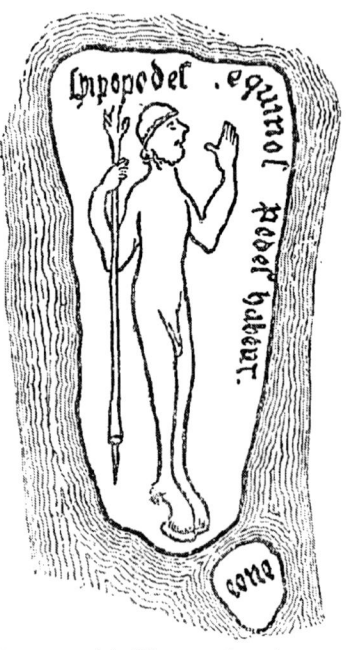

Island with Hippopod or horse-footed man (from the Hereford map)

"In the bay which we have called Codanus is amongst the islands Codanovia, which is still inhabited by the Teutons, and it surpasses the others both in size and in fertility. The part which lies towards the Sarmatians seems sometimes to be islands and sometimes connected land, on account of the backward and forward flow of the sea, and because the interval which separates them is now covered by the waves, now bare. Upon these it is asserted that the Œneans dwell, who live entirely on the eggs of fen-fowl and on oats, the Hippopods with horses' feet, and the Sanalians, who have such long ears that they cover the whole body with them instead of clothes, since they

IN NORTHERN MISTS

CHAPTER III

otherwise go naked. For these things, besides what is told in fables, I find also authorities whom I think I may follow. Towards the coast of the Belgæ [1] lies Thule, famous in Greek poems and in our own; there the nights in any case are short, since the sun, when it has long been about to set, rises up; but in the winter the nights are dark as elsewhere ... But at the summer solstice there is no night at all, because the sun then is already clearer, and not only shows its reflection, but also the greater part of itself."

Thus we see here, as in so many of the classical authors, and later in Pliny, old legends and more trustworthy information hopelessly mixed together. The legends, whose Greek origin is disclosed by the form of the names, may be old skippers' tales, or the romances of merchants who went northward from the Black Sea, but they may also in part be derived from Pytheas. A fable like that of the long-eared Sanali (otherwise called Panoti) originally came from India and is later than his time. The statement about the Œneæ, or, doubtless more correctly, Œonæ (i.e., egg-eaters), who live on eggs and oats, may, on the other hand, have reached him from the north, where the eggs both of fen-fowl (plovers' eggs, for example) and of sea-birds were eaten from time immemorial. Cæsar had heard or read of people who lived on birds' eggs and fish on the islands at the mouth of the Rhine, but he may indeed have derived his knowledge from Greek sources [cf. Müllenhoff, i., 1870, p. 492].

Island with long-eared man (from the Hereford map)

What Mela says about Thule probably comes from Pytheas, as already mentioned (p. 90), and it is very possible that the remarkable statements about the immense bay of

---

[1] These "Belgæ" are, of course, the same as the "Belcæ" already mentioned by Mela as the Scythian people in the northernmost part of Scythia (see above, p. 89). What people is meant is uncertain.

ANTIQUITY, AFTER PYTHEAS

Codanus are likewise derived from him, although they may also be ascribed to the circumnavigation of the Skaw under Augustus, or to other voyages in these waters of which we have no knowledge.

CHAPTER III

Whether Codanovia (which is not found in any other known author) is the same name as the later Scadinavia in Pliny, must be regarded as uncertain. It is the first time that such an island or that the bay of Codanus is mentioned in literature. This "immense bay" must certainly be the Cattegat with the southern part of the Baltic; and the numerous islands which close it in to a curved strait or sound must be for the most part the Danish islands and perhaps southern Sweden. Whence the name is derived we do not know for certain.[1]

Codanovia

Ptolemy mentions three peoples in southern Jutland, and calls the easternmost of them "Kobandoi." It is not likely that three peoples can have lived side by side in this narrowest part of the peninsula, and we must believe that some of them lived among the Danish islands, where Ptolemy does not give the name of any people. The "Kobandoi" would then be on the easternmost island, Sealand [cf. Much, 1893, pp. 198 f.]. Now it will easily be supposed

---

[1] Sophus Bugge [1904, pp. 156 f.] thinks that Codanus may come from an Old Norse word "Koð," which meant a shallow fjord or a shallow place in the water (equivalent to old Indian "gādhâ-m") and which according to him is akin to the root "Kað" in some Norwegian place-names. "Codanus sinus" ("Kōda," accus. "Kōdan") is then the shallow sea, or Cattegat, especially near the Belts. "Codan-ovia" is the island in "Kōdan." Mullenhoff [1887, ii. p. 284] and Much [1893, p. 207] have connected "Codanus" with Old High German "quoden" (=femina, interior pars coxæ) from the same root as the Anglo-Saxon "codd" (=serpent, sack, bag), Middle Low German "koder" (=belly, abdomen), Old Norse "koðri" (=scrotum). It would then mean a sack-inlet or sack-bay, equal to the Frisian "Jâde," or else a narrower inlet to an extended bay of the sea (the Baltic?). The explanation does not seem quite natural. R. Keyser [1868, p. 82] derives the name from "Godanus," i.e., the Gothic, although the Goths at that time were usually called "Gutones" by the Romans. Ahlenius's suggestion [1900, p. 24] that Codanus might be an old copyist's error for "Toutonos" (Teutons), because one MS. reads Thodanus, does not sound probable. Detlefsen [1904, p. 31] thinks that the name Codanus is preserved in Katte(n)-gat, which would mean the inlet (gat) to Codanus, which would then come to include the whole of the Baltic. If Bugge's explanation given above is correct, it might however mean the shallow gat or inlet.

93

IN NORTHERN MISTS

CHAPTER III

that "Codanus" and "Kobandoi" have some connection or other; the latter might be a corruption of the name of a people, "Kodanoi" or "Kodanioi."[1] But as precisely these islands and the south of Sweden were inhabited by tribes of the Danes—of whom several are mentioned in literature: South Danes, North Danes, Sea Danes, Island Danes, etc.—it may be further supposed that "Kodanioi" is composed of "ko" or cow[1] and "Daner" (that is, Cow-Danes), and means a tribe of the latter who were remarkable for the number of their cows, which would be probable enough for a people in fertile Sealand (or in Skåne).[2] In this case "Codanus" must be derived from the name of this people, just as most of the names of seas and bays in these regions were taken from the names of peoples (e.g., "Oceanus Germanicus," "Mare Suebicum," "Sinus Venedicum," "Quænsæ"). The name "Daner" is one of those names of peoples that are so ancient that their derivation must be obscure.[3] Procopius uses it as a common name for many nations ("ethne"), in the same way as he names the "ethne" of the Slavs (see later, p. 146). It is also used in the early Middle Ages as a common name for the people of the North, like Eruli, and later Normans. It is therefore natural that there should have been special names for the tribes, like Sea-Danes, Cow-Danes, etc. "Kodanovia" ("ovia," equivalent to Old High German "ouwa" or "ouwia" for island, Gothic "avi," Old Norse "ey" [cf. Grimm, 1888, p. 505], must be the island on which this tribe lived, and this might then be Sealand (though Skåne is also possible).

That the Cimbri lived in Codanus suits very well, as their home was Jutland;[4] on the other hand, we know less about the country inhabited by the Teutons. They must have been called in Germanic "*þeodonez" (Gothic "*þiudans" means properly kings), and the name has been

---

[1] Professor Alf Torp calls my attention to R. Much's [1895, p. 37] explanation of "Kobandoi" as a Germanic "*Kōwandōz," a derivation from the word cow. This should therefore be divided "Kōw-and-," where "and" is a suffix, and the meaning would be a cow-people.

[2] I have proposed this explanation to Professor Alf Torp; he finds that it "might indeed be possible, but not altogether probable."

[3] It has been sought to derive "Daner" from an original Germanic word, equivalent to Anglo-Saxon "denu" (Gothic "*danei") and "dene" for dale, and its meaning has been thought to be "dwellers in dales or lowlands" [cf. Much, 1895, p. 40; S. Bugge, 1890, p. 236].

[4] That they lived in the sea or bay must, of course, mean that they lived on islands; and the northern part of Jutland, north of the Limfiord, was probably looked upon as an island, but the Cimbrian Promontory is not mentioned; it occurs first in Pliny. The Germanic form of the name, "himbrōz," perhaps still survives in the Danish district of Himmerland, the old Himbersyssel, with the town of Aalborg [cf. Much, 1905, p. 100].

ANTIQUITY, AFTER PYTHEAS

connected with Old Norse "þiód," now Thy (Old Danish "Thythesyssel") with its capital Thisted, and the island Thyholm, in north-western Jutland [cf. Much, 1893, pp. 7 ff.; 1905, p. 100].

Whether the Vistula had its outlet into Codanus or farther east Mela does not say, nor does he tell us whether Sarmatia was bounded by this gulf; but this is not impossible, although Codanus is described at the end of the chapter on Germania. Strangely enough, he says, according to the MSS. [iii. c. 4], that "Sarmatia is separated from the following [i.e., Scythia] by the Vistula"; it would thus lie on the western side of the river, which seems curious. It might be possible that the islands off the coast of Sarmatia are among the many which lay in Codanus(?). As Sarmatia lay to the east of Germania, these islands would in any case be as far east as the Baltic, if not farther; but there is no ebb and flood there by which the connecting land between them might be alternately covered and left dry; on the other hand, the description suits the German North Sea coast. Either Mela's authority has heard of the low-lying lands—the Frische Nehrung and the Kurische Nehrung, for instance—off the coast of the amber country, and has added the tidal phenomena from the North Sea coast, or, what is more probable, the Frisian islands, for example, may by a misunderstanding have been moved eastwards into Sarmatia, since older writers, who as yet made no distinction between Germania, Sarmatia and Scythia, described them as lying far east, off the Scythian coast (perhaps taken from the voyage of Pytheas).[1]

[1] There is a resemblance of name which may be more than accidental between Mela's "Œneæ," or Pliny's "Œonæ," and Tacitus's "Aviones" ["Germania," c. 40], who lived on the islands of North Frisia and the neighbouring coast. "Aviones" evidently comes from a Germanic "*awjonez," Gothic "*aujans," Old High German "ouwon" (cf. Old Norse "ey," Old High German "ouwa" for island), which means islanders. In the Anglo-Saxon poem "Widsid" they are called "eowe" or "eowan" [cf. Grimm, 1880, p. 330 (472), Much, 1893, p. 195; 1905, p. 101]. It is possible that the Greeks, on hearing the Germanic name, connected it with the Greek word "Œonæ" (=egg-eaters), and thereby

IN NORTHERN MISTS

CHAPTER III
Voyage to Samland, circa 60 A.D.

The emperor Nero's (54-68 A.D.) love of show led, according to Pliny [Nat. Hist., xxxvii. 45], to the amber coast of the Baltic becoming "first known through a Roman knight, whom Julianus sent to purchase amber, when he was to arrange a gladiatorial combat for the emperor Nero. This knight visited the markets and the coasts and brought thence such a quantity that the nets which were hung up to keep the wild beasts away from the imperial tribune had a piece of amber in every mesh; indeed the weapons, the biers, and the whole apparatus of a day's festival were heavy with amber. The largest piece weighed thirteen pounds." This journey must have followed an undoubtedly ancient trade-route from the Adriatic to Carnuntum (in Pannonia), the modern Petronell on the Danube, where the latter is joined by the March, and from whence Pliny expressly says that the distance was 600,000 paces to the amber coast, which agrees almost exactly with the distance in a straight line to Samland. From Carnuntum the route lay along the river March, thence overland to the upper Vistula, and so down this river to Samland. It may easily be understood that much fresh knowledge reached Rome as a result of this journey.

Pliny, 23-79 A.D.

The elder Pliny's (23-79 A.D.) statements about the North, in his great work "Naturalis Historia" (in thirty-seven books), are somewhat obscure and confused, and so far are no advance upon Mela; but we remark nevertheless that fresh knowledge has been acquired, and it is as though we get a clearer vision of the new countries and seas through the northern mists. He himself says, moreover, that he "has received information of immense islands which have recently been discovered from Germania." His work is in great part the fruit of an unusually extensive acquaintance with older writers, mostly Greek, but also Latin. He repeats a good deal of what Mela says, or draws from the same sources, probably Greek.

the whole idea of egg-eating may have arisen, without anything having been related about it.

ANTIQUITY, AFTER PYTHEAS

His information about the North must have been obtained, so far as I can see, mainly in three different ways : (1) Directly through the Romans' connection with Germania and through their expeditions to its northern coasts (under Augustus and Nero, for example). Pliny himself lived in Germania for several years (45-52 A.D.) as a Roman cavalry commander, and may then have collected much information. (2) He has drawn extensively from Greek sources, whose statements about the North may have come partly by sea, chiefly through Pytheas (perhaps also through later trading voyages) ; partly also by land, especially through commercial intercourse between the Black Sea and the Baltic.[1] (3) Finally he received information from Britain about the regions to the north. This may be derived partly from Greek sources, partly also from later Roman connection with Britain. Mela expressly says of this country that new facts will soon be known about it, " for the greatest prince [the Emperor Claudius] is now opening up this country, which has so long been closed . . . he has striven by war to obtain personal knowledge of these things, and will spread this knowledge at his triumph." The information obtained by Pliny through these different channels is often used by him uncritically, without remarking that different statements apply to the same countries and seas.

His theory of the universe was the usual one, that the universe was a hollow sphere which revolved in twenty-four hours with indescribable rapidity. " Whether by the continual revolution of such a great mass there is produced an immense

[1] To this it might be objected that he ought in that case to have obtained much information also about the interior of Scythia and Sarmatia ; but in the first place this is not certain, as the special goal of the merchants was the amber countries, and they would therefore keep to the known routes and travel rapidly through—and in the second, Pliny actually mentions a good many tribes in the interior. He says, it is true [iv. 26, 91], of Agrippa's estimate of the size of Sarmatia and Scythia, that he considers such estimates too uncertain in these parts of the earth ; but to conclude from this, as Detlefsen [1904, p. 34] has done, that Pliny's Greek authorities cannot have received their information by the land route, seems to me unreasonable, since Pliny perhaps did not even know how his authorities had obtained their knowledge.

IN NORTHERN MISTS

CHAPTER III

noise, exceeding all powers of hearing, I am no more able to assert than that the sound produced by the stars circulating about one another and revolving in their orbits, is a lovely and incredibly graceful harmony." The earth stood in the centre of the universe and had the form of a sphere. The land was everywhere surrounded by sea, which covers the greater part of the globe.

In his description of the North [iv. 12, 88 f.] Pliny begins at the east, and relies here entirely on Greek authorities.

> Far north in Scythia, beyond the Arimaspians, "we come to the 'Ripæan' Mountains and to the district which on account of the ever-falling snow, resembling feathers, is called Pterophorus. This part of the world is accursed by nature and shrouded in thick darkness; it produces nothing else but frost and is the chilly hiding-place of the north wind. By these mountains and beyond the north wind dwells, if we are willing to believe it, a happy people, the Hyperboreans, who have long life and are famous for many marvels which border on the fabulous. There, it is said, are the pivots of the world, and the uttermost revolution of the constellations." The sun shines there for six months; but strangely enough it rises at the summer solstice and sets at the winter solstice, which shows Pliny's ignorance of astronomy. The climate is magnificent and without cold winds. As the sun shines for half the year, "the Hyperboreans sow in the morning, harvest at midday, gather the fruit from the trees at evening, and spend the night in caves. The existence of this people is not to be doubted, since so many authors tell us about them."

Having then mentioned several districts bordering on the Black Sea, Pliny continues [iv. 13, 94 f.]:

> "We will now acquaint ourselves with the outer parts of Europe, and turn, after having gone over the Ripæan Mountains, towards the left to the coast of the northern ocean, until we arrive again at Gades. Along this line many nameless islands are recorded. Timæus mentions that among them there is one off Scythia called Baunonia, a day's sail distant, upon which the waves cast up amber in the spring. The remaining coasts are only known from doubtful rumours. Here is the northern ocean. Hecatæus calls it Amalcium, from the river Parapanisus[1] onwards and as far as it washes the coast of Scythia, which name [i.e., Amalcium] in the language of the natives means frozen.[2]

---

[1] This river is not mentioned elsewhere and must be invented, Hecatæus of Abdera (circa 300 B.C.) having imagined that it rose in mountains of this name in the interior of Asia and fell into the northern ocean.

[2] This is certainly wrong. The name "Amalcium" cannot come from any northern language, but must come from the Greek "malkios" (μάλκιος),

98

ANTIQUITY, AFTER PYTHEAS

Philemon [1] says that it was called by the Cimbri Morimarusa, that is, the dead sea; from thence and as far as the promontory Rusbeas, farther out, it is called Cronium. Xenophon of Lampsacus says that three days' sail from the Scythian coast is an island, Balcia, of enormous size; Pytheas calls it Basilia." He goes on to mention the Œonæ, Hippopods, and Long-eared men in almost the same terms as Mela.

CHAPTER III

This mention of lands and seas in the North is of great interest. But in attempting to identify any of them in Pliny's description we must always remember that to him and his Greek authorities, and to all writers even in much later times, all land north of the coasts of Scythia, Sarmatia and Germania was nothing but islands in the northern ocean. Further, it must be remembered that the ancient Greeks did not know the name Germania, which was not introduced until about 80 B.C. To them Scythia and Celtica (Gaul) were conterminous, and their Scythian coast might therefore lie either on the Baltic or the North Sea.

It has not been possible to decide where the name "Rusbeas" (called by Solinus "Rubeas") comes from; [2] but it is best understood if we take it to be southern Norway or Lindesnes. As the description begins at the east on the Scythian coast, it follows that "Amalcium" is the Baltic as far as the Danish islands and the land of the Cimbri. "Morimarusa," [3] which extends from Amalcium to Lindesnes, will be

which means "stiffening," "freezing"; "a" must here be an emphatic particle.

[1] This Greek is given as an authority in several passages of Pliny; he is also mentioned by Ptolemy, but is not otherwise known. He may have lived about 100 B.C. [cf. Detlefsen, 1904, pp. 23-25].

[2] On account of the syllable "rus," which is found in Phœnician names (e.g., Rusazus, Ruscino, Ruspino) and which means headland, cape, it has been sought to derive it from the Semitic; but Detlefsen [1904, p. 24] thinks it more reasonable to suppose it Germanic. Not the smallest trace of Phœnician names has been found in the north. R. Keyser [1868, p. 165] thinks the name, which he reads "Rubeas," "is without doubt the Welsh 'rhybyz'" (rhybudd = sign, warning); but the word cannot have had this form in Pliny's time.

[3] The name may be either Celtic or Old Germanic. In Celtic "mori," Irish "muir," Cymric "môr," is sea; but R. Much [1893, p. 220] thinks that Germanic "mari" and Gothic "marei" (German "Meer," Latin "mare")

IN NORTHERN MISTS

CHAPTER III

the Cattegat (in part, at any rate) and the Skagerak. Cronium will be the North Sea and the Northern Ocean beyond Lindesnes.[1] We must believe that Philemon has obtained his information about the Cimbri (at the Skaw), about Morimarusa, and about Rusbeas either from Pytheas—whose mention thereof we must then suppose to have been accidentally omitted by other authors—or else from later Greek merchants. In the same way Xenophon must have got his Balcia, which is here named for the first time in literature. As these two Greek authors (probably of about 100 B.C.) are expressly mentioned as authorities, the statements cannot be derived from the circumnavigation of the Skaw in the time of Augustus, nor from any other Roman expedition. It is clear enough that Pliny himself did not know where Rusbeas and Balcia were, but simply repeated uncritically what he had read. On the other hand, he knew from another source that the sea he calls Cronium lay far north of Britain, and must therefore be sought for to the north-west of the Scythian coast.

may also have been pronounced formerly with "o." "Marusa" is related to Irish "marb," Cymric "marw" for dead, but according to Much it may be of Germanic origin and have had the form "* marusaz" (cf. "* marwaz") with the meaning of motionless, lifeless. "Morimarusa" would thus be the "motionless sea," which reminds one of Pytheas's kindred ideas of the sluggish, congealed sea ("mare pigrum, prope immotum mare"). If the name is of Germanic origin, this does not debar its being derived from Pytheas (and taken from him by Philemon); he may have got it from Norway. If Rusbeas is southern Norway, this would point in the same direction. But it is doubtless more reasonable to suppose that the name is derived from the Cimbri, who are mentioned in connection with it, while Pliny does not mention any people in Norway.

[1] Hergt [1893, p. 40] thinks that "Morimarusa" would be the Baltic (and the Cattegat), which was called dead because it had no tides and was frozen in winter. "Rusbeas" would thus be the point of the Skaw. In this way he has two names for the Baltic, and two, if not three, for the Skaw. This interpretation seems to be even less consistent than that given above. Pliny in another passage mentions (see pp. 65, 106) that the sea called "Cronium" was a day's sail beyond Thule, which lay to the north of Britain and within the Arctic Circle. This in itself makes it difficult for Cronium to begin at Lindesnes, but if it has to begin at Skagen, and thus be the Skagerak, it becomes still worse.

ANTIQUITY, AFTER PYTHEAS

Balcia must be looked for most probably in the Baltic. As already mentioned (p. 72) it may be Jutland; but as it is described as an island of immense size and three days' sail from the Scythian coast, it suits southern Sweden better, although Pliny has also the name Scadinavia for this from another source.

CHAPTER III

After these doubtful statements about the north coast of Scythia, taken from Greek sources and interwoven with fables, Pliny reaches firmer ground in Germania, when he continues [iv. 13, 96]:

"We have more certain information concerning the Ingævones people who are the first [that is, the most north-eastern] in Germania. There is the immense mountain Sævo, not less than the Riphæan range, and it forms a vast bay which goes to the Cimbrian Promontory [i.e., Jutland], which bay is called Codanus and is full of islands, amongst which the most celebrated is Scatinavia, of unknown size; a part of it is inhabited, as far as is known by the Hilleviones, in 500 cantons ('pagis'), who call it [i.e., the island] the second earth. Æningia is supposed to be not less in size. Some say that these regions extend as far as the Vistula and are inhabited by Sarmatians [i.e., probably Slavs], Venedi [Wends], Scirri, and Hirri; the bay is called Cylipenus, and at its mouth lies the island Latris. Not far from thence is another bay, Lagnus, which borders on the Cimbri. The Cimbrian Promontory runs far out into the sea and forms a peninsula called Tastris." Then follows a list of twenty-three islands which are clearly off the North Sea coast of Sleswick and Germany. Among them is one called by the soldiers " Glæsaria " on account of the amber (" glesum "),[1] but by the barbarians " Austeravia " [i.e., the eastern island], or " Actania."

Here are a number of new names and pieces of information. The form of some of the names shows that here too Pliny has borrowed to some extent from Greek authors; but his information must also partly be derived from Roman sources, and from Germany itself. His " Codanus " must be the same as that of Mela, and is the sea adjacent to the country of the Cimbri, which is here for the first time clearly referred to as a promontory (promunturium). It is the Cattegat, and, in part at any rate, the Skagerak. The enormous mountain

[1] This must come from an Old Germanic word "*glez," Anglo-Saxon " glær," for amber. It is the same word as the Norwegian " glas " or Danish " glar," which has come to mean glass.

IN NORTHERN MISTS

CHAPTER III

"Sævo" will then be most probably the mountains of Scandinavia, especially southern Norway, which forms the bay of Codanus in such a way that the latter is bounded on the other side by the Cimbrian Promontory.[1] It will then be in the same mountainous country that we should look for the promontory of Rusbeas (see above).

Scandinavia

The name "Scatinavia" or "Scadinavia" (both spellings occur in the MSS. of Pliny) is found here certainly for the first time; but, curiously enough, we also find the name "Scandia" in Pliny; it is used of an island which is mentioned as near Britain (see below, p. 106). "Scandia" has often been taken

---

[1] The origin of the name "Sævo" cannot be determined with certainty. Forbiger [1848, iii. p. 237] thinks it is Kjolen, and asserts that it is a Norwegian name which is still found in the form of "Seve," ridge; but no such name is known in Norway. It seems possible that the name may be connected with the Gothic "saivs" for sea (cf. Old Norse "sær"); but it may also be supposed to have arisen from a corruption of "svevus", in any case it was so regarded in the Middle Ages. Solinus says [c. 20, 1], following Pliny, that "Mons Sævo ... forms the commencement of Germany," but Isidore Hispalensis says that "Suevus Mons" forms the north-east boundary of Germany, and on the Hereford Map (about 1280) a mountain chain, "Mons Sueuus," runs in northeast Germany to a bay of the sea called "Sinus Germanicus," which may be the Baltic. On the Ebstorf map (1284) "Mons Suevus" has followed the Suevi southwards to Swabia. It is also possible that Ptolemy's mountain chain "Syēba" ($\Sigma \acute{v} \eta \beta a$, vi. c. 14) in northernmost Asia (62° N. lat.) has something to do with Pliny's "Sævo." There has been much guessing as to where the latter is to be sought: some [cf. Detlefsen, 1904, p. 28] think it was Kjolen, although it is quite incomprehensible how this far northern range could be connected with Codanus; others [cf. Lonborg, 1897, p. 20] that it was in Mecklenburg or Pomerania or even in Jutland [Geijer, 1825, p. 77], where no mountain is to be found, least of all an immense one ("inmensus"). Pliny's words could be most simply connected with the Norwegian mountains [cf. Holz, 1894, p. 25]. It may indeed be supposed, as Mullenhoff [iv., 1900, p. 600] thinks, that the men of Augustus's fleet, in 5 A.D., may have seen in the Cattegat or heard of the "Sea-mountains" of the Scandinavian (or rather, Swedish) coast, "*Saivabergo" or "*Saivagabergia," which rose up over the sea, and the name of which became in Latin "Mons Sævo"; but perhaps it is just as reasonable to suppose that the information may be derived from the Germans of Jutland, who had communication with Norway and knew its high mountainous country, and that therefore it did not originate with the low west coast of Sweden.

ANTIQUITY, AFTER PYTHEAS

for a shortened form of "Scadinavia"; but if we consider the occurrence of both names in Pliny in conjunction with the fact that Mela has not yet heard either, but has, on the other hand, a large island, "Codanovia," in the bay of Codanus, then it may seem possible that originally there were two entirely different names: "Codanovia," for Sealand (and perhaps for south Sweden), and "*Skânovia" ("Skáney," latinised into "Scandia") for Skåne. By a confusion of these two the form "Scadinavia" for south Sweden may have resulted in Pliny, instead of Mela's "Codanovia," while at the same time he got the name "Scandia" from another source. The latter is the only one used by Ptolemy both for south Sweden and the Danish islands; he has four "Scandiæ," three smaller ones and one very large one farther east, "Scandia" proper (see below, p. 119). By further confusion of the two names, "Scadinavia" has become "Scandinavia" in later copyists and authors.[1]

CHAPTER III

[1] One might be tempted to connect the name "Scadinavia" with the old Norse goddess Skade or Skaði, who was of Finnish race; she was black-haired, lived in the mountains in the interior of the country, and was amongst other things the goddess of ski-running. The name Scadinavia would then be of Finnish origin. This derivation has also been put forward [cf. Mullenhoff, ii., 1887, pp. 55 f., 357 f.]. The termination "avi," "avia," must then be the same as "ovia" (see p. 94). This explanation would take for granted an original non-Germanic, so-called "Finnish" population in south Sweden (which does not appear impossible; see below); but it will then be difficult to explain why the name should have survived only in the most southern part, Skåne. Sophus Bugge [1896, p. 424] thought that "Scadinavia" (later "Scadanavia") is related to the common Norwegian place-name "Skoðvin" or Skoien ("vin" = pasture) and may come from a lost Old Norse word "*skaða" (old Slavonic "skotŭ") for cattle. "Skoðvin" would then be cattle-pasture. From "*skaða" the word "*skaðanaz" may be regularly derived, with the meaning of herdsman; and "Skadan-avia" or "Skadinavia" will be herdsman's pastures, since the termination "avia" may have the same meaning as the German "Au" or "Aue" (good pasture, meadow). The Old Norse "Skáney" ("Skáni," now "Skåne") would then come from Skaðney, where the "ð" has been dropped as in many similar instances. Bugge himself afterwards [1904, p. 156] rejected this explanation and derived "Scadinavia" from the same word as "Codanus" (see p. 93), taking it to mean the island or coast-land by "Kōdan," which has had a prefixed "s," while the long "o" has been

IN NORTHERN MISTS

CHAPTER III

In conflict with this is the hitherto accepted opinion among philologists that the name "Skåne" must be derived from "Scadinavia," which would regularly become by contraction "*Skadney," and this by losing the "d" would become "Skåney." But this similarity may after all be accidental, and it is difficult to reconcile the hypothesis with the fact that the form "Scandia" (and not "*Skadnia") already appears in Pliny and later in Ptolemy. To this must be added that the form "*Skadney," or a similar one, is not known; the first time we find the word Skåne in literature is in the story of Wulfstan the Dane to King Alfred (about 890, see later), where it takes the form "Scôn eg," which is the same as "Skåney." "Skania," which is a latinised form of "Skåney," is found in a Papal letter of 950, and a Swedish runic inscription of about 1020 reads "a Skanu," which also is the same as "Skåney." It therefore appears probable that this is the original form, the same as the Norwegian name "Skåney," and that it has not resulted from a contraction of "Skadinavia." Professor Torp agrees that a form "*Skånovia" might possibly be the original.

What may be the meaning of the name "Hilleviones" in Scadinavia is difficult to make out; it does not occur in any other writer, but is in all likelihood a common term for all Scandinavians. One is reminded of the "Hermiones" who occur in Mela in the same connection, but a little later Pliny mentions these also. "Æningia," which is said to be no smaller than Scadinavia, is a riddle. Could it be a corruption of a Halsingia or Alsingia (the land of the Helsingers), a name for northern Sweden, which thus lay farther off and was less known than Scadinavia?[1] When we read that these regions were supposed to extend as far as the Vistula, this might indicate a vague idea that Scadinavia and Æningia were connected with the mainland, whereby a bay of the sea was formed, called "Cylipenus,[2] which will thus be yet another

---

changed into short "a." This explanation may be very doubtful. In many parts of Norway a name "Skåney" is known, which comes from "skán" (meaning crust), and it may therefore not be improbable that the Swedish "Skåney" or Skåne is the same name.

[1] Ahlenius [1900, p. 31] has tried to explain the name as a copyist's error for "Æstingia," which he connects with the "Æstii" (Esthonians) of Tacitus; but the people would then have been called Æstingii rather than Æstii. One might then be more inclined to think of Jordanes' "Astingi" or "Hazdingi," the same as the Old Norse Haddingjar (Hallinger).

[2] R. Keyser [1868, p. 89] explains the name as the same as in the Old Norse name for a people, "Kylpingar," in northern Russia, neighbours of the

ANTIQUITY, AFTER PYTHEAS

name for the Baltic, taken from a new source; but the whole may be nothing more than an obscure statement.

"Latris," which lay at the mouth of Cylipenus, may be one of the Danish islands, and one may perhaps be reminded of Sealand with the ancient royal stronghold of "Lethra" or Leire, Old Norse "Hleidrar." The bay of "Lagnus,[1] which borders on the Cimbri, must then be taken as a new name for the Cattegat, while "Tastris" may be Skagen. According to the sources Pliny has borrowed from, we thus get the following names for the same parts: for the Baltic or parts thereof, "Amalcium" and "Cylipenus," and perhaps in part "Codanus"; for the Cattegat, "Lagnus" and "Codanus"; for the Skagerak, "Morimarusa," in part also "Codanus"; for south Sweden, "Scadinavia" and "Balcia"; for Jutland or Skagen, "Promunturium Cimbrorum" and "Tastris." At any rate, this superfluity of names discloses increased communication, through many channels, with the North. Communication with the North is also to be deduced from Pliny's mention [viii. c. 15, 39] of an animal called "achlis," as a native of those countries.

> It had "never been seen among us in Rome, though it had been described by many." It resembles the elk [alcis], "but has no knee-joint, for which reason also it does not sleep lying down, but leaned against a tree, and if the tree be partly cut through as a trap, the animal, which otherwise is remarkably fleet, is caught. Its upper lip is very large, for which reason it goes backwards when grazing, so as not to get caught in it if it went forward." It might be thought that this elk-like animal was a reindeer; but the mention of the long upper lip and the trees suits the elk better, and it may have been related of this animal that it was caught by means of traps in the forest. The fable that it slept leaning against a tree may be due to the similarity between the name "achlis" (which may be some corruption or other, perhaps of "alces") and "acclinis" (= leaning on).

Finally, Pliny had a third source of knowledge about the North through Britain, which to him was a common name for

CHAPTER III

Finns. He thinks that there may have been an Old Norse name "Kylpinga-botn" for the Baltic; but it is not likely that this word Kylpingar existed at that time.

[1] Keyser [1868, p. 80] derives the word from Gothic "lagus" (corresponding to Old Norse "logr") for sea

CHAPTER III all the islands in that ocean. Some of the statements from this quarter originated with Pytheas; but later information was added; Pliny himself mentions Agrippa as an authority. Among the British Isles he mentions [iv. 16, 103]: "40 'Orcades' separated from each other by moderate distances, 7 'Acmodæ,' and 30 'Hebudes.'" His 7 "Acmodæ" (which in some MSS. are also called "Hæcmodæ") are, clearly enough, Mela's 7 Hæmodæ, and probably the Shetland Islands, while the 30 "Hebudes" are the Hebrides, which are thus mentioned here for the first time in any known author.

After referring to a number of other British islands "and the 'Glæsiæ,' scattered in the Germanic Ocean, which the later Greeks call the 'Electrides,' because amber (electrum) is found in them,"[1] Pliny continues [iv. 16, 104]: "The most distant of all known islands is 'Tyle' (Thule), where at the summer solstice there is no night, and correspondingly no day at the winter solstice."[2] ... "Some authors mention yet more islands, 'Scandia,' 'Dumna,' 'Bergos,' and the largest of all, 'Berricen,' from which the voyage is made to Tyle. From Tyle it is one day's sail to the curdled sea which some call 'Cronium.'" We do not know from what authors Pliny can have taken these names, nor where the islands are to be looked for; but as Thule is mentioned, we must suppose that in any case some of them come originally from Pytheas. As Scandia comes first among these islands, one is led to think that Dumna and the two other enigmatical names are of Germanic origin. "Dumna" might then remind us of

---

[1] The same islands which are here spoken of as British, have been previously referred to (see above, p. 101) by Pliny as Germanic, or rather as a single island with the name "Glæsaria." This is another proof of how he draws directly from various sources without even taking the trouble to harmonise the statements. In this case he has probably found the islands mentioned in connection with facts about Britain, or a journey to that country. And it may be supposed that the original source is Pytheas.

[2] In his ignorance of astronomy Pliny adds that "this is said to continue alternately for six months."

ANTIQUITY, AFTER PYTHEAS

Scandinavian names such as Duney, Donna (in Nordland), or the like; but it is more probable that it comes from the Celtic "dubno" or "dumno" (= deep), and may be the name of an island off Scotland. "Bergos" may remind us of the Old Norse word "bjarg" or "berg."[1] It is not so easy with the strange name "Berricen," which in some MSS. has the form "Verigon" or "Nerigon" (cf. above, p. 58). If the first reading is the correct one, it suggests an origin in an Old Norse "ber-ig" ("ber" = bear; the meaning would therefore be "bear-y," full of bears), not an unsuitable name for southern Norway, whence the journey was made to Thule or northern Norway; but this is doubtful. If "Nerigon" is the correct reading, it will not be impossible, in the opinion of Professor Torp, that this, as Keyser supposed, may be the name Norway, which in Old Norse was called, by Danes for example, "*Norþravegaʀ" (like "Austravegaʀ" and "Vestravegaʀ"). If any of the names of these islands are really Germanic, like Scandia, then they cannot, as some have thought, refer to islands off Scotland or to the Shetlands, as these were not yet inhabited by Norsemen. The islands in question must therefore be looked for in Norway. It is important that Scandia is mentioned first among them in connection with Britain, and that at the same time another is described as the largest of them all, and as lying on the way to Thule. This again points to communication by sea between the British Isles and Scandinavia, of which we found indications four hundred years earlier.

CHAPTER III

In 84 A.D. Agricola, after his campaign against the Caledonians, sent his fleet round the northern point of Scotland, "whereby," Tacitus[2] tells us, "it was proved that Britain is an island. At the same time the hitherto unknown islands which are called 'Orcadas' (the Orkneys) were discovered and subdued. Thule also could be descried in the distance; but

Agricola, 84 A.D.

---

[1] Some MSS. read "Vergos."
[2] Tacitus, "Agricola," c. 10; see also c. 38. Cf. also Bunbury, 1883, ii. p. 342

IN NORTHERN MISTS

CHAPTER III

the fleet had orders not to go farther, and winter was coming on. Moreover the water is thick and heavy to row in ; it is said that even wind cannot stir it to much motion. The reason for this may be the absence of land and mountains, which otherwise would give the storms increased power, and that the enormous mass of continuous ocean is not easy to set in motion." This Thule must have been Fair Island or the Shetland Isles, and this is the most northern point reached by the Romans, so far as is known. The idea of the heavy sea, which is not moved by the winds, is the same that we met with in early antiquity (see pp. 40, 69).

In the preceding summer some of Agricola's soldiers—a cohort of Usippii, enlisted in Germania and brought to Britain—had mutinied, killed their centurion and seized three ships, whose captains they forced into obedience. "Two of them aroused their suspicions and were therefore killed , the third undertook the navigation," and they circumnavigated Britain. "They were soon obliged to land to provide themselves with water and to plunder what they required ; thereby they came into frequent conflict with the Britons, who defended their possessions ; they were often victorious, but sometimes were worsted, and finally their need became so great that they took to eating the weakest ; then they drew lots as to which should serve the others as food. Thus they came round Britain [i.e. round the north], were driven out of their course through incompetent navigation, and were made prisoners, some by the Frisians and some by the Suevi, who took them for pirates. Some of them came to the slave-markets and passed through various hands until they reached Roman Germania, becoming quite remarkable persons by being able to relate such marvellous adventures."[1] It is possible that certain inaccurate statements may have found their way to Rome as the result of this voyage.

Tacitus, 98 A.D.

Cornelius Tacitus, who wrote his "Germania" in the year 98 A.D., was a historian and ethnographer, not a geographer. His celebrated work has not, therefore, much to say of the northern lands ; he has not even a single name for them. On the other hand, he has some remarkable statements about the peoples, especially in Sweden, which show that since the time of Pliny fresh information about that part of the world must have reached Rome.

Tacitus makes the "Suebi," or "Suevi," inhabit the greater part of Germany as far as the frontier of the Slavs

[1] Tacitus, "Agricola," c. 28.

ANTIQUITY, AFTER PYTHEAS

(Sarmatians) and Finns on the east (and north?). The name, which possibly means the "hovering" people and is due to their roving existence, is perhaps rather to be regarded as a common designation for various Germanic tribes. After them he called the sea on the eastern coast of Germany, i.e., the Baltic, the Suebian Sea ("Suebicum mare"). On its right-hand (eastern) shore dwelt the "Æstii" (i.e., Esthonians; perhaps from "aistan" = to honour, that is, the honourable people [?]). "Their customs and dress

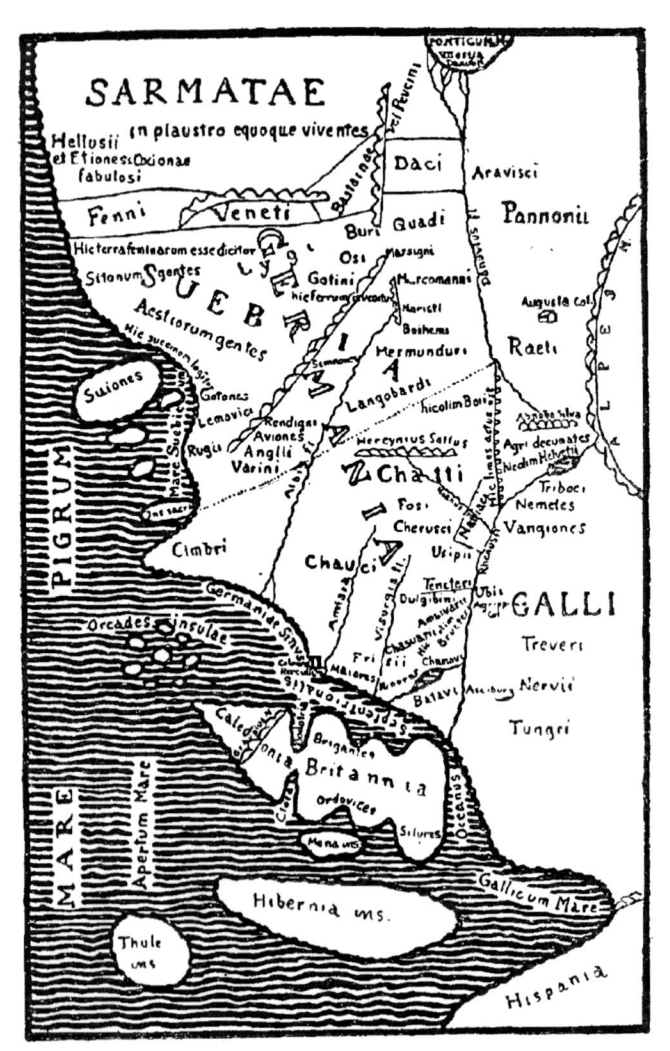

The nations of Tacitus (after K. Miller)

are like those of the Suevi, but their language more nearly resembles the British" (!). "The use of iron is rare there, that of sticks [i.e., clubs, fustium] common. They also explore the sea and collect amber in shallow places and on the shore itself. But they do not understand its

CHAPTER III nature and origin, and it long lay disregarded among things cast up by the sea, "until our luxury made it esteemed." "They have no use for it,[1] they gather it in the rough, bring it unwrought, and are surprised at the price they receive" [c. 45]. From this it may be concluded that there was constant trading communication between the Mediterranean and the Baltic, and that Roman merchants had probably penetrated thither.

"In the Ocean itself (ipso in Oceano) lie the communities of the Suiones, a mighty people not only in men and arms, but also in ships." The Suiones, who are first mentioned by Tacitus, are evidently of the same name as the Svear (Old Norse "svíar," Anglo-Saxon "sveon") or Swedes.[2] Their ships were remarkable for having a prow, "prora," at each end (i.e., they were the same fore and aft); they had no sail, and the oars were not made fast in a row, but were loose, so that they could row with them now on one side, now on the other, "as on some rivers."[3] In other words, they had open rowlocks, as in some of the river boats of that time, and as is common in modern boats; the oars were not put out through holes as in the Roman ships, and as in the Viking ships (the Gokstad and Oseberg ships). The boat of the

Boat found at Nydam, near Flensburg. Third century A.D. 70 feet long (after C. Engelhardt)

[1] Here Tacitus is mistaken, as amber was extensively employed for amulets and ornaments even in the Stone Age (see above, p. 32).

[2] Much [1905, p. 133] connects the name with "ge-swio" = "related by marriage." It may be just as reasonable to suppose that the name means "burners" ("svier"), since they cleared the land by setting fire to the forests [cf. Müllenhoff, iv., 1900, p. 499].

[3] Cf. Müllenhoff, iv., 1900, p. 502.

ANTIQUITY, AFTER PYTHEAS

Iron Age which was dug up at Nydam had just such open rowlocks.

The Suiones (unlike the other Germanic peoples) esteemed wealth, and therefore they had only one lord; this lord governed with unlimited power, so much so that arms were not distributed among the people, but were kept locked up, and moreover in charge of a thrall,[1] because the sea prevented sudden attacks of enemies, and armed idle hands (i.e., armed men unemployed) are apt to commit rash deeds [c. 44].

The neighbours of the Suiones, probably on the north, are the "Sitones" [c. 45], whom Tacitus also regards as Germanic. "They are like the Suiones with one exception, that a woman reigns over them; so far have they degenerated not only from liberty, but also from slavery. Here Suebia ends (Hic Suebiæ finis)." Suebia was that part of Germany inhabited by the Suevi. It looks as though Tacitus considered that courage and manliness decreased the farther north one went. The Suiones allow themselves to be bullied by an absolute king, who sets a thrall to guard their weapons, and the Sitones are in a still worse plight, in allowing themselves to be governed by a woman. The Sitones are not mentioned before or after this in literature, and it seems as though the name must be due to some misunderstanding.[2] It has been supposed that

[1] This might be thought to show that arms of metal, especially of iron, were still rarities in Scandinavia, which only rich and powerful chiefs could obtain, and this might agree with the statement about the esteem in which wealth was held among this particular people. But perhaps the more probable explanation is that the idea may have arisen through foreign merchants (South Germans or Romans) having been present at the great annual "things" and fairs at some well-known temple, e.g., Upsala [cf. Mullenhoff, 1900, p. 503], where for the sake of peace and on account of the sacredness of the spot it was forbidden to carry arms, and where arms were therefore left in a special "weapon-house," like those which were later attached to churches in Norway, and there guarded by a thrall. The foreigners may have seen this without understanding its meaning, and Tacitus may have given his own explanation.

[2] The name "Sitones" reminds one forcibly of the "Sidones" mentioned by Strabo and Ptolemy [cf. Geijer, 1825, p. 82]; but the difficulty is that Strabo includes the latter among the Bastarni, with the Peucini who lived on the north and east of the Carpathians and therefore far to the south of the Baltic [cf.

IN NORTHERN MISTS

CHAPTER III

they were Finns ("Kvæns")[1] in northern Sweden, and their name may then have been taken as the word for woman ("kvæn," or "kván," mostly in the sense of wife [cf. English queen]), and from this the legend of womanly government may have been formed[2] in the same way as Adam of Bremen later translates the name Cvenland (Kvænland) by "Terra feminarum," and thus forms the myth of the country of the Amazons. But this explanation of the statement of Tacitus may be doubtful.[3] We have already seen that Mela mentions a people in Scythia, the "Mæotides," who were governed by women, and, as we have said, it would not have seemed unreasonable to him that the government of women increased farther north.

Of the regions on the north Tacitus says: "North of the Suiones lies another sluggish and almost motionless sea (mare

Ahlenius, 1900, p. 36]. Ptolemy's "Sidones" also lived in the neighbourhood of the Carpathians, and to the north of them. But it is nevertheless possible that Tacitus may have heard a similar word and confused it with this name, or he may have heard a story of a reigning woman or queen among Strabo's Sidones, somewhere north of the Carpathians, and thought that anything so unheard of could only be found in the farthest north. It is also to be noted that Tacitus himself mentions "Peucini" or "Bastarnæ" as neighbours of the "Fenni" (Finns), and therefore inhabiting some distant tract bordering on the unknown in the north-east; on the other hand he does not mention the Sidones in this connection, though they are spoken of in conjunction with the Bastarnæ both by Strabo before him and by Ptolemy after him. Add to this the similarity of names between Sitones and Suiones, and it seems likely that he thought they must be near one another. Mullenhoff [ii., 1887, p. 9] supposes that the word "Sitones" may have been an appellative which has been mistaken for the name of a people, and he connects it with Gothic "*sitans," Old Norse "*setar," from the same root as the Norwegian "sitte" (to sit, occupy). If this is correct we might suppose it to be used in the sense of colonists (cf. Norwegian "opsitter"). Much [1905, p. 31] suggests that perhaps it may be derived from Old Norse "siða" = to practise witchcraft (cf. "seid"), and mean sorcerers. On the "Sidones" cf. Much, 1893, pp. 135, 187, 188; Mullenhoff, 1887, pp. 109, 325.

[1] Wiklund [1895, pp. 103-117] thinks that the "Kvæns" in north Sweden were not Finns, but colonists from Svearike (middle Sweden).

[2] Cf. Zeuss, 1837, p. 157; Mullenhoff, ii., 1887, p. 10

[3] Cf. Lonborg, 1897, p. 136; Ahlenius, 1900, p. 37.

ANTIQUITY, AFTER PYTHEAS

pigrum ac prope immotum); that this encircles and confines the earth's disc is rendered probable by the fact that the last light of the setting sun continues until the sun rises again, so clearly that the stars are paled thereby. Popular belief also supposes that the sound of the sun emerging from the ocean can be heard, and that the forms of the gods are seen and the rays beaming from his head. There report rightly places the boundaries of nature." As mentioned above (see p. 108), he thought that even to the north of the Orkneys the sea was thick and sluggish.

Tacitus is the first author who mentions the Finns (Fenni), but whether they are Lapps, Kvæns or another race cannot be determined. He says himself: " I am in doubt whether to reckon the Peucini, Venedi and Fenni among the Germans or Sarmatians (Slavs)." He speaks of the Fenni apparently as dwelling far to the north-east, beyond the Peucini, or Bastarnæ, from whom they are separated by forests and mountains, which the latter overrun as robbers.

"Among the Fenni amazing savagery and revolting poverty prevail. They have no weapons, no horses, no houses ['non penates,' perhaps rather, no homes]; [1] their food is herbs, their clothing skins, their bed the ground. Their only hope is in their arrows, which from lack of iron they provide with heads of bone. Hunting supports both men and women; for the women usually accompany the men everywhere and take their share of the spoils. Their infants have no other protection from wild beasts and from the rain than a hiding-place of branches twisted together; thither the men return, it is the habitation of the aged. Nevertheless this seems to them a happier life than groaning over tilled fields, toiling in houses and being subject to hope and fear for their own and others' possessions. Without a care for men or gods they have attained the most difficult end, that of not even feeling the need of a wish. Beyond them all is fabulous, as that the 'Hellusii' and 'Oxionæ' have human heads and faces, but the bodies and limbs of wild beasts, which I leave on one side as undecided."

These Fenni of Tacitus consequently live near the outer limits of the world, where all begins to be fable. The name itself carries us to northern Europe, or rather Scandinavia, for it was certainly only the North Germans, especially the Scandinavians, who used the word as a name for their non-

[1] Cf. Baumstark, 1880, p. 329; Müllenhoff, iv., 1900, p. 516.

Aryan neighbours. No doubt it appears from the description that they lived in northern Russia, and were only separated from the Peucini by forests and mountains; but, as was said above, Tacitus had neither sense for nor interest in geography. If he heard of a savage and barbarous Finn-people far in the North, and if it suited him on other grounds to bring them in beyond the Peucini or Bastarnæ, but before the Hellusii and Oxiones, who not only led the life of beasts, but even had their bodies and limbs, then certainly no geographical difficulties would stop him. It is of interest that these Fenni are described as a typical race of hunters, using the bow as their special weapon. As Tacitus only states that they had no horses, he had doubtless heard of no other domestic animals amongst them. Consequently it is not likely that they were reindeer-nomads. The interweaving of branches that the children were hidden in, to which the men returned, and which was the dwelling of the old men, must be the tent of the Finns, which was raised upon branches or stakes. As early as Herodotus [iv. 23] we read of the Argippæans, who were also Mongols, that "every man lived under a tree, over which in winter he spread a white, thick covering of felt." It is clearly a tent that is intended here also [cf. Müllenhoff, ii., 1887, pp. 40, 352]. The idea that among the barbarians men and women frequently did the same work does not seem to have been uncommon in antiquity, and it can scarcely have been regarded as something peculiar to the Finns; in this connection it is no doubt derived from the legends of the Amazons. Herodotus, and after him Mela (see above, pp. 87 f.), describes such a similarity between men and women among the Scythian people and the Sauromatians; and Diodorus [iv. 20, v. 39] says of the Ligurians that men and women shared the same hard labour.

The so-called Dionysius Periegetes wrote in the time of the emperor Hadrian (117–138 A.D.) a description of the earth in 1187 verses, which perhaps on account of its simple brevity and metrical form was used in schools and widely

ANTIQUITY, AFTER PYTHEAS

circulated [cf. K. Miller, vi., 1898, p. 95]. But unfortunately the author has merely drawn from obsolete Greek sources, such as Homer, Hecataeus, Eratosthenes and others, and has nothing new to tell us. The whole continent was surrounded by ocean like an immense island; it was not quite circular, but somewhat prolonged in the direction of the sun's course (i.e., towards the east and west).

After Greek scientific geography had had its most fruitful life in the period ending with Eratosthenes and Hipparchus it still sent out such powerful shoots as the physical-mathematical geographer Posidonius and the descriptive geographer Strabo; but after them a century and a half elapses until we hear of its final brilliant revival in Marinus of Tyre and Claudius Ptolemy, whose work was to exercise a decisive influence upon geography thirteen centuries later.

Marinus's writings are lost, and we know nothing more of him than is told us by his younger contemporary Ptolemy, who has relied upon him to a considerable extent, and whose great forerunner he was. He must have lived in the first half of the second century A.D. He made an exhaustive attempt to describe every place on the earth according to its latitude and longitude, and drew a map of the world on this principle. He also adopted Posidonius's insufficient estimate of the earth's circumference (instead of that of Eratosthenes), and his exaggerated extension of the " oecumene " towards the east; and as this was passed on from him to Ptolemy he exercised great influence upon Columbus, amongst others, who thus came to estimate the distance around the globe to India at only half its real length. In this way Marinus and Ptolemy are of importance in the discovery not only of the West Indies, but also of North America by Cabot, and in the earliest attempts to find a north-west passage to China. Thus " accidental " mistakes may have far-reaching influence in history.

Claudius Ptolemæus marks to a certain extent the highest point of classical geographical knowledge. He was

CHAPTER III

Marinus of Tyre

Ptolemy, circa 150 A.D.

IN NORTHERN MISTS

CHAPTER III

perhaps born in Egypt about 100 A.D. He must have lived as an astronomer at Alexandria during the years 126 to 141, and perhaps longer; and he probably outlived the emperor Antoninus Pius, who died in 161 A.D., but we do not know much more of him. In his celebrated astronomical work, most generally known by its Arabic title of " Almagest " (because it first reached mediæval western Europe in an Arabic translation), he gave his well-known account of the universe and of the movements of the heavenly bodies, which had such great influence in the later Middle Ages, and on Columbus and the great discoveries. His celebrated " Geography " in eight books (written about 150 A.D.) is, as he himself tells us, for the most part founded upon the now lost work of Marinus, and shows a great advance in geographical comprehension upon the practical but unscientific Romans. With the scientific method of the Greeks an attempt is here made to collect and co-ordinate the geographical knowledge of the time into a tabulated survey, for the most part dry, of countries, places and peoples, with a number of latitudes and longitudes, mostly given by estimate. His information and names are in great part taken from the so-called " Itineraries," which were tabular and consisted chiefly of graphic routes for travellers with stopping-places and distances, and which were due for the most part to military sources (especially the Roman campaigns), and in a less degree to merchants and sailors.

Cartographical representation was by him radically improved by the introduction of correct projections, with converging meridians, of which a commencement had already been made by Hipparchus. His atlas, which may originally have been drawn by himself, or by another from the detailed statements in his geography, gives us the only maps that have been preserved from antiquity, and thus has a special interest.

As to the North, we find remarkably little that is new in Ptolemy, and on many points he shows a retrogression even, as it seems, from Pytheas; but the northern coast

ANTIQUITY, AFTER PYTHEAS

of Europe begins to take definite shape past the Cimbrian Peninsula to the Baltic. His representation of Britain and Ireland (Ivernia), which is based upon much new information,[1] was certainly a great improvement on his predecessors, even though he gives the northern part of Scotland (Caledonia) a strange deflection far to the east, which was retained on later maps (in the fifteenth century). He mentions five Ebudes (Hebrides) above Ivernia, and says further [ii. 3]:

"The following islands lie near Albion off the Orcadian Cape; the island of Ocitis (32° 40′ E. long., 60° 45′ N. lat.), the island of Dumna (30° E. long., 61° N. lat.), north of them the Orcades, about thirty in number, of which the most central lies in 30° E. long., 61° 40′ N. lat. And far to the north of them Thule, the most western part of which lies in 29° E. long., 63° N. lat., the most eastern part in 31° 40′ E. long., 63° N. lat., the most northern in 30° 20′ E. long., 63° 15′ N. lat., the most southern in 30° 20′ E. long., 62° 40′ N. lat., and the central part in 30° 20′ E. long., 63° N. lat."

Ptolemy calculates his degrees of longitude eastwards from a meridian O which he draws west of the Fortunate Isles (the Canaries), the most western part of the earth. It will be seen that he gives Thule no very great extent. His removing it from the Arctic Circle south to 63° is doubtless due to the men of Agricola's fleet having thought they had sighted Thule north of the Orkneys. In his eighth book [c. 3] he says:

Thule has a longest day of twenty hours, and it is distant west from Alexandria two hours. Dumna has a longest day of nineteen hours, and is distant westward two hours.

It is evident that these "hours" are found by calculation, and are merely a way of expressing degrees of latitude and longitude; they cannot therefore be referred to any local observation of the length of the longest day, etc. It is curious that Ptolemy only mentions Ebudes and Orcades, and not the Shetland Isles; perhaps they are included among his thirty Orcades.

He represents the Cimbrian Peninsula (Jutland) with

---

[1] Many of his place-names in Ireland especially point to frequent communication, probably due to trade, between this island and the continent, perhaps with Gaul.

CHAPTER III

remarkable correctness, though making it lean too much towards the east, like Scotland. Upon it " dwelt on the west the Sigulones, then the Sabalingii, then the Cobandi, above them the Chali, and above these again and farther west the Phundusii, and more to the east the Charudes

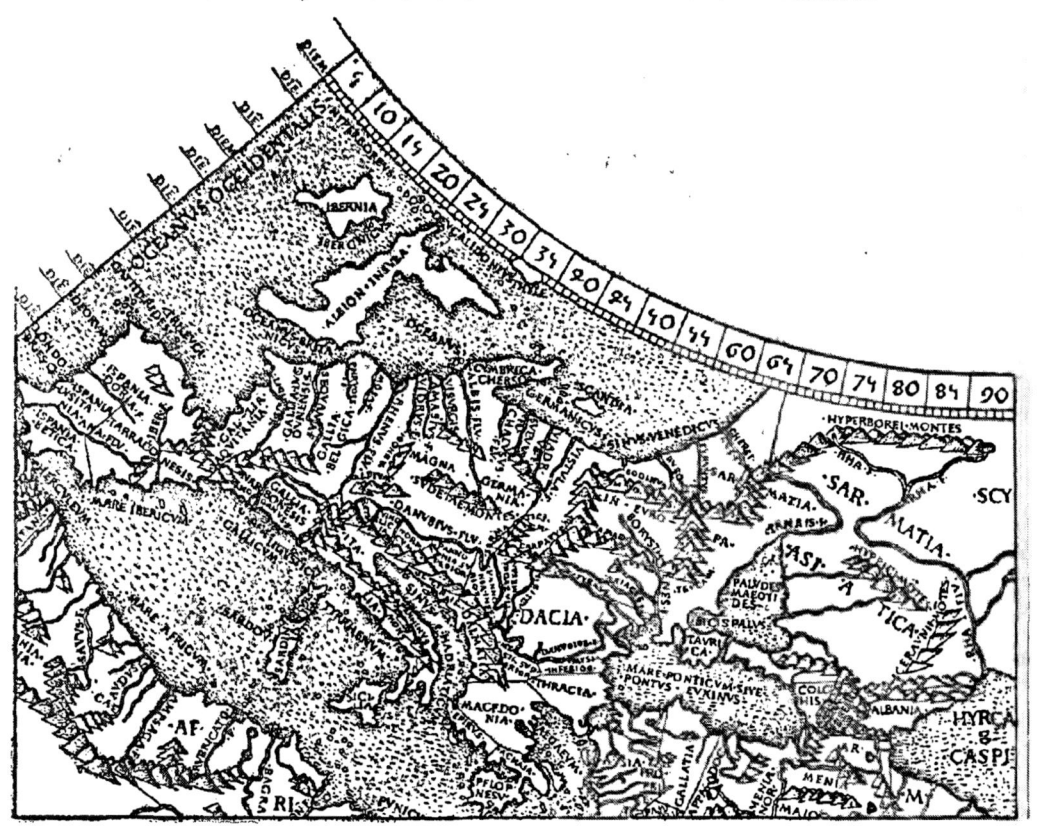

The northern part of Ptolemy's map of the world, Europe and Asia.

[Harudes or Horder; cf. p. 85], and to the north of all the Cimbri." It was suggested above (p. 94) that possibly the name Cobandi might be connected with the Codanus of Mela and Pliny. The Sabalingii, according to Much [1905, p. 11], may be the same name as Pytheas's Abalos (cf. p. 70), which may have been written Sabalos or Sabalia, and may have been inhabited by Aviones. To the north of the Cimbrian Chersonese Ptolemy places three islands, the "Alociæ,"

ANTIQUITY, AFTER PYTHEAS

which may be taken from the Halligen islands, properly "Hallagh" [cf. Detlefsen, 1904, p. 61], off the coast of Sleswick.[1]

CHAPTER III

To the east of the peninsula are the four so-called "Scandiæ," three

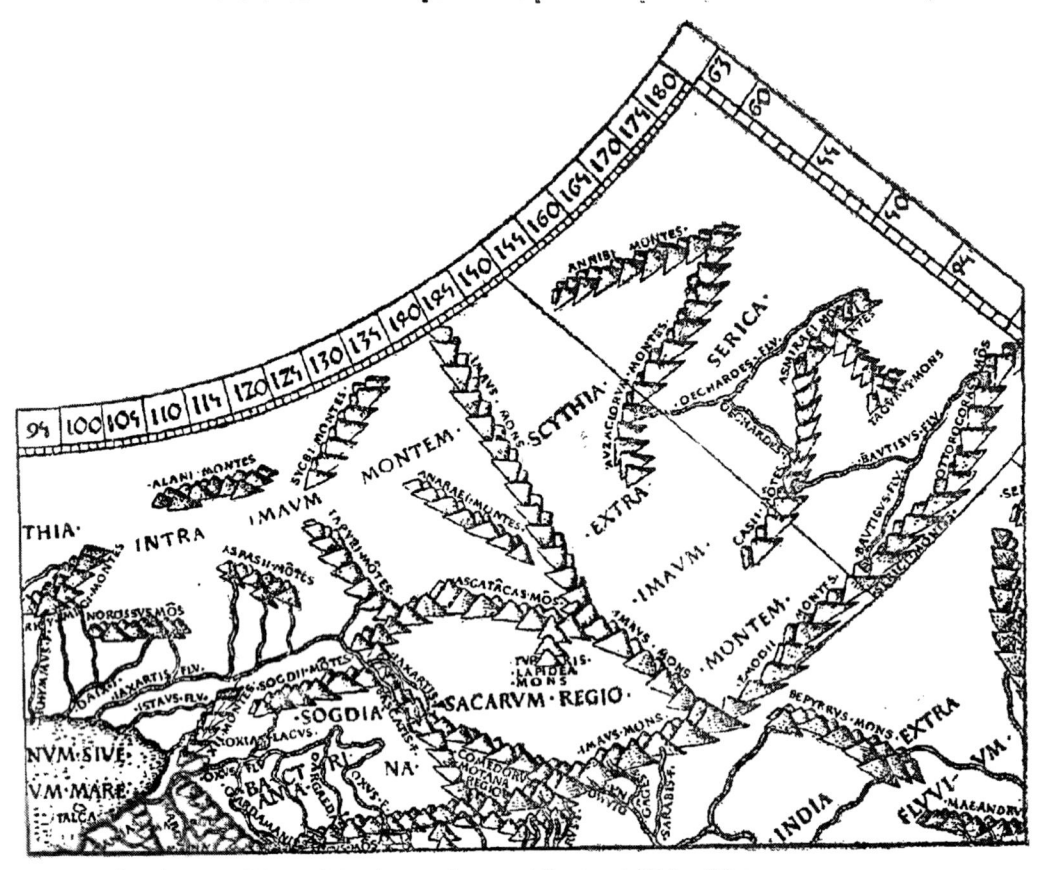

From the Rome edition of Ptolemy of 1490 (Nordenskiöld, 1889)

small [the Danish islands], of which the central one lies in 41° 30′ E. long., 58° N. lat.; but the largest and most eastern lies off the mouths of the Vistula;

---

[1] Much [1895, a, p. 34] thinks that the "Alociæ" may have been some small rocky islands which have now disappeared. Upon them he supposes there may have been colonies of auks, which have given them their name, as in Gothic, for instance, they may have been called "*alakô." The hypothesis is improbable; even if any such rocky islets had been washed away by the sea they must have left behind submerged rocks, and none such are known in the sea off Jutland.

119

CHAPTER III the westernmost part of this island lies in 43° E. long., 58° N. lat., the easternmost in 46° E. long., 58° N. lat., the northernmost in 44° 30′ E. long., 58° 30′ N. lat., the southernmost in 45° E. long., 57° 40′ N. lat.   But this one [i.e., south Scandinavia] is called in particular Scandia, and the western part of it is inhabited by the Chædini, the eastern by the Phavonæ and Phiresii, the northern by the Phinni, the southern by the Gutæ and Dauciones, and the central by the Levoni.

It will be seen that Scandia would not be much larger than Thule : 20′ longer from west to east, and only 10′ longer from north to south.

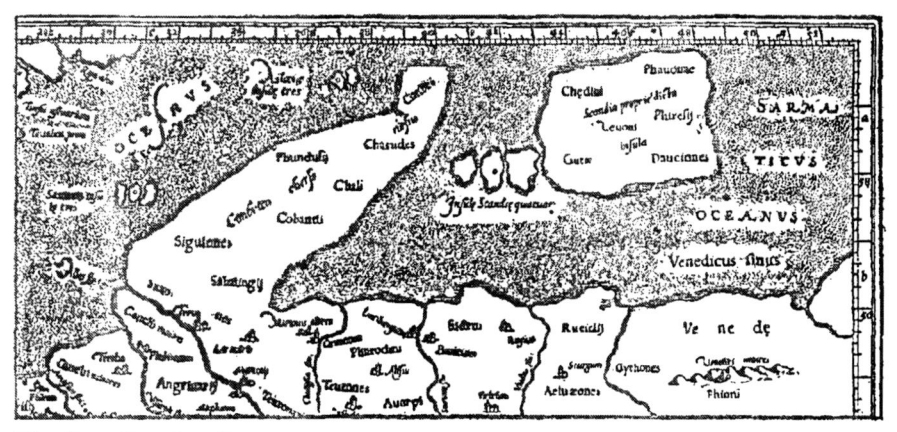

The Scandinavian North according to Ptolemy. The most northern people in Scandinavia, the Phinni, are omitted in this map, as in most MSS.

The " Chædini " must be the Norwegian " Heiðnir " or " Heinir," whose name is preserved in Heiðmork, Hedemarken [cf. Zeuss, 1837, p. 159 ; Much, 1893, p. 188 ; Müllenhoff, 1900, p. 497]. This is the first time that an undoubtedly Norwegian tribe is mentioned in known literature. " Phinni " (Finns) is only found in one MS. ; but as Jordanes (Cassiodorus) says that Ptolemy mentions seven tribes in Scandia, it must have been found in ancient MSS. of his work, and it occurs here for the first time as the name of a people in Scandinavia. Ptolemy also mentions " Phinni " in another place as a people in Sarmatia near the Vistula (together with Gythones or Goths) ; but these must be connected with the " Fenni " of Tacitus, and doubtless also belong originally to Scandinavia. The " Gutæ " must be the Gauter or Göter, unless they are

120

ANTIQUITY, AFTER PYTHEAS

the Guter of Gotland (?). The "Dauciones," it has been supposed, may possibly be the Danes, and the "Levoni" might perhaps be the Hilleviones mentioned by Pliny, whose name does not otherwise occur. Thus a knowledge of Scandinavia slowly dawns in history.

To the north of the known coasts and islands of Europe there lay, according to Ptolemy and Marinus, a great continuous ocean, which was a continuation of the Atlantic. On the extreme north-west was "the Hyperborean Ocean, which was also called the Congealed ($πέπηγος$) or 'Cronius' or the Dead ($νεκρός$) Sea." North of Britain was the Deucaledonian Ocean, and east of Britain the Germanic Ocean as far as the eastern side of the Cimbrian Chersonese, that is, the North Sea and a part of the Baltic. This was joined by the Sarmatian Ocean, with the Venedian (i.e., Wendish) Gulf, from the mouths of the Vistula north-eastwards. The Baltic was still merely an open bay of the great Northern Ocean. But whether the latter extended farther to the east, round the north of the œcumene, making it into an island, was unknown. Ptolemy and Marinus therefore put the northern boundary of the known continent at the latitude of Thule, and made this continent extend into the unknown on the north-east and east; they thus furnish the latest development of the doctrine that the œcumene was not an island in the universal ocean, since they considered that guesses about the regions beyond the limits of the really known were

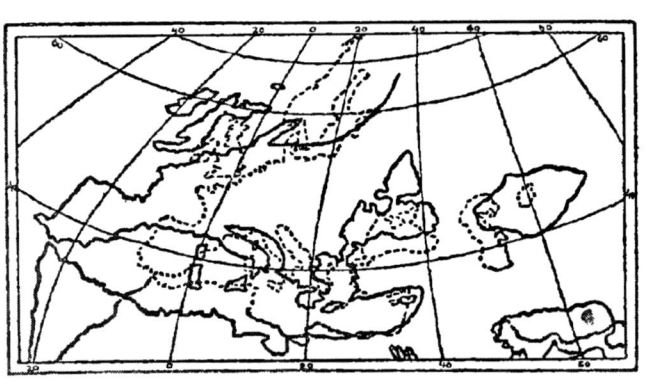

Ptolemy's map of Europe, etc., compared with the true conditions (in dotted line)

CHAPTER III inadmissible, and no one had reached any coast in those directions; for the Caspian Sea was closed and not connected with the Northern Ocean. In the same way the extent of Africa towards the south was uncertain, and they connected it possibly with south-eastern Asia, to the south of the Indian Ocean, which thus also became enclosed.

Ptolemy wrote at a time when the Roman Empire was at its height, and he had the advantage of being able, as a Greek, to combine the scientific lore of the older Greek literature with the mass of information which must inevitably have been collected from all parts of the world by the extensive administration of this gigantic empire. His work, like that of Marinus, was therefore a natural fruit which grew by the stream of time. But the stream had just then reached a backwater; he belonged to a languishing civilisation, and represents the last powerful shoot which Greek science put forth. Some thirteen centuries were to elapse before, by the changes of fate, his works at last made their mark in the development of the world's civilisation. In the centuries that succeeded him the Roman Empire went steadily backwards to its downfall, and literature degenerated rapidly; it sank into compilation and repetition of older writers, without spirit or originality. It is therefore not surprising that the literature of later antiquity gives us nothing new about the North, although communication therewith must certainly have increased.

The geographical author of antiquity most widely read

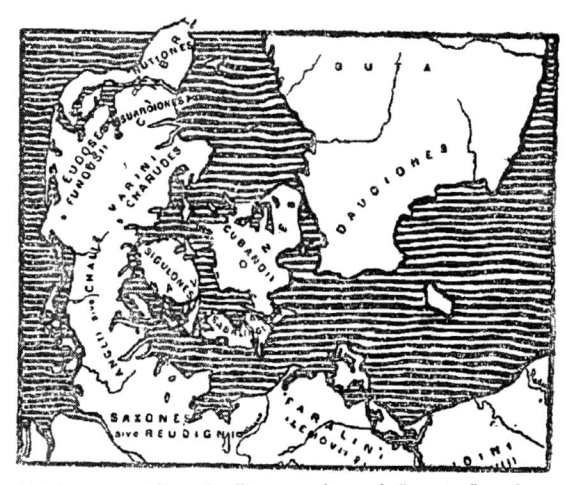

Ptolemy's tribes in Denmark and South Sweden

ANTIQUITY, AFTER PYTHEAS

in the Middle Ages was C. Julius Solinus (third century A.D.), who for the most part repeated passages from Pliny, with a marked predilection for the fabulous. All that is to be found in the MSS. of his works about Thule, the Orcades and the Hebudes, beyond what we read in Pliny, consists, in the opinion of Mommsen [1895, p. 219], of later additions by a copyist (perhaps an Irish monk) of between the seventh and ninth centuries, and as this has a certain interest for our country it will be dealt with later under this period.

CHAPTER III
Solinus, 3rd century A.D.

Rufus Festus Avienus lived in the latter half of the fourth century A.D. and was proconsul in Africa in 366 and in Achæa in 372. His poem " Ora Maritima " is mainly a translation of older Greek authors and, as mentioned above (p. 37), is of interest from his having used an otherwise unknown authority of very early origin. His second descriptive poem is a free translation of Dionysius Periegetes.

Avienus, circa 370 A.D.

Amongst other authors who in this period of literary degeneration compiled geographical descriptions may be named: Ammianus Marcellinus (second half of the fourth century) in his historical works, Macrobius[1] (circa 400 A.D.), the Spaniard Paulus Orosius, whose widely read historical work (circa 418 A.D.) has a geographical chapter, Marcianus of Heraclea (beginning of the fifth century), Julius Honorius (beginning of the fifth century), Marcianus Capella (about 470 A.D.), Priscianus Cæsariensis (about 500 A.D.) and others.

Macrobius, Orosius, Capella, etc.

Their statements about the northern regions are repetitions of older authors and contain nothing new.

Much of the geographical knowledge of that time was included in the already mentioned (p. 116) " Itineraries," which were probably illustrated with maps of the routes. Partial copies of one of them are preserved in the so-called " Tabula Peutingeriana " [cf. K. Miller, vi. 1898, pp. 90 ff.], which came to be of importance in the Middle Ages.

Itineraries

---

[1] Macrobius's division of the earth into zones after Parmenides with an equatorial ocean like Mela, in graphic representation, had great influence during the Middle Ages.

IN NORTHERN MISTS

CHAPTER III

Thus at the close of antiquity the lands and seas of the North still lie in the mists of the unknown. Many indications point to constant communication with the North, and now and again vague pieces of information have reached the learned world. Occasionally, indeed, the clouds lift a little, and we get a glimpse of great countries, a whole new world in the North, but then they sink again and the vision fades like a dream of fairyland. It seems as though no one felt scientifically impelled to make an effort to clear up these obscure questions.

Then followed restless times, with roving warlike tribes in Central Europe. The peaceful trading communication between the Mediterranean and the northern coasts was broken off, and with it the fresh stream of information which had begun to flow in from the North. And for a long time men chewed the cud of the knowledge that had been collected in remote antiquity. But Greek literature was more and more forgotten, and it was especially the later Roman authors they lived on.

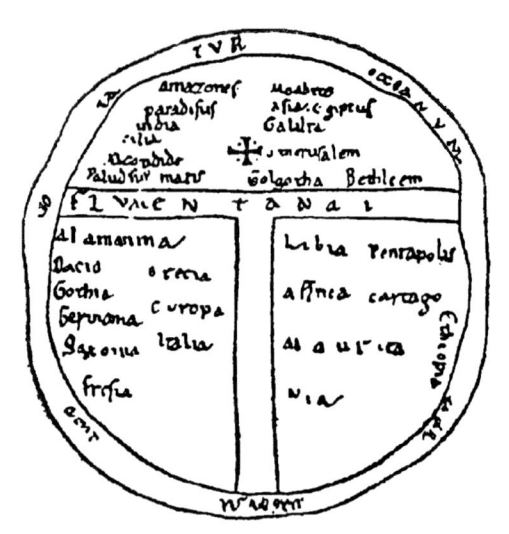

Map of the World from a ninth-century MS. (in the Strasburg Library)

CHAPTER IV

THE EARLY MIDDLE AGES

THUS it came about that the geographical knowledge of later antiquity shows nothing but a gradual decline from the heights which the Greeks had early reached, and from which they had surveyed the earth, the universe and their problems with an intellectual superiority that inclines one to doubt the progress of mankind. The early Middle Ages show an even greater decline. Rome, in spite of all, had formed a sort of scientific centre, which was lost to Western Europe by the fall of the Roman Empire. To this must be added the introduction of Christianity, which, for a time at any rate, gave mankind new values in life, whereby the old ones came into disrepute. Knowledge of distant lands, or of the still more distant heavens, was looked upon as something like folly and madness. For all knowledge was to be found in the Bible, and it was especially commendable to reconcile all profane learning therewith. When, for instance, Isaiah says of the Lord that He " sitteth upon the circle of the earth "

CHAPTER IV

(i.e., the round disc of the earth), and "stretcheth out the heavens as a curtain, and spreadeth them out as a tent to dwell in" [xl. 22], and that He "spread forth the earth" [xlii. 5, xliv. 24], and when in the Book of Job [xxvi. 10] it is said that "He has compassed the waters with bounds, where light borders on darkness," such statements did not agree with the doctrine of the spherical form of the earth; this was therefore regarded with disfavour by the Church; the circular disc surrounded by Ocean, which was the idea of the childhood of Greece, was more suitable, and according to Ezekiel [v. 5–6] Jerusalem lay in the centre of this disc. It was inevitable that knowledge of the earth and of its farthest limits should be still more crippled in such an age, and this is especially true of knowledge of the North.

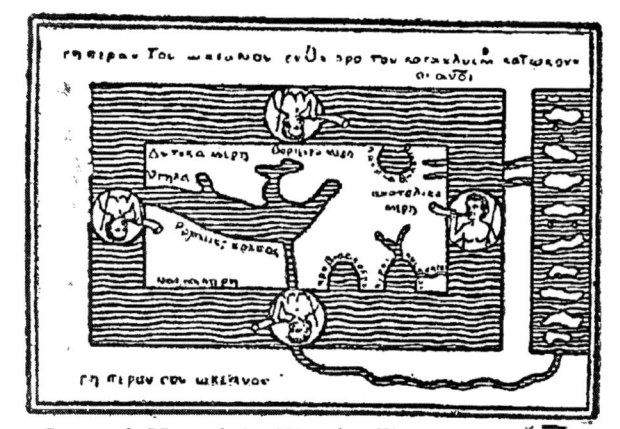

Cosmas's Map of the World. The surface of the earth is rectangular and surrounded by ocean, which forms four bays: the Mediterranean on the west (with the Black Sea), the Caspian above on the right, the Red Sea, and the Persian Gulf below on the right. The Nile (below), the Euphrates and the Tigris flow from the outer world under the ocean to the earth's surface

Those writers who in the early part of the Middle Ages occupied themselves with such worldly things as geography, confined themselves mostly to repeating, and in part further confusing, what Pliny and later Latin authors had said on the subject. The most widely read and most frequently copied were Solinus and Capella, also Macrobius and Orosius. This was the intellectual food which replaced the science of the Greeks. Truly the course of the human race has its alternations of heights and depths!

THE EARLY MIDDLE AGES

But even if the migrations had for a time interrupted peaceful trading intercourse with the North, they were also the means of new facts becoming known, and it was inevitable that in the long run these migrations, and subsequent contact with the northern peoples, should leave their mark on the science of geography. The knowledge of the North shown in the literature of the early Middle Ages is thus to be compared with two streams, often quite independent of one another; the one has its source in classical learning and becomes ever thinner and more turbid; the other is the fresh stream of new information from the North, which we find in a Cassiodorus or a Procopius. Sometimes these two streams flow together, as in an Adam of Bremen, and they may then form a mixture of like and unlike, in which it is often hopeless to find one's way.

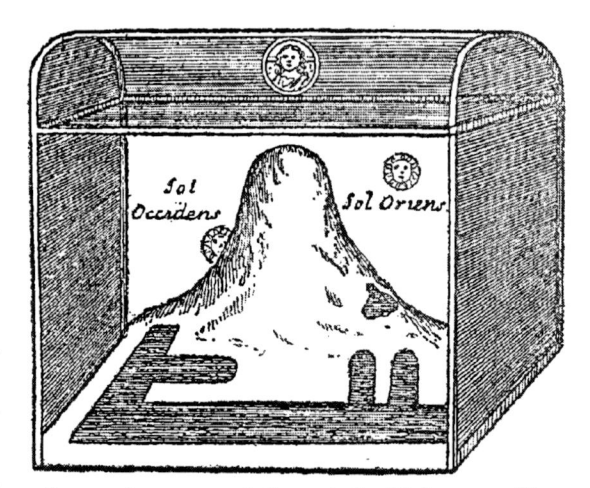

Cosmas's representation of the Universe, with the mountain in the north behind which the Sun goes at night. The Creator is shown above

It is true that some were found, even in the early Middle Ages, who maintained the doctrine of the earth's spherical form, whereas early Christian authors, such as Lactantius (ob. 330) and Severianus (ob. 407), had asserted that it was a disc; the latter also thought that the heaven was divided into two storeys, an upper and a lower, with the visible heaven as a division; the earth formed the floor of this celestial house. One ancient notion (in Empedocles, Leucippus, Democritus) was that this disc of the earth stood on a slant, increasing in height towards the north, which was partly

IN NORTHERN MISTS

<small>CHAPTER IV
Cosmas Indicopleustes, 6th century</small>

covered by high mountains, the Rhipæan and Hyperborean ranges (as in Ptolemy's map). These childish ideas took their most remarkable shape in the "Christian Topography," in twelve books, of the Alexandrine monk, Cosmas Indicopleustes (sixth century). In his younger days he had travelled much as a merchant and seen many wonderful things, amongst others the wheel-ruts left by the Children of Israel during their wanderings in the wilderness. The Jews' tabernacle, he thought, was constructed on the same plan and in the same proportions as the world. Consequently the earth's disc had to be made four-cornered, with straight sides, and twice as long as it was broad. The ocean on the west formed a right angle with the ocean on the south. On the north was a high mountain; behind it the sun was hidden in its course during the night.[1] As the sun in winter traverses the sky in a lower orbit, it appears to us as though it receded behind the mountain near its foot, and it stays away longer than in summer, when it is higher. The whole vault of heaven was like a four-cornered box with a vaulted lid, which was divided by the firmament into two storeys. In the lower one were the earth, the sea, the sun, moon and stars; in the upper one the waters of the sky. The stars were carried round in circles by angels, whom God at the creation appointed to this heavy task. It was impossible for the earth to revolve, simply because its axle must be supported by something, and of what kind of material could it be made? He had nothing else worth mentioning to say about the North. But notions such as these had their influence on the earliest mediæval maps.

<small>Cassiodorus, 468-570 A.D.</small>

The first mediæval author who, so far as we know, definitely gave new information of value about the countries and peoples of the North, was the Roman senator and historian Cassiodorus (born at Scylaceum, it is supposed about 468), who was an eminent statesman under Theodoric, King of the Goths

---

[1] Similar conceptions are to be found in Avienus ("Ora Maritima," vv., 644-663), and are derived from ancient Greek geographers (Anaximenes, cf. Mullenhoff, i., 1870, p. 77).

THE EARLY MIDDLE AGES

(493–526). After the victories of Belisarius in Italy, Cassiodorus retired into a monastery in southern Italy (Bruttium), which he himself had founded, and died there, perhaps 100 years old (about 570). He wrote several valuable works, amongst them, probably by order of Theodoric, one in twelve books on "The Origin and Deeds of the Goths," which was perhaps completed about 534. This work has unfortunately been lost, and we only know it through the Goth Jordanes, who has made excerpts from it. There is reason to believe [cf. Mommsen, 1882, Proœmium, p. xxxvii.] that Cassiodorus's knowledge of Gothic was defective, and that he has borrowed his information about the North, especially Scandinavia, from a contemporary, or perhaps somewhat older writer, Ablabius, who is referred to in Jordanes' book as "the distinguished author of a very trustworthy history of the Goths," but who is otherwise unknown. Through the Norwegian king Rodulf and his men (see below, under Jordanes), or other Northerners who visited Theodoric, and who were "mightier than all the Germans in courage and size of body," first-hand information was brought concerning the countries of the North, which Ablabius, who certainly knew Gothic, may have written down, and from him Cassiodorus has thus derived his statements, which again are taken from him by Jordanes. In addition to various classical authors, some Latin and some Greek, of whom Jordanes mentions many more than he has made use of, it is probable that Cassiodorus has also drawn upon the maps of Roman itineraries [cf. Mommsen, 1882, Proœmium, p. xxxi.], and perhaps also Greek maps.

The Gothic monk (or priest) Jordanes lived in the sixth century, and wrote about 551 or 552 a book on "The Origin and Deeds of the Goths" ("De origine actibusque Getarum"), which for the most part is certainly a poor repetition of the substance of Cassiodorus's great work on the same subject; and in fact he tells us this himself, with the modest addition that "his breath is too weak to fill the trumpet of such a

IN NORTHERN MISTS

CHAPTER IV

man's mighty speech." It is true that Jordanes asserts in his preface that he has only had the loan of the work to read for three days, for which reason he cannot give the words but only the sense, and thereto, he says, he has added what was suitable " from certain histories in the Greek [which he did not understand] and Latin tongues," and he has mixed it with his own words. But this is only said to hide his lack of originality; for the book evidently contains long literal excerpts from the work of Cassiodorus, while Jordanes' Latin becomes markedly worse when he tries to walk alone. Not even the preface to the work is original; this is copied from Rufinus's translation of Origines' commentary on the Epistle to the Romans.

Of the uttermost ocean we read in Jordanes :

"Not only has no one undertaken to describe the impenetrable uttermost bounds of the ocean, but it has not even been vouchsafed to any one to explore them, since it has been experienced that on account of the resistance of the seaweed and because the winds cease to blow there, the ocean is impenetrable and is known to none but Him who created it." This conception has a striking resemblance to Avienus's "Ora Maritima" (see above, pp. 37-40), and may very probably be derived from it.

Of the western ocean he says, amongst other things :

"But it has also other islands farther out in the midst of its waves, which are called the Balearic Isles, and another Mevania; likewise the Orcades, thirty-three in number, and yet not all of them are cultivated [inhabited]. It has also in its most western part another island, called Thyle, of which the Mantuan [i.e., Virgil] says : 'May the uttermost Thule be subject to thee.' This immense ocean has also in its arctic, that is to say, northern, part, a great island called Scandza, concerning which our narrative with God's help shall begin; for the nation [the Goths] of whose origin you inquired, burst forth like a swarm of bees from the lap of this island, and came to the land of Europe."

After having spoken of Ptolemy's (also Mela's) mention of this island, which according to his version of the former had the shape of "a citron leaf, with curved edges and very long in proportion to its breadth" (this cannot be found in Ptolemy), and lay opposite the three mouths of the Vistula, he continues :

"This [island] consequently has on its east the greatest inland sea in the world, from which the River Vagi discharges itself, as from a belly, profusely into

THE EARLY MIDDLE AGES

the Ocean.[1] On the western side it [the island of Scandza] is surrounded by an immense ocean and on the north it is bounded by the before-mentioned unnavigable enormous ocean, from which an arm extends to form the Germanic Ocean ('Germanicum mare'), by widening out a bay. There are said to be many more islands in it, but they are small,[2] and when the wolves on account of the severe cold cross over after the sea is frozen, they are reported to lose their eyes, so that the country is not only inhospitable to men but cruel to animals. But in the island of Scandza, of which we are speaking, although there are many different peoples, Ptolemy nevertheless only gives the names of seven of them. But the honey-making swarms of bees are nowhere found on account of the too severe cold. In its northern part live the people Adogit, who, it is said, in the middle of the summer have continuous light for forty days and nights, and likewise at the time of the winter solstice do not see the light for the same number of days and nights; sorrow thus alternating with joy, so are they unlike others in benevolence and injury; and why? Because on the longer days they see the sun return to the east along the edge of the axis [i.e., the edge of the pole, that is to say, along the northern horizon], but on the shorter days it is not thus seen with them, but in another way, because it passes through the southern signs, and when the sun appears to us to rise from the deep, with them it goes along the horizon. But there are other people there, and they are called Screrefennæ, who do not seek a subsistence in corn, but live on the flesh of wild beasts and the eggs of birds,[3] and such an enormous number of eggs [lit., spawn] is laid in the marshes that

CHAPTER IV

---

[1] This description would best suit the Baltic (and the Belts) as forming the eastern side of Scandza; but the term inland sea ("lacus") does not agree well with Scandza being an island and lying just opposite the Vistula, which "with its three mouths discharged itself into the Ocean"; and in the rear of the Vidivarii at the mouths of the Vistula "dwelt likewise on the Ocean the Æstii, that very peace-loving people" [v. 36, cf.Tacitus]. Besides which Jordanes' Germanic Ocean may be the Baltic, although his very obscure description may equally well suit the North Sea, or both together. The supposition that the great inland sea and the River Vagi might be Lake Ladoga and the Neva [cf. Geijer, 1825, p. 100] or Lake Vener and the Gota River [cf. Lonborg, 1897, p. 25, and Ahlenius, 1900, p. 44] does not agree with the description of Jordanes, which distinctly asserts that it lay on the east side of Scandza in contradistinction to the immense ocean on the west and north. The fact must be that Jordanes had very obscure ideas on this point, and this has made his description confusing.

[2] These small islands have been taken to be the Danish islands [cf. Ahlenius, 1900, p. 43]; but as we hear in immediate connection with them of severe cold and of the wolves losing their eyes on crossing the frozen sea ("congelato mari"), our thoughts are led farther north and we would be inclined to take them for the Åland islands.

[3] This reminds us of Mela's statement respecting the Œneans, who lived on fen-fowl's eggs (see above, pp. 91, 95).

CHAPTER IV

Screrefennæ or Skridfinns

it serves both for the increase of their kind [i.e., of the birds] and for a plentiful supply for the people."

The "Screrefennæ" of Jordanes (in other MSS. "Crefenne," "Rerefennæ," etc.) are certainly a corruption of the same word as Procopius's "Scrithifini" (Skridfinns), and were a non-Germanic race inhabiting the northern regions (see later). The mention of these people, together with their neighbours the "Adogit," who had the midnight sun and a winter night of forty days (cf. also Procopius), shows without a doubt that Jordanes', or rather Cassiodorus's, authority had received fresh information from the most northern part of Scandinavia, possibly through the Norwegian king Rodulf and his men.

Adogit

The mysterious name "Adogit" is somewhat doubtful. P. A. Munch [1852, p. 93], and later also Müllenhoff [ii., 1887, p. 41], thought that it might be a corruption of Hálogi ("Háleygir," or Helgelanders) in northern Norway. Sophus Bugge [1907] does not regard this interpretation as possible, as this name cannot have had such a form at that time; he (and, as he informs us, Gustav Storm also independently) thinks that "adogit" is corrupted from "ādogii," i.e., "andogii," meaning inhabitants of And or Ando in Vesterålen.[1] The termination -ogii he takes to be a mediæval way of writing what was pronounced -oji, i.e., islanders.[2] But it should be remembered how much the name "Screrefennæ" has been corrupted, and that it is very possible that other names may have been so equally.

[1] And or Amd was used formerly not only for the island of And (Andö), but for a great part of Vesterålen and Hinno.

[2] I will mention as yet another possibility a corruption of Ptolemy's islands, the "Alociæ," which lay at the extreme north of his map, north of the Cimbrian Chersonese and farther north than the island of Scandia (see above, pp. 119 f.). A Greek capital lambda, Λ, may easily be mistaken for a capital delta, Δ, especially in maps, and in such corrupted form may have been transferred to Roman maps, and thence have been used for the name of a people who were said to live specially far north. Läffler [1894, p. 4] thinks that "Adogit" was a Lappish people, and that the name certainly cannot be of Scandinavian-Germanic origin, but he does not say why.

THE EARLY MIDDLE AGES

The statement that the Adogit had forty days' daylight in summer and a corresponding period of night in winter is, unfortunately, of no assistance in the form in which it is given for deciding the locality inhabited by them, for no such phenomenon occurs anywhere on the earth. If we suppose that the Adogit people themselves observed the rising and setting of the sun above a free horizon, then we must believe that they reckoned the unbroken summer day from the first to the last night on which the upper limb of the sun did not disappear below the edge of the sea. And they would have reckoned the unbroken winter night from the first day on which the sun's upper limb did not appear above the horizon at noon, until the first day when it again became visible.

CHAPTER IV
Impossibility of forty days' daylight in summer and night in winter

If we reckon in this way, and take into account the horizontal refraction and the fact that the obliquity of the ecliptic about the year 500 was approximately 11' greater than now, we shall find that at that time the midnight sun was seen for forty days (i.e., from June 2 to July 12) in about 66° 54' N. lat., or in the neighbourhood of Kunna, south of Bodö; but at the same place more than half the sun's disc would be above the horizon at noon at the winter solstice; it was therefore not hidden for a single day, much less for forty days. But, on the other hand, it was not until 68° 51' N. lat., or about Harstad on Hinnö, that they had an unbroken winter night, without seeing the rim of the sun, for forty days (from December 2 to January 11); but there they had the midnight sun in summer for about sixty-three days. The fable of a summer day of the same length as the unbroken winter night cannot therefore have originated with the Northerners; it must have been evolved in an entirely theoretical way by astronomical speculations (in ignorance of refraction) which were a survival of Greek science, where the length of the northern summer day was always assumed to be equal to that of the winter night. But that information had been received at this time from the Northerners is probable, since the statement of a forty days' summer day and winter night is not

IN NORTHERN MISTS

CHAPTER IV

found in any known author of earlier date,[1] and Jordanes' contemporary, Procopius, has an even more detailed statement, especially of this winter night (see later). The probability is that what the Northerners took particular notice of was the long night, during which, as Procopius also relates, they kept an accurate account of the days during which they had to do without the light of the sun, a time in which "they were very depressed, since they could not hold intercourse." This must also have been what they told to the Southerners, while they did not pay so much attention to the length of the summer day, when of course they would in any case have plenty of sunlight. We must therefore suppose that the latitude worked out according to the winter night of forty days is the correct one, and this gives us precisely Sophus Bugge's And—Andö, or, better still, Hinnö.

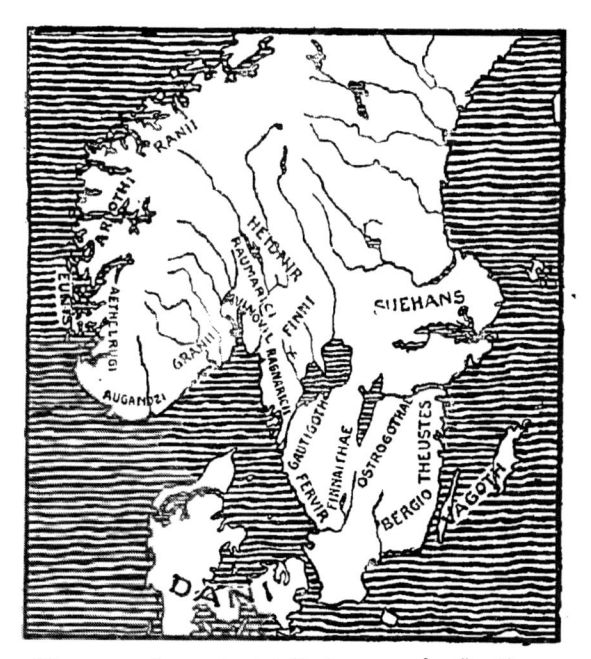

The more important tribal names in Southern Scandinavia, according to Jordanes

Northern Tribal Names

Jordanes counts about twenty-seven names of tribes or peoples in Sweden and Norway; a number of them are easily recognised, while others must be much corrupted and are difficult to interpret.[2] He mentions first the peoples of Sweden,

---

[1] Cleomedes says that the summer day in Thule lasted a month, while the astronomically ignorant Pliny puts it at six months.

[2] As to these tribal names see especially Läffler [1894, 1907] and Sophus Bugge [1907], besides P. A. Munch [1852], Müllenhoff [1887], and others.

THE EARLY MIDDLE AGES

then those of Norway. "Suehans" is certainly the Svear.

> They, "like the Thuringians, have excellent horses. It is also they who through their commercial intercourse with innumerable other peoples send for the use of the Romans saphherine skins ('sappherinas pelles'), which skins are celebrated for their blackness.[1] While they live poorly they have the richest clothes."[1]

We see then that at this time the fur trade with the North was well developed, as the amber trade was at a much earlier date. Adam of Bremen tells us of the "proud horses" of the Svear as though they were an article of export together with furs. In the Ynglinga Saga it is related [cf. Sophus Bugge, 1907, p. 99] that Adils, King of the Svear at Upsalir,

> "was very fond of good horses, he had the best horses of that time." He sent a stallion "to Hålogaland to Godgest the king, Godgest the king rode it, and could not hold it, so he fell off and got his death; this was in Omd [Amd] in Hålogaland."

The original authority for the statement in Jordanes was probably King Rodulf, who perhaps came from the northern half of Norway, and it looks as though the Norwegians even at that time were acquainted with Swedish horses

Jordanes further mentions five tribes who "dwell in a flat, fertile land [i.e., south Sweden], for which reason also they have to protect themselves against the attacks of other tribes ('gentium')." Among the tribes in Sweden are mentioned also the "Finnaithæ"—doubtless in Finn-heden or Finn-veden (that is, either Finn-heath or Finn-wood), whose name must be due to an aboriginal people called Finns—further, the "Gautigoth," generally taken for the West Göter, who were a specially "brave and warlike people," the "Ostrogothæ" [East Göter] and many more.

Then he crosses the Norwegian frontier and mentions

> "The 'Raumarici' [of Romerike] and 'Ragnaricii' [of Ranrike or Bohuslen], the very mild [peaceful] 'Finns' ('Finni mitissimi'), who are milder than all

---

[1] The origin of the word "sappherinas" is uncertain. Lonborg [1897, p. 26] proposes that it may have meant deep sapphire blue, and have been used of the skins of blue foxes. Probably it is rather a northern word, not Germanic, but either Slavonic or Finnish (?).

CHAPTER IV

IN NORTHERN MISTS

CHAPTER IV

the other inhabitants of Scandza,[1] further their equals the 'Vinoviloth'; the 'Suetidi' are known among this people ['hac gente' must doubtless mean the Scandinavians] as towering above the rest in bodily height, and yet the 'Danes,' who are descended from this very race [i.e., the Scandinavians?] drove out the 'Heruli' from their own home, who claimed the greatest fame [i.e., of being the foremost] among the peoples ['nationes'] of Scandia for very great bodily size. Yet of the same height as these are also the 'Granii' [of Grenland, the coast-land of Bratsberg and Nedenes], the 'Augandzi' [people of Agder],[2] 'Eunix' [islanders, Holmryger in the islands?], 'Ætelrugi' [Ryger on the mainland in Ryfylke], 'Arochi' [= 'arothi,' i.e., Harudes, Horder of Hordaland], 'Ranii' [in other MSS. 'Rannii' or 'Rami,' Sophus Bugge (1907) and A. Bugge see in this a corruption of '*Raumi,' that is, people of Romsdal], over whom not many years ago Roduulf was king, who, despising his own kingdom, hastened to the arms of Theodoric king of the Goths, and found what he had hankered after. These people fight with the savageness of beasts, more mighty than the Germans in body and soul."

The small (?), "very mild" Finns must, from the order in which they are named, have lived in the forest districts—Solör, Eidskogen, and perhaps farther south—on the Swedish border. P. A. Munch [1852, p. 83] saw in their kinsmen the "Vinoviloth" the inhabitants of "Vingulmark" (properly "vingel-skog," thick, impenetrable forest), which was the forest country on Christiania fjord from Glommen to Lier. Müllenhoff agrees with this [ii., 1887, pp. 65 f.], but thinks that "-oth," the last part of the word, belongs to the next name, Suetidi, and that "Vinovil" may be a corruption of Vingvili or Vinguli (cf. Paulus Warnefridi's "Vinili"?). But however this may be, we must regard this people and the foregoing as "Finnish" and as inhabiting forest districts,

---

[1] Müllenhoff, Mommsen, Läffler, and others think that the "mitiores" (milder) of the MSS. may be an error for "minores" (smaller), which gives better sense, in contradistinction to the "Suetidi" who come just after and were taller than all the rest. Sophus Bugge proposes that "mitissimi" and "mitiores" may be errors for "minutissime" and "minutiores," and that it should therefore be translated "the very small Finns who are smaller than all the other, etc." [cf. also A. Bugge, 1906, p. 18]; but the necessity for so great a change is doubtful [cf. Läffler, 1907, p. 109].

[2] S. Bugge thought [1907, p. 101] at one time that these might be people of Gond or Gand, i.e., Hoiland, south of Stavanger, but afterwards changed this view [cf. 1910, p. 97].

THE EARLY MIDDLE AGES

as hunters, as well as a third Finnish people, "Finnaithæ" in Småland. We shall return later to these "Finns" in Scandinavia. It has been thought that "Suetidi" may be from the same word as "Sviþjoð"; but as Jordanes has already mentioned the Svear ("Suehans"), and as the name occurs among the Norwegian tribes, and there is evidently a certain order in their enumeration, Müllenhoff may be right in seeing in it a corruption of a Norwegian tribal name. He thinks that "Othsuetidi" may be a corruption of "Æthsævii," i.e., "Eiðsivar" (cf. Eidsivathing), "Heiðsævir" or "Heiðnir" in Hedemarken, who were certainly a very tall people. The mention of the Norwegian warriors has a certain interest in that it is due to the Roman statesman Cassiodorus (or his authority), who glorified the Goths and had no special reason for praising the Northmen.[1] It shows that even at that time our northern ancestors were famed for courage and bodily size, and that too above all other Germanic peoples, who were highly esteemed by the Romans. It is not clear whether Rodulf was King of the "Ranii" (Raumer?) alone, or of all the Norwegian tribes from Grenland to Romsdal. It may be supposed that he was a Norwegian chief who migrated south through Europe at the head of a band of warriors, composed of men from the tribes mentioned, and that finally on the Danube, hard pressed by other warlike people, he sought alliance and support from the mighty king of the Goths, Theodoric or Tjodrik (Dietrich of Berne). This may have been just before 489, when the latter made his expedition to Italy. Many circumstances combine to make such a hypothesis probable.[2]

We know that about 489 the Eruli were just north of the Danube, and were the Goths' nearest neighbours. Now, as we shall see later, Eruli was perhaps at first a common name for bands of northern warriors, and these Eruli on the

---

[1] Jordanes, who was a Goth, had even less reason for glorifying the Northmen at the expense of the Germans or Goths.

[2] Cf. Mommsen, 1882, p. 154; A. Bugge, 1906, pp. 21, 33 f.

Danube may therefore certainly have consisted to a greater or less extent of Norwegians. We know, further, that at this time there was a king of the Eruli to whom Theodoric sent as a gift a horse, sword and shield, thereby making him his foster-son [cf. Cassiodorus, Varia iii. 3, iv. 2]. Finally, we know from Procopius that the Eruli just at this time had a king, Rodulf, who fell in battle against the Langobards (about 493). When we compare this with what Jordanes says about the Norwegian king Rodulf, who hastened to Theodoric's arms and found there what he sought, it will be easy to conclude that this Norwegian chief is the same as the chief of Eruli here spoken of. Rodulf, or "Hrodulfr," is a known Norwegian name. "Rod-," or "Hrod," is the same as the modern Norwegian "ros" (i.e., praise), and means probably here renowned.

One is further inclined to believe that it was from this Rodulf or his men, of whom some may have come from And in Hålogaland, that Cassiodorus or his authority obtained the information about Scandinavia and northern Norway, which is also partly repeated in Procopius.

Sophus Bugge [cf. 1910, pp. 87 ff.; see also A. Bugge, 1906, pp. 35 f.] has suggested that the "Råðulfr," who is mentioned in the runic inscription on the celebrated Rok-stone in Ostergotland (of about the year 900), in which Theodoric ("Þiaurikr") is also mentioned, may be the same Norwegian chief Rodulf who came to Theodoric and who fell in battle with the Langobards. He even regards it as possible that it is an echo of this battle which is found in the inscription, where it is said that "twenty kings lie slain on the field"; in that case the battle has been moved north from the Danube to "Siulunt" (i.e., Sealand). There are other circumstances which agree with this: it is said of the Eruli that they had peace for three years before the battle [cf. Procopius]; on the Rok-stone it is stated that the twenty kings stayed in Siulunt four winters; the latter must have been Norwegian warriors of different tribes: Ryger, Horder, and Heiner (from Hedemarken), perhaps under a paramount king Råðulfr, who settled in Sealand—while the Eruli were bands of northern warriors, who under a king Rodulf had established themselves on the north bank of the Danube. Bugge's supposition may be uncertain, but if it be correct it greatly strengthens the view (see p. 145) that the Eruli were largely Norwegian warriors, since in that case the king of the Eruli, Rodulf (= Råðulfr), would have been in command of tribes for the most part Norwegian: Ryger, Horder, and Heiner.

THE EARLY MIDDLE AGES

The Byzantine historian Procopius, of Cæsarea (ob. after 562), became in 527 legal assistant, "assessor," to the general Belisarius, and accompanied him on his campaigns until 549, amongst others that against the Goths in Italy. In his work (in Greek) on the war against the Goths ("De bello Gothico," t. ii. c. 14 and 15), written about 552, he gives information about the North which is of great interest. He tells us of the warlike Germanic people, the Eruli, who from old time[1] were said to have lived on the north bank of the Danube, and who, with no better reason than that they had lived in peace for three whole years and were tired of it, attacked their neighbours the Langobards, but suffered a decisive defeat, and their king, Rodulf, fell in the battle (about 493).[2]

CHAPTER IV
Procopius, circa 552 A.D.

"They then hastily left their dwelling-places, and set out with their women and children to wander through the whole country [Hungary] which lies north of the Danube. When they came to the district where the Rogians had formerly dwelt, who had joined the army of the Goths and gone into Italy, they settled there; but as they were oppressed by famine in that district, which had been laid waste, they soon afterwards departed from it, and came near to the country of the Gepidæ [Siebenburgen]. The Gepidæ allowed them to establish themselves and to become their neighbours, but began thereupon, without the slightest cause, to commit the most revolting acts against them, ravishing their women, robbing them of cattle and other goods, and omitting no kind of injustice, and finally began an unjust war against them." The Eruli then crossed the Danube to Illyria and settled somewhere about what is now Servia under the eastern emperor Anastasius (491-518). Some of the Eruli would not "cross the Danube, but decided to establish themselves in the uttermost ends of the inhabited world. Many chieftains of royal blood now undertaking their leadership, they passed through all the tribes of the Slavs one after another, went thence through a wide, uninhabited country, and came to the so-called Varn. Beyond them they passed by the tribes of the Danes [in Jutland], without the barbarians

---

[1] This is certainly incorrect; probably they came from the north and established themselves near the Danube in the neighbourhood of the Langobards.

[2] Paulus Warnefridi gives a mythical account of the cause of the war and of the battle and death of king Rodulf [Bethmann and Waitz, 1878, pp. 57 ff]; the fight and king Rodulf are also referred to in the "Origo Gentes Langobardorum" (of about 807). In both these works it is stated that it was the Langobards (and not the Eruli) who had lived in this country (by the Danube?) in peace for three years.

CHAPTER IV

there using violence towards them. When they thence came to the ocean [about the year 512] they took ship, and landed on the island of Thule [i.e., Scandinavia] and remained there. But Thule is beyond comparison the largest of all islands; for it is more than ten times as large as Britain. But it lies very far therefrom northwards. On this island the land is for the most part uninhabited. But in the inhabited regions there are thirteen populous tribes, each with a king. Every year an extraordinary thing takes place; for the sun, about the time of the summer solstice, does not set at all for forty days, but for the whole of this time remains uninterruptedly visible above the earth. No less than six months later, about the winter solstice, for forty days the sun is nowhere to be seen on this island; but continual night is spread over it, and therefore for the whole of that time the people are very depressed, since they can hold no intercourse. It is true that I have not succeeded, much as I should have wished it, in reaching this island and witnessing what is here spoken of, but from those who have come thence to us I have collected information of how they are able [to count the days] when the sun neither rises nor sets at the times referred to," etc. When, during the forty days that it is above the horizon, the sun in its daily course returns "to that place where the inhabitants first saw it rise, then according to their reckoning a day and a night have passed. But when the period of night commences, they find a measure by observation of the moon's path, according to which they reckon the number of days. But when thirty-five days of the long night are passed, certain people are sent up to the tops of mountains, as is the custom with them, and when from thence they can see some appearance of the sun, they send word to the inhabitants below that in five days the sun will shine upon them. And the latter assemble and celebrate, in the dark it is true, the feast of the glad tidings. Among the people of Thule this is the greatest of all their festivals. I believe that these islanders, although the same thing happens every year with them, nevertheless are in a state of fear lest some time the sun should be wholly lost to them.

"Among the barbarians inhabiting Thule, one people, who are called Skridfinns [Scrithifini], live after the manner of beasts. They do not wear clothes [i.e., of cloth] nor, when they walk, do they fasten anything under their feet, [i.e., they do not wear shoes], they neither drink wine nor eat anything from the land, because they neither cultivate the land themselves nor do the women provide them with anything from tilling it, but the men as well as the women occupy themselves solely and continually in hunting; for the extraordinarily great forests and mountains which rise in their country give them vast quantities of game and other beasts. They always eat the flesh of the animals they hunt and wear their skins, and they have no linen or anything else that they can sew with. But they fasten the skins together with the sinews of beasts, and thus cover their whole bodies. The children even are not brought up among them as with other peoples; for the Skridfinns' children do not take women's milk, nor do they touch their mothers' breasts, but they are nourished solely with the marrow of slain beasts. As soon therefore as a woman has given birth, she winds the child in a skin, hangs it up in a tree, puts marrow into its mouth,

THE EARLY MIDDLE AGES

and goes off hunting; for they follow this occupation in common with the men. Thus is the mode of life of these barbarians arranged.

"Nearly all of the remaining inhabitants of Thule do not, however, differ much from other peoples. They worship a number of gods and higher powers in the heavens, the air, the earth and the sea, also certain other higher beings which are thought to dwell in the waters of springs and rivers. But they always slay all kinds of sacrifice and offer dead sacrifices. And to them the best of all sacrifices is the man they have taken prisoner by their arms. Him they sacrifice to the god of war, because they consider him to be the greatest. But they do not sacrifice him merely by using fire at the sacrifice; they also hang him up in a tree, or throw him among thorns, and slay him by other cruel modes of death. Such is the life of the inhabitants of Thule, among whom the most numerous people are the Gauti (Goter), with whom the immigrant Eruli settled."

This description by Procopius of Thule (Scandinavia) and its people bears the stamp of a certain trustworthiness. If we ask whence he has derived his information, our thoughts are led at once to the Eruli, referred to by him in such detail, who in part were still the allies of the Eastern Empire, and of whom the emperor at Byzantium had a bodyguard in the sixth century. There were many of them in the army of the Eastern Empire both in Persia and in Italy; thus Procopius says that there were two thousand of them in the army under the eunuch Narses, which came to Italy to join Belisarius. Procopius thus had ample opportunity for obtaining first-hand information from these northern warriors, and his account of them shows that the Eruli south of the Danube kept up communication with their kinsmen in Scandinavia, for when they had killed their king "Ochon" without cause, since they wished to try being without a king, and had repented the experiment, they sent some of their foremost men to Thule to find a new king of the royal blood. They chose one and returned with him; but he died on the way when they had almost reached home, and they therefore turned again and went once more to Thule. This time they found another, "by name 'Datios' [or 'Todasios' = Tjodrik?]. He was accompanied by his brother 'Aordos' [= Vard?] and two hundred young men of the Eruli in Thule." Meanwhile, as they were so long absent, the Eruli of

CHAPTER IV

Erulian sources of Procopius

IN NORTHERN MISTS

CHAPTER IV

Singidunum (the modern Belgrade) had sent an embassy to the emperor Justinianus at Byzantium asking him to give them a chief. He sent, therefore, the Erulian "Svartuas" (= Svartugle, i.e., black owl?), who had been living with him for a long time. But when Datios from Thule approached, all the Eruli went over to him by night, and Svartuas had to flee quite alone, and returned to Byzantium. The emperor now exerted all his power to reinstate him; "but the Eruli, who feared the power of the Romans, decided to migrate to the Gepidæ." This happened in Procopius's own time, and may therefore be regarded as trustworthy; it shows how easy communication must have been at that time between Scandinavia and the south, and also with Byzantium, so that Procopius may well have had his information by that channel. But he may also have received information from another quarter. His description of Thule shows such decided similarities with Jordanes' account of Scandza and its people that they point to some common source of knowledge, even though there are also dissimilarities. Among the latter it may be pointed out that Jordanes makes a distinction between Thule (north of Britain) and Scandza, while Procopius calls Scandinavia Thule, which, however, like Jordanes, he places to the north of Britain, and he does not mention Scandia. It may seem surprising that Jordanes' authority, Cassiodorus (or Ablabius?), should have known Ptolemy better than the Greek Procopius. The explanation may be that when Procopius heard from the statements of the Eruli themselves that some of them had crossed the ocean from the land of the Danes (Jutland) to a great island in the north, he could not have supposed that this was Scandia, which on Ptolemy's map lay east of the Cimbrian peninsula and farther south than its northern point; it would seem much more probable that it was Thule, which, however, as he saw, must lie farther from Britain and be larger than it was shown on Ptolemy's map; for which reason Procopius expressly asserts that Thule was much larger than Britain and lay far to the north of it. As it was not Procopius's habit to

Common source of Procopius and Jordanes

THE EARLY MIDDLE AGES

make a show of unnecessary names, he keeps the well-known name of Thule and does not even mention Scandia. It may even be supposed that it was to west Norway itself, or the ancient Thule, that the Eruli sailed. If their king Rodulf was a Norwegian, as suggested above, this would be probable, as in that case many of themselves would have come from there too; besides which, we know of a people, the Harudes or Horder, who had formerly migrated by sea from Jutland to the west coast of Norway; there had therefore been an ancient connection, and perhaps, indeed, Horder from Norway and Harudes from Jutland may have been among Rodulf's men, and there may also have been Harudes among the Eruli whom the Danes, according to Jordanes, drove out of their home (in Jutland?). There was also, from the very beginning of Norwegian history, much connection between Norway and Jutland.

Another disagreement between the descriptions of Procopius and Jordanes is that according to the former there were thirteen tribes, each with a king, in Thule, while Jordanes enumerates twice as many tribal names in Scandza, but of these perhaps several may have belonged to the same kingdom.[1]

A remarkable similarity between the two authors is the summer day forty days long and the equally long winter night among the people of Thule as with the Adogit, and the fact that in immediate connection therewith the Scrithifini and Screrefennæ, which must originally be the same name, are mentioned. The description in Procopius of festivals on the reappearance of the sun, etc., points certainly to information from the North; but, as already pointed out, the statement in this form, that the summer day was of the same length as the winter night, cannot be due to the Norsemen themselves; it is a literary invention, which points to a common literary

[1] It is probable that the mention of the tribes in Jordanes is taken from two different sources; for he begins by saying that Ptolemy only has the names of seven, without mentioning any of these, and later on he gives a whole series of others, which may have been added from another author who supplemented the one from whom the mention of Ptolemy is taken.

origin; for it would be more than remarkable if it had arisen independently both with the authority of Procopius and with that of Jordanes. An even more striking indication in the same direction is the resemblance which we find in the order of the two descriptions of Thule and of Scandza. First comes the geographical description of the island, which in both is of very great size and lies far out in the northern ocean; then occurs the statement that in this great island are many tribes.[1] Next we have in both the curious fact that the summer day and the winter night both last for forty days. Then follows in both a more detailed statement of how the long summer day and winter night come about, and of how the sun behaves during its course, etc. Immediately after this comes the description of the Skridfinns, who have a bestial way of life, and do not live on corn, but on the flesh of wild beasts, etc., with an addition in Jordanes about fen-fowl's eggs (perhaps taken from Mela), while Procopius has a more detailed description of their mode of life, which reminds one somewhat of Tacitus. Finally, there is a reference to the Germanic people of Thule or Scandza; but while Procopius mentions their religious beliefs and human sacrifices, and only gives the name of the most numerous tribe, the Gauti, Jordanes has for the most part a rigmarole of names.

Even if the method of treating the material is thus very different in the two works, the order in which the material is arranged, and to some extent also the material itself, are in such complete agreement that there must be a historical connection, and undoubtedly a common literary source, through a greater or less number of intermediaries, is the basis of both descriptions. One might think of the unknown Ablabius, or perhaps of the unknown Gothic scholar Aithanarit, whom the Ravenna geographer mentions in connection with his reference to the Skridfinns, if indeed he did not live later than Procopius. It

---

[1] Jordanes here repeats Ptolemy, from whom the name of Scandza, =Scandia, is taken (and the statement as to the shape of the island?), while Procopius has nothing about it.

THE EARLY MIDDLE AGES

is striking also that the passage about Thule in Procopius gives rather the impression of having been inserted in the middle of his narrative about the Eruli, without any very intimate connection therewith, and it may therefore be for the most part taken from an earlier author, perhaps with alterations and additions by Procopius himself; but it is not his habit to inform us of his authorities.

CHAPTER IV

Procopius's description of the Eruli is of great interest. It is a remarkable feature in the history of the world that at certain intervals, even from the earliest times, roving warrior peoples appear in Europe, coming from the unknown North, who for a time fill the world with dread, and then disappear again. One of these northern peoples was perhaps, as already mentioned, the "Cimmerians," who in the eighth century B.C. made an inroad into Asia Minor. Six hundred years later, in the second century B.C., bands of Cimbri and Teutones came down from northern Europe and were pressing towards Rome, till they were defeated by Marius and gradually disappeared. Five hundred years later still, in the third to the fifth centuries A.D., the Eruli come on the scene, and after they have disappeared come the Saxons and Danes, and then the Normans. We may perhaps suppose, to a certain extent at all events, that the races which formed these restless and adventurous bands were in part the same, and that it is the names that have changed. The Eruli are also mentioned by Jordanes and by many other authorities besides Procopius. Together with the Goths they played a part in the "Scythian" war in the third century, but afterwards disappear to the north of the Black Sea. They must have been the most migratory people of their time; we find them roaming over the whole of Europe, from Scandinavia on the north to Byzantium on the south, from the Black Sea on the east to Spain on the west; from the third to the fifth century we find Eruli from Scandinavia as pirates on the coasts of western Europe, and even in the Mediterranean itself, where in 455 they reached Lucca in Italy [cf. Zeuss, 1837, p. 477 f.; Müllenhoff, 1889,

The Eruli are Norsemen

IN NORTHERN MISTS

CHAPTER IV

p. 19]. When we read in Procopius that some of the Eruli would not "cross the Danube, but determined to establish themselves in the uttermost ends of the world," this means, of course, that they had come from thence, and that rather than be subject to the Eastern Empire they would return home to Scandinavia. The name also frequently appears in its primitive Norse form, "erilaR," in Northern runic inscriptions.[1] Since "erilaR" (in Norwegian "jarl," in English "earl") means leader in war, and is not known in Scandinavia as the original name of a tribe which has given its name to any district in the North, we must suppose that it was more probably an appellative in use in the more southern parts of Europe for bands of northern warriors of one or more Scandinavian tribes [cf. P. A. Munch, 1852, p. 53]. They may have called themselves so; it was, in fact, characteristic of the Scandinavian warrior that he was not disposed to acknowledge any superior; they were all free men and chiefs in contradistinction to thralls. Gradually these bands in foreign countries may have coalesced into one nation [cf. A. Bugge, 1906, p. 32]. But as expeditions of Eruli are spoken of in such widely different parts of Europe, the name must, up to the end of the fifth century, have often been used for Norsemen in general, to distinguish them from the nations of Germany, like the designation Normans, and sometimes also Danes, in later times. That the latter was used as an appellative as early as the time of Procopius seems to result from his mentioning the tribes ("ethne") of the Danes in just the same way as he speaks of those of the Slavs. What is said about the Eruli suits the Scandinavians: they were very tall

---

[1] The name appears in the runic inscriptions to be often a designation of the author of the inscription. Sophus Bugge thought that the Eruli had obtained their knowledge of runes from the Goths, and that they kept them a secret (this reappears in the word "run" itself, which means secret), especially in the leading families, who turned them to account. During their centuries of roving life they carried the knowledge of runes with them to various parts of Denmark, Sweden and Norway. In this way the uniformity of language in the inscriptions from widely separated places may also be explained.

THE EARLY MIDDLE AGES

(cf. Jordanes, above, p. 136) and fair, were specially famed for their activity, and were lightly armed; they went into battle without helmet or coat of mail, protected only by a shield and a thick tunic, which they tucked up into a belt. Their thralls, indeed, had to fight without shields; but when they had shown their courage they were allowed to carry a shield [Procopius, De bello Pers., ii. 25]. "At that time," says Jordanes, "there was no nation that had not chosen the light-armed men of its army from among them. But if their activity had often helped them in other wars, they were vanquished by the slow steadiness of the Goths," and they had to submit to Hermanaric, King of the Goths by the Black Sea, the same who is called Jörmunrek in the Völsunga Saga. The people here described can scarcely have been typical dwellers in plains, who are usually slow and heavy; we should rather think of them as tough and active Scandinavian mountaineers, who by their hard life in the hills had become light of foot and practised in the use of their limbs; but who, on the other hand, had been ill-supplied with heavier weapons and had had scant opportunities of exercise as heavy-armed men, for which indeed they had no taste. This also explains their remarkable mobility. We are thus led once more to think of Norway as the possible home of some of the Eruli. To sum up, we find then that they had a king with the Norse name Rodulf, and there are many indications that he was the same as the Norwegian king Rodulf (from Romsdal?) who came to Theodoric. They returned through Jutland and sailed thence to Thule, where they settled by the side of the Gauti, i.e., to the west of them in Norway, which from old time had had frequent communication with Jutland, from whence the Horder (and probably also the Ryger?) had immigrated. They are described as having characteristics which are typical of mountaineers, but not of lowlanders. An Erulian name, "Aruth" ('Αρουθ), mentioned by Procopius [De bello Goth., iv. 26], also points to Norway, since it appears to be the same as the Norwegian tribal name "Horder"

CHAPTER IV

IN NORTHERN MISTS

CHAPTER IV

("* Haruðr," gen. "Haruþs," on the Rök-stone [cf. S. Bugge, 1910, p. 98], or "Arothi" in Jordanes).

Other Erulian names in Procopius may be common to the northern Germanic languages. In the opinion of Professor Alf Torp it is probable that "Visandos" is bison, "Aluith" is Alvid or Alvith (all-knowing); in "Fanitheos" the first syllable may be "fan" or "fen" (English, fen) and the second part "-theos" may be the Scandinavian termination "-ther"; "Aordos" may be Vard. The King's name "Ochon" seems to resemble the Norwegian Håkon; but the latter name cannot have had such a form at that time, it must have been longer.

What Procopius tells us [De bello Goth., ii. 14] about the manners and customs of the Eruli agrees with what we know of the Norsemen generally. They worshipped many gods, whom they considered it their sacred duty to propitiate with human sacrifices. Aged and sick persons were obliged to ask their relatives to help them to get rid of life;[1] they were killed with a dagger by one who did not belong to the family, and were burnt on a great pile, after which the bones were collected and buried, as was the custom in western Norway amongst other places. "When an Erulian died, his wife, if she wished to show her virtue and leave a good name behind her, had to hang herself not long after with a rope by her husband's grave and thus make an end of herself. If she did not do this, she lost respect for the future, and was an offence to her husband's family. This custom was observed by the Eruli from old time." Their many gods and human sacrifices agree, as we see, with Procopius's description of the inhabitants of Thule, and with what we know of the Scandinavians from other quarters. As human sacrifices with most peoples were connected with banquets, at which slain

---

[1] It appears to have been a general custom among the Germans to put old people to death (cf. p. 18). Herodotus [1. 216] relates of the Massagetæ, who may have been a Germanic tribe, that "when any one has grown very old all his relatives come together and slaughter him, and with him other small cattle; they then cook the flesh and hold a banquet. This is considered by them the happiest end. But they do not eat one who dies of sickness, but bury him underground, and lament that he did not live to be slaughtered."

THE EARLY MIDDLE AGES

enemies were eaten,[1] the assertion that our Germanic ancestors did not practise cannibalism rests upon uncertain ground. When, therefore, in finds of the Stone Age in Denmark, Sweden and Norway broken or scraped human bones occur, which point to cannibalism, it cannot be argued from this, as is done by Dr. A. M. Hansen [1907], that the finds belong to a non-Germanic people.

For the rest, Procopius paints the Eruli in crude colours; they are covetous, domineering and violent towards their fellow men, without being ashamed of it. They are addicted to the grossest debauchery, are the most wicked of men, and utterly depraved.

The "Scrithifini" of Procopius (and Jordanes' corrupted form, "Screrefennæ" or "Scretefennæ") are undoubtedly a people of the same kind as Tacitus's "Fenni" (Ptolemy-Marinus's "Finni"); but they have here acquired the descriptive prefix "scrithi-," which is generally understood as the Norse "skriða" (= to slide, e.g., on the ice, to glide; cf. Swedish "skridsko," skate). The Norsemen must have characterised their Finnish (i.e., Lappish) neighbours on the north as sliding (walking) on ski ("skriða á skiðum"), to distinguish them from other peoples in the outlying districts whom they also called Finns. If this is so, it is the first time that a reference to ski-running is found in literature. There is, moreover, considerable similarity between Procopius's description of these hunters and Tacitus's account of the "Fenni," who must certainly also have lived in Scandinavia (see above, p. 113), and who may have been the same people. They have many peculiar characteristics in common, e.g., that both men and women go hunting; and the statement that while the mothers go hunting, the children, in Tacitus, are hidden in a shelter of boughs (i.e., a tent), and in

CHAPTER IV

Skridfinns

[1] This widespread form of anthropophagy is due to the superstition that by eating something of another, beast or man, or particular parts, e.g., the heart (cf. Sigurd Favnesbane), one acquired the peculiar properties of the other, such as strength, courage, goodness, etc. It is thus a similar idea to that in the Christian sacrament.

IN NORTHERN MISTS

CHAPTER IV

Procopius are hung up in a tree (perhaps the Lapps' "komse," i.e., a cradle made of wood to hang up in the tent). Procopius himself probably did not know Tacitus's "Germania," but it is possible that his unknown authority did so, although this work was generally forgotten at that time.

But even if the description of Procopius may thus be partly derived from Tacitus, in any case fresh information has been added, the name Skridfinns itself to begin with, and certain

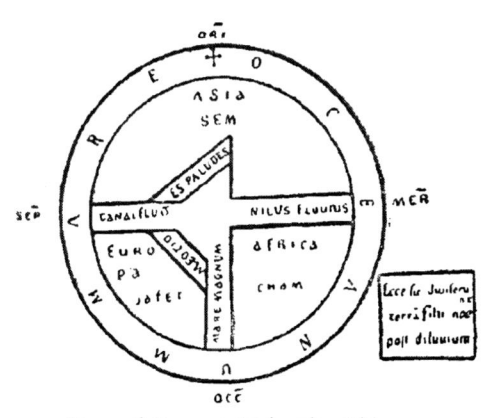

Map of the world in the MS. of Isidore, tenth century, St. Gallen (K. Miller)

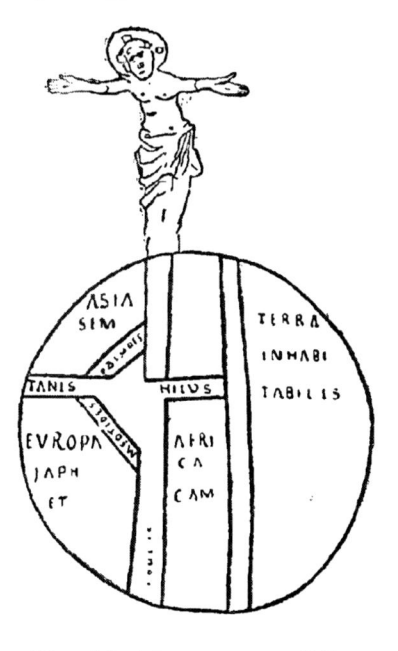

The oldest known map of the world, from the MS. of Isidore of the end of the seventh century, St. Gallen (K. Miller)

correct details, such as their fastening the skins together with the sinews of beasts. The fable that the children did not touch their mothers' breasts may (like the masculine occupation of the women) be due to legends about the Amazons, who were not brought up on their mothers' milk. That the children were given marrow instead may be due to the fact that this people of hunters, like the Lapps of the present day, ate much animal fat and marrow. The Eskimo often give their children raw blubber to chew.

Thus while valuable information about the North is to be

THE EARLY MIDDLE AGES

found in the early mediæval authors we have mentioned, this is not the case with the well-known Isidorus Hispalensis of Seville (ob. 636, as bishop of that city), who, however, exercised the greatest influence on the geographical ideas of the Middle Ages. His geographical knowledge was derived from late Latin authors, especially Orosius, Hieronymus and Solinus, and contributed nothing new of value. But as he was one of the most widely read authors of the early Middle Ages, he is of importance for having in that dark time continued the thread of the learning of antiquity, even though that thread was thin and weak. He was also to have an influence on cartography. With his fondness for bad etymological interpretations he derived the word "rotunditas," for the roundness of the earth, from "rota," wheel, and he taught that " the word ' orbis ' is used on account of the roundness of the circumference, since it is like a wheel. For in every part the circumfluent ocean surrounds its borders in a circle." Hence the conception of the earth's disc as a wheel came to be general in the early Middle Ages, and hence the designation of wheel-maps. Isidore divided the earth's disc into three parts, Asia (including Paradise) at the top of the wheel-map, and Europe and Africa, also called Lybia, at the bottom ; and the boundaries between these continents formed a T with the rivers Tanais and Nile horizontally at the top, and the Mediterranean ("Mare Magnum") below. Therefore maps of this type, which was maintained for a long time, are also called T-maps.[1] Otherwise Isidore declared clearly enough in favour of the spherical form of the earth.

The Anglo-Saxon monk and scholar, Beda Venerabilis (673-735), who in his work "Liber de natura rerum" also mentions the countries of the earth, but without making any fresh statement about the North, was strongly influenced by Isidore. He asserts, however, the spherical form of the earth in an intelligent way, giving, amongst other reasons, that of the ancient Greeks, that earth and water are attracted towards

CHAPTER IV
Isidorus Hispalensis, before 636 A.D.

Bede, 673-735

---

[1] They were also called O T maps ; O T being the initials of Orbis Terrarum.

IN NORTHERN MISTS

CHAPTER IV

a central point. The form of a sphere was also the only one that would explain why certain stars were visible in the north, but not in the south.

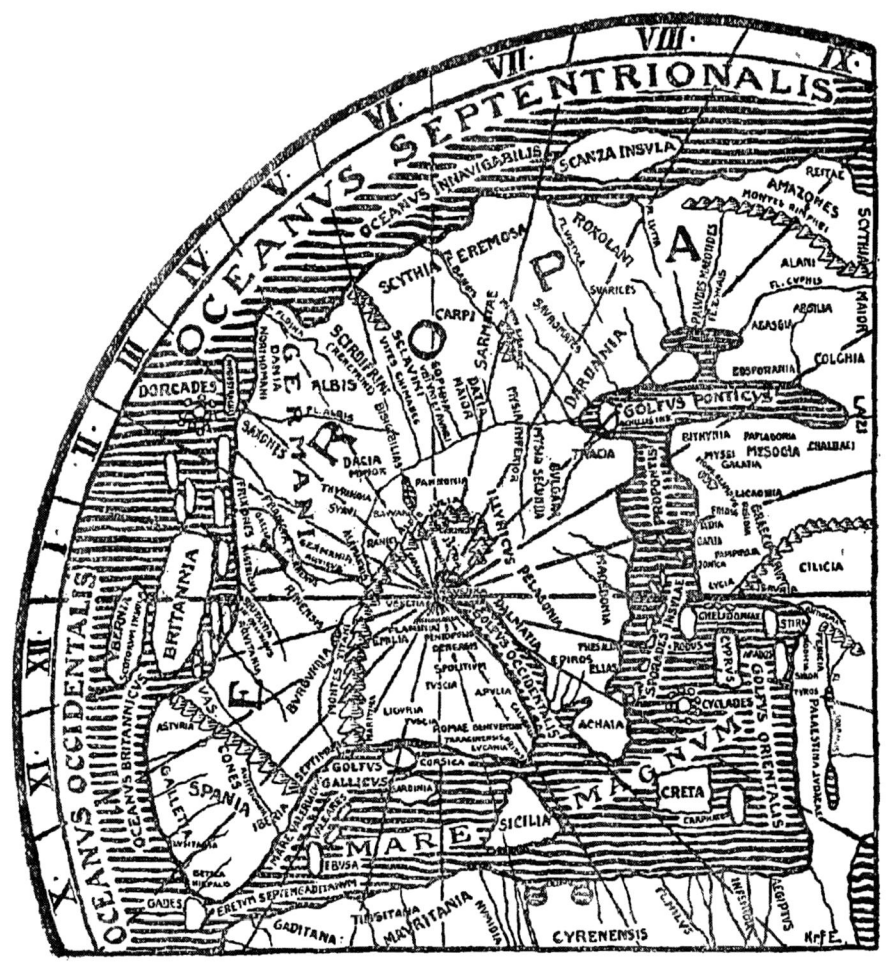

Europe on the reconstructed map of the world of the Ravenna geographer (after K. Miller)

The Ravenna geographer, seventh century

A few new facts about the North are to be found in the anonymous author who wrote a cosmography at the close of the seventh century. As, according to his own statement, he was born at Ravenna, he is usually known as the Ravenna geographer, but otherwise nothing is known of him, except that he was probably a priest. He bases his work on older

152

THE EARLY MIDDLE AGES

authors; the Bible, some Latin, some Greek, and some later writers; but he certainly had a Roman itinerary map like the Tabula Peutingeriana. His statements about the North are in part taken from Jordanes, but he also quotes three other "Gothic scholars," who are otherwise entirely unknown. One of them, Aithanarit (or Athanaric ?), is mentioned particularly in connection with the Skridfinns. The other two, Eldevaldus (or Eldebald ?) and Marcomirus (or Marcomeres ?), have also described western Europe; the latter is specially used in the description of the countries of the Danes, Saxons and Frisians.

The Ravenna geographer regarded the earth's disc as approximately round, and surrounded by ocean, but the latter was not entirely continuous, for it did not extend behind India. It was true that some cosmographers had described it so, but no Christian ought to believe this, for Paradise was in the extreme East, near to India; and as the pollen is wafted by the breath of the wind from the male palm to the female near it, so does a beneficent perfume from Paradise blow upon the aromatic flowers of India. Some thought that the sun in its course returned to the east under the depths of ocean; but the Ravenna geographer agreed with those who said that the sun moved all night along paths which cannot be traced, behind lofty mountains, in the north beyond the ocean, and in the morning it came forth again from behind them.

[iv. 12.] "In a line with Scythia and the coast of the ocean is the country which is said to be that of the 'Rerefeni' and 'Sirdifeni' ('Scirdifrini'). The people of this country, according to what the Gothic scholar Aithanarit says, dwell among the rocks of the mountains, and both men and women are said to live by hunting, and to be entirely unacquainted both with meat and wine. This land is said to be colder than all others. Farther on by the side of the Serdifenni on the coast of the ocean is the land which is called Dania; this land, as the above-mentioned Aithanaridus and Eldevaldus and Marcomirus, the Gothic scholars, say, produces people who are swifter than all others." [These must be the Eruli.] "This Dania is now called the land of the Nordomanni." This is the first time the name Norman is used, so far as is known.

[v. 30.] "In the northern ocean itself, after the land of the Roxolani, is an island which is called Scanza, which is also called Old Scythia by most cosmographers. But in what manner the island of Scanza itself lies, we will with God's help relate."

He says, following Jordanes (see above, p. 130), that from this island other nations, amongst them the Goths and the Danes, besides the Gepidæ, migrated.

It will be seen that the Ravenna geographer's statements

CHAPTER IV

IN NORTHERN MISTS

CHAPTER IV

about the Skridfinns, whose name is varied and corrupted even more than in Jordanes, bear a striking resemblance to those of Procopius, although he says he derived them from the Goth Aithanarit; if this is correct, then the latter must either have borrowed from Procopius, which is very probable, or he is older and was the common authority both of Procopius and the Ravenna geographer, and, if so, perhaps also of Cassiodorus (?).

Æthicus Istricus, seventh century (?)

An enigmatical work, probably dating from about the seventh century, which was much read in the Middle Ages, professes to be a Latin translation, by a certain Hieronymus, from a Christian book of travel by a Greek commonly called Æthicus Istricus.[1] He is said to have travelled before the fourth century. The translator asserts that Æthicus had related many fabulous things, which he has not repeated, as he wished to keep to the sure facts; but among them we find many remarkable pieces of information, as that Æthicus had seen with his own eyes on the north of the Caspian Sea the Amazons give the breast to Centaurs and Minotaurs, and when he was living in the town of Choolisma, built by Japhet's son Magog, he saw the sea of bitumen which forms the mouth of Hell and from which the cement for Alexander's wall of iron came. In Armenia he looked in vain for Noah's ark; but he saw dragons, ostriches, griffins, and ants as large and ferocious as dogs. He also mentioned griffins and treasures of gold in the north between the Tanais and the northern ocean. "The Scythians, Griffins, Tracontians and Saxons built ships of wattles smeared over with pitch" (perhaps it is meant that they were also covered with hides). These ships were extraordinarily swift. Among the Scythians there was said to be an able craftsman and great teacher, Grifo, who built ships with prows in the northern ocean. He was like the griffins or the flying fabulous birds. Æthicus visited an island called Munitia north of Germania. There he found "Cenocephali" (dog-headed men). They were a hideous race. The Germanic peoples came to the island as merchants and called the people "Cananei."

Cynocephali on a peninsula northeast of Norway
(from the Hereford map)

---
[1] Cf. Wuttke, 1854.

THE EARLY MIDDLE AGES

They go with bare calves, smear their hair with oil or fat and smell foully. They lead a dirty life and feed on unclean animals, mice, moles, etc. They live in felt tents in the woods far away by fens and swampy places. They have a number of cattle, fowls and eggs.[1] They know no god and have no king. They use more tin than silver. One might be tempted to think that this fable of dog-headed people in the north had arisen from the word "Kvæn" (Finn), which to a Greek like Æthicus would sound like "cyon" (dog). The name "Cenocephali" may have been introduced in this way, while that of "Cananei" may have arisen by a sort of corrupt similarity of sound between Kvæn and the Old Testament people of Canaan. It might thus be Kvænland or Finland that is here spoken of. Their going with bare calves and living in felt tents may remind us of the Argippæi of Herodotus, who were bald (while in Mela they went bare-headed) and had felt tents in winter.

The Langobard author Paulus Warnefridi, also called Diaconus (about 720–790), gives for the most part more or less confused extracts from earlier authors, but he seems besides to have obtained some new information about the North. Just as the Goth Jordanes (or Cassiodorus, or Ablabius) makes the Goths emigrate from Ptolemy's Scandza, so Paulus, following earlier authors,[2] makes the Langobards proceed from Pliny's

The Seven Sleepers in the Cave by the North Sea (from Olaus Magnus)

CHAPTER IV

Paulus Warnefridi, 720-790

[1] The text has "ovium" (=sheep), but this is doubtless a copyist's error for "ovum" (=egg). This may remind us of the Œonæ of Mela and Pliny, who lived on the eggs of fen-fowl (see above, p. 92).

[2] Cf. the "Origo Gentis Langobardorum" (of the second half of the seventh century), where the "Winnilians," who were later called Langobards, live originally on an island called "Scadanan," or in another MS. "Scadan." The latter name, with the addition of a Germanic word for meadow or island, might become Scadanau, Scadanauge, or Scadanovia. Cf. also Fredegar Scholasticus's abbreviated history after Gregory of Tours, where it is related that the Langobards originated in "Schatanavia," or in one MS. "Schatanagia."

155

IN NORTHERN MISTS

CHAPTER IV

island Scatinavia, far in the north. It looks as though at that time a northern origin was held in high esteem. But Paulus describes the country, from the statements of those who have seen it, as not "really lying in the sea, but the waves wash the low shores." This points to a confusion here with a district called Scatenauge by the Elbe, which in a somewhat later MS. (about 807) of the Langobardic Law is mentioned as the home of the Langobards [cf. Lönborg, 1897, p. 27]. Paulus further relates that on the coast "north-west towards the uttermost boundaries of Germany" there lie seven men asleep in a cave, for how long is uncertain. They resemble the Romans in appearance, and both they and their clothes are unharmed, and they are regarded by the inhabitants as holy. The legend of the Seven Sleepers is already found in Gregory of Tours, who has it from Asia Minor, where it arose in the third century and was located at Ephesus [cf. J. Koch, 1883]. The legend was very common in Germania, and we find it again later in tales of shipwreck on the coast of Greenland.[1]

"Near to this place [i.e., the cave with the seven men] dwell the 'Scritobini';[2] thus is this people called; they have snow even in summer time, and they eat nothing but the raw flesh of wild beasts, as they do not differ from the beasts

---

[1] It is difficult to understand how Paulus has managed to transfer the legend to the North. It might be thought that the idea, which already appears in Herodotus, that the people of the North sleep for the six winter months (see p. 20), is connected with it. Plutarch ["De defectu oraculorum," c. 18] relates that in the ocean beyond Britain there was according to the statement of Demetrius an island "where Cronos was imprisoned and guarded, while he slept, by Briareus. For sleep had been used as a bond, and there were many spirits about him as companions and servants." According to another passage in Plutarch ["De facie in orbe Lunæ," 941] this island was north-west of the isle of Ogygia, which was five days' sail west of Britain. It is possible that this myth of the sleeping Cronos has also helped to locate the legend of the Seven Sleepers on the north-west coast of Europe. Viktor Rydberg [1886, i. pp. 529 ff.] thought that the legend and its localisation in the North might be connected with Mimer's seven sons, who in the Volospǫ's description (st. 45) of Ragnarok were to spring up at the sound of the horn Gjallar, after having lain asleep for long ages. But this interpretation of the strophe: "Leika Mims synir" is improbable.

[2] In other MSS. Scridowinni and Scritofinni, etc.

THE EARLY MIDDLE AGES

themselves in intelligence, and they also make themselves clothes of their skins with the hair on. Their name is explained from the word 'to leap' in the foreign tongue [i.e., Germanic], for by leaping with a certain art they overtake the wild beasts with a piece of wood bent like a bow. Among them is an animal which is not much unlike a stag, and I have seen a dress made of the hide of this animal, just as if it was bristling with hairs, and it was made like a tunic and reached to the knees, as the above-mentioned Scritobini wear it, as I have told. In these parts, at the summer solstice, there is seen for several days, even at night, the clearest light, and they have there much more daylight than elsewhere, as on the other hand, about the winter solstice, even if there is daylight, the sun itself is not seen there, and the day is shorter than in any other place, the nights also are longer; for the farther one goes away from the sun, the nearer the sun appears to the earth [the horizon], and the shadows become longer." ...

"And not far from the shore which we before spoke of [by the cave] on the west, where the ocean extends without bounds, is that very deep abyss of the waters which we commonly call the ocean's navel. It is said twice a day to suck the waves into itself, and to spew them out again; as is proved to happen along all these coasts, where the waves rush in and go back again with fearful rapidity. Such a gulf or whirlpool is called by the poet Virgil Caribdis, and in his poem he says it is in the strait by Sicily, as he says :

The oldest known picture of a ski-runner (from the Hereford map's representation of Norway, thirteenth century)

> 'Scilla lies on the right hand
> and the implacable Caribdis on the left.
> And three times it sucks the vast billows
> down into the abyss with the deep whirlpool
> of the gulf, and it sends them up again into the air,
> and the wave lashes the stars.'

"By the whirlpool of which we have spoken it is asserted that ships are often drawn in with such rapidity that they seem to resemble the flight of arrows through the air; and sometimes they are lost in this gulf with a very frightful destruction. Often just as they are about to go under, they are brought back again by a sudden shock of the waves, and they are sent out again thence with the same rapidity with which they were drawn in. It is asserted that there is also another gulf of the same kind between Britain and the Gallician province"

CHAPTER IV

CHAPTER
IV
[i.e., northern Spain], whereupon there follows a description of the tides on the south coast of France and at the mouths of the rivers, after which there is a highly coloured account of the horrors of the Ebudes, where they can hear the noise of the waters rushing towards a similar Caribdis.

Paulus Warnefridi evidently had a very erroneous idea of ski-running, which he made into a leaping instead of a gliding motion. He may have imagined that they jumped about on pieces of wood bent like bows. That the abyss of waters or navel of the sea is thought to be in the North may be due to reports either of the current in the Pentland Firth or of the

The Maelstrom near the Lofoten Islands
(from Olaus Magnus)

Mosken-ström or the Salt-ström, which thus make their appearance here in literature, and which were afterwards developed into the widespread ideas of the Middle Ages about maelstroms and abysses in the sea, perhaps by being connected with the ancient Greek conception of the uttermost abyss (Tartarus, Anostus, Ginnungagap; see pp. 11, 12, 17), and as here with the description of the current in the Straits of Messina.

Viktor Rydberg [1886, pp. 318, 425, ff.] supposed Paulus's description of the whirlpool to be derived from the Norse legends of the world's well, "Hvergelmer"—which causes the tides by the water flowing up and down through its

THE EARLY MIDDLE AGES

subterranean channels—and of the quern "Grotte" at the bottom of the sea, which forms whirlpools when the waters run down into the hole in the mill-stone.[1] But it is perhaps just as probable that it is the southern, originally classical ideas which have been localised in the Norse legends. As we have seen, we find in Virgil the same conception of a gulf in the sea which sucks the water into itself and sends it up again. Isidore says of the abyss (also repeated in Hrabanus Maurus):

"Abyssus is the impenetrable deep of the waters, or the caves of the hidden waters, from whence springs and rivers issue forth, but also those which run concealed beneath the ground. Therefore it is called Abyssus, for all streams return by hidden veins to their mother Abyssus."

It is credible that ideas such as this may have originated, or at any rate coloured, the myth of "Hvergelmer" (i.e., the noisy or bubbling kettle). Isidore was early known in England, Ireland and Scandinavia. The whirlpool is also found among Orientals; thus Sindbad is drawn into it. Paulus's mention of whirlpools not only in the North, and off the Hebrides, but also between Britain and Spain and in the Straits of Messina, does not show that he derived the legend solely from the North. Later, on the other hand, in Adam of Bremen, the whirlpool becomes more exclusively northern, and later still we shall get it even at the North Pole itself.

Paulus Warnefridi also mentions Greek fabulous people such as the Dog-heads (Cynocephali) and the Amazons in North Germania. He says that the Langobards fought with a people called "Assipitti," who lived in "Mauringa," and that they frightened them by saying that they had Cynocephali in their army, who drank human blood, their own if they could not get that of others. The Langobards were said to have been stopped by the Amazons at a river in Germany. The

[1] According to the "Grottasongr," Mysing carried off the quern and the two female thralls, Fenja and Menja, on his ship and bade them grind salt, and they ground until the ship sank (according to some MSS. it was in the Pentland Firth), and there was afterwards a whirlpool in the sea, where the water falls into the hole in the quern. Thus the sea became salt. This is the same legend which is repeated in the tale of the mill which grinds at the bottom of the sea.

IN NORTHERN MISTS

<small>CHAPTER IV</small>

Langobard king, Lamissio, fought with the bravest of them, while he was swimming in the river, and slew her; and according to a prearranged agreement he thereby obtained for his people the right of crossing unhindered. Paulus regards the story as untrue, as the Amazons were supposed to have been destroyed long before; but he had nevertheless heard that there was a tribe of such women in the interior of Germany. The same idea of a female nation in Germany occurs again later in literature (cf. King Alfred's " Mægða-land ").

<small>Interpolation in Solinus, circa eighth century</small>

It has already been mentioned (p. 123) that in the MSS. of Solinus of the ninth century and later there is found a mention of the Ebudes, the Orcades and Thule which in the opinion of Mommsen is a later addition; and as it is not found in Isidore Hispalensis, who made extensive use of Solinus, it must have been introduced after his time (seventh century), but before the ninth century, when it occurs in a MS. As the addition about Thule, so far as I can judge, must show that this country is regarded as Norway, and as there are many indications that it was made by an Irish monk, it is further probable that it belongs to the period before the Irish discovery of Iceland, which then, according to Dicuil's book, became regarded as Thule. I think, therefore, we can place the addition at the beginning of the eighth century, and it will then be evidence of the knowledge of Norway which prevailed in the British Isles at that time. After having mentioned Britain and the neighbouring islands the account proceeds [Solinus, c. 22]:

"From the Caledonian Promontory it is two days' sail for those who voyage to Tyle [Thule]. From thence begin the Ebudes islands [Hebrides], five in number [the five principal islands]. Their inhabitants live on fruits, fish and milk. Though there are many islands, they are all separated by narrow arms of the sea. They all together have but one king. The king owns nothing for himself alone, all is common property. Justice is imposed upon him by fixed laws, and lest he should be led away from the truth by covetousness, he learns righteousness by poverty, since he has no possessions; he is therefore supported by the people. No woman is given him in marriage, but he takes in turn her who pleases him at the moment. Thus he has neither the desire nor the hope of children. The second station for the voyager [to Thule] is provided by the

THE EARLY MIDDLE AGES

Orcades. But the Orcades lie seven days' and the same number of nights' sail from the Ebudes, they are three in number [i.e., the three principal isles of the Shetlands]. They are uninhabited ('vacant homines'). They have no woods, but are rough with reeds and grass, the rest is bare sandy beach and rocks. From the Orcades direct to Thule is five days' and nights' sail. But Thule is fertile and rich in late-ripening fruits. The inhabitants there live from the beginning of spring with their cattle, and feed on herbs and milk ; the fruits of the trees they keep for winter. They have women in common, regular marriage is not known among them."

This description cannot well be pure invention, and unless it may be thought to be transferred from another place, we must believe it to be derived from a distant knowledge of Norway. Their living with the cattle in spring is in accordance with this, but not their subsistence on the fruits of the trees. Here one would rather be led to think of the Hesperides and their golden apples, unless we are to suppose that they collected nuts and berries. That the inhabitants of Thule had women in common might be connected with the predilection of the Scandinavians for polygamy, of which we also hear from other sources ; but this is uncertain. Even the Greeks and Romans saw in the absence of regular marriage a sign of barbarism, which brought man near to the beasts, and which they therefore attributed to people at the extreme limits of the earth ; cf. Herodotus, and Strabo's description of the Irish (p. 81). If the Caledonian Promontory means Scotland, it is surprising that it should be two days' sail to the Hebrides, and that these were the first and the Orcades the second station on the way to Thule. We must then suppose that there has been a jumbling together of several authorities, which is not very probable if this is a later interpolation, since we must doubtless believe the interpolating copyist to have thought himself possessed of knowledge of these matters. If, however, we suppose him to have been an Irishman, and to have looked upon the voyage to Thule with Ireland as a starting-point, then it becomes more consistent. It is then two days' sail from Ireland to the Hebrides, seven days thence to the Shetlands, and then five to Thule ; that is, the whole voyage

IN NORTHERN MISTS

CHAPTER IV

will last fourteen days; and this may be about right. It is undeniably somewhat surprising that there should be no inhabitants on the Orcades, or Shetland, at that time.

THE DISCOVERY OF THE FAROES AND ICELAND BY THE IRISH IN THE EIGHTH CENTURY

Dicuil, circa 825

The earliest voyages northward to the Arctic Circle, of which there is certain literary mention in the early Middle Ages, are the Irish monks' expeditions across the sea in their small boats, whereby they discovered the Faroes and Iceland, and, at all events for a time, lived there. Of these the Irish monk Dicuil gave an account, as early as about the year 825, in his description of the earth, "De Mensura Orbis Terræ" [cf. Letronne, 1814, pp. 38 f., 131 f.]. It is characteristic of the spiritual tendency of that period of the Middle Ages that these remarkable voyages were not, like other voyages of discovery, undertaken from love of gain, thirst for adventure, or desire of knowledge, but chiefly from the wish to find lonely places, where these anchorites might dwell in peace, undisturbed by the turmoil and temptations of the world.[1] In this way the unknown islands near the Arctic Ocean must have seemed to satisfy all their requirements; but their joy was short-lived; the disturbers of the North, the Vikings from Norway, soon came there also and drove them out or oppressed them.

What Dicuil tells us of the Scandinavian North is chiefly derived from Pliny, and contains nothing new. But of the unknown islands in the northern ocean he writes [7, 3]:

Discovery of the Faroes by the Irish

"There are many more islands in the ocean north of Britain, which can be reached from the northern British Isles in two days' and two nights' direct sailing with full sail and a favourable wind. A trustworthy priest ('presbyter religiosus') told me that he had sailed for two summer-days and an intervening night in a little boat with two thwarts [i.e., two pairs of oars],[2] and landed on

---

[1] As will be mentioned later, the islands were possibly inhabited by Celts before the arrival of the monks. In that case the latter must doubtless have visited them with the additional object of spreading Christianity.

[2] It has also been translated: "two rows of oars," which is improbable.

THE EARLY MIDDLE AGES

one of these islands. These islands are for the most part small; nearly all are divided from one another by narrow sounds, and upon them anchorites, who proceeded from our Scotia [i.e., Ireland], have lived for about a hundred years ('in centum ferme annis'). But as since the beginning of the world they had always been deserted, so are they now by reason of the Northman pirates emptied of anchorites, but full of innumerable sheep and a great number of different kinds of sea-birds. We have never found these islands spoken of in the books of authors."[1]

This description best suits the Faroes,[1] where, therefore, Irish monks had previously lived, and from whence they had been driven out by Norwegian seafarers, probably at the close of the eighth century. As, however, Dicuil is so well aware of the islands being full of sheep, the Irish may have continued to visit them occasionally, like the trustworthy priest referred to, who sailed there in a boat with two thwarts. Dicuil's statement that they were then "emptied of anchorites" must doubtless be interpreted to mean that they were uninhabited; but this does not sound very probable. Rather, there are many indications that the islands had an original Celtic population, which continued to live there after the settlement of the Norsemen.

The Faroes

There are some Celtic place-names, such as "Dímon" (the islands "Stora Dímon" and "Litla Dímon," or "Dímun meiri" and "Dímun minni") from the Celtic "dimun" (=double neck, thus like Norwegian "Tviberg").[2]

---

[1] Some writers have thought that they might be the Shetlands; but this seems less probable.

[2] Cf. A. Bugge, 1905, pp. 55 f. Several names of fishing-banks, which A. Bugge gives from Dr. Jakobsen, are also of interest. Off Sandey is a fishing-bank called "Knokkur" (or "á Knokki"), and one of the same name lies west

163

IN NORTHERN MISTS

CHAPTER IV

As such Celtic place-names cannot have been introduced later, the Norwegians must have got them from the Celts who were there before, and with whom they had intercourse. The language of the Faroes has also many loan-words from Celtic, mostly for agriculture and cattle-farming, and for the flora and fauna of the islands. These might be explained by many of the Norwegian settlers having previously lived in the Scottish islands or in Ireland, or having had frequent communication with those countries [cf. A. Bugge, 1905, p. 358]; but it seems more natural to suppose that the loan-words are derived from a primitive Celtic population. To this must be added that the people of the Southern Faroes are still dark, with dark eyes and black hair, and differ from the more Germanic type of the northern islands [cf. D. Bruun, 1902, p. 5]. The name "Færöene" (sheep-islands) shows that there probably were sheep before the Norsemen came, which so far agrees with Dicuil; these sheep must then have been introduced by the earlier Celts.

According to this it seems possible that the Irish monks came to the islands not merely as anchorites, but also to spread Christianity among a Celtic population. The Norwegians arrived later, took possession of the islands, and oppressed the Celts.

Irish Discovery of Iceland

But the bold Irish monks extended their voyages farther north. Dicuil has also to tell us how they found Iceland, which he calls Thule, and lived there. After having mentioned what Pliny, Solinus, Isidore (Hispalensis) and Priscianus say about Thule (Thyle), he continues [7, 2, 6]:

"It is now thirty years since certain priests, who had been on that island from the 1st of February to the 1st of August, told that not only at the time of the summer solstice, but also during the days before and after, the setting sun at evening conceals itself as it were behind a little mound, so that it does

---

of Syd-Straumsey. West of Sudrey is a fishing-place called "Knokkarnir." The fishing-banks are called after the landmarks; "cnoc" is Celtic for hill, and must have been the name of the heights that formed landmarks for the fishing-places in question; on land these names have given way to more modern Norse ones, but have held their own out to sea. A. Bugge thinks that the Celtic place-names may be due to Norwegians who before they came to the Faroes had lived with Irish-speaking people in the Scottish islands or in Ireland; but it nevertheless seems very improbable that they should have used a foreign language to give names to their new home. A more natural explanation is that they had the names from the earlier Celtic inhabitants, whether these were only the Irish monks, or whether there were others. Names of islands and hills are usually among the most ancient of place-names.

THE EARLY MIDDLE AGES

not grow dark even for the shortest space of time, but whatsoever work a man will do, even picking the lice out of his shirt (pediculos de camisia extrahere), he may do it just as though the sun were there, and if they had been upon the high mountains of the island perhaps the sun would never be concealed by them [i.e., the mountains]. In the middle of this very short time it is midnight in the middle of the earth, and on the other hand I suppose in the same way that at the winter solstice and for a few days on either side of it the dawn is seen for a very short time in Thule, when it is midday in the middle of the earth. Consequently I believe that they lie and are in error who wrote that there was a stiffened (concretum) sea around it [i.e., Thyle], and likewise those who said that there was continuous day without night from the vernal equinox till the autumnal equinox, and conversely continuous night from the autumnal equinox till the vernal, since those who sailed thither reached it in the natural time for great cold, and while they were there always had day and night alternately except at the time of the summer solstice; but a day's sail northward from it they found the frozen (congelatum) sea."

This description, written half a century before the Norwegians, according to common belief, came to Iceland, shows that the country was known to the Irish, at any rate before the close of the eighth century (thirty years before Dicuil wrote in 825), and how much earlier we cannot say. With the first-hand information he had received from people who had been there, Dicuil may have blended ideas which he had obtained from his literary studies. The sun hiding at night behind a little mound reminds us of the older ideas that it went behind a mountain in the north (cf. Cosmas Indicopleustes and the Ravenna geographer); but of course it may also be due to local observation. The idea that the frozen sea ("congelatum mare") had been found a day's sail north of this island is precisely the same as in the Latin and Greek authors, where, according to Pytheas, the stiffened sea ("concretum mare") or the sluggish sea ("pigrum") lay one day's sail beyond Thule (cf. p. 65). But this does not exclude the possibility of the Irish having come upon drift-ice north of Iceland; on the contrary, this is very probable.

Dicuil's statement of the Irish discovery of Iceland is confirmed by the Icelandic sagas. Are Frode (about 1130) relates that at the time the Norwegian settlers first came to Iceland,

"there were Christians here whom the Norwegians called 'papar' [priests];

CHAPTER IV

but they afterwards went away, because they would not be here together with heathens, and they left behind them Irish books, bells and croziers, from which it could be concluded that they were Irishmen." In the Landnámabók, which gives the same statement from Are, it is added that "they were found east in Papey and in Papyli. It is also mentioned in English books that at that time there was sailing between the countries" [i.e., between Iceland and Britain].

In many other passages in the sagas we hear of them,[1] and the Norwegian author Tjodrik Monk (about 1180) has a similar statement. Many places in south Iceland, such as "Papafjörðr" with "Papos," and the island of "Papey," still bear names derived from these first inhabitants. A former name was "Pappyli," which is now no longer used. But besides these place-names there are many others in Iceland which are either Celtic or must be connected with the Celts. Thus, among the first that are mentioned in the Landnámabók are "Minþakseyrr" and "Vestmanna-eyjar." "Minþak" is an Irish word for a dough of meal and butter, and Westmen were the Irish. It is true that in the Landnámabók [cf. F. Jónsson, 1900, pp. 7, 132, 265] these names are placed in connection with the Irish thralls whom Hjorleif, the associate of Ingolf, had brought with him, and who killed him; but, as the more particular circumstances of the tale show, *it is probable that it is the place-names that are original, and that have given rise to the tale of the thralls, and not the reverse.* A. Bugge [1905, pp. 359 ff.] gives a whole list of Icelandic place-names of Celtic origin, mostly derived from personal names;[2] he

[1] Cf. Landnáma, Prologue. Further on in the Landnáma places are frequently mentioned where priests had formerly lived, and where in consequence heathens dared not settle.

[2] It is explicable that places and estates may be called after the personal names of Irish land-takers; but it is more difficult to understand how the Norwegians should have come by Celtic names, *derived from appellatives, for mountains, fjords, and rivers*—which are everywhere among the earliest of place-names—if the Celts had not been there before they came. Among such place-names of Celtic origin, or which indicate a Celtic population, may be mentioned: "Dímunarvág, Dímunar-klakkar" (an inlet and two rocky islets in Breidifjord); "Dímon," in many places as the name of a ridge, a mountain, and an islet; "Katanes"; "Katadalr"; "Kúðafljót," the name of a

THE EARLY MIDDLE AGES

endeavours to explain them as due to Celtic influence, through Irish land-takers; but the most natural explanation is certainly here as with the Faroes, that there was a primitive Celtic population in Iceland, and not merely a few Irish monks, when the Norwegians arrived; and that from these Celts the Icelanders are in part descended, while they took their language from the ruling class, the Norwegians, who also became superior in numbers. Future anthropological investigations of the modern Icelanders may be able to throw light on these questions. The original Celtic population may have been small and dispersed, but may nevertheless have made it easier for the Norwegians to settle there, as they did not come to a perfectly uncultivated country, and to subdue men takes less time than to subdue Nature. As to how, and how early, the Celts first came to Iceland, we know in the meantime nothing.

Einhard (beginning of the ninth century), the biographer of Charlemagne, speaks of the Baltic as a bay eastwards from the western ocean of unknown length and nowhere broader than 100,000 paces (about ninety miles), and mentions the peoples of those parts: "'Dani' and 'Sueones,' whom we call 'Nordmanni,'" live on the northern shore and on all the islands, while Slavs and Esthonians and other peoples dwell on the southern shore. The well-known German scholar, Hrabanus Maurus (circa 776-856), Archbishop of Mayence (847-856), bases his encyclopædic work, "De Universo" (completed in 847), in twenty-two books, chiefly upon Isidore, from whom he makes large extracts, and has little to say about the North. Rimbertus (end of the ninth century), on the other hand, in his biography of Ansgarius, gives much information about Scandinavia and its people, while the nearly contemporary Bavarian geographer ("geographus Bawarus") describes the Slavonic peoples.

CHAPTER IV

Einhard, ninth century

Hrabanus Maurus

Rimbertus

confluence of several rivers into a large piece of water, in Vester-Skaftarfells district, from Irish "cud" (=head). "Minþakseyrr" is mentioned above. Further, there are many names after Irishmen: a river "Irá," two places "Irageröi," a channel into Hvammsfjord "Irska leið," "Irsku buðir," a hill "Irski hóll," besides "Vestmanna-eyjar," etc.

CHAPTER V

THE AWAKENING OF MEDIÆVAL KNOWLEDGE OF THE NORTH

KING ALFRED, OTTAR, ADAM OF BREMEN

IN the ninth century the increasingly frequent Viking raids, Charlemagne's wars and conquests in the North, and the labours of Christian missionaries, brought about an increase of intercourse, both warlike and peaceful, between southern Europe and the people of the Scandinavian North. The latter had gradually come to play a certain part on the world's stage, and their enterprises began to belong to history. Their countries were thereby more or less incorporated into the known world. Now for the first time the mists that had lain over the northern regions of Europe began to lift, to such an extent that the geographical knowledge of the Middle Ages became clearer, and reached farther than that of the Greeks a thousand years earlier.

But while in the foregoing centuries the clouds had moved slowly, they were now rapidly dispelled from large tracts of the northern lands and seas. This was due in the first place

AWAKENING OF MEDIÆVAL KNOWLEDGE

to the voyages of the Scandinavians, especially of the Norwegians. By their sober accounts of what they had found they directed geographical science into new and fruitful channels, and freed it little by little from the dead weight of myths and superstitions which it had carried with it through the ages from antiquity. We find the first decisive step in this direction in the Anglo-Saxon king Alfred the Great of England (849–circa 901 A.D.).

King Alfred had Orosius's Latin history done into Anglo-Saxon, and himself translated large portions of the work. By about 880 he was at peace with the Danish Vikings, to whom he had been obliged to cede the north-eastern half of England. He died about 901. His literary activity must no doubt have fallen within the period between these dates. Finding the geographical introduction to Orosius's work inadequate, especially as regards northern Europe, he added what he had learnt from other sources. Thus, from information probably obtained from Germans, he gives a survey of Germany, which he makes extend northwards " to the sea which is called ' Cwên-sǽ.' " What is meant by this is not quite clear; it might be the Polar Sea or the White Sea; on the other hand, it may be the Baltic or the Gulf of Bothnia; for the text does not make it certain whether King Alfred regarded Scandinavia as a peninsula connected with the continent or not. He speaks of countries and peoples on the " Ost-sǽ ",[1] and he mentions amongst others the South Danes and North Danes both on the mainland (Jutland) and the islands—both peoples with the Ost-sǽ to the north of them—further the " Osti " (probably the Esthonians, who also had this arm of the sea, the Ost-sǽ, to the north), Wends and Burgundians (Bornholmers?),

[1] The "Ost-sǽ" is the southern and western part of the Baltic with the Cattegat and a part of the Skagerak, as distinguished from the sea to the west of Jutland (the land of the South Danes), which is "the arm of the sea which lies round the country of Britain." The sea west of Norway he also calls the "West-sǽ." As the Ost-sǽ is called an arm of the sea, it might be urged that King Alfred therefore regarded Scandinavia as a peninsula; but we see that he also calls the sea round Britain, which he knew better, an arm of the sea.

CHAPTER V

King Alfred, 849-901

CHAPTER V

who "have the same arm of the sea to the west of them, and the Sveones (Svear) to the north." "The Sveones have south of them the Esthonian ['Osti'] arm of the sea, and east of them the Sermende [Sarmatians? or Russians?]; and to the north, beyond the uninhabited tracts ['wêstenni'], is 'Cwênland'; and north-west of them are the 'Scride-Finnas,' and to the west the Norwegians ('Norðmenn')."

Ottar's voyage to the White Sea, ninth century

King Alfred's most important contribution to geographical knowledge of the North is his remarkable account of what the Norwegian Ottar (or "Ohthere" in the Anglo-Saxon text) told him about his voyage to the North. The brief and straightforward narrative of this sober traveller forms in its clearness and definiteness a refreshing contrast to the vague and confused ideas of earlier times about the unknown northern regions. We see at once that we are entering upon a new period.

Map of Northern Scandinavia and the White Sea

"Ottar told his lord, Alfred the king, that he dwelt farthest north of all the Norwegians.[1] He said that he dwelt on the northern side of the land by the 'West-sæ.' He said however that the land extends very far to the north from there; but that it is quite uninhabited ('weste'), except that in a few places

---

[1] In another passage somewhat later he says that "no men [i.e., Norsemen, Norwegian chiefs] lived to the north of him." This may have been somewhere about Malangen or Senjen, which archæological remains show to have formed the approximate northern boundary of fixed Norwegian habitation at that time. Norwegians may have lived here and there farther north to about Loppen [cf. A. Bugge, 1908, pp. 407 ff.]; but Ottar doubtless means that no nobles or people of importance lived to the north of him.

AWAKENING OF MEDIÆVAL KNOWLEDGE

the Finns[1] live, hunting in the winter and fishing in the sea in summer. He said that once he wished to find out how far the land extended due north, and whether any man lived north of the waste tracts. So he went due north[2] along the coast; the whole way he had the uninhabited land to starboard and the open sea to port for three days. Then he was as far north as the whalers go.[3] Then he went on due north as far as he could sail in the next three days. There the land turned due east, or the sea turned into the land,[4] he did not know which; but he knew that there he waited for a west wind, or with a little north in it, and sailed thence eastward, following the coast as far as he could sail in five days. Then he had to wait for a due north wind, because the land there turned due south, or the sea into the land, he did not know which.[5] Then he sailed thence due south along the coast, as far as he could sail in five days. There lay a great river going up into the land, so they turned up into the river, because they dared not sail past it for fear of trouble, since all the country was inhabited on the other side of the river. He had not met with inhabited country before, since he left his own home; but all the way there was waste land to starboard, except for fishermen, fowlers and hunters, and they were all Finns, and there was always sea to port. The land of the Beormas was well inhabited; but they [i.e., Ottar and his men] dared not land there; but the land of the Terfinnas was entirely waste, except where hunters or fishers or fowlers had their abode.

"The Beormas told him many stories both about their own country and the countries that were about it, but he knew not what was true, because he had not seen it himself. The Finns and the Beormas, as it seemed to him, spoke almost the same language. He went thither chiefly to explore the country, and

---

[1] It may be explained that the Lapps are called "Finns," both in Old Norse and modern Norwegian. As it is not absolutely certain to what race these ancient "Finns" belonged, it has been thought best to retain Ottar's name for them here.

[2] It is clear Ottar reckoned north and south according to the direction of the land, and not according to the meridian; this is a common habit among coast-dwellers who live on a coast that lies approximately north and south. Ottar's north is consequently nearly north-east.

[3] This would be, according to the number of days' sail given, about midway between Malangen and the North Cape, that is, about Loppen.

[4] That is to say, made a bay of the sea into the land. Ottar has now reached the North Cape.

[5] This was at the entrance to the White Sea, near Sviatoi Nos, or a little farther south-east. If Ottar took as much as six days on the voyage from Malangen to the North Cape, but only four from the North Cape to the entrance to the White Sea, which is nearly double the distance, this may possibly be explained by his sailing the first part within the skerries, among islands, thus making the distance longer and stopping oftener, while on the latter part of the voyage, where there are no islands, he may have sailed much faster with open sea and a favourable wind, and have had less temptation to stop.

CHAPTER V

IN NORTHERN MISTS

CHAPTER V

for the sake of the walruses, for they have much valuable bone in their tusks—some such tusks he brought to the king—and their hide is very good for ships' ropes. This whale is much smaller than other whales, not more than seven cubits long; but in his own country is the best whaling, there they are forty-eight cubits, and the largest fifty cubits long; of them ('þara'), said he, he with six others ('syxa sum') had killed sixty in two days."[1]

Since King Alfred, as has been said, must have written between 880 and 901, Ottar may have made his voyage about 870 to 890. This remarkable man, who according to his own statement undertook his expedition principally from desire of knowledge, is the second northern explorer of whom we have definite information in history. The first was the Greek Pytheas, who went about as far as the Arctic Circle. Some twelve hundred years later the Norwegian Ottar continues the exploration farther north along the coasts of Norway and sails right into the White Sea. He thereby determined the extent of Scandinavia on the north, and is the first known discoverer of the North Cape, the Polar Sea (or Barents Sea), and the White Sea; but he did not know whether the latter

[1] The most reasonable way of reading this last much-contested statement is to take "of them" as referring to the walruses, which were seven cubits long, and to understand the sentence about the Norwegian whales, which are larger, as an inserted parenthesis [cf Japetus Steenstrup, 1889]; for it is impossible that six men could kill sixty large whales in two days, and the sobriety of Ottar's narrative makes it very improbable that he made boasts of this sort. King Alfred evidently did not grasp the essential difference between walrus and whale. Another explanation might be that these sixty were a school of a smaller species of whale, which were caught by nets in a fjord, so that King Alfred has only confused their size with that of the larger whales of which he had also heard Ottar speak. An attempt has been made to save the sense by proposing that instead of "with six others" we should read "with six harpoons" ("syx asum") or "with six ships" ("syx ascum"); but even if such an emendation were permissible, it does not make the statement more credible. What should Ottar do with sixty large whales, even if he could catch them? It must have been the blubber and the flesh that he wanted, but he and his men could not deal with that quantity of blubber and flesh in weeks, to say nothing of two days. Even a large whaling station at the present time, with machinery and a large staff of workmen, would have all it could do to deal with sixty large whales ("forty-eight" or "fifty" cubits long) before they became putrid, if they were all caught in two days.

AWAKENING OF MEDIÆVAL KNOWLEDGE

was a bay of the ocean or not. It is unlikely that Ottar was the first Norwegian to *discover* the coasts along which he sailed. It is true that the expressions "that he wished to find out how far the land extended due north, or whether any man dwelt to the north of the uninhabited tracts," might be taken to mean that this was hitherto unknown to the Norwegians; but it should doubtless rather be understood as a general indication of the object of the voyage: this was of interest to King Alfred, but not whether it was absolutely the first voyage of discovery in those regions. The names Terfinnas and Beormas are given as something already known, and when Ottar reaches the latter he understands at once that he ought not to proceed farther, for fear of trouble; it may be supposed that he knew them by report as a warlike people. A. Bugge [1908, p. 409] quotes K. Rygh to the effect that the names of fjords in Finmark must be very ancient, e.g., those that end in "-angr." This termination is not found in Iceland, and would consequently be older than the Norwegian colonisation of that country; nor does "angr" (= fjord) as an appellative occur in the Old Norse literary language. It may therefore be possible that these names are older than Ottar. Bugge also, from information given by Mr. Qvigstad, calls attention to the fact that the Lapps call Magarö "Makaravjo," and a place on Kvalö (near Hammerfest) "Rahkkeravjo." The latter part of these names must be the primary Germanic word "awjô" for island or land near the shore. According to this the Norsemen must have been as far north as this and have given names to these places, while this form of the word was still in use, and the Finns or Lapps have taken it from them.

The land of the Terfinnas, which was uninhabited, is the whole Kola peninsula. Its name was "Ter" (or "Turja"), whence the designation Ter-Finns. The common supposition that the river Ottar came to was the Dvina cannot be reconciled with Ottar's narrative given above, which expressly states that he followed the coast round the peninsula all the

CHAPTER V

CHAPTER V

way, " and there was always open sea to port."[1] He cannot, therefore, have left the land and sailed straight across the White Sea; moreover he could not be aware that there was land on the other side of this wide bay of the ocean.[2] The river which " went up into the land " was consequently on the Kola peninsula, and formed the boundary between the unsettled land of the Terfinnas and that of the Beormas with fixed habitation. The river may have been the Varzuga, although it is also possible that Ottar sailed farther west along the southern coast of the Kola peninsula, without this alteration of course appearing in Alfred's description. He may then have gone as far as the Kandalaks.

What kind of people Ottar's Beormas[3] may have been is uncertain. We only hear that they lived in the country on the other side of the river, that their country was well settled (i.e., was permanently inhabited by an agricultural population?), that they were able to communicate with Ottar, and that they spoke almost the same language as the Finns. The

---

[1] Cf. G. Storm, 1894, p. 95. S. E. Lonborg's reasons [1897, p. 37] for rejecting Storm's view and maintaining the Dvina as the river in question have little weight. Lonborg examines the statements of direction, south, north, etc., as though King Alfred and Ottar had had a map and a modern compass before them during the description. He has not remarked that Ottar has merely confined himself to the chief points of the compass, north, east, and south, and that he has not even halved them; how otherwise should we explain, for instance, that he sailed " due north along the coast " from Senjen to the North Cape ? This course is no less incorrect than his sailing due south, for example, from Sviatoi Nos to the Varzuga. To one sailing along a coast, especially if it is unknown, the circumstance that one is following the land is far more important than the alterations of course that one makes owing to the sinuosities of the coast. The statement that they had the uninhabited land to starboard all the way is consequently not to be got over.

[2] His own words, that he did not know whether the land (at Sviatoi Nos) turned towards the south, or whether the sea made a bay into the land, show also that Ottar cannot have sailed across the White Sea and discovered the land on the other side.

[3] Alfred's word "Beormas" is perhaps linguistically of the same origin as "Perm" or "Perem," which the Russians, at any rate in later times, apply to another Finno-Ugrian people, the Permians, of Kama in north Russia [cf. Storm, 1894, p 96].

AWAKENING OF MEDIÆVAL KNOWLEDGE

description may suit the East Karelians, whom we find, at any rate somewhat later, established on the south and west side of the White Sea, as far north as the Kandalaks, perhaps also as far as the Varzuga. If this is correct, we must suppose that Ottar's Finns and Terfinns spoke a Finno-Ugrian language, very like Karelian. As Ottar knew the Finns well, his statement about the language deserves consideration.

This view, that the Beormas were Karelians, agrees with Egil Skallagrimsson's Saga, which doubtless was put into writing much later, but which mentions Ottar's contemporary, Thorolf Kveldulfsson, and his expeditions among the Finns or Lapps to collect the Finnish or Lappish tribute (about 873 and 874). We read there: "East of Namdal lies Jemtland, and then Helsingland, and then Kvænland, and then Finland, then Kirjalaland. But Finmark lies above all these countries." Kirjalaland is Karelia, which thus lies quite in the east upon the White Sea, and must be Ottar's Bjarmeland (Beormaland). On his Finnish expedition of 874 Thorolf came far to the east, and was then appealed to by the Kvæns for help against the Kirjals (Karelians), who were ravaging Kvænland. He proceeded northward against them and overcame them; returned to Kvænland, went thence up into Finmark, and came down from the mountains in Vefsen. This mention of the ravages of the Kirjals agrees with the impression of Ottar's Beormas, who were so warlike that he dared not pass by their country.

Ottar's account of himself was that

"he was a very rich man in all classes of property of which their wealth [i.e , the wealth of those peoples] consists, that is, in wild beasts ('wildrum'). He had further, when he came to the king, six hundred tame, unsold animals. These animals they called reindeer. There were six decoy reindeer ('stæl hranas'), which are very dear among the Finns, for with them they catch the wild reindeer. He was among the principal men in that country [Hålogaland], although he had no more than twenty horned cattle, and twenty sheep, and twenty pigs; and the little ploughing he did was done with horses [i.e., not with oxen, as among the Anglo-Saxons]. But their largest revenue is the tribute paid them by the Finns; this tribute consists of pelts and birds' feathers [down] and whalebone [walrus tusks], and they gave ships' ropes made of whales' [walrus] hide, and of seals'. Each one pays according to his rank ; the chiefs have to pay fifteen martens' skins, five reindeers' skins, one bear's skin, ten ankers of feathers, a kirtle of bear- or otter-skin, and two ships' ropes, each sixty cubits long, one made of whales' [i.e., walrus] hide, and the other of seals'.[14]

This description gives a valuable picture of the state of society in northernmost Norway at that time. Ottar's Finns had tame and half-tamed reindeer, and their hunting even of such sea-beasts as walrus and seal was sufficiently productive to enable them to pay a considerable tribute. These early inhabitants of the most northerly regions of the old world will be treated of later in a separate chapter.

Ottar's mention of walrus-hunting is of great interest, as showing that it was regularly carried on both by Norwegians and Finns even at that time. Of about the same period (about the year 900) is the well-known Anglo-Saxon casket, called the Franks Casket, of which the greater part is now in the British Museum, one side being in Florence. The casket, which on account of its rich decoration is of great historical value, is made of walrus ivory. It has been thought that it might be made of the tusks that Ottar brought to King Alfred. If this was so, it is in any case improbable that so costly a treasure should be worked in a material the value and suitability of which were unknown. We must therefore suppose that walrus ivory sometimes found its way at that time to this part of Europe, and it could come from no other people but the Norwegians. They certainly carried on walrus-hunting long before Ottar's time. This appears also from his narrative, for men who were not well practised could not kill sixty of these large animals in a couple of days, even if we are to suppose that they were killed with lances on land where they lie in big herds. If these sixty animals were really whales (i.e., small whales), and not walruses, it is still more certain evidence of long practice. We see, too, that walrus ivory and ships' ropes of walrus hide had become such valuable objects of commerce as to be demanded in tribute. So difficult and dangerous an occupation as this hunting, which requires an

AWAKENING OF MEDIÆVAL KNOWLEDGE

equipment of special appliances, does not arise among any people in a short time, especially at so remote a period of history, when all independent development of a new civilisation, which could not come from outside, proceeded very slowly. It is therefore an interesting question whether the Norwegians developed this walrus-hunting themselves or learned it from an earlier seafaring people of hunters, who in these northern regions must consequently have been Ottar's Finns. To find an answer to this, it will be necessary to review the whole difficult question of the Finns and Lapps connectedly, which will be done in a later section.

The walrus, called in Norwegian " rosmal "[1] or " rosmål " (also " rosmar," and in Old Norse " rostungr "), is an arctic animal which keeps by preference to those parts of the sea where there is drift-ice, at any rate in winter. It is no longer found in Norway, but probably it visited the coasts of Finmark not unfrequently in old times, to judge from place-names such as " Rosmålvik " at Loppen, and " Rosmålen " by Hammerfest. Even in the seventeenth and eighteenth centuries its visits to the northern coasts of the country were frequent, perhaps annual [cf. Lillienskiold, 1698]. But as these places were certainly the extreme limit of its distribution, it can never have been very numerous here; like the herds of seals in our own time, it must have appeared only for more or less short visits. Curiously enough, so far as is known, walrus bones have not been observed in finds below ground in the North, while bones of other arctic animals, such as the ring-seal (Phoca fœtida), are found.

Since, therefore, the walrus cannot be supposed to have been common on the northern coasts of Norway at any time during the historical period, and since its hunting gave such valuable products, we must suppose that the Norwegian walrus-hunters were not long in looking for better and surer hunting-grounds eastward in the Polar Sea, where there is plenty of walrus. It

---

[1] " Rosmal " comes from Old Norse " rosm-hvalr "=horse-whale, of the same meaning therefore as " hval-ross."

CHAPTER V

was there too that Ottar went, for this very reason (probably because there was not enough walrus in his home waters) and, as he says, to find out how far the land extended; but it is also probable that walrus-hunters had been in these waters long before him. It is true that the statement that after three days' sail from home he "was as far north as the farthest point reached by whalers" ("þā hwælhuntan firrest farraþ") might mean that walrus-hunting was not carried on farther east than Loppen (where there is still a "Rosmål-vik"), that is, if by these whalers is meant walrus-hunters; but doubtless these expressions are not to be taken so literally, and perhaps the meaning is rather that this was the usual limit of their voyages. Unfortunately, we have no information as to Ottar's own catch on the eastward voyage.

Norwegian whaling

From Ottar's statement that "in his own country there is the best whaling, they are forty-eight cubits long, and the largest are fifty cubits long," we must conclude that the Norwegians, and perhaps the Finns also, carried on a regular whaling industry, with great whales as well as small (see later, chap. xii.).

Ottar's voyage to South Norway and Sleswick

Of Ottar's statements about Norway we read further in King Alfred:

"He said that Nordmanna-Land was very long and very narrow. All that is fitted either for grazing or ploughing lies on the sea, and that, however, is in some places very rocky, with wilderness [mountainous waste] rising above the cultivated land all along it. In the wilderness dwell the Finns. And the inhabited land is broadest eastward, and always narrower farther north. On the east it may be sixty leagues broad, or a little broader; and midway thirty or more, and on the north, he said, where it was narrowest, it may be three leagues to the waste land; and the wilderness in some places is so broad that it takes two weeks to cross it; and in others so broad that one can cross it in six days.

"There is side by side with the land in the south, on the other side of the wilderness, Sveoland, extending northwards, and side by side with the land in the north, Cwêna-Land. The Cwênas sometimes make raids upon the Norsemen over the wilderness, sometimes the Norsemen upon them; and there are very great freshwater lakes in this wilderness; and the Cwênas carry their ships overland to these lakes, and from thence they harry the Norsemen. They have very small ships and very light.

AWAKENING OF MEDIÆVAL KNOWLEDGE

"Ottar said that the part of the country where he lived was called Halgoland [Hálogaland]. He said that no man [i.e., no Norseman] lived farther north than he. Then there is a harbour in the southern part of that country which men call 'Sciringes heale' [Skiringssal [1] in Vestfold]. Thither, said he, one could not sail in a month, anchoring at night, with a favourable wind every day; and all the while he must sail near the land: and to starboard of him would be first 'Iraland,'[2] and then the islands which lie between Iraland and this country [Britain?]. Afterwards there is this country [to starboard] until he comes to Sciringesheal; and all the way on the port side there is Norway (Norðweg).[3] South of Sciringesheal a very great sea [the Skagerak and

CHAPTER V

---

[1] Sciringesheal had a king's house and a well-known temple; it may have been situated on the Viksfjord, east of Larvik, where the name Kaupang (i.e., "kjøpstad" = market town) still preserves its memory [cf. Munch, 1852, pp. 377, 380]. Possibly the name may be connected with the Germanic tribe of "Skirer," who are mentioned on the shores of the Baltic, near the Ruger (or Ryger). Connected with Sciringesheal was a kingdom in South Jutland, with the port of "Sliesthorp" (mentioned by Einhard about 804), "Sliaswic" [Ansgarii Vita, c. 24] or "Slesvik," also called "Heidaby." It is possible that Sciringesheal may have been originally founded by Skirer who had immigrated from South Jutland (?). Another hypothesis has been put forward by S. A. Sorensen, who thinks that Sciringesheal may be a translation into Norse of "baptisterium" ("skíra" = to baptize); and that the place was situated near Sandefjord. In that case we should look for a church rather than a heathen temple, and we should have to suppose that attempts had been made to introduce Christianity even before Ottar's time.

[2] Dr. Ingram, in 1807, and Rask [1815, p. 48] propose to read "Isaland" (i.e., Iceland, which was discovered by the Norsemen just at this time), but this does not improve the sense. Besides which, the form "Isaland" for Iceland is not known, and it would mean the land of "ices" and not of ice. That the true Ireland should be intended would seem to betray greater geographical ignorance than we are disposed to attribute to Ottar or Alfred. Alfred himself mentions "Ibernia" or "Igbernia" (i.e., Ireland) as lying west of Britain, and says that "we call it Scotland." He does not use the name Ireland elsewhere; but here he is quoting Ottar, and the latter may possibly have meant Scotland (?) [cf. Langebek, Porthan and Forster], which was colonised by Irishmen, although it would then be difficult to understand the reference which follows to islands lying "between Iraland and this country" (i.e., Britain). Meanwhile it must be remembered that it was not unusual at that time to place Ireland to the north of Britain (cf. later Adam of Bremen), and there may here be a confusion of this sort. The simplest supposition would be to take "Iraland" for Shetland; but it is difficult to understand how the islands could have received such a designation.

[3] So far as I can discover this is the first time this name for Norway occurs

CHAPTER V

Cattegat] goes up into the land; it is broader than any man can see across; and 'Gôtland' [Jutland] is on the opposite side, and then 'Sillende.'[1] This sea goes many hundred leagues up into the land.

"And from Sciringesheal he said that it was five days' sail to the harbour which is called 'Hæðum' [Heidaby or Sleswick]; it lies between the Wends and the Saxons and the Angles, and belongs to the Danes. When he sailed thither from Sciringesheal, he had on the port side Denmark[2] [i.e., southern Sweden, which then belonged to Denmark], and on the starboard open sea for three days; and for the two days before he came to Heidaby he had to starboard Gôtland and Sillende, and many islands. In those countries dwelt the Angles before they came to this land. And for these two days he had on the port side the islands which belong to Denmark."

This account of Ottar's of his southward voyage is remarkable for the same sober lucidity as his narrative of the White Sea expedition; and as, on all the points where comparison is possible, it agrees well with other independent statements, it furnishes strong evidence of his credibility.

Alfred next gives a description of Wulfstan's (= Ulfsten's) voyage from Heidaby eastward through the southern Baltic to Prussia, with references to Langeland, Laaland, Falster and Skåne ("Scóneg"), which all belonged to Denmark and lay to port. After them came on the same side Bornholm ("Burgenda land"), which had its own king, then Blekinge, "Mēore," Öland and Gotland, and these countries belonged to Sweden ("Swēom"). To starboard he had the whole way Wendland

Anglo-Saxon Map of the World, "Cottoniana," perhaps of the eleventh century (from K. Miller)

in literature. Lönborg [1897, p. 142] is consequently incorrect in saying that the name "Norvegia" first occurs in the eleventh century.

[1] Einhard calls it "Sinlendi," and it was a part of South Jutland or Sleswick [cf. Munch, 1852, p. 378].

[2] "Denemearc" is mentioned by Alfred for the first time in literature.

AWAKENING OF MEDIÆVAL KNOWLEDGE

("Weonodland" = Mecklenburg and Pomerania) as far as the mouths of the Vistula ("Wislemūðan"). Then follows a description of "Estmẹre" (Frisches Haff), Esthonia, which was approximately East Prussia, and the Esthonians. Henceforward we can count these parts of Europe as belonging to the known world.

CHAPTER V

In the old German poem "Meregarto," which is a sort of description of the earth and probably dates from the latter half of the eleventh century [Müllenhoff and Scherer, 1892, ii. p. 196], we find the following remarkable statements about the "Liver sea" and about Iceland :[1]

"Meregarto," eleventh century

"There is a clotted sea in the western ocean.
When the strong wind drives ships upon that course,
Then the skilled seamen have no defence against it,
But they must go into the very bosom of the sea.
Alas! Alas!
They never come out again.
If God will not deliver them, they must rot there.

I was in Utrecht as a fugitive.
For we had two bishops, who did us much harm.
Since I could not remain at home, I lived my life in exile.
When I came to Utrecht, I found a good man,
The very good Reginpreht, he delighted in doing all that was good.
He was a wise man, so that he pleased God,
A pious priest, of perfect goodness.
He told me truly, as many more there [also said],
He had sailed to Iceland—there he found much wealth—
With meal and with wine and with alder-wood.
This they buy for fires, for wood is dear with them.
There is abundance of all that belongs to provisions and to sport [pleasure]
Except that there the sun does not shine—they lack that delight—
Thereby the ice there becomes so hard a crystal,
That they make a fire above it, till the crystal glows.
Therewith they cook their food, and warm their rooms.
There a bundle of alder-wood is given [sold] for a penny."

We find in this poem the same idea of a curdled or clotted sea—here probably in the north-west near Iceland—as appeared early among the Greeks and Romans, perhaps even among the

[1] Professor Alf Torp has kindly given me a [Norwegian] translation of the poem.

CHAPTER V

Carthaginians and Phœnicians (see pp. 40, 66 f.).[1] It is possible that it may have found its way into this poem by purely literary channels from classical authors; but the description seems to bear traces of more life, and it rather points to a legend which lived in popular tradition.

In this poem and in Adam of Bremen Iceland is mentioned for the first time in literature,[2] in both works as a country that was known, but of which strange things were told, which is natural enough, since it lay near the borders of the unknown. The pious Reginbrecht may have travelled to Iceland as a missionary or clerical emissary, which would not be unnatural, as the country was under the archbishopric of Hamburg. On the other hand, it is surprising that people as early as that time sailed thither from Germany with meal, wine and wood. But as these articles must have been precisely those which

[1] It may be of interest in this connection to remind the reader that Plutarch ["De facie in orbe Lunæ," 941] mentions that the island of Ogygia lay five days' sail west of Britain, and that upon one of the islands in the north-west lay Cronos imprisoned (cf. above, p. 156), for which reason the sea was called Cronium. According to the statements of the barbarians "the great continent [i.e., that which lies beyond the ocean, cf. above, p. 16] by which the great ocean is enclosed in a circle" lies nearer to these islands, "but from Ogygia it is about five thousand stadia when one travels with rowing-boats; for the sea is heavy to pass through, and muddy on account of the many currents; but the great land sends out the streams and they stir up the mud, and the sea is heavy and earthy, for which reason it is held to be curdled." These are similar conceptions to those we have already found in Aristotle's Meteorologica (cf. above, p. 41), and Plutarch is also inclined to place this sluggish sea towards the north-west. Moreover, it seems as though the ancients imagined the stiffened sea (usually in connection with darkness) everywhere on the outer limits of the world. Curtius (of the time of Augustus) in a speech makes Alexander's soldiers (when they try to force him to turn back) use such expressions as that this leads to nowhere, all was covered with darkness and a motionless sea, and dying Nature disappears. Similar conceptions of a curdled and stinking sea and an ocean of darkness near the outer limits of the world are also found in Arabic literature [cf. Edrisi, 1154 A.D.].

[2] On maps the name possibly appears earlier. On an English map of the world (Cottoniana), possibly of the close of the tenth century (992–994), there is an "Island" (see p 183), but the possibility is not excluded that the existing copy of this map may be later, and may have taken some names from Adam of Bremen [cf. K. Miller, iii. 1895, p. 37].

AWAKENING OF MEDIÆVAL KNOWLEDGE

would be valuable in Iceland, with its lack of corn and poverty in trees, it points to knowledge of the facts, and does not seem improbable. That there should be great wealth there does not agree with Adam's description, which tends in the con-

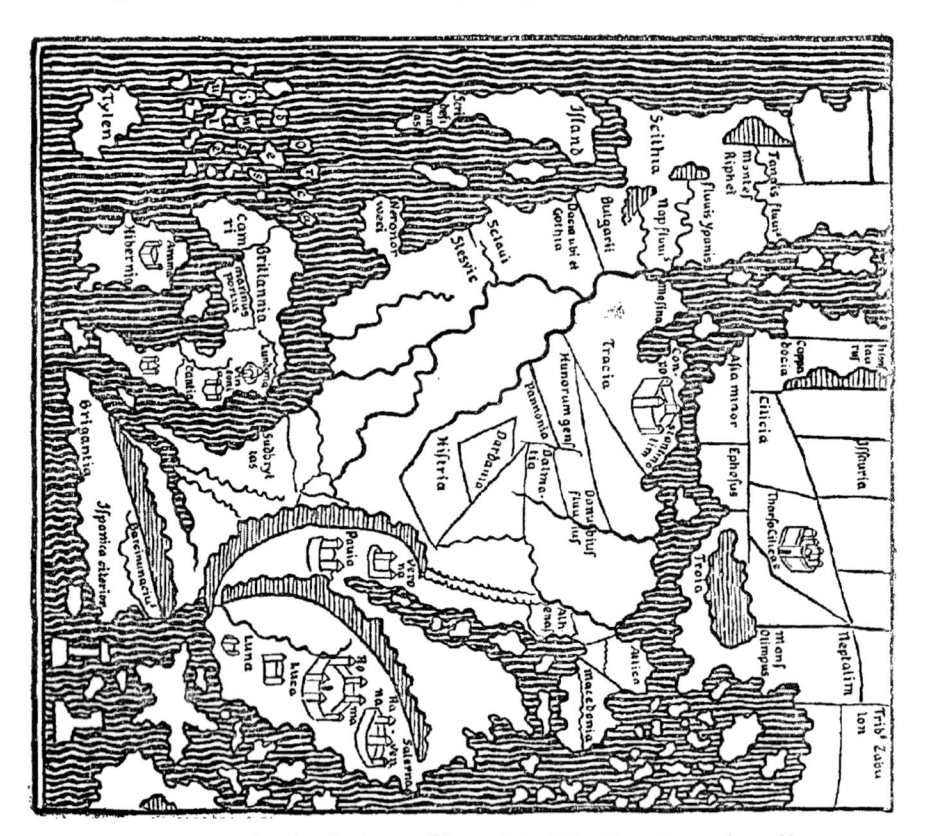

Europe on the Anglo-Saxon Map of the World, "Cottoniana"
(eleventh century?)

trary direction; but as immediately afterwards abundance of provisions is spoken of, it is probable that the rich fisheries were meant, and perhaps the breeding of sheep, which was already developed at that time.

The strange idea that the ice becomes so hard that it can be made to glow, which occurs again in another form in Adam of Bremen, is difficult to understand. Can it have arisen, as Professor Torp has proposed to me, from a misunderstanding

IN NORTHERN MISTS

CHAPTER V

of statements that the Icelanders heated stones for their baths ? In some parts of Norway red-hot stones are also used for heating water for brewing and cooking [cf. A. Helland: Hedemarkens Amt]. Perhaps tales of their sometimes using melted ice for drinking water may also have contributed to the legend (?). In any case, as Adam's account shows still better, diverse statements about ice, fire (volcanoes), and steam (boiling springs ?), etc., may have been confused to form these legends about the ice in Iceland.

Adam of Bremen, about 1070

The first author after King Alfred to make valuable contributions to the literature of the North is Adam of Bremen, who not only gives much information about the Scandinavian North and its people, but mentions Iceland, and for the first time in literature also Greenland and even Wineland, as distant islands in the great ocean. Of the life of the learned magister Adam we know little more than that he came to Bremen about 1067 and became director of the cathedral school, and that he spent some time at the court of the enlightened Danish king Svein Estridsson. This king, who had spent twelve years campaigning in Sweden, "knew the history of the barbarians by heart, as though it had been written down," and from him and his men Adam collected information about the countries and peoples of the North. On his return to Bremen he wrote his well-known history of the Church in the North under the archbishopric of Bremen and Hamburg ("Gesta Hammaburgensis," etc.), which in great part seems to have been completed before the death of Svein Estridsson in 1076. In the fourth book of this work is a "description of the islands [i.e., countries and islands] in the North" ("Descriptio insularum aquilonis"). Adam's most important literary geographical sources seem to have been the following: besides the Bible, Cicero and Sallust, he has used Orosius, Martianus Capella, Solinus, Macrobius and Bede ; he was also acquainted with Paulus Warnefridi's history of the Langobards, and probably Hrabanus Maurus, possibly also with some of Isidore. In the archiepiscopal archives he

AWAKENING OF MEDIÆVAL KNOWLEDGE

was able to collect valuable materials from the missions to heathens in the North, and to these was added the verbal information he had obtained at the Danish court.

Adam's work has thus become one of the most important sources of the oldest history of the North. It would carry us too far here to go into this side of it, and we shall confine ourselves for the most part to his geographical and ethnographical statements.

He describes Jutland, the Danish islands, and other countries and peoples on the Baltic. This too he calls [iv. 10] the Baltic Sea, "because it extends in the form of a belt ('baltei')[1] along through the Scythian regions as far as 'Grecia' [here = Russia]. It is also called the Barbarian or Scythian Sea." He quotes Einhard's description of the Baltic, and regards it as a gulf ("sinus"), which, in the direction of west to east, issues from the Western Ocean. The length of the gulf [eastwards] was according to Einhard unknown. This, he says,

"has recently been confirmed by the efforts of two brave men, namely Ganuz [also Ganund] Wolf, Earl (satrapæ) of the Danes, and Harald [Hardråde], King of the Norwegians, who, in order to explore the extent of this sea, made a long and toilsome voyage, perilous to those who accompanied them, from which they returned at length without having accomplished their object, and with double loss on account of storms and pirates. Nevertheless the Danes assert that the length of this sea (ponti) has frequently been explored and by many different travellers, and even that there are men who have sailed with a favourable wind from Denmark to Ostrogard in Ruzzia."

It therefore looks as if Adam had understood that Scandinavia was connected with the continent, which also appears from his words [iv. 15]:

"Those who are acquainted with these regions also declare that some have reached as far as Græcia [i.e., Russia] by land from Sueonia [Sweden]. But the barbarous people, who live in the intervening parts, are a hindrance to this journey, wherefore they rather attempt this dangerous route by sea."

---

[1] This name appears here for the first time in literature (cf. "Balcia" in Pliny, pp. 71, 99, above). It has also been sought to derive it from the Old Prussian (Lettish and Lithuanian) "baltas," white; it would then mean the white sea, and the name would be due to the sandy coasts of the south-east [cf. Schafarik, Slav. Alt., i. pp. 451 ff.].

CHAPTER V

But he nevertheless speaks of the countries of the North as islands, and he seems to draw no sharp distinction between island and peninsula. Kurland and Esthonia he seems to regard as true islands.

The entrance to the Baltic, he says [iv. 11], "between Aalborg, a headland

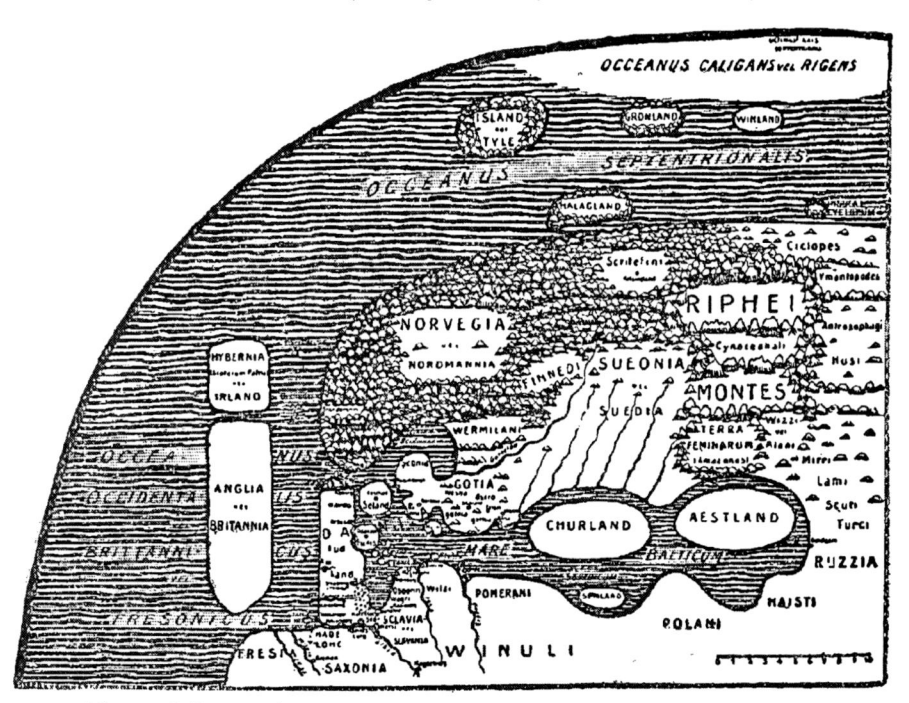

Adam of Bremen's geographical idea of the countries and islands of the North, as represented by A. A. Björnbo (1910)

of Denmark [i.e., the Skaw], and the skerries of Nortmannia [Norway], is so narrow that boats easily sail across it in one night."

There are in the Baltic [iv. 19] "many other islands, all full of savage barbarians, and therefore they are shunned by sailors. On the shores of the Baltic Sea the Amazons are also said to live in the country which is now called the Land of Women ('terra feminarum')."

The Land of Women

This designation is a translation of the name "Kvænland," which was thought to be formed of the Old Norse word for woman: "kvæn" or "kván" (chiefly in the sense of wife; modern English "queen"); and it is very possible that the name was really derived from this, and not from the

AWAKENING OF MEDIÆVAL KNOWLEDGE

Finnish "Kainulaiset." We have seen that Alfred called it in Anglo-Saxon "Cwên-Land" or "Cwêna-Land," which also means woman-land. Here it is probably Southern Finland. Adam probably took the idea from earlier authors.[1] To him this name is a realisation of the Greeks' Amazons, who have been moved northward to the Gulf of Bothnia, just as the Scandinavians become Hyperboreans. In this way ancient geographical myths come to life again and acquire new local colour. Of these Amazons, he says:

"some assert that they conceive by drinking water. Others however say that they become pregnant through intercourse with seafaring merchants, or with their own prisoners, or with other monsters, which are not rare in those parts; and this appears to us more credible.[2] If their offspring are of the male sex, they are Cynocephali; but if of the female, beautiful women. These women live together and despise fellowship with men, whom indeed they repulse in manly fashion, if they come. Cynocephali are those who have their head in their breast; in Russia they are often to be seen as prisoners, and their speech is a mixture of talking and barking."

It has already been mentioned (p. 154) that the Greek writer Æthicus had already placed the Cynocephali on an

---

[1] We may compare with this the tale of the Arab author Qazwinî, of the thirteenth century [cf. G. Jacob, 1896, pp. 9, 37]: "The City of Women is a great city with a wide territory on an island in the western ocean. At-Tartûshî says: its inhabitants are women, over whom men have no authority. They ride horses, and themselves wage war. They show great bravery in conflict. They have also slaves. Every slave in turn visits his mistress at night, remains with her all night, rises at dawn, and goes out secretly at daybreak If then one of them gives birth to a boy she kills him on the spot; but if a girl she lets her live. At-Tartûshî says: the City of Women is a fact of which there is no doubt." This, as we see, is an adaptation of the Greek legend of the Amazons, and of the Scythian women who had children by their slaves [cf. Herodotus, vi. 1]. As a similar story of the City of Women, "west of the Russians," is attributed to the Jew Ibrâhîm ibn Ja'qûb (of the tenth century), which he says he had from the emperor Otto (the Great), it probably dates from the tenth century. Jacob thinks the legend here was due to the name of Magdeburg, which was translated "civitas virginum"; but as the women lived in an island in the ocean it is more probable that it may be derived from Kvænland. Similar legends seem to have been common in the Middle Ages, and occur in many authors. (Cf. Paulus Warnefridi, above, p. 160). Isidore is said to have made Sweden the original home of the Amazons.

[2] Cf. Plutarch, Thes. 26; Strabo, xi. 504; and others.

IN NORTHERN MISTS

CHAPTER V

island north of Germania. The revival of the Greek-Indian fable of dog-headed men seems, on the one hand, to be due to Greeks who had understood the word "Kvæn" as Greek κύων (dog), and either through Æthicus or some other channel the idea thus formed must have reached Adam. On the other hand, the notion of them as prisoners in Russia may be due to Germanic-speaking peoples, who misinterpreted the national name "Huns," which was used both for Magyars and Slavs, and have taken it to mean Hund (dog).[1] But Adam himself did not understand the Greek name's meaning of dog-heads, and confuses it with another fable of men with heads in their breasts [cf. Rymbegla, 1780, p. 350 ; Hauksbók, 1892, p. 167]. Of the Scandinavians Adam says [iv. 12] :

Nortmanni or Hyperboreans

"The Dani and Sueones and the other peoples beyond Dania are all called by the Frankish historians Normans ('Nortmanni'), whilst however the Romans similarly call them Hyperboreans, of whom Martianus Capella speaks with much praise."

It does not seem as though Adam made any distinction between the names Norman and Norseman.

[iv. 21.] "When one has passed beyond the islands of the Danes a new world opens in Sueonia [Sweden] and Nordmannia [Norway], which are two kingdoms of wide extent in the north, and hitherto almost unknown to our world. Of them the learned king of the Danes told me that Nordmannia can scarcely be traversed in a month, and Sueonia not easily in two. This, said he, I know from my own experience, since I have lately served for twelve years in war under King Jacob in those regions, which are both enclosed by high mountains, especially Nordmannia, which with its Alps encircles Sueonia."

Sweden he describes as a fertile land, rich in crops and honey, and surpassing any other country in the rearing of cattle :

"It is most favoured with rivers and forests, and the whole land is everywhere full of foreign [i.e., rare ?] merchandise." The Swedes were therefore well-to-do, but did not care for riches. "Only in connection with women they know no moderation. Each one according to his means has two, three or more

---

[1] Adam's statement (immediately afterwards in the same section) that the land of the Alani or Wizzi was defended by an army of dogs, must be due to a similar misinterpretation of the name "Huns."

at the same time; the rich and the chiefs have them without number. For they count also as legitimate the sons which are born of such a connection. But it is punished with death, if any one has had intercourse with another man's wife, or violated a virgin, or robbed another of his goods or done him wrong. Even if all the Hyperboreans are remarkable for hospitality, our Sueones are pre-eminent; with them it is worse than any disgrace to deny a wayfarer shelter," etc.

[iv. 22.] "Many are the tribes of the Sueones; they are remarkable for strength and the use of arms, in war they excel equally on horseback and in ships."

Adam relates much about these people, their customs, religion, and so forth:

[iv. 24.] "Between Nordmannia and Sueonia dwell the Wermelani and Finnédi (or 'Finvedi') and others, who are now all Christians and belong to the church at Skara. In the borderland of the Sueones or Nordmanni on the north live the Scritefini, who are said to outrun the wild beasts in their running. Their greatest town ['civitas,' properly community] is Halsingland, to which Stenphi was first sent as bishop by the archbishop. . . . He converted many of the same people by his preaching." Helsingland was inhabited by Helsingers, who were certainly Germanic Scandinavians and not Skridfinns; but Adam seems to have thought that all the people of northern Sueonia or Suedia (he has both forms) belonged to the latter race.

"On the east it [i.e., Sweden] touches the Riphæan Mountains, where there are immense waste tracts with very deep snow, where hordes of monstrous human beings further hinder the approach. There are the Amazons, there are the Cynocephali, and there the Cyclopes, who have one eye in their forehead. There are those whom Solinus calls 'Ymantopodes' [one-footed men], who hop upon one leg, and those who delight in human flesh for food, and just as one avoids them, so is one rightly silent about them.[1] The very estimable king of the Danes told me that a people were wont to come down from the mountains into the plains; they were of moderate height, but the Swedes were scarcely a match for them on account of their strength and

Uniped
(from the Hereford map)

---

[1] This passage is undoubtedly taken from Solinus, and we see how Magister Adam confuses together what he has heard and what he finds in classical authors.

CHAPTER V

activity, and it is uncertain from whence they come. They come suddenly, he said, sometimes once a year or every third year, and if they are not resisted with all force they devastate the whole district, and go back again. Many other things are usually related, which I, since I study brevity, have omitted, so that they may tell them who assert that they have seen them."

It is probably the roving mountain Lapps that are here described. Descending suddenly into the plains with their herds of reindeer, they must then, as now, have done great damage to the peasants' crops and pastures ; and the peasants were certainly not content with killing the reindeer, as they sometimes do still, but also attacked the Lapps themselves. Although the latter are not a warlike people, they were forced to defend themselves, and that the Swedes and Norwegians are scarcely a match for them in strength and activity may be true even now.

Cannibals in Eastern Europe
(from the Hereford map)

Nortmannia or Nordvegia

[iv. 30.] "Nortmannia [Norway], as it is the extreme province of the earth, may also be suitably placed last in our book. It is called by the people of the present day 'Norguegia' [or 'Nordvegia'] . . . This kingdom extends to the extreme region of the North, whence it has its name." From " projecting headlands in the Baltic Sound it bends its back northwards, and after it has gone in a bow along the border of the foaming ocean, it finds its limit in the Riphean Mountains, where also the circle of the earth is tired and leaves off. Nortmannia is on account of its stony mountains or its immoderate cold the most unfertile of all regions, and only suited to rearing cattle. The cattle are kept a long time in the waste lands, after the manner of the Arabs. They live on their herds, using their milk for food and their wool for clothes. Thus the country rears very brave warriors, who, not being softened by any superfluity in the products of their country, more often attack others than are themselves disturbed. They live at peace with their neighbours, namely the Sveones, although they are sometimes raided, but not with impunity, by the Danes, who are equally poor. Consequently, forced by their lack of possessions, they wander over the whole world and by their piratical expeditions bring home the greater part of the wealth of the countries." But after their conversion to Christianity they improved, and they are " the most temperate of all men both in their diet and their morals." They are very pious, and the priests turn this to account and fleece them. " Thus the purity of morals is destroyed solely through the avarice of the clergy."

AWAKENING OF MEDIÆVAL KNOWLEDGE

"In many parts of Nordmannia and Suedia people even of the highest rank are herdsmen,[1] living in the style of the patriarchs and by the labour of their hands. But all who dwell in Norvegia are very Christian, with the exception of those who live farther north along the coast of the ocean [i.e., in Finmark]. It is said they are still so powerful in their arts of sorcery and incantations, that they claim to know what is done by every single person throughout the world. In addition to this they attract whales to the shore by loud mumbling of words, and many other things which are told in books of the sorcerers, and which are all easy for them by practice.[2] On the wildest alps of that part I heard that there are women with beards,[3] but the men who live in the forests [i.e., the waste tracts?] seldom allow themselves to be seen. The latter use the skins of wild beasts for clothes, and when they speak to one another it is said to be more like gnashing of teeth than words, so that they can scarcely be understood by their neighbours.[4] The same mountainous tracts are called by the Roman authors the Riphean Mountains, which are terrible with eternal snow. The Scritefingi [Skridfinns] cannot live away from the cold of the snow, and they outrun the wild beasts in their chase across the very deep snowfields. In the same mountains there is so great abundance of wild animals that the greater part of the district lives on game alone. They catch there uri [= aurochs; perhaps rather 'ursi' = bears?], bubali [antelopes = reindeer?], and elaces [elks] as in Sueonia; but in Sclavonia and Ruzzia bisons are taken; only Nortmannia however has black foxes and hares, and white martens and bears of the same colour, which live under water like uri (?),[5] but as many things here seem altogether

CHAPTER V

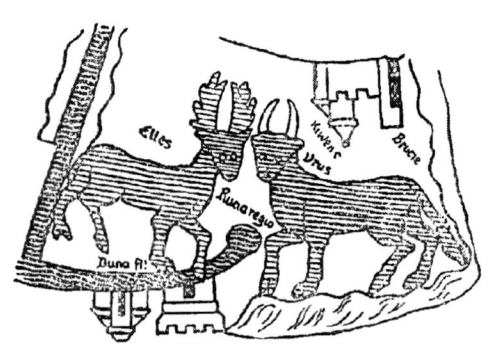

Elles (elk) and Urus (aurochs) in Russia (from the Ebstorf map, 1284)

---

[1] It seems very probable, as Mr. F. Schiern [1873, s. 13] suggests, that this conception of even the noblest men (nobilissimi homines) being herdsmen may be due to a misunderstanding of the old Norse word "fehirðir," which might mean herdsman, but was also the usual word for treasurer, especially the king's treasurer.

[2] This description refers, probably, to the Lapps and their magic arts.

[3] This must be another misunderstanding of tales about Kvæns, whom Adam took for women.

[4] These skin-clad hunters, who spoke a language unintelligible to the Norwegians, were certainly Lapps.

[5] It might be thought that "uri" was here a corruption for "lutræ" (otters); but as "uri" is found in two passages without making sense in its

191

IN NORTHERN MISTS

CHAPTER V

different and unusual to our people, I will leave these and other things to be related at greater length by the inhabitants of that country."

Then follows a reference to Trondhjem and the ecclesiastical history of the country, etc.

The Western Ocean

Of the Western Ocean, from which the Baltic issues, Adam says [iv. 10] that it

"seems to be that which the Romans called the British Ocean, whose immeasurable, fearful and dangerous breadth surrounds Britannia on the west ... washes the shores of the Frisians on the south ... towards the rising of the sun it has the Danes, the entrance to the Baltic Sea, and the Norsemen, who live beyond Dania; finally, on the north this ocean flows past the Orchades [i.e., the Shetlands, with perhaps the Orkneys], thence endlessly around the circle of the earth, having on the left Hybernia, the home of the Scots, which is now called Ireland, and on the right the skerries ('scopulos') of Nordmannia, and farther off the islands of Iceland and Greenland, there the ocean, which is called the dark ['caligans' = shrouded in darkness or mist], forms the boundary."

Later [iv. 34], after the description of Norway, he says of the same ocean:

"Beyond ('post') Nortmannia, which is the extreme province of the North, we find no human habitations, only the great ocean, infinite and fearful to behold, which encompasses the whole world. Immediately opposite to Nortmannia it has many islands which are not unknown and are now nearly all subject to the Norsemen, and which therefore cannot be passed by by us, since consequently they belong to the see of Hamburg. The first of them are the Orchades insulæ [the Shetlands and Orkneys], which the barbarians call Organas" ... and which lie "between Nordmannia and Britannia and Hibernia, and they look playfully and smilingly down upon the threats of the foaming ocean. It is said that one can sail to them in one day from the Norsemen's town of Trondhjem ('Trondemnis'). It is said likewise to be a similar distance from the Orchades both to Anglia [England] and to Scotia [Ireland?]" ...

The Orkneys

---

proper meaning, aurochs, it may also be supposed that it is here used as a name for walrus, as proposed by A M. Hansen; and then the last sentence will be quite simple, that the white bear lives under water like the walrus The confusion may have arisen through a belief that the tusks of the walrus were aurochs' horns. The horns in the picture of the "Urus" on the Ebstorf map (1284) are very like walrus tusks. But it is striking that the common land bear is not mentioned, while the white bear is spoken of. As the latter seldom comes to Finmark, its mention points to the Norwegians having hunted it in the Polar Sea; if it be not due to the connection of Norway with Iceland and Greenland, but as these lands are mentioned separately this seems less probable.

AWAKENING OF MEDIÆVAL KNOWLEDGE

[iv. 35.] "The island of Thyle, which is separated from the others by an infinite distance, lies far out in the middle of the ocean and, as is said, is scarcely known. Both the Roman authors and the barbarians have much to say of it which is worth mentioning. They say that Thyle is the extreme island of all, where at the summer solstice, when the sun is passing through the sign of Cancer, there is no night, and correspondingly at the winter solstice no day. Some think that this is the case for six months at a time. Bede also says that the light summer nights in Britain indicate without doubt that, just as at the summer solstice they have there continuous day for six months, so it is nights at the winter solstice, when the sun is hidden. Pytheas of Massalia writes that this occurs in the island of Thyle, which lies six days' sail north of Britain, and it is this Thyle which is now called Iceland from the ice which there binds the sea. They report this remarkable thing about it, that this ice appears to be so black and dry that, on account of its age, it burns when it is kindled.[1] This island is immensely large, so that it contains many people who live solely upon the produce of their flocks and cover themselves with their wool. No corn grows there, and there is only very little timber,[2] for which reason the inhabitants are obliged to live in underground holes, and share their dwellings with their cattle.

CHAPTER V
Thule or Iceland

---

[1] This idea may possibly be due on the one hand to the mist, which may have been regarded as brought about by heat; for in a scholium (possibly by Adam himself, or not much later) we read: "By Iceland is the Ice Sea, and it is boiling and shrouded in mist ('caligans')." On the other hand it may be due to statements about volcanoes and boiling springs which have been confused with it. The black colour and dryness of the ice may be due to confusion with lava or with floating pumice-stone in the sea, and statements about the lignite of Iceland ("surtarbrand") may also have given rise to this idea [cf. Baumgartner, 1902, p. 503]. Lönborg's suggestion [1897, p. 165] that it may be due to driftwood is less probable. Compare also the idea in the "Meregarto" (above, p. 181) of the ice as hard as crystal, which is heated. In two MSS. of Solinus, of which the oldest is of the twelfth century [cf. Mommsen's edition of Solinus, 1895, pp. xxxiv., xxxvii., 236; Lappenberg, 1838, pp. 887 f.], there is an addition about the northern islands in which we read of Iceland: "Yslande. The sea-ice on this island ignites itself on collision, and when it is ignited it burns like wood. These people also are good Christians, but in winter they dare not leave their underground holes on account of the terrible cold. For if they go out they are smitten by such severe cold that they lose their colour like lepers and swell up. If by chance they blow their nose, it comes off and they throw it away with what they have blown out." This passage cannot be derived from Adam of Bremen (nor has it any resemblance to the Meregarto); it may indicate that similar ideas of the ice of Iceland were current at that time. Saxo's remarkable allusion to this ice (in the introduction to his work) also shows that it was connected with much superstition.

[2] The woods consisted then as now solely of birch-trees, which were however larger at that time.

IN NORTHERN MISTS

CHAPTER V

They thus lead a holy life in simplicity, as they do not strive after more than what nature gives; they can cheerfully say with the Apostle: 'if we have clothing and food, let us be content therewith!' for their mountains are to them in the stead of cities, and their springs serve them for pleasure. I regard this people as happy, whose poverty none covets, but happiest in that they have now all adopted Christianity. There is much that is excellent in their customs, especially their good disposition, whereby everything is shared, not only with the natives, but with strangers." After referring to their good treatment of their bishop, etc., he concludes: "Thus much I have been credibly informed of Iceland and extreme Thyle, but I pass over what is fabulous."

Greenland

[iv. 36.] "Furthermore there are many other islands in the great ocean, of which Greenland is not the least; it lies farther out in the ocean, opposite ('contra') the mountains of Suedia, or the Riphean range. To this island, it is said, one can sail from the shore of Nortmannia in five or seven days, as likewise to Iceland. The people there are blue ['cerulei,' bluish-green] from the salt water; and from this the region takes its name. They live in a similar fashion to the Icelanders, except that they are more cruel and trouble seafarers by predatory attacks. To them also, as is reported, Christianity has lately been wafted.

Hålogaland

"A third island is Halagland [Hálogaland], nearer to Nortmannia, in size not unlike the others.[1] This island in summer, about the summer solstice, sees the sun uninterruptedly above the earth for fourteen days, and in winter it has to be without the sun for a like number of days.[2] This is a marvel and a mystery to the barbarians, who do not know that the unequal length of days results from the approach and retreat of the sun. On account of the roundness of the earth ('rotunditas orbis terrarum') the sun must in one place approach and bring the day, and in another depart and leave the night. Thus when it ascends towards the summer solstice, it prolongs the days and shortens the nights for those in the north, but when it descends towards the winter solstice, it does the same for those in the southern hemisphere ('australibus').[3] Therefore

---

[1] In a scholium, possibly by Adam himself, there is this correction: "According to what others report, Halagland is the extreme part of Norway, which borders on the Skridfinns and is inaccessible by reason of the forbidding mountains and the harshness of the cold."

[2] This statement that the summer day and the winter night were of the same length cannot here, any more than in Jordanes and Procopius, be due to direct observation on the part of Northerners, but must be an echo of classical astronomical speculations (cf. above, pp. 134, 144). It is strange, too, that while in Jordanes (and Procopius) the length of the summer day and winter night was forty days (among the "Adogit" in Hálogaland), it is here given as fourteen days in Hálogaland. Possibly the number fourteen may be due to a confusion or a copyist's error for forty.

[3] Probably Adam has taken this explanation from Bede [cf. Kohlmann, 1908, pp. 45 ff.].

the ignorant heathens call that land holy and blessed, which has such a marvel to exhibit to mortals. But the king of the Danes and many others have stated that this takes place there as well as in Suedia and Norvegia and the other islands which are there."

[iv. 38.] "Moreover he mentioned yet another island, which had been discovered by many in that ocean, and which is called 'Winland,' because vines grow there of themselves and give the noblest wine. And that there is abundance of unsown corn we have obtained certain knowledge, not by fabulous supposition, but from trustworthy information of the Danes. (Beyond ('post') this island, he said, no habitable land is found in this ocean, but all that is more distant is full of intolerable ice and immense mist ['caligine,' possibly darkness caused by mist]. Of these things Marcianus has told us: 'Beyond Thyle,' says he, 'one day's sail, the sea is stiffened.' This was recently proved by Harold, prince of the Nordmanni, most desirous of knowledge, who explored the breadth of the northern ocean with his ships, and when the boundaries of the vanishing earth were darkened before his face, he scarcely escaped the immense gulf of the abyss by turning back.)[1]

[iv. 39.] "Archbishop Adalbert, of blessed memory, likewise told us that in his predecessor's days certain noblemen from Friesland, intending to plough the sea, set sail northwards, because people say there that due north of the mouth of the river Wirraha [Weser] no land is to be met with, but only an infinite ocean. They joined together to investigate this curious thing, and left the Frisian coast with cheerful song. Then they left Dania on one side, Britain on the other, and reached the Orkneys. When they had left these behind on the left, and had Nordmannia on the right, they reached after a long voyage the frozen Iceland. Ploughing the seas from this land towards the extreme axis of the north, after seeing behind them all the islands already mentioned, and confiding their lives and their boldness to Almighty God and the holy preacher Willehad, they suddenly glided into the misty darkness of the stiffened ocean, which can scarcely be penetrated by the eye. And behold! the stream of the unstable sea there ran back into one of its secret sources, drawing at a fearful speed the unhappy seamen, who had already given up hope and only thought of death, into that profound chaos (this is said to be the gulf of the abyss) in which it is said that all the back-currents of the sea, which seem to abate, are sucked up and vomited forth again, which latter is usually called flood-tide. While they were then calling upon God's mercy, that He might receive their souls, this backward-running stream of the sea caught some of their fellows' ships, but the rest were shot

---

[1] This passage, from "Beyond this island," is not found in all the MSS., whence Lappenberg [1876, p. xvii.] thinks it is a later addition—but by Adam himself, as the style resembles his. To this latter reason it may be objected that when Adam mentions Harold Hardråde earlier in his work, he is disposed to disparage him, which is not the case here. But since he does not disparage him either in his mention of the Baltic voyage (see p. 185), this is of little importance.

out by the issuing current far beyond the others. When they had thus by God's help been delivered from the imminent danger, which had been before their very eyes, they saved themselves upon the waves by rowing with all their strength.

[iv. 40] "And being now past the danger of darkness and the region of cold they landed unexpectedly upon an island, which was fortified like a town, with cliffs all about it. They landed there to see the place, and found people who at midday hid themselves in underground caves; before the doors of these lay an immense quantity of golden vessels and metal of the sort which is regarded by mortals as rare and precious; when therefore they had taken as much of the treasures as they could lift, the rowers hastened gladly back to their ships. Then suddenly they saw people of marvellous height coming behind them, whom we call Cyclopes, and before them ran dogs which surpassed the usual size of these animals. One of the men was caught, as these rushed forward, and in an instant he was torn to pieces before their eyes; but the rest were taken up into the ships and escaped the danger, although, as they related, the giants followed them with cries nearly into deep sea. With such a fate pursuing them, the Frisians came to Bremen, where they told the most reverend Alebrand everything in order as it happened, and made offerings to the gentle Christ and his preacher Willehad for their safe return."

As will be seen, Adam obtained from the people of Scandinavia much new information and fresh ideas about the geography of the North, which add considerably to the knowledge of former times; but unfortunately he confuses this information with the legends and ancient classical notions he has acquired from reading the learned authors of late Roman and early mediæval times; and this confusion reaches its climax in the last tale, which is chiefly of interest to the folk-lorist. The first part of it (section 39) is made up from Paulus Warnefridi's description of the earth's navel, to some extent with the same expressions (see above, p. 157); the second part (section 40) is based upon legends on the model of the Odyssey, of which there were many in the Middle Ages. While his description gives a fairly clear picture of his views regarding the countries on the Baltic, it is difficult to get any definite idea of the relative position of the more distant islands; but it is probable, as proposed by Gustav Storm, that he imagined them as lying far in the north.

Wineland

As Wineland is mentioned last, and as it is added that beyond this island there is no habitable land in this ocean, but that all

AWAKENING OF MEDIÆVAL KNOWLEDGE

is full of ice and mist, it might be thought that this is regarded as lying farthest out in a northern direction. But this would not agree with Adam's earlier statement [iv. 10], where Iceland and Greenland are given as the most distant islands, and "there this ocean, which is called the dark one, forms the boundary." The explanation must be that, as already remarked (p. 195), his statement about the ocean beyond Wineland is probably a later addition, though possibly by Adam himself. It is obviously inserted somewhat disconnectedly, and perhaps has been put in the wrong place, and this is also made probable by the quotation from Marcianus about Thyle, which has nothing to do with Wineland, but refers on the contrary to Iceland (cf. p. 193).[1] Omitting this interpolation, the text says of the geographical position merely that the King of the Danes also mentioned the island of Wineland, as discovered by many in that ocean, i.e., the outer ocean, and so far as this goes it might be imagined as lying anywhere. That no importance is attached to the order in which the islands are named appears also from the fact that Halagland is put after Iceland and Greenland, although it is expressly stated that it lay nearer Norway. That Adam, after having described the last-named country a long while before, here gratuitously mentions Halagland (Hålogaland) as an island by itself[2] together with Iceland and Greenland, shows how deficient his information about the northernmost regions really was.

As will be further shown in the later chapter on Wineland, Adam's ideas of that country, of the wine and the corn there,

[1] While this sheet is in the press I happen to see that the same opinion has been advanced, almost in the same words, by Sven Lonborg [1897, p. 168].

[2] Adam's idea of Hålogaland (Halagland) as an island may be due to its similarity of sound to the "Heiligland" (Heligoland) mentioned by him. As one of these lands was an island it must have been easy to suppose that the other was one also. The interpretation of the name as meaning holy may come from the same source. Heiligland was regarded as holy on account of the monastery established there. A corresponding name, "Eyin Helga," is applied in the sagas to two islands: Helgeo in Mjosen, and the well-known Iona in the Hebrides [Magnus Barfot's Saga, cap. 10]. The latter was holy on account of Columcille's church.

must be derived from legends about the Fortunate Isles, which were called by the Norsemen " Vínland hit Góða." This legend must have been current in the North at that time, and possibly it may already have been connected with the discovery of countries in the west. But it is, perhaps, not altogether accidental that Wineland should be mentioned immediately after Halagland. For as the latter name was regarded as meaning the Holy Land,[1] it may be natural that Wineland or the Fortunate Isles, originally the Land of the Blest, should be placed in its neighbourhood. To this the resemblance in sound between Vinland and Finland (or, more correctly, Finmark, the land of the Finns or Lapps) may, consciously or unconsciously, have contributed ; later in the Middle Ages these names were often confused and interchanged.[2] Finns and Finland were sometimes spelt in German with a V; and V and F were transposed in geographical names even outside Germany, as when, in an Icelandic geographical tract attributed to Abbot Nikulás Bergsson of Thverá (ob. 1159), Venice is transformed by popular etymology to "Feneyjar" [cf. F. Jónsson, 1901, p. 948]. It is particularly interesting that the Latin "vinum" (wine) became in Irish legendary poetry "fín," and the vine was called "fíne," as in the poem of the Voyage of Bran [Kuno Meyer, 1895, vol. i., pp. xvii., 9, 21].

Conception of the earth and the ocean

It is not clear from Adam's description whether he altogether held the conception of the earth, or rather the "œcumene," as a circular island or disc divided into three, surrounded by the outer ocean (the Oceanus of the Greeks, see p. 8), as represented on the wheel-maps of earlier times (cf. p. 151, and the Beatus map) ; but his expression that the

---

[1] See note 2, p. 197.

[2] Adam did not apparently know the name "Finn," he only mentions Finnédi and Scritefini. It might then seem natural that he should intermix the names Vinland and Finland, and believing that this Fin- or Vin- had something to do with Wine, he may have applied to this land Isidore's description of the Fortunate Isles, in a similar manner as he applied the Greek story about the Amazons to Kvænland with the Cynocephali, etc.

AWAKENING OF MEDIÆVAL KNOWLEDGE

Western Ocean extends northwards from the Orchades "infinitely around the circle of the earth" ("infinites orbem terræ spaciis ambit") may point to this. It is true that immediately afterwards he has an obscure statement that at Greenland "ibi terminat oceanus qui dicitur caligans," which has usually been translated as "there ends the ocean, which is called the dark one" (?); but it is difficult to get any sense

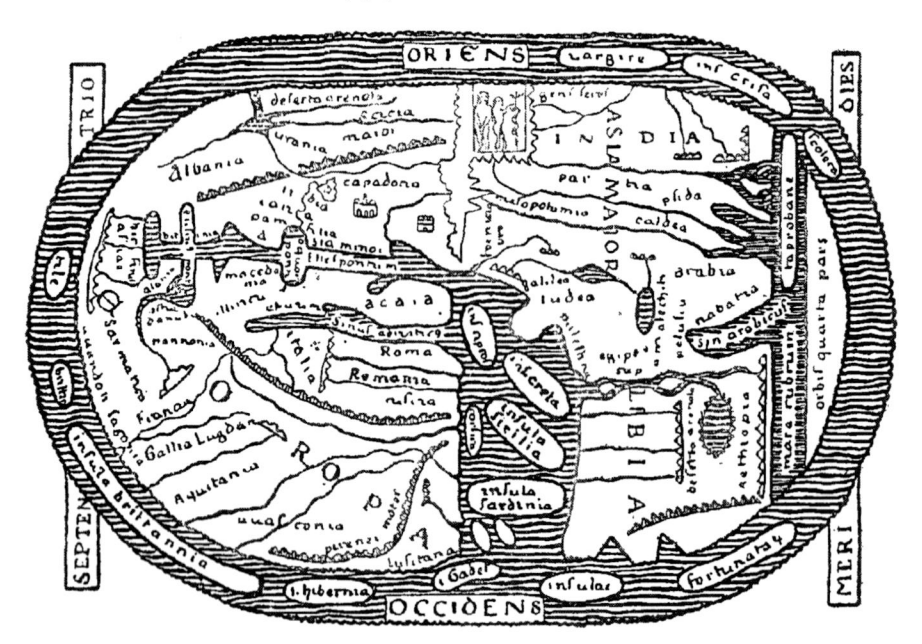

The so-called St. Severus version, of about 1050, of the Beatus map (eighth century)

out of it. One explanation might be that he imagined Greenland as lying out on the extreme edge of the earth's disc, near the abyss, and that thus the ocean (which in that region was called dark?) ended here in that direction (i.e., in its breadth), while in its length it extended farther continuously around "the circle of the earth." This view would, no doubt, conflict with his statement in another place that the earth was round, which can only be understood as meaning that it had the form of a globe. But this last idea he took from Bede, and he has scarcely assimilated it sufficiently for it to permeate his views of the circle of the earth and the universal ocean, as also appears from his mention of the gulf at its outer limit. If we had been able to suppose that Adam really thought the Western Ocean on the north flowed past the Orchades, and thence infinitely towards the west around the globe of the earth (instead of the circle of the earth), this would better suit the statement that Ireland lay to the left, Norway to the right, and Iceland and Greenland farther out (also to the right ?). This would agree with the statement that Norway was the extreme land on the north, and that beyond it (i.e., farther north ?) there was no human habitation, but only the infinite ocean which surrounds the whole world, and in which opposite ("ex adverso") Norway lie many islands, etc. According to this, these islands must be imagined as lying to the west, and not to the north of Norway. But besides the fact that such a view of the extent of the ocean towards the west would conflict with the prevailing cartographical representation of that time, it is contradicted by his assertion that Greenland lies farther out in the ocean (than Iceland) and opposite the mountains of Suedia and the Riphean range, which must be supposed to lie on the continent to the north-east of Norway; this cannot very well be possible unless these islands are to be placed out in the ocean farther north than Norway, and there is thus on this point a difficult contradiction in Adam's work. The circumstance that Hâlogaland is spoken of as an island after Iceland and Greenland is also against the probability that the ocean, in which these islands lay, was imagined to extend infinitely towards the west; the direction is, in this manner, given as northerly. The same thing appears from the description of the voyage of the Frisian noblemen: when they steered northward with the Orkneys to port and Norway to starboard they came to the frozen Iceland, and when they proceeded thence towards the North Pole, they saw behind them all the islands previously mentioned. Dr. A. A. Björnbo has suggested to me that according to Adam's way of expressing himself "terminat"

AWAKENING OF MEDIÆVAL KNOWLEDGE

must here mean "forms the boundary," whereby we get the translation given above (p. 192), which seems to give better sense; but in any case Adam's description of these regions is not quite clear.

We are told that Magister Adam obtained information about the countries and peoples of the North from Svein Estridsson and his men; but as regards Iceland he might also have had trustworthy information from the Archbishop of Bremen, Adalbert, who had educated an Icelander, Isleif Gissursson, to be bishop. The latter (who is also mentioned by Are Frode) might also have told him about Greenland and Wineland; but Adam says distinctly that he had been informed about the latter country and the wine and corn there, which must have seemed very remarkable to him, if he imagined the country to be in the north, by the Danish king, and that the information had been confirmed by Danes. We shall return later to these countries, to Adam's ideas of Wineland, and to the alleged polar expeditions of King Harold and of the Frisian noblemen.

Just as these pages are going to press I have received from Dr. Axel Anthon Björnbo his excellent essay on "Adam of Bremen's view of the North" [1909]. By Dr. Björnbo's exhaustive researches the correctness of the views just set forth seems to be confirmed on many points; but he gives a far more complete picture of Adam's geographical ideas. The reasons advanced by Dr. Björnbo for supposing that Adam imagined the ocean as surrounding the earth's disc, with Iceland, Greenland, etc., in the north, are of much interest. His map of the North according to Adam's description is of great value, and gives a clear presentation of the main lines of Adam's conceptions. With his kind permission it is reproduced here (p. 186). But, as will appear from my remarks above (pp. 197 f.), I am not sure that one is justified in placing Winland so far north, in the neighbourhood of the North Pole, as Dr. Björnbo has done in his map. Possibly he has also put the other islands rather far north, and has curved the north coast of Scandinavia somewhat too much in a westerly direction.

Through Dr. Björnbo's book I have become acquainted with another recently published work on Adam of Bremen by Hermann Krabbo [1909], of which I have also been unable to make use; it also has a map, but not so complete a one as Björnbo's as regards the northern regions.

CHAPTER VI

FINNS, SKRIDFINNS (LAPPS), AND THE FIRST SETTLEMENT OF SCANDINAVIA

BEFORE we proceed to the Norwegians' great contributions to the exploration of the northern regions, we shall attempt to collect and survey what is known, and what may possibly be concluded, about the most northern people of Europe, the Finns, and the earliest settlement of Scandinavia.

The Finns are mentioned, as we have seen (p. 113), for the first time in literature by Tacitus, who calls them "Fenni," and describes them as exclusively a people of hunters. Procopius does the same, but calls them "Skridfinns," and removes their home to the northernmost Thule or Scandinavia. Cassiodorus (Jordanes) also mentions the "Skridfinns" as hunters in the same northern regions, but speaks moreover of "Finns" and "Finaiti," and another people resembling the Finns ("Vinoviloth"?) farther south in Scandinavia. The Ravenna geographer also mentions the "Skridfinns" (after Jordanes). Then comes Paulus Warnefridi, who speaks of the ski-running

CHAPTER VI

Earliest mention of the Finns

of the Skridfinns, though indeed in a way which shows he did not understand it very well, and mentions a deer of whose skin they made themselves clothes, but does not say that this deer was domesticated. Next King Alfred mentions "Skridfinns," "Finns," and "Ter-Finns," and in the information he obtained from Ottar he speaks of the hunting, fishing and whaling of the "Finns," and of their keeping reindeer in the north of Norway. This description is in accordance with what we learn of the Lapps from later history, with this difference only, that on account of the killing-off of the game their hunting in recent times became of small importance. Lastly we have Adam of Bremen's description of the Finns, which contains nothing new of note. He mentions "Finnédi" or "Finvedi" between Sweden and Norway (near Vermeland) and "Skridfinns" in northern Scandinavia. Besides these he speaks of a small people who come down at intervals, once a year or every three years, from the mountains, and who are probably the Mountain Lapps with their reindeer. He mentions also a people skilled in magic on the shores of the northern ocean [Finmark], and skin-clad men in the forests of the north, who may be Fishing Lapps or Forest Lapps. In connection with this we may also refer to the mention of the Lapps in the "Historia Norvegiæ":

> Norway "is divided lengthways into three curved zones [i.e., parallel to the curved coast-line]: the first zone, which is very large and lies along the coast; the second, the inland zone, which is also called the mountain zone; the third, the forest zone, which is inhabited by Finns [Lapps], but is not ploughed." The Lapps, in the third zone, which was waste land, "were very skilled hunters, they roam about singly and are nomads, and they live in huts made of hides instead of houses. These houses they take on their shoulders, and they fasten smoothed pieces of wood [literally, balks, stakes] under their feet, which appliances they call 'ondrer,' and while the deer [i.e., reindeer] gallop along carrying their wives and children over the deep snow and precipitous mountains, they dash on more swiftly than the birds. Their dwelling-place is uncertain [it changes] according as the quantity of game shows them a hunting-ground when it is needed."

From the earliest accounts referred to, especially from that of Adam of Bremen, it looks as though there were

FINNS AND SKRIDFINNS

Fishing Lapps and Reindeer Lapps in northern Scandinavia in those remote times, as there are now, and they were called Finns or Skridfinns; but besides these there were people who were called Finns in southern Scandinavia, from whence they have since disappeared. This has led to the hypothesis that the primitive population in southern Scandinavia also was composed of the same Finns (Lapps) as are now found in the northern part, to which they were compelled to retreat by the later Germanic immigrants [cf. Geijer, 1825, pp. 411 ff.; Munch, 1852, pp. 3 ff.; Sven Nilsson]. But for various reasons this hypothesis has had to be abandoned, and the question has become difficult.

CHAPTER VI

Men of the Woods in Northern Scandinavia (from Olaus Magnus)

The word " Finn " as the name of a people does not occur, so far as is known, outside Scandinavia. The only place farther south where there are place-names which remind one of it is in Friesland, where we find a Finsburg. The origin of the national name " Finn " is unknown. Some have thought that it might be connected with the word "finna" (English, to find), and that it means one who goes on foot.

The name " Finn "

Since in Swedish and Norwegian the name has come to be applied to two such entirely different peoples as, in Norway, the Fishing Lapps and Reindeer Lapps and, in Sweden, the people of Finland, we must suppose that in the primitive Norse language it was a common designation for several non-Germanic races, whom the later Germanic immigrants in south Scandinavia drove into the wastes and forest tracts, where they lived by hunting and fishing. This would provide a natural explanation of the curious circumstance that Jordanes, as well as Adam of Bremen (later also Saxo), mentions Finns, Finvedi, and other Finn-peoples in many parts of south Scandinavia ; in our saga literature there are also many references to Finns far south. But the most decisive circumstance is, perhaps, that the word Finn occurs in many place-names of south Scandinavia, from Finnskog and Finnsjö in Uppland, and Finnheden or Finnveden in Småland, to Finnö in the Bokn-fjord [cf. Müllenhoff, ii. 1887, p. 51 ; A. M. Hansen, 1907]. It may be quoted as a strong piece of evidence that a people called Finns must have lived in old times in south Norway, that the oldest Christian laws, of about 1150, for the most southern jurisdictions, the Borgathing and Eidsivathing, visit with the severest penalty of the law the crime of going to the Finns, or to Finmark, to have one's fortune told [cf. A. M. Hansen, 1907, p. 79]. It may seem improbable that here (e.g., as far south as Bohuslen) this should have referred to Finns (Lapps) in the north, in what is now called Finmark ; and we should be rather inclined to believe it to refer to the Finns (and Finnédi) mentioned by Jordanes and Adam of Bremen nearer at hand, in the forest tracts between Norway and Sweden, where we still have a Finnskog, which, however, is generally connected with the later immigration of Kvæns or Finns from Finland (the so-called wood-devils ; compare also Finmarken between Lier and Modum). But it might be thought that these Christian laws were compiled more or less from laws enacted for northern Norway, and thus provisions of this kind, which were only adapted for that part of the country, were included. And it must be borne in mind that the northern Finns (Lapps) in particular had an ancient reputation for proficiency in magic and soothsaying, and, further, that Finmark in those times was often regarded as extending much farther south than now, as far as Jemteland and Herjedalen.

Immigration to Scandinavia   It is difficult to decide with certainty what kind of people the "Finns" who were found in many parts of south

FINNS AND SKRIDFINNS

Scandinavia may have been. The supposition that they were the same people as the Finns (Lapps) of our time has had to be abandoned, as we have said, in the face of more recent archæological, anthropological and historical-geographical researches. Müllenhoff [ii. 1887, pp. 50 ff.] has proposed that the word "Finn" may originally have been a Scandinavian common name for several peoples who were diffused in south Scandinavia, but who in his opinion were Ugro-Finnish, like the Kvæns, Lapps and others [cf. also Geijer, 1825, pp. 415 f.]. He even goes so far as to suppose that the very name of Scandinavia may be due to them (like that of the ski-goddess "Skaði,"[1] who was a Finn-woman, cf. p. 103). But it has not been possible to point either to linguistic or anthropological traces of any early Finno-Ugrian people in any part of south Scandinavia, and there are many indications that the southern diffusion of the Mountain Finns (Reindeer Lapps) is comparatively late.

Dr. A. M. Hansen, therefore, in his suggestive works, "Landnám" [1904] and "Oldtidens Nordmænd" ["The Norsemen of Antiquity," 1907], has put forward the hypothesis that the Finns of earliest history, whom he would include under the common designation of "Skridfinns," were a non-Aryan people, wholly distinct both from the Finno-Ugrian tribes and from the Aryan Scandinavians, who formed the primitive population of northern Europe and were related to the primitive peoples of southern Europe, the Pelasgians, Etruscans, Basques and others. In Scandinavia they were forced northwards by the Germanic tribes, and have now disappeared through being partly absorbed in the latter. In the east and north-east they were displaced by the Finno-Ugrian peoples who immigrated later. The last remnants of them would be found in the Fishing Lapps of our time, and in the so-called Yenisei Ostyaks of north-western Siberia. This bold hypothesis has the disadvantage, amongst others, of forcing us

---

[1] S. Bugge has since maintained the probability that the name "Skaði" is of Germanic origin.

CHAPTER VI
to assume the existence of a vanished people, who are otherwise entirely unknown. In the next place, Dr. Hansen, in arbitrarily applying the name of Skridfinns to all the "Finns" in Scandinavia, does not seem to have laid sufficient weight on the difference which early writers make between Skridfinns in the north and the other Finns farther south.

In earlier times there was a strong tendency, due to old Biblical notions, to imagine all nations as immigrants to the regions where they are now found. But when a zoologist finds a particular species or variety of animal distributed over a limited area, he makes the most natural assumption, that it has arisen through a local differentiation in that region. The simplest plan must be to look upon human stocks and races in the same way. When we have tried in Europe to distinguish between Celts, Germans, Slavs, Ugro-Finns, etc., the most reasonable supposition will be that these races have arisen through local "evolution," the home of their differentiation being within the area in which we find them later. As such centres of differentiation in Europe we might suppose: for the Celts, western Central Europe; for the Germans, eastern Central Europe; for the Slavs, Eastern Europe; for the Ugro-Finns, northern East Europe and western Siberia, etc.

This is doubtless a linguistic division, but to a certain extent it coincides with anthropological distinctions. Since the North was covered with ice till a comparatively recent period, we cannot expect any local differentiation of importance there since that time, but must suppose an immigration to the north and to Scandinavia of already differentiated races, from southern Europe. We may thus suppose that tribes belonging to the parent-races of brachycephalic Celts and Slavs, and dolichocephalic Germans, came in from the south and south-east, and Ugro-Finns and Mongoloid tribes immigrated from the south-east and east. In this way we may expect, at the commencement of the historical period, to find Celto-Slavs and Germans in southern and central Scandinavia, and Mongoloid and Finno-Ugrian people in the northernmost regions and

FINNS AND SKRIDFINNS

towards the north-east and east (Finland and North Russia). This agrees fairly well with what is actually found. If we except the northernmost districts, anthropological measurements (principally by Brigade-Surgeon Arbo) show that the people of Norway are descended not only from the tall, fair, and pronouncedly dolichocephalic Germanic race, but also from at least one brachycephalic race, which was of smaller stature and dark-haired.[1] Measurements in Sweden and Denmark show a similar state of things, but in Denmark and the extreme south of Sweden the short-skulls are more numerous than in the rest of Scandinavia. In order to explain these anthropological conditions, we must either suppose that the various Germanic tribes which have formed the people of Scandinavia were more or less mixed with brachycephalic people, even before they immigrated,[2] in proportions similar to those now obtaining, or that tribes immigrated to Scandinavia belonging to at least two different races, one specially dolichocephalic and one specially brachycephalic. The latter hypothesis will be, to a certain extent at all events, the more natural, and as it is not probable that the short-skulls arrived later than the long-skulled Germanic tribes, it is most reasonable to suppose that there was at least one short-skulled primitive people before they came. These primitive people were hunters and fishermen, and must therefore in most districts have wandered over a wide area to find what was necessary to support life. It was only the more favourable conditions of life in certain districts —for instance, the abundance of fish along the west coast of Norway—that allowed a denser population with more permanent habitation. As the taller and stronger Germanic tribes spread along the coasts, the older short-skulled hunters, who

CHAPTER VI

Southern Finns in Scandinavia

---

[1] We shall not here enter into the difficult question of the blond short-skulls, as it has no bearing on our argument.

[2] It might, for instance, be supposed that the Ryger and Horder, who came from north-eastern Germania, were already mixed with short-skulled Slavs before their immigration to western Norway.

CHAPTER VI may have been Celts,[1] were in most districts forced towards the forest tracts of the interior, where there was abundance of game and fish. In districts where they lived closer together and had more permanent settlements, as on the west coast of Norway, they were not altogether displaced. For this dark primitive people, who were shorter of stature than themselves, and who hunted and fished in the outlying districts, the Germanic tribes may, in one way or another, have found the common name of "Finns," whether the people called themselves so or the name arose in some other way.[2] When the Germanic people then came across another short, dark-haired people of hunters and fishermen in the north, they applied the name of "Finn" to them too, although they belonged to an entirely different linguistic family, the Finno-Ugrian, and to an even more different Mongoloid race. But to distinguish them from the southern Celtic people of hunters, the northern were sometimes called "Skridfinns." Gradually, as the southern Finns became absorbed into the Germanic population and disappeared as a separate people, the name in Norway remained attached to the other race and country (Finmark) in the north, and in Sweden to the very different people and country (Finland) in the north-east.

The southern Finns were an Aryan people, and as the Aryan languages at that remote time, when they became detached from the more southern short-skulls of Europe, the

[1] Among the known brachycephalic peoples of Europe we have the Celts and the western Slavs, Poles, Czecks, etc. These are linguistically far apart, but it is a question whether the brachycephalic element in both is not originally the same. It must be borne in mind that, at the remote period of which we are now speaking, the linguistic difference between them was certainly small, and for that matter it is of little importance from which of them the first immigration into Scandinavia came.

[2] As Professor Alf Torp has pointed out to me, the word "Fin" must, on account of the Germanic mutation of sounds, be expected to have sounded something like "Pen" at that remote time. "Pen" in Celtic means head, and it is not altogether impossible that such a word might have been transformed into a national name.

FINNS AND SKRIDFINNS

Celts and Slavs, did not vary very much, it is easily explicable that scarcely a single ancient place-name can be found in southern Norway which can be said with certainty to bear a non-Germanic character. If, on the other hand, the southern Finns, who are mentioned so late as far on in the Middle Ages, had been a Finno-Ugrian or other non-Aryan people, it is incredible that we should not be able easily to point to foreign

CHAPTER VI

Skridfinns hunting (from Olaus Magnus)

elements in the place-names, which would be due to their language.

Scandinavian finds of skulls of the Stone Age, and later, are so few and so casual that we can conclude very little from them as regards the race to which the primitive population belonged. Further, it must be remarked that the early people of hunters, the short-skulled "Finns," must have been very few in number, and have lived scattered about the country, in contrast to the later Germanic tribes who had a fixed habitation. That among the earliest skulls found there should only be a few short ones is, therefore, what we should expect. It must also be remembered, of course, that the proportion of skulls left by each people depends in a great degree on its burial customs.

We now come to the northern Finns, of whom Ottar gives

CHAPTER VI
Northern "Finns" in Finmark

a sufficiently detailed description to enable us to form a fairly accurate picture of their culture. Since they were able to pay a heavy annual tribute in walrus-tusks, ropes of walrus-hide and seal-hide, besides other skins and products of fishery, we must conclude that they were skilled hunters and fishermen even at sea, and such skill can only have been acquired through the slow development and practice of a long period, unless they learned it from the Norsemen. But on the other hand they also kept reindeer, resembling in this the eastern reindeer nomads. These two ways of living are so distinct that they can scarcely have been originally developed in one and the same people, and we must therefore conclude that a concurrence of several different cultures has here taken place.

Now as regards whaling and sealing, it is remarkable that along the whole northern coast of Europe and Asia there is no trace of any other race of seafaring hunters. Not until we come to the Chukches, near Bering Strait, do we find a sea-fishery culture, but this is borrowed from the Eskimo farther east, and originally came from the American side of Bering Strait. In Novaya Zemlya, it is true, there is a small tribe of Samoyeds who live by hunting both on sea and land, and who do not keep reindeer, but on the other hand use dogs for sleighing; but their sea-hunting is primitive, like the more casual sealing and walrus-hunting I have seen practised by the reindeer Samoyeds along the shores of the Kara Sea, with firearms, but without special appliances and with extremely clumsy boats. It is difficult to see in this the remains of an older, highly developed people of hunters.

This sealing culture which was found in Ottar's time in northernmost Norway and on the Murman coast cannot, therefore, have come from the east along the coast of Siberia, but must have been a local development, perhaps arising from the amalgamation of the original hunting culture of these "Finns" with a higher European culture from the south.

It fortunately happens that at Kjelmö, on the southern

FINNS AND SKRIDFINNS

side of the Varanger Fjord, a rich find of implements has been made, which must belong to the very same people of "Finns" who, as Ottar says, lived here and there along the coast (of Finmark and Terfinna Land) as hunters, fishermen and fowlers. Dr. O. Solberg in particular has in the last few years made valuable excavations on this island.[1] The many objects found lay evenly distributed in strata, the thickness of which shows that they must be the result of many centuries of accumulation. Solberg refers them to the period between the seventh and about the eleventh centuries.

In North Varanger many heathen graves containing implements have been found. By the help of the latter Solberg has been able to show that the graves are partly of the same age and partly of a somewhat later time than the Kjelmö find, and certainly belong to the same people. By comparing these various finds we can form a picture of this people's culture and its associations.

In addition to a number of bones of fish, birds and mammals, the Kjelmö find contains a variety of implements, mostly made of reindeer-horn and bone, which have been remarkably well preserved in the lime-charged sand, while on the other hand the iron, with few exceptions, has rusted entirely away. There are also many fragments of pottery, baked at an open fire and made of clay found on the island. These hunters and fishermen, therefore, understood the art of the potter as well as that of the smith, and thus the culture of this northern district on the shores of the Polar Sea was not on such a very low level. But it was not of independent growth; the pottery shows a connection with that of the older Iron Age in south Scandinavia; while on the other hand a couple of bronze objects, especially the small figure of a bear, found in a grave in North Varanger, are typically representative of the early

CHAPTER VI — Archæological relics of "Finns" in Varanger

---

[1] Cf. O. Solberg, 1909. The particulars here given of this remarkable find are for the most part taken from Solberg's interesting paper, the proofs of which he has allowed me to see. He has also been kind enough to give me an opportunity of examining the objects.

CHAPTER VI

part of the Permian Iron Age in eastern Russia (from the eighth century). Many other objects found in the graves also point to connection with the south-east, partly with Russia or Ottar's Beormaland, and perhaps with Finland; while on the other side there may have been communication westwards

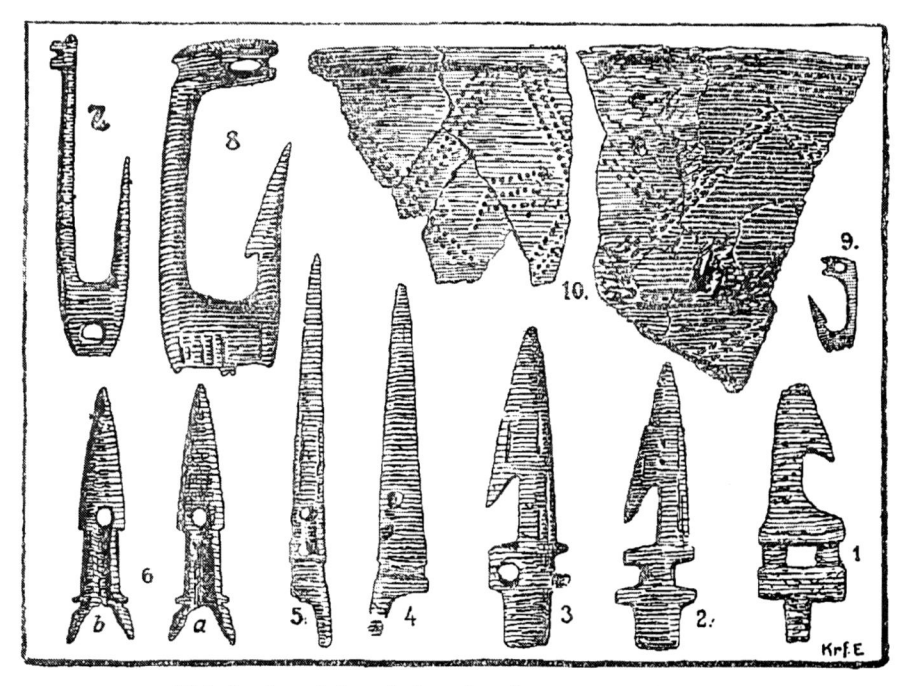

7-9, Fish-hooks (of reindeer-horn); 10, potsherds; 1-6, harpoon-points (of reindeer-horn), from Kjelmö; less than half natural size (after O. Solberg, 1909)

and south-westwards (Ottar's route) with Norway. Solberg has found marks of ownership on the Kjelmö implements which he shows to have much resemblance to those still in use among the Skolte-Lapps.[1] But the use of owner's marks was an ancient and universal custom among the Germanic peoples, and the Finns probably derived it from them. The owner's marks found by Solberg bear a resemblance to many ancient Germanic ones [cf. Hofmeyer, 1870; Michelsen,

[1] Lapps belonging to the Greek Church, who live in a Russian enclave on the Pasvik, Varanger Fjord. (TR.)

214

FINNS AND SKRIDFINNS

1853], and seem rather to point to cultural connection with the Norsemen.

Among the implements of reindeer-horn and bone in the Kjelmö find there are especially many fish-hooks, which show that fishing played an important part in the life of these people on the island, probably mostly in the summer months. Possibly there are also some stone sinkers which would show that they had nets. There are also fish-spears of reindeer-horn, which were used for salmon-fishing in the rivers. Further, there is a quantity of arrow-heads; but of special interest to us are a number of harpoon-points of various form, which doubtless do not show so highly developed a sealing culture as that of the Eskimo, but which are nevertheless quite ingenious and bear witness to much connection with the sea. It is worth mentioning that, while some of these harpoon-points (Figs. 2 and 3 above) resemble old, primitive Eskimo forms, which are found in Greenland, another still more primitive form (Fig. 1 above) bears a striking resemblance to harpoon-points of bone which are in use, amongst other places, in Tierra del Fuego, and which are also known from the Stone Age in Europe. This proves how the same implements may be developed quite independently in different places.

Probable mode of using the harpoon-points from Kjelmö

CHAPTER VI

It is curious that among the same people such different forms of harpoon-points should be found, from the most primitive to more ingenious ones. This may tend to show that their sealing culture was not so old as to have acquired fixed and definite forms like that of the Eskimo.

It is remarkable that by far the greater number of harpoon-points were made entirely of reindeer-horn, without any iron tip. Only on two of them (see Fig. 2, p. 214) are there marks of such a tip, which was let in round the fore-end, but which has rusted completely away. There is nowhere a sign of the use of any blade of iron (or stone), such as is used by the Eskimo. All these harpoon-points were made fast to a thong by deep notches at the base, or by a hole; and they have either a tang at the base which was stuck into a hole in the end of the harpoon-shaft, or else they have a hole or a groove at the base, which was surrounded by an iron ring, and into which a tang at the end of the shaft was inserted. As no piece of reindeer-horn or bone has been found which might serve as a tang for fixing the harpoon-points, it is possible that these were fastened directly on to the wooden shaft. With the help of the thong, which was probably made tightly fast (on a catch ?) to the upper part of the shaft, the point was held in its place. But when the harpoon was cast into the animal, the point remained fixed in its flesh and came away from the shaft, which became loose, and the animal was caught by the thong, the end of which was either made fast to the boat or held by the hunter; for it is improbable that it was made fast to a buoy or bladder, which is an invention peculiar to the Eskimo. All the harpoons found at Kjelmö are remarkably small, and cannot have been used for any animal larger than a seal. Among the objects found there is only one piece cut off a walrus-tusk, and none of the implements were made of this material, except, perhaps, one arrow-head. The explanation of this cannot be merely that the walrus was not common in the neighbourhood of Kjelmö; it shows rather that these Finns did not practise walrus-hunting at all; for if they had

FINNS AND SKRIDFINNS

done so, we should expect their weapons and implements to be made to a large extent of walrus-tusk, which has advantages over reindeer-horn.

Whether the harpoons, which we know to have been used later by the Norsemen, resembled those from Kjelmö, and whether they learned the use of them from the Finns, or the Finns had them from the Norsemen, are points on which it is difficult to form an opinion. Nothing has been found which might afford us information as to the kind of boats these northern sealers used. It is possible that they were light wooden boats, somewhat like the Lapps' river-boats, and that they used paddles. Nor do the Kjelmö finds tell us whether these people kept tame reindeer. It is true that bones of dogs have been found, like the modern Lapp-hound; but whether they were used for herding reindeer cannot be determined, nor can they have been common on the island, since otherwise the animal bones would have shown marks of having been gnawed by dogs.

The masses of bones found show that the people lived on fish to a great extent, many kinds of birds, among them the great auk (Alca impennis), reindeer, fjord-seal (Phoca vitulina), the saddleback seal (Ph. grœnlandica), grey-seal (Halichœrus grypus),[1] porpoise, beaver, etc.

It will be seen that everything we learn from this find agrees in a remarkable way with the statements of Ottar, with the single exception that there are no indications of walrus-hunting, beyond the one piece of tusk mentioned.[2]

As has been said, this sealing of the Finns must be regarded as a locally developed culture, which was not diffused farther east than Ter or the Kola peninsula. But with their reindeer-keeping the opposite is the case; this has its greatest predominance in Asia and north-eastern Europe, and

---

[1] Curiously enough, no bones of the great bearded seal (Phoca barbata) are mentioned; but its absence may perhaps be accidental.

[2] In a grave in North Varanger some fragments were found, probably of walrus-tusk [cf. Solberg, 1909, p. 93].

IN NORTHERN MISTS

CHAPTER VI

Ottar's "Finns"

is specially associated with the Samoyeds. It seems, therefore, most probable that it was brought to north Scandinavia from the east.

If, then, Ottar's description of his Finns' and Terfinns' diffusion towards the east (as well as the description in Egil's Saga) tallies almost exactly with the diffusion of the Fishing Lapps and Reindeer Lapps of our time, and if what he tells us of the Finns' manner of life agrees in all essentials with what we know of the life of the Lapps long after that time, down to the sixteenth and seventeenth centuries, then this in itself points to Ottar's "Finns" having been essentially the same people as the present-day Lapps. But to this may be added the statement of Ottar, who must have known the Finns and their language well: that they and the Beormas spoke approximately the same language. Since, then, the Lapps of our time—who live in the same district as Ottar's Finns—and the East Karelians—who live in the same district, on the western side of the White Sea, as Ottar's Beormas—speak closely related languages, and since, further, the Karelians are a people with fixed habitation like the Beormas, then it will be more natural to suppose that they are the same two peoples who lived in these districts at that early time, instead of proposing, like Dr. A. M. Hansen, to replace them both by an unknown people, who spoke an unknown language.[1]

[1] Professor G. Storm [1894, s. 97] and others have thought that the Karelian-Finnish name "Kantalaksi" ("Kandalaks") and "Kantalahti" for the north-western bay of the White Sea, and the town at its inner end, may be a corrupted translation of the Norwegian name "Gandvik" for the White Sea, as "kanta" ("kanda") might be the Finnish-Karelian pronunciation of the Norwegian "gand," and the Finnish-Karelian "lahti" or "laksi" has the same meaning as the Norwegian "vik" (bay). Dr. Hansen, considering this explanation probable, takes it as proof that the Karelians must have come to the region later than the Norwegians, and later than the Beormas of Ottar's time. But if the Karelians had immigrated thither after the Norwegians had given it this name, it would be equally incomprehensible that they should not have taken their place-names from the settled Beormas instead of from the casually visiting Norwegians. Storm's explanation of the name "Kandalaks" is, however,

FINNS AND SKRIDFINNS

The correctness of this hypothesis is also supported, as we have seen, by the rich Kjelmö find, which shows that in Ottar's time there was in the Varanger Fjord a well-developed sealing culture, to which we know no parallel from finds farther south, and which both in date and characteristics is distinct from the Arctic Stone Age. Through grave-finds in North Varanger, belonging to later centuries, we have, as Solberg shows [1909], a possible transition from the Kjelmö culture to that of the Lapps of our own time, and there is thus a connected sequence.

In old heathen burial-places on the islands of Sjåholmen and Sandholmen, in the Varanger Fjord, Herr Nordvi found a number of skulls and portions of skeletons, which probably belonged to the same people as the dwellers on Kjelmö. Some of these skulls are in the collection of the Anatomical Institute at Christiania, and have been described by Professor J. Heiberg [1878]. They are brachycephalic with a cephalic index between 82 and 85 ; one was mesocephalic with an index of 78. Dr. O. Solberg has also found a few such skulls. Time has not

CHAPTER VI

Ancient Lappish skulls

---

in my opinion highly improbable ; the casually visiting Norwegians cannot possibly have given the settled Beormas or Karelians the name of their own home. It is then, according to my view, much more probable that the Norwegian " Gandvik " is some kind of " popular etymological " translation of " Kantalaksi," which must then be a name of Finnish-Karelian origin. I have asked Professor Konrad Nielsen, of Christiania, about this, and he has also discussed the question with Professor E. Setàla and Professor Wichmann, of Helsingfors. All three are of my opinion. The meaning of " Kantalaksi " (or " Kannanlaksi," from an older word " Kanðanlaksi," where the first part is genitive) seems to Nielsen to be quite certain : " kanta " (genitive, " kannan ") is heel, basis. The name should, according to Setàla, be translated, " the broad bay." The Norwegians must consequently have corrupted the first part of the name in a " popular etymological " manner to their " gand " (which means sorcery), and the latter part of the name they have translated by " vik " (bay). The name " Gandvik " may already have been known in Norway in the tenth century, as it is mentioned by the heathen skald, Eilif Gudrunsson, in Thorsdrápa. This seems to prove that the Beormas of the tenth century (and then evidently also of Ottar's time) were Karelians, using the Karelian name " Kantalaksi " for the White Sea. This name consequently leads to conclusions contrary to those of Dr. Hansen, and it goes against the correctness of his views.

permitted me to subject these heathen skulls at the Anatomical Institute to a detailed examination; I have only made a purely preliminary comparison between them and half a dozen skulls of modern Reindeer Lapps and Skolte-Lapps, and found that in certain features they differ somewhat from the latter. Doubtless the Lapps and Skolte-Lapps of our time are very mixed, partly with the Finns (Kvæns) and partly with Norwegians and others; but the typical Reindeer Lapp skulls are nevertheless quite characteristic, and as they are somewhat more brachycephalic than the skulls from the heathen graves, it is difficult to suppose that this is due to any such recent mixture of race. As possible differences the following may be noted: the heathen skulls as compared with the Reindeer Lapp skulls are not quite so typically brachycephalic; seen from the side they are somewhat lower (i.e., the length-height index is less, according to Heiberg's measurements it would be about as 77 to 86); the forehead recedes somewhat more from the brow-ridges, which are more prominent than in the typical Reindeer Lapp skulls. The Skolte-Lapp skulls examined were of more mixed race, and were more mesocephalic; but they bore most resemblance to the Reindeer Lapp skulls, although some of them also showed a transition to the heathen skulls. According to this it does not look as though the heathens to whom these graves belonged can be accepted offhand as the ancestors of our Reindeer Lapps. They may have been an earlier, kindred race who, to judge by Ottar's statements, spoke a similar language, closely related to Karelian. The Reindeer Lapps must in that case have immigrated later.

It remains to examine what place-names can tell us. It is remarkable, as Qvigstad [1893, p. 56 f.] has pointed out, that while the Lapps have genuine Lappish names for the inner fjord coasts—e.g., Varanger, Tana, Lakse, Porsanger, and Alten fjords—all their place-names for the outer sea-coasts, even in Finmark, are of Norwegian origin, if we except the names of a few large islands, such as "Sallam," for

FINNS AND SKRIDFINNS

Sörö in West Finmark and for Skogerö in Varanger, and "Sievjo," for Seiland in West Finmark. It would therefore seem as though the Norwegians arrived on the outer coasts before either the Fishing Lapps or Reindeer Lapps, while the latter came first to the inner fjord coasts. This conclusion may be supported by the fact that the Lapps' names for sea-fish and sea-birds are throughout loan-words from Norwegian, as also are their words for appliances belonging to modern boats and sailing, which may indicate that they learned fishing and navigation from the Norwegians. Their name for walrus has probably also originally come from Norwegian, but on the other hand, the names of river fish, and their numerous names for seals, are as a rule genuine Lappish [Qvigstad, 1893, p. 67]. This conclusion, however, does not agree with Ottar's description, which distinctly says that "Finns," who were hunters and fishermen, lived scattered along the coasts of Finmark and the Kola peninsula, while the Norwegians (i.e., Norwegian chiefs) did not live farther north than himself, and did not practise whaling farther north than, probably, about Loppen. Dr. Hansen therefore thought to find in this a support for his theory, that the "Finns" of that time, whom he called Skridfinns, were a non-Aryan primitive people entirely distinct from the Reindeer Lapps of our day. But this bold hypothesis is little adapted to solve the difficulties with which we are here confronted. Thus, in order to explain the Lappish loan-words from Norwegian, one is obliged to assume that these Skridfinnish ancestors of the Fishing Lapps first lost their own language and their own place-names and words for the implements they used and the animals they hunted, etc., and adopted the Norwegian language entirely; and then again lost this language and adopted that of the later immigrant Reindeer Lapps, who chiefly lived in the mountainous districts of the interior. At this later change of language, however, they retained a number of Norwegian words, especially those used in navigation and place-names; but strangely enough they acquired new, genuinely Lappish names for certain large islands, and moreover they adopted the many names for seals, which were the most important object of their fishery, from the nomadic Reindeer Lapps, who previously had known nothing about such things. The question arises of itself: but if these Skridfinns were capable of undergoing all these remarkable linguistic revolutions, why may they not just as well have begun by speaking a language resembling Lappish, and gradually adopted their loan-words and place-names from Norwegian ? This will be a simpler explanation. Nor, as we have seen, is Dr. Hansen's assumption probable, that the Beormas also belonged to these same Skridfinns, and spoke their language, while they were not replaced by the Karelians until later ;[1] but still less so is the hypothesis which is thereby forced upon us, that the Reindeer Lapps came as reindeer nomads from the district east of the White Sea, and learned their language, allied to Karelian, through coming in contact with the Karelians on their journey westward round the south of the White Sea. This contact cannot have lasted very long, as the country on the south side of the White Sea is not particularly favourable to reindeer nomads. And if in so short a time they lost their old language and adopted an entirely new one, it will seem strange that they have been able to keep this new language comparatively unchanged through their later contact with the Norwegians, to whom moreover they were in a position of subjection. In any case it must be considerably less improbable that an original people of hunters, established in Finmark, who from the beginning spoke Karelian-Lappish, should have adopted loan-

---

[1] Dr. Hansen seeks to explain the difficulty that the Beormas near the Dvina, according to the name of the goddess "Jomale" in the tale of Tore Hund's journey to Beormaland, must have spoken Karelian, by supposing that the Beormas on the Dvina and those on the Gulf of Kandalaks were two entirely different peoples, although in the old narratives no support for such an assertion is to be found. Besides, we have above found evidence that the Beormas at Kandalaks also spoke Karelian, because this name is a Karelian word, which was used already in the tenth century.

FINNS AND SKRIDFINNS

words and place-names from the later immigrant and settled Norwegians, to whom they were subject, and who were skilled sailors with better seagoing boats. In more or less adopting the Norwegians' methods of navigation and fishery, with better appliances, they also acquired many loan-words from them. But on the whole we must not attach too much weight to such linguistic evidence, when we see that the Lapps have such a great quantity of loan-words from other languages.

To sum up what has been said here, the following explanation may be the most natural: in prehistoric times the coasts and inland districts of north Scandinavia and the Kola peninsula were inhabited by a wandering people of hunters, who belonged to the same race or family as the Fishing and Reindeer Lapps, and who were thus related to the Samoyeds farther east; but through long contact with the Karelians on the White Sea and with the Kvæns they had acquired a Karelian-Finnish language. Their language, however, as Konrad Nielsen has shown, contains also many words which resemble Samoyed, whether this be due to original kinship or to later influence. These people were called by the Norsemen Finns, or, to distinguish them from the other sort of Finns farther south, Skridfinns, because they were in the habit of travelling on ski in the winter. People of this race of hunters learned the domestication of reindeer from contact with reindeer nomads, the Samoyeds, farther east. Most of them continued their life of hunting, sealing and fishing, but adopted reindeer-keeping to some extent as an auxiliary means of subsistence. The Eskimo are a good example of how, in northern regions, a wandering people of hunters may have a fairly uniform culture and language throughout a much greater extent of territory than is here in question; for they have essentially the same culture and language from west of Bering Strait to the east coast of Greenland. A tribe related to these hunter Finns, who spoke very nearly the same language but lived farther east, where there was certainly hunting to be had on land but little at sea, gradually became transformed entirely into reindeer nomads, and diffused themselves at a comparatively late period over the mountainous tracts westward, and along the Kjölen range southward. As the Norsemen pressed northward along the coast of Nordland they encountered the hunter Finns or Fishing Lapps. Through this contact with a higher culture these Lapps learned much, but on the other hand the Norsemen learned something from their sealing and hunting culture, which was well adapted to these surroundings. Thus a higher development of sea-hunting arose. Originally the Lapps had a light boat, the planks of which were fastened together with osiers, with a paddle, which was well adapted to sea-fishing, and for which they still have a genuine Lappish word in their language. From the Norsemen they learned to build larger boats and to use sails, whence most of their words for the new kind of navigation were Norse loan-words. We see from Peder Claussön Friis's description that in the sixteenth century the Fishing Lapps even "had much profit of their shipbuilding, since they are good carpenters, and build all the sloops and ships for the northward voyage themselves at their own cost and to a considerable amount. . . . They also build many boats. . . . " In other words, we see that they had completely adopted the Norwegians' boat- and ship-building, and with it the words connected therewith. In the same way they certainly acquired better appliances for sea-fishing than those they originally had; consequently in this too they learned of the Norwegians, and it was therefore natural that they gradually adopted Norse names for sea-fish too, even if they had names for them before; besides which they were always selling this fish to the Norwegians. It was otherwise, however, with sealing, which had previously been their chief employment on the sea. In this they were superior to the Norsemen, as the implements of the Kjelmö find show, and here the Norsemen became their pupils. For this reason then they kept their own names for seal, and the many genuine

FINNS AND SKRIDFINNS

Lappish words they have for them prove that this was an important part of their original culture. If we should imagine that the Lappish language came in at a comparatively late period with the Reindeer Lapps, as Dr. Hansen thinks, we should be faced by incomparably greater difficulties in explaining how they acquired these many genuine Lappish words for seal, than would confront us in explaining how they got loan-words for reindeer-keeping from the Norwegians, or how the original Fishing Lapps took Norse loan-words for sea-fishing and the use of boats. And now as regards place-names, it is not improbable that these were determined for later times principally by the permanent settlements of the Norsemen, along the outer sea-coast, and not by the scattered Finns (Lapps), who led a wandering life as hunters and fishermen, and who no doubt were driven out by the Norsemen. If we suppose that these Finns were kept away from a place, a fishing-centre or a district, by the Norwegian settlement, it would only require the passing of one or two generations for them to forget their old place-names, and in future they would use those of the Norwegians settled there. But that they once had names of their own is shown by the genuine Lappish names for some of the larger islands. Within the fjords, where the Norwegians were late in establishing themselves, and where the Finns (Lapps) could live with less interference, it was different, and there they kept their own names.

We do not seem therefore to have any information or fact which is capable of disproving the unbroken connection between Ottar's Finns, along the coasts of Finmark and Ter, and the Fishing Lapps of our time, although the latter at present consist to a large extent of impoverished Reindeer Lapps, especially in West Finmark. The original culture of the Fishing Lapps and the distinction between it and that of the Reindeer Lapps who immigrated later have been preserved to recent times in their broader features. It is true that the Fishing Lapp no longer keeps reindeer; he only has a poor cow

IN NORTHERN MISTS

CHAPTER VI

or a few sheep to milk [cf. A. Helland, 1905, p. 147]; but amongst other descriptions we see from that of the Italian Francesco Negri of his travels in Norway in 1664-5 [L. Daae, 1888, p. 143] that the Fishing Lapps of Nordland and Finmark still kept reindeer in the latter part of the seventeenth century. He says of the Finns [i.e., Fishing Lapps] in Finmark that

> "they live either along the coast or in the forests of the interior. They are, like their neighbours the Lapps, small in stature, and they resemble them in face, clothing, customs and language. The only way in which they differ from the Lapps is, that the latter are nomads, while the Finns of this part have fixed dwellings. They possess only a few reindeer and a little cattle. They are also called Sea Lapps, while the other nomads are called Mountain Lapps. . . ."

Fishing Lapps and Reindeer Lapps

This distinction between Finns (i.e., Fishing Lapps) and Lapps (i.e., Reindeer Lapps) seems to have been common. Thus in the royal decree of September 27, 1726, both Finns and Lapps are mentioned, and in mediæval maps of the fifteenth century, beginning with that of Claudius Clavus, of about 1426, we find on the Arctic Ocean in north-east Sweden "Findhlappi," and farther north "Wildhlappelandi," and in later Clavus maps [Nordenskiold, 1889, Pl. xxx.] we find to the north-east of Norway a "Finlappelanth," and farther north an extensive "Pillappelanth," sometimes also "Phillappelanth," besides a "Finlanth" in the east. Pillappelanth is the same as Claudius Clavus's "Wildlappenland."[1] This word may be thought to have arisen through a misunderstanding of the word "Fjeldlap" (Mountain Lapp), which Clavus may have seen written as Viellappen and taken to mean Wild Lapp (he calls them "Wildlappmanni"). But, as Mr. Qvigstad has pointed out to me, the name "Wild Lapps" for Mountain (Reindeer) Lapps is also found in Russian. Giles Fletcher (English Ambassador to Russia in 1588) writes:[2]

---

[1] Cf. Bjornbo and Petersen, 1904, p. 178. In Michel Beheim's travels in Norway in 1450 "Wild lapen" are also mentioned, cf. Vangensten, 1908, pp 17, 30 f.

[2] Hakluyt: "The Principal Navigations, etc." (1903), iii. p. 404.

FINNS AND SKRIDFINNS

"The Russe divideth the whole nation of the Lappes into two sortes. The one they call 'Nowremanskoy Lapary,' that is, the Norvegian Lappes. ... The other that have no religion at all but live as bruite and heathenish people, without God in the worlde they cal 'Dikoy Lapary,' or the wilde Lappes."

CHAPTER VI

There is, however, a possibility that this Russian name may have come from the maps or in a literary way. In any case we have as early as the fifteenth century a distinction between Finnlapps (i.e., Fishing Lapps) and Mountain Lapps or Wild Lapps, besides Finns in Finland; but this shows at the same time that they must have been nearly akin, since both are called Lapps.

Of great interest is Peder Claussön Friis's description of the Lapps, which is derived from the Helgelander, Judge Jon Simonssön (ob. 1575). He draws a distinction between "Sea Finns," who live on the fjords, and "Lappe-Finns" or "Mountain Finns," "who roam about the great mountains,"

"and both sorts are also called 'Gann-Finns' on account of the magic they use, which they call 'Gan.'" "The Finns [i.e., Lapps] are a thin and skinny folk, and yet much stronger than other men, as can be proved by their bows, which a Norse Man cannot draw half so far as the Finns can. They are very black and brown on their bodies, and are hasty and evil-tempered folk, as though they had the nature of bears."

"The Sea Finns dwell always on Fjords, where there is sufficient fir and spruce, so that they may have firing and timber to build ships of, and they live in small houses or huts, of which the half is in the ground, albeit some have fine houses and rooms. ... They also row out to fish like other Northern sailors, and sell their fish to the merchants, who come there, for they do not sail to Bergen, and they are not fond of going where there are many people, nor do people wish to have them there, and they apply themselves greatly to shooting seal and porpoise, that they may get their oil, for every Finn must have a quart of oil to drink at every meal. . . ."

"They keep many tame reindeer, from which they have milk, butter, and cheese . . . they also keep goats, but no sheep.

"They shoot both elks and stags and hinds, but for the most part reindeer, which are there in abundance; and when one of them will shoot reindeer, he holds his bow and arrow between the horns of a tame reindeer, and shoots thus one after another, for it is a foolish beast that cannot take care of itself."

"The Finns are remarkably good archers, but only with handbows, for which they have good sharp arrows, for they are themselves smiths, and they shoot

CHAPTER VI

so keenly with the same bows that they can shoot with them great bears and reindeer and what they will. Moreover they can shoot so straight that it is a marvel, and they hold it a shame at any time to miss their mark, and they accustom themselves to it from childhood, so that the young Finn may not have his breakfast until he has shot three times in succession through a hole made by an auger.

"They are called Gann-Finns for the witchcraft they use, which they call 'Gann,' and thence the sea or great fjord which is between Russia and Finmark, and stretches to Karelestrand, is called Gandvig.

"They are small people and are very hairy on their bodies, and have a bear's nature. . . ."

"The Sea Finns can for the most part speak the Norse language, but not very well. . . . And they have also their own language which they use among themselves and with the Lapps, which Norse Men cannot understand, and it is said that they have more languages than one; of their languages they have however another to use among themselves which some[1] can understand, so it is certain that they have nine languages, all of which they use among themselves."[2]

Skridfinn Archer (from Olaus Magnus)

---

[1] Gustav Storm [1881, p. 407] altered "some" to "none," evidently thinking it would make better sense of this obscure passage; following him therefore Magnus Olsen, J. Qvigstad and A. M. Hansen have recently discussed the passage as though it read: "which none can understand." It appears to me that "which some [i.e., a few] can understand" gives clearer sense.

[2] This passage seems somewhat confused and it is difficult to find a logical connection in it. The first part is simple; most of the Sea Finns (Fishing Lapps) speak Norwegian, but badly. Among themselves and with the Mountain Finns (Reindeer Lapps) they do not use this, but their own language. The language of the latter people must consequently have been the same, unless we are to make the improbable assumption that the Fishing Lapps had a language different from that of the Reindeer Lapps, which the latter however had learned, although they are still in our time very bad linguists, and speak imperfect Norwegian. So far there cannot be much doubt of the meaning, but it is different when we come to the statement that they had more languages than one, and that of "their languages they have however another to use among themselves." It seems to me that the certain examples

FINNS AND SKRIDFINNS

"Of the Mountain Finns the same is to be understood as has now been noted of the Sea Finns; the others [i.e., the former] are small, hairy folk and evil, they have no houses and do not dwell in any place, but move from one place to another, where they may find some game to shoot.[1] They do not eat bread, nor do the Sea Finns either. . . . And he [the Mountain Finn] has tame reindeer and a sledge, which is like a low boat with a keel upon it. . . ."

CHAPTER VI

From this description it appears with all desirable clearness that, on the one hand, there was no noticeable external difference in the sixteenth century between the small Fishing Lapps and the small Reindeer Lapps, and on the other there was no essential difference between the Lapps of that time and the Finns described by Ottar—we even find the decoy reindeer still used in the sixteenth century; further, that the Lapps were unusually skilful hunters and archers, for which they were

mentioned by Qvigstad [1909] of the Lapps having been in the habit of inventing jargons at the beginning of the eighteenth century give a natural explanation of this passage [cf. also Magnus Olsen, 1909]. A. M. Hansen's interpretation [1907 and 1909], that the original mother-tongue of the Fishing Lapps (called by him "Skridfinnish"), which was quite different from that which they spoke with the Reindeer Lapps, is here meant, cannot be reconciled with the words of the text, for in that case they must have had two mother-tongues; it is expressly said that the second language was "their own," which they spoke among themselves; if it was only the language of the Reindeer Lapps, then it was precisely *not* their own, nor would they have any reason to speak it among themselves. I understand the passage thus: "of their [own] language they have also another [i.e., another form, variant, or jargon] to use among themselves, which [only] some [of them] can understand." But how it should result from this that "it is certain that they have nine languages" is difficult to explain; for even if we assume with Hansen that nine is an error for three, it does not improve matters, for in any case they did not use all three languages, including Norwegian, "among themselves." It is probable enough, as indeed both Hansen and Magnus Olsen have assumed, that there is a reference here to the magic arts of the Lapps; and we must then suppose that this mention of the nine languages was an expression commonly understood at the time, which did not require further explanation, to be compared with the nine tongue-roots of the poisonous serpent [cf. M. Olsen, 1909, p. 91]. Nine was a sacred number in heathen times, cf. Adam of Bremen's tale of the festivals of the gods every ninth year at Upsala, where nine males of every living thing were offered, etc. Thietmar of Merseburg mentions the sacrificial festival which was held every ninth year at midwinter at Leire, etc.

[1] Remark the resemblance between this passage and the mention of the Lapps in the "Historia Norvegiæ" (above, p. 204).

IN NORTHERN MISTS

CHAPTER VI

also praised by earlier authorities (we read in many places of Finn-bows, Finn-arrows, etc. Some thought that the man who at the battle of Svolder shot and hit Einar Tambarskelve's bow so that it broke, was a Lapp). We see too that the Reindeer Lapp was not exclusively a reindeer nomad, but practised hunting to such an extent that he moved about for the sake of game, and it even looks as if this was his chief means of livelihood, which is therefore mentioned first. That the reindeer-keeping mentioned by Ottar should have been so essentially different from that of the present day, as A. M. Hansen asserts, is difficult to see. That the decoy reindeer which Ottar tells us were used for catching wild reindeer, and which were so valuable, are no longer to be found in our day is a matter of course, simply because the wild reindeer in northern Scandinavia has practically disappeared from the districts frequented by the Lapps with their tame reindeer. Furthermore, with the introduction of firearms decoy reindeer became less necessary for getting within range of the wild ones; but we see that they were still used in the sixteenth century, when the Lapps continued to shoot with the bow. So long as there was abundance of game, before the introduction of the rifle, the Reindeer Lapp also lived, as we have seen, to a large extent by hunting; but then he was not able to look after large herds of reindeer. It is therefore probable that a herd of 600 deer, as mentioned by Ottar, must then have been regarded as constituting wealth, although to the Reindeer Lapps of the present day, who live exclusively by keeping reindeer, it would be nothing very great.[1]

[1] Ottar's statement that he owned 600 reindeer is, as pointed out by O. Solberg [1909, p. 127], evidence against the correctness of A. M Hansen's assumption that the Finns mentioned by Ottar had learned to keep reindeer by imitating the Norwegian's cattle-keeping, and that they kept their reindeer on the mountain pastures in summer, but collected them together for driving home in winter; it would have been a difficult matter to manage several hundred reindeer in this fashion, unless they were divided up into so many small herds that we cannot suppose them all to have been the property of one man. Large herds of many deer must have been half wild and have been kept in a similar way to the Reindeer Lapps' reindeer now.

FINNS AND SKRIDFINNS

Those of the modern Lapps whose manner of life most reminds us of Ottar's "Finns" are perhaps the so-called Skolte-Lapps on the south side of the Varanger Fjord. Helland [1905, p. 157] says of them: "They have few reindeer and keep them not so much for their flesh and milk as for transport. Their principal means of subsistence is salmon and trout fishing in the river, and a little sea-fishing in the fjord on Norwegian ground. They are also hunters."

We must suppose that the "Finns" who according to Ottar, or to Alfred's version of him, paid tribute in walrus-hide ropes, etc., lived by the sea and engaged in sealing and walrus-hunting, and in any case they cannot have kept reindeer except as a subsidiary means of subsistence, like the Fishing Lapps in the sixteenth and seventeenth centuries. But Alfred's expressions do not exclude the possibility of there having been amongst the "Finns" some who were reindeer nomads like the Reindeer Lapps of our time. That they already existed at that time and somewhat later seems to result from the statements in the sagas of the sheriffs of Hálogaland (e.g., Thorulf Kveldulfsson), who in order to collect the "Finn" tribute travelled into the interior and up into the mountains. It cannot have been only wandering hunters who paid this tribute, and they must certainly also have had herds of reindeer.

That the Lapps have degenerated greatly as hunters and sealers in the last few centuries, and that the Fishing Lapps no longer enjoy anything like the same prosperity as they did in Ottar's time, and even as late as the seventeenth century, is easily explained. For on the one hand the game both in the sea and on land has decreased to such an extent that it can no longer support any one, and on the other it is a well-known fact that a people originally of hunters loses its skill in the chase to a considerable extent through closer contact with European civilisation, while at the same time it becomes impoverished. How this comes about may be accurately observed among the Eskimo of Greenland in our time. So

CHAPTER VI

Decline of hunting

long as the Lapps were heathens, as in Peder Claussön Friis's time, and were still without firearms and, what is perhaps equally important, without fire-water, and not burdened with schooling and book-learning, they retained their old hunting culture and their hereditary skill in sealing and hunting; but with the new culture and its claims, the new objects, demands and temptations of life, their old accomplishments suffered more or less; nor were they any longer held in such high esteem that the Lapp child had to shoot three times running through an auger-hole before he might have his breakfast. And just as the Eskimo of the west coast of Greenland have been obliged to take more and more to fishing and bird-catching, which were looked down upon by the old harpooners, so have our Fishing Lapps become more and more exclusively fishermen.

Snæfells Glacier in Iceland

CHAPTER VII

THE VOYAGES OF THE NORSEMEN: DISCOVERY OF ICELAND AND GREENLAND

SHIPBUILDING

THE discovery of the Faroes and Iceland by the Celts and the Irish monks, and their settlement there, give evidence of a high degree of intrepidity; since their fragile boats were not adapted to long voyages in the open sea, to say nothing of carrying cargoes and keeping up any regular communication. Nor did they, in fact, make any further progress; and neither the Irish nor the Celts of the British Isles as a whole ever became a seafaring people. It was the Scandinavians, and especially the Norwegians, who were the pioneers at sea; who developed an improved style of shipbuilding, and who, with their comparatively good and seaworthy craft, were soon to traverse all the northern waters and open up a prospect into a new world, whereby the geographical ideas of the times should undergo a complete transformation. It has been asserted that the Phœnicians in their day ventured out into the open ocean far from land; ut this lacks proof and is improbable. The Norwegians are

IN NORTHERN MISTS

CHAPTER VII

The First Viking Expeditions

the first people in history who definitely abandoned the coast-sailing universally practised before their time, and who took navigation away from the coasts and out on to the ocean. From them other people have since learnt.

First they crossed the North Sea and sailed constantly to Shetland, the Orkneys, North Britain and Ireland; then to the Faroes, Iceland and Greenland, and at last they steered straight across the Atlantic itself, and thereby discovered North America. We do not know how early the passage of the North Sea originated; but probably, as we have seen, it was before the time of Pytheas and much earlier than usually supposed. J. E. Sars [1877, i. (2nd ed.), p. 191] concluded on other grounds that it was at a very remote period, and long before the Viking age.

The beginning of the more important Viking expeditions is usually referred to the end of the eighth century, or, indeed, to a particular year, 793. But we may conclude from historical sources [1] that as early as the sixth century Viking voyages certainly took place over the North Sea from Denmark to the land of the Franks, and doubtless also to southern Britain,[2] and perhaps by the beginning of the seventh century the Norwegians had established themselves in Shetland and even plundered the Hebrides and the north-west of Ireland (in 612).[3] We know further from historical sources that as

---

[1] Gregory of Tours; "Gesta Francorum"; the Anglo-Saxon poems "Beowulf" and "Widsið," etc

[2] Zeuss, 1837, p. 501; Mullenhoff, 1889, pp. 18 f, 95 f.; A. Bugge, 1905, pp 10 f.

[3] Cf. H. Zimmer [1891, 1893, p. 223] and A. Bugge [1905, pp. 11 f.]. In a life of St. Gildas, on an island off the Welsh coast ["Vita Gildæ, auctore Carodoco Lancarbanensi," p. 109], we read that he was plundered by pirates from the Orcades islands, who must be supposed to have been Norwegian Vikings. This is said to have taken place in the sixth century, but the MS. dates from the twelfth. The island of Sark, east of Guernsey, was laid waste by the Normans, according to the "Miracula Sancti Maglorii," cap. 5. [A. de la Borderie, "Histoire de Bretagne," Critique des Sources, iii. 13, p. 236.] This part of the "Miracula" was composed, according to Borderie, before 851, but even in the saint's lifetime (sixth century) the "Miracula" places an attack by

THE VOYAGES OF THE NORSEMEN

early as the third century and until the close of the fifth century the roving Eruli sailed from Scandinavia, sometimes in company with Saxon pirates, over the seas of Western Europe, ravaging the coasts of Gaul and Spain, and indeed penetrating in 455 into the Mediterranean as far as Lucca in Italy.[1] From these historical facts we are able to conclude that long before that time there had been intercommunication by sea between the countries of Northern Europe. Scandinavia, and especially Norway, was in those days very sparsely inhabited, and all development of culture that was not due to direct influence from without must have taken place with extreme slowness at such an early period of history, even where intercourse was more active than in the North. As we are not acquainted with any other European people who at that time possessed anything like the necessary skill in navigation to have been the instructors of the Scandinavians, we are forced to suppose that it was after centuries of gradual training and development in seamanship that the latter attained the superiority at sea which they held at the beginning of the Viking age, when they took large fleets over the North Sea and the Arctic Ocean as though these were their home waters. When we further consider how, since that time, the type of ships, rigging and sails has persisted almost without a change for eleven hundred years, to the ten-oared and eight-oared boats of our own day—which until a few years ago were the almost universal form of boat in the whole of northern Norway—it will appear improbable that the type of ship and the corresponding skill in seamanship required a much shorter time for their development.[2]

CHAPTER VII

Earliest navigation of the Scandinavians

the "Normans" (cap. 2). It has been suggested [cf. Vogel, "Die Normannen und das Fränkische Reich," 1896, p. 353] that this might refer to Saxon pirates; but doubtless incorrectly.

[1] Cf. Zeuss, 1837, pp 477 f.; Mullenhoff, 1889, p. 19.

[2] What an enormous time such a development requires is demonstrated by the history of the rudder. The most ancient Egyptian boats were evidently steered by two big oars aft, one on each side. These oars were later, in Egyptian and Greek ships, transformed into two rudders or rudder oars,

IN NORTHERN MISTS

CHAPTER VII

The Ships of the rock-carvings

The first literary mention of the Scandinavians' boats occurs in Tacitus, who speaks of the fleets and rowing-boats without sails of the Suiones (see above, p. 110). But long before that time we find ships commonly represented on the rock-carvings which are especially frequent in Bohuslen and in the districts east of Christiania Fjord. If these were naturalistic representations they would give us valuable information about the form and size of the ships of those remote times. But the distinct and characteristic features which are common to all these pictures of ships, from Bohuslen to as far north as Beitstaden, show them to be conventional figures, and we cannot therefore draw any certain conclusions from them with regard to the appearance of the ships.

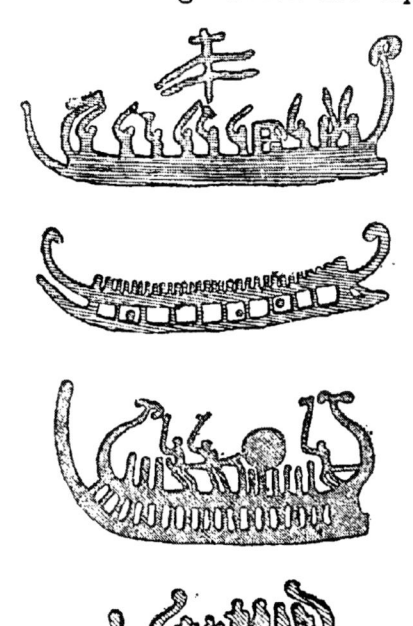

Rock-carvings in Bohuslen

Dr. Andr. M. Hansen [1908], with his usual imaginativeness, has pointed out the resemblance between the rock-carvings and the vase-paintings of the Dipylon period in Attica, and thinks there is a direct connection between them. It appears highly probable that the style of the rock-carvings is not a wholly native northern art, but is due more or less to influence from the countries of the Mediterranean or the East, in the same way as we have seen that the burial customs (dolmens, chambered barrows, etc.) came from these. Dr. Hansen has, however, exaggerated the resemblance between the Dipylon art and the rock-carvings; many of the resemblances are clearly due to the fact that the

---

one on each side aft (see illustrations, pp. 7, 23, 35, 48). On the Viking ships we find only one of these rudders on the starboard side, but fixed exactly in the same way. Then at last, towards the end of the Middle Ages, the rudder was moved to the stern-post. But the rudder of the boats of Northern Norway has still a "styrvold" (instead of an ordinary tiller), which is a remnant of the rudder of the Viking ships.

THE VOYAGES OF THE NORSEMEN

same subjects are represented (e.g., spear-throwing, fighting with raised weapons, rowers, horsemen, chariots, etc.); it may also be mentioned that such signs as the wheel or the solar symbol (the eye) are common to wide regions of culture. On the other hand, there are differences in other important features; thus, the mode of representing human beings is not the same, as asserted by Hansen; the characteristic "Egyptian" style of the men depicted in the Dipylon art, with broad, rectangular shoulders and narrow waists, is just what one does not find in the rock-carvings, where on the contrary men are depicted in the more naturalistic style which one recognises among many other peoples in a savage state of culture. Hansen also lays stress upon resemblances to figures from Italy. But what most interests us here is the number of representations of ships in the rock-carvings, which for the most part show a remarkable uniformity as regards their essential features, while they differ from all pictures of ships, not only in the art of the Dipylon and of the Mediterranean generally, but also in that of Egypt and Assyria-Babylonia. The boats or ships depicted in the rock-carvings are so strange-looking that doubts have been expressed whether they are boats or ships at all, or whether it is

CHAPTER VII

Rock-carving at Björnstad in Skjeberg, Smålenene. The length of the ship is nearly fifteen feet (from a photograph by Professor G. Gustafson)

not something else that is intended, sledges, for instance. There is no indication of the oars, which are so characteristic of all delineations of ships in Greece, Italy, Egypt and Assyria; nor is there any certain indication of sails or rudders, which are also characteristic of southern art. Moreover, the lowest line, which should answer to the keel, is often separated at both ends from the upper line, which should be the top strake. On the other hand the numerous figures in the "boats" can with difficulty be regarded as anything but men, and most probably rowers, sometimes as many as fifty in number, besides the unmistakable figures of men standing, some of them armed; and it must be added that if these pictures represented nothing but sledges, it is inconceivable that there should never be any indication of draught animals. But one remarkable point about these numerous carvings is the typical form both of the prow and of the stern-post. With comparatively few exceptions the prow has two turned-up beaks, which are difficult to understand. It has been attempted to explain one of these as an imitation of the rams of Greek and Phœnician warships; but in that case it ought to be directed forward and not bent up. The shape of the stern-post is also curious: for what one must regard as the keel of the ship has in all these representations a blunt after end, curiously like a sledge-runner; while the upper line of the ship, which should correspond to the top strake, is bent upward and frequently somewhat forward, in a more or less even curve, sometimes ending in a two- or three-leaved ornament, somewhat like the stern-post of Egyptian ships (see p. 23). This mode of delineation became so uniformly fixed that besides occurring in

IN NORTHERN MISTS

CHAPTER VII

almost all the rock-carvings it appears again in an even more carefully executed form in the knives of the later Bronze Age. Such a type of ship, with a keel ending bluntly aft, is not known in ancient times in Europe, either in the Mediterranean or in the North.[1] Egyptian, Assyro-Phœnician, Greek and Roman representations of ships (see pp. 7, 23, 35, 48, 241, 242), all show a keel which bends up to form a continuously curved stern-post; and both the Nydam boat from Sleswick (p. 110) and the Norwegian Viking ships that have been discovered agree in having a similar turned-up stern-post, which forms a continuous curve from the keel itself (pp. 246, 247); it is the same with delineations of the later Iron Age (p. 243). Even Tacitus expressly says that the ships of the Suiones were alike fore and aft. The only similar stern-posts to be found are possibly the abruptly ending ones of the ship and boats on the grave-stone from Novilara in Italy; but here the prows are quite unlike those of the rock-carvings.

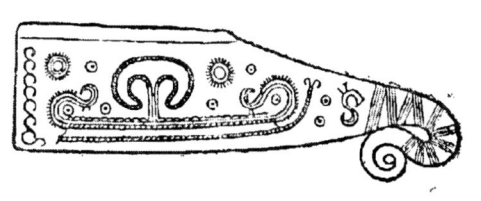

Bronze knife with representation of a ship, of the later Bronze Age. Denmark

As therefore this representation of the ship's stern-post does not correspond to any known type of ancient boat or ship, as it is also difficult to understand how the people of the rock-carvings came to represent a boat with two upturned prows, and as further there is a striking similarity between the lowest line of the keel and a sledge-runner, one might be tempted to believe that by an association of ideas these delineations have become a combination of ship and sledge. These rock-carvings may originally have been connected with burials, and the ship, which was to bear the dead, may have been imagined as gliding on the water, on ice, or through the air, to the realms of the departed, and thus unconsciously the keel may have been given the form of a runner. It may be mentioned as a parallel that in the "kennings" of the far later poetry of the Skalds a ship is called, for instance, the "ski" of the sea, or, vice versa, a ski or sledge may be called the ship of the snow. The sledge was moreover the earliest form of contrivance

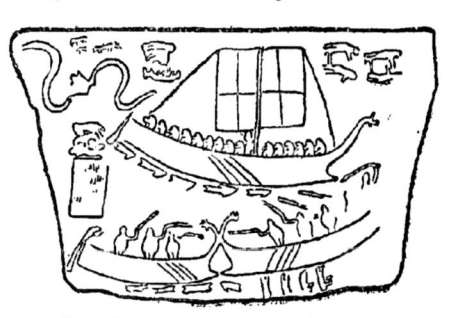

Carvings on a grave-stone at Novilara, Italy

---

[1] The types of Scandinavian craft it most reminds one of are the fjord and Nordland "jagt," in western and northern Norway, and the "pram," which is now in use in south-eastern Norway. It is conceivable that it represents an ancient boat type resembling the form of the "jagt."

THE VOYAGES OF THE NORSEMEN

for transport. In this connection there may also be a certain interest in the fact that in Egypt the mummies of royal personages were borne to the grave in funereal boats upon sledges. That the rock-carvings were originally associated with burials may also be indicated by the fact that the carved stones of the Iron Age, which in a way took the place of the rock-carvings, frequently represent the dead in boats on their way to the underworld or the world beyond the grave (see illustration, p. 243). That ships played a prominent part in connection with the dead appears also from the remarkable burial-places formed by stones set up in the form of a ship, the so-called ship-settings, in Sweden and the Baltic provinces, as well as in Denmark and North Germany. These belong to the early Iron Age. The usual burial in a ship covered by a mound, in the later Iron Age, is well known. We seem thus to be able to trace a certain continuity in these customs. A certain continuity even in the representation of ships may also be indicated by the striking resemblance that exists between the two- or three-leaved, lily-like prow ornament on the rock-carvings, on the knives of the later Bronze Age, on the grave-stone of Novilara, and on such late representations as some of the ships of the Bayeux tapestry. The upturned prows of the ships of the rock-carvings also frequently end in spirals like the stern-post on the stone at Stenkyrka in Gotland (p. 243), and both prows and stern on other stones of the later Iron Age from Gotland.

CHAPTER VII

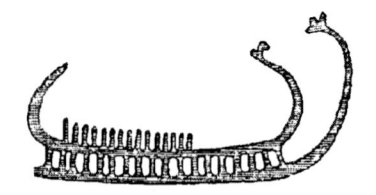

Ship from the Bayeux tapestry (eleventh century), and rock-carving

All are agreed in referring the rock-carvings to the Bronze Age; but while O. Montelius, for example, puts certain of them as early as between 1450 and 1250 B.C., A. M. Hansen has sought to bring them down to as late as 500 B.C. In any case they belong to a period that is long anterior to the beginning of history in the North. From whence and by what route this art came it is difficult to say. Along the same line of coasts by which the megalithic graves, dolmens and chambered barrows made their way from the Mediterranean to the North (see p. 22) rock-carvings are also to be found scattered through North Africa, Italy (the Alps), Southern France,

CHAPTER VII
Spain, Portugal, Brittany, England, Ireland and Scotland. It may be reasonable to suppose that this practice of engraving figures on stone came first from Egypt at the close of the Stone Age; but the rock-carvings of the west coast of Europe and of the British Isles are distinct in their whole character from those of Scandinavia, and do not contain representations of ships [1] and men, which are such prominent features of the latter; but common to both are the characteristic cup-markings, besides the wheel, or solar signs (with a cross), foot-soles, and also spirals. There may thus be a connection, but we must suppose that the rock-carvings underwent an independent development in Scandinavia (like the Bronze Age culture as a whole)—if it could not be explained by an eastern communication with the south through Russia, which however is not probable—and as the representation of ships came to be so common, we must conclude it to be here connected with a people of strong seafaring tendencies. Since the ships depicted on the rock-carvings cannot, so far as we know at present, have been direct imitations of delineations of ships derived from abroad—even though they may be connected with forms of religion and burial customs that were more or less imported—we are, as yet at least, bound to believe that the people who made the rock-carvings had boats or ships which furnished the models for their conventional representations. And when we see that these people went to work to engrave on the rocks pictures of ships which are fifteen feet in length, and have as many as fifty rowers,[2] we are bound to believe that in any case they were able to imagine ships of this size. It is also remarkable that rock-carvings are most numerous

[1] Professor Gustafson informed me that in the summer of 1909 he saw in a megalithic grave in Ireland a representation of a ship, which might have some resemblance to a Scandinavian rock-carving; but he regarded this as very uncertain.

[2] Professor G. Gustafson has in recent years examined and figured many Norwegian rock-carvings for the University of Christiania. The illustration reproduced here (p. 237) is from a photograph which he has kindly communicated to me.

THE VOYAGES OF THE NORSEMEN

precisely in those districts, Viken and Bohuslen, where we may expect that the seamanship of the Scandinavians first attained a higher degree of perfection if it was first imported from the south-east. With this would also agree Professor Montelius's theory : that at a very much earlier time, about the close of the Stone Age, direct communication already existed between the west coast of Sweden and Britain, which he concludes from remarkable points of correspondence in stone cists with a hole at the end, and other features.

CHAPTER VII

Shipment of tribute. From the bronze doors from Babavat, Assyria (British Museum)

It is difficult to say how the Scandinavians at the outset arrived at their boats and ships, such as we know them from the boats found at Nydam in Sleswick and the Viking ships discovered in Norwegian burial-mounds. They are of the same type that in Norway, in the districts of Sunnmör and Nordland, has persisted to our time, and they show a mastery both in their lines and in their workmanship that must have required a long period for its development. From the accounts of many contemporaries, as well as from archæological finds, we know that even so late as the first and second centuries A.D. large canoes, made of dug-out tree trunks, were in common use on the north coast of Germany between the Elbe and the Rhine, and there can be no doubt that this was the original form of boat in the north and west of Central Europe. In England similar canoes made of the dug-out trunks of oaks have been found with a length of as much as forty-eight feet ; they have also been found in Scotland, in Bremen and in Sleswick-

The earliest boats of Northern Europe

CHAPTER VII

Holstein (in many cases over thirty-eight feet long), with holes for oars. It is related of the Saxons north of the Elbe, who at an early period made piratical raids on coasts to the south of them, that they sailed in small boats made of wickerwork, with an oaken keel and covered with hides. Besides these they clearly had dug-out canoes; but in the third century A.D. it is recorded that they built ships on the Roman model. The only people north of the Mediterranean of whom we know with certainty that they had their own well-developed methods of shipbuilding are, as already mentioned (p. 39), the Veneti at the mouth of the Loire, whose powerful and seaworthy ships of oak are described by Cæsar. That the Scandinavians should have derived their methods from them cannot be regarded as probable, unless it can be proved that the intervening peoples possessed something more than primitive canoes and coracles. We must therefore believe, either that the Scandinavians developed their methods of shipbuilding quite independently, or that they had communication with the Mediterranean by some other route than the sea. Now in many important features there is such a great resemblance between the Norwegian Viking ships and pictorial representations of Greek ships, and of even earlier Egyptian and Assyrian ships, that it is difficult to avoid the conclusion that some connection must have existed. For instance, the resemblance between the strikingly lofty prows and stern-posts, sometimes bent back, with characteristic ornamentation, and animal heads, which are already to be found in Egyptian and Assyrian representations, cannot be explained offhand as coincidences occurring in types independently developed. They are decorations, and cannot have

Warship of Ramses III., circa 1200 B.C.

THE VOYAGES OF THE NORSEMEN

contributed to the seaworthiness of the boats or had any practical purpose, unless the animal heads were intended to frighten enemies (?). It is true that lofty and remarkable prows are to be found in boats from such a widely separated region of culture as Polynesia; but in the first place it is not impossible that here too there may be a distant connection with the Orient, and in the second, the Mediterranean and Scandinavian forms of ship are so characteristic, compared with those of other parts of the world, that we necessarily place them apart as belonging to a distinct sphere of culture. Another characteristic of these boats and ships is the oars with rowlocks (open or closed), instead of paddles. The rudder of the Viking ship (see illustrations, pp. 246, 247, 248, 250) is also in appearance and mode of use so remarkably like the Egyptian rudder of as early as circa 1600 B.C. (see illustrations, pp. 7, 23), and the Greek (p. 48),[1] that it is not easy to believe that this, together with all the other resemblances, were independent discoveries of the North. The square sail and mast of the Scandinavian boat also closely resemble those of Egyptian, Phœnician, Greek and Italian ships as depicted.

Stone from Stenkyrka in Gotland (ninth century)

---

[1] The Viking ships had, however, only one rudder on the starboard side, while the ancient Egyptian, Phœnician and Greek ships had two rudders, one on each side.

CHAPTER VII

It may be supposed that the communication which originally produced these resemblances did not take place by the sea-route, round the coasts of western Europe, but overland between the Black Sea and the Baltic. It is thus possible that the Scandinavian type of boat first began to be developed in the closed waters of the Baltic. It is here too that the boats of the Scandinavians (Suiones) are first mentioned in literature by Tacitus, and it is here that the earliest known boats of Scandinavian type have been found; these are the three remarkable boats of about the third century A.D. which were discovered at Nydam, near Flensburg. The best preserved of them (p. 110) is of oak, about seventy-eight feet long, with fourteen oars on each side, and it carried a crew of about forty men. The boats terminated in exactly the same way fore and aft, agreeing with what Tacitus says of the boats of the Suiones; and they could be rowed in both directions. They had rowlocks with oar-grummets like those in use on the west coast and in the northern part of Norway. There is no indication of the boats having had masts and sails, which also agrees with Tacitus. There can be no doubt that we have here the typical Scandinavian form of boat, with such fine lines and such excellent workmanship that it can only be due to an ancient culture the development of which had extended over many centuries.

From the Baltic this form of boat may have spread to Norway, where it gradually attained its greatest perfection; and it is worth remarking that in that very district where the Baltic type of boat derived from the south-east reached a coast with superior harbours, richer fisheries, and better opportunities for longer sea voyages, namely, in Bohuslen and Viken, we find also the greater number of rock-carvings with representations of ships. It is moreover a question whether the very name of "Vikings" is not connected with this district, and did not originally mean men from Viken, Vikværings; as they were specially prominent, the name finally became a common designation for all Scandinavians,

THE VOYAGES OF THE NORSEMEN

as had formerly been the case with the names Eruli, Saxons, Danes.[1] In the course of their voyages towards the southwest the Scandinavians may also have met very early with ships from the Mediterranean, which, for instance, were engaged in the tin trade with the south of England, or may even have reached the amber coast, and thus fresh influence from the Mediterranean may have been added. When we see how in the fifth century roving Eruli reached as far as Italy in their ships, this will not appear impossible; and if there is any contrivance that we should expect to show a certain community of character over a wide area, it is surely the ship or boat.

Tacitus says that the fleets of the Suiones consisted of row-boats without sails. It is difficult to contest the accuracy of so definite a statement, especially as it is supported by the Nydam find, and by the circumstance that the Anglo-Saxons appear to have crossed the sea to Britain in nothing but rowboats; but Tacitus is speaking of warships in particular, and it is impossible that sails should not have been known and used in Scandinavia, and especially in Norway, at that time. There are possibly indications of sails even in the rock-carvings (see the first example in illustration, p. 236), and in the ornaments on the knives of the Bronze Age (see illustration, p. 238). In the case of a people whose lot it was to live to so great an extent on and by the sea, it is scarcely to be supposed that any very long time should elapse before they thought of making use of the wind, even if they did not originally derive the invention of sails from the Mediterranean.

Just as the Phœnicians and the Greeks had swift-sailing longships for war and piracy, and other, broader sailing-ships for trade (see p. 48), so also did the Scandinavians gradually develop two kinds of craft: the swift longships, and the broader and heavier trading-vessels, called "bosses" and "knars."

CHAPTER VII

---

[1] But "Viking" is also explained as derived from a Celtic word, and is said to mean warrior [cf. A. Bugge].

CHAPTER VII
Shipbuilding in Norway

But even if northern shipbuilding exhibits a connection with that of the Mediterranean, and thus was no more spontaneous in its growth than any other form of culture in the world, the type of ship produced by the Scandinavians was nevertheless undoubtedly superior to all that had preceded it, just as they themselves were incontestably the most skilful seamen of their time. The perfection and refinement of form, with fine lines, which we find in the three preserved boats from Nydam, and in the three ships of the beginning of the Viking age, or about the year 800, give evidence in each case of centuries of culture in this province; and when we see the richness of workmanship expended on the Oseberg ship and all the utensils that were found with it, we understand that it was no upstart race that produced all this, but a people that may well have sailed the North Sea even a thousand years earlier, in the time of Pytheas.

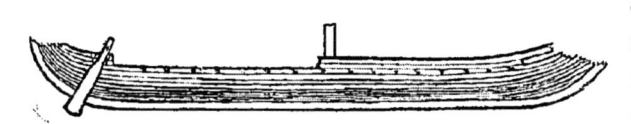

The preserved portion of the Viking ship from Gokstad, near Sandefjord (ninth century)

The immigration to Norway of many tribes may itself have taken place by sea. Thus the Horder and Ryger are certainly the same tribes as the "Harudes" (the "Charudes" of the emperor Augustus and of Ptolemy), dwelling in Jutland and on the Rhine (cf. Cæsar), and the "Rugii" west of the Vistula on the south coast of the Baltic (from whom possibly Rügen takes its name).[1] They came by the sea route to western Norway straight from Jutland and North Germany, and there must thus have been communication between these countries at that time; but how early we do not know; it may have been at the beginning

[1] Cf. P. A. Munch, i., 1852; Müllenhoff, ii., 1887, p. 66; iv., 1900. pp. 121, 467, 493, etc.; Much, 1905, pp. 124, 135; Magnus Olsen, 1905, p. 22; A. Bugge, 1906, p. 20.

THE VOYAGES OF THE NORSEMEN

of our era, and it may have been earlier.[1] But the fact that whole tribes were able to make so long a migration by sea indicates in any case a high development of navigation, and again it is on the Baltic that we first find it.

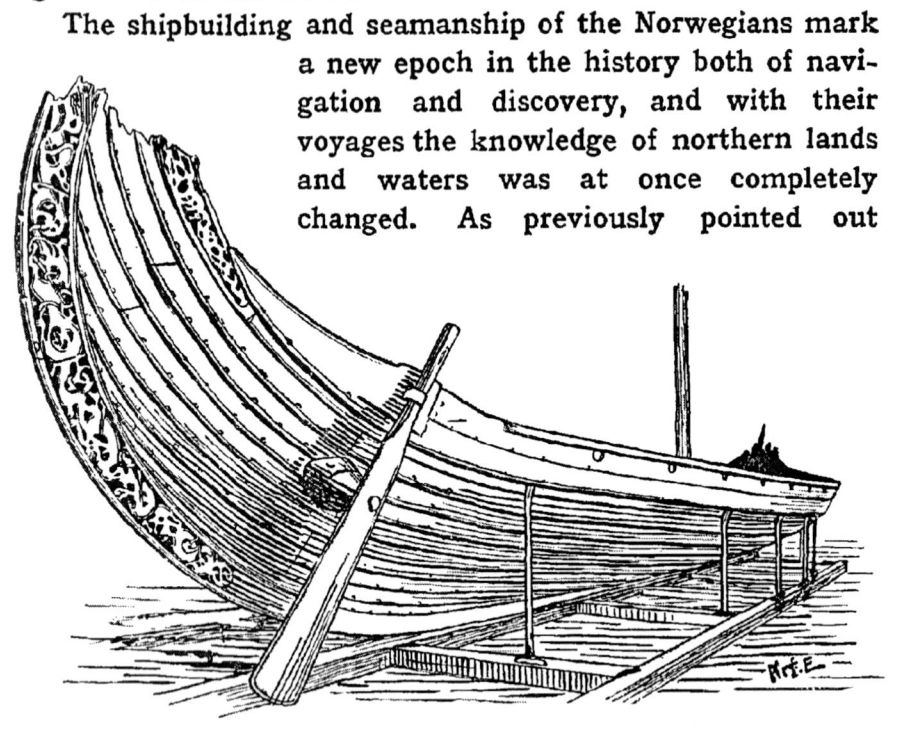

The shipbuilding and seamanship of the Norwegians mark a new epoch in the history both of navigation and discovery, and with their voyages the knowledge of northern lands and waters was at once completely changed. As previously pointed out

The Viking ship from Oseberg, near Tönsberg (ninth century)

(p. 170), we notice this change of period already in Ottar's communications to King Alfred, but their explorations of land and sea begin more particularly with the colonisation of

---

[1] H. Koht [1908] has suggested the possibility that the name "Håløiger" (Háleygir) from Hålogaland (Northern Norway) may be the same as the Vandal tribe Lugii, which about the year 100 inhabited the region between the upper course of the Elbe and Oder. With the prefix "há" they are distinguished as the high Lugii. Moltke Moe thinks that "Hallinger" or "Haddingjar" may come from another Vandal tribe, the "Hasdingi" (Gothic "Hazdiggôs"), which had its name from the Gothic "*hazds," long hair [cf. Müllenhoff, iv., 1900, p. 487; Much, 1905, p. 127]. It may also be possible that the name of Skiringssal in Vestfold was connected with the Sciri in eastern Germany [cf. Munch, 1852].

247

IN NORTHERN MISTS

CHAPTER VII

Iceland, which in its turn became the starting-point for expeditions farther west.

We find accounts of these voyages of discovery in the old writings and sagas, a large part of which was put into writing in Iceland. A sombre undercurrent runs through these narratives of voyages in unknown seas; even though they may be partly legendary, they nevertheless bear witness in their terseness to the silent struggle of hardy men with ice, storms, cold and want, in the light summer and long, dark winter of the North.

The Norwegians' appliances for navigation

They had neither compass, nor astronomical instruments, nor any of the appliances of our time for finding their position at

Ships from the Bayeux tapestry (eleventh century)

sea; they could only sail by the sun, moon and stars, and it seems incomprehensible how for days and weeks, when these were invisible, they were able to find their course through fog and bad weather; but they found it, and the open craft of the Norwegian Vikings, with their square sails, fared north and west over the whole ocean, from Novaya Zemlya and Spitsbergen to Greenland, Baffin's Bay, Newfoundland and North America, and over these lands and seas the Norsemen extended their dominion. It was not till five hundred years later that the ships of other nations were to make their way to the same regions.

The lodestone, or compass, did not reach the Norwegians till the thirteenth century.[1] As to what means they had before

---

[1] O. Irgens [1904] thinks the Norwegians may have had the compass very early (lodestone on a straw or a strip of wood floating on water in a bowl),

THE VOYAGES OF THE NORSEMEN

that time for finding their course at sea, Norse-Icelandic literature contains extremely scanty statements. We see that to them, as to the Phœnicians before them, the polestar was the lodestar, and that they sometimes used birds —ravens—to find out the direction of land; but we also hear that when they met with fog or cloudy weather they drifted without knowing where they were, and sometimes went in the opposite direction to that they expected, as in Thorstein Ericson's attempt to make Wineland from Greenland, where they arrived off Iceland instead of off America. Even when after a long period of dull weather they saw the sun again, it could not help them to determine their direction at all accurately, unless they knew the approximate time of day; but their sense of time was certainly far keener than ours, which has been blunted by the use of clocks. Several accounts show that on land the Scandinavians knew how to observe the sun accurately, in what quarter and at what time it set, how long the day or the night lasted at the summer or winter solstice, etc. From this they formed an idea of their northern latitude. Amongst other works a treatise of the close of the thirteenth century or later included in the fourth part of the collection " Rymbegla " [1780, pp. 472 ff.] shows that they may even have understood how to take primitive measurements of the sun's altitude at noon with a kind

CHAPTER VII

Landing of William the Conqueror's ships in England. Bayeux tapestry (eleventh century)

---

perhaps even in the eleventh century; indeed, he considers it not impossible that the lodestone may have been brought to the North even much earlier than this by Arab traders. But the expression often used in the sagas that they drifted about the sea in thick and hazy weather (without seeing the heavenly bodies), and did not know where they were, seems to contradict this.

CHAPTER VII of quadrant. But they can scarcely have been able to take observations of this kind on board ship during their long voyages in early times, and they still less understood how to compute the latitude from such measurements except perhaps at the equinoxes and solstices. It is true that from the narrative, to be mentioned later, of a voyage in the north of Baffin's Bay, about 1267, it appears that at sea also they attempted to get an idea of the sun's altitude by observing where the shadow of the gunwale, on the side nearest the sun, fell on a man lying athwartships when the sun was in the south. With all its imperfection this shows that at least they observed the sun's altitude.[1] In order to form some idea of their western or eastern longitude they cannot have had any other means than reckoning; and so long as the sun and stars were visible, and they knew in what direction they were sailing, they undoubtedly had great skill in reckoning this. In thick weather

Seal of the town of Dover, 1284

they could still manage so long as the wind held unaltered; but they could not know when it changed; they were then obliged to judge from such signs as birds, of what country they were, and in what direction they flew;

[1] O. Irgens [1904] has suggested the possibility that they might measure the length of the shadow of the gunwale by marks on the thwart, and determine when the boat lay on an even keel by a bowl of water, and that thus they might obtain a not untrustworthy measurement of the sun's altitude even at sea. He further supposed that the Norwegians might have become acquainted with the hour-glass from Southern Europe or from the plundering of monasteries, and that thus they were able to measure the length of the day approximately at sea. But no statements are known that could prove this.

THE VOYAGES OF THE NORSEMEN

we hear occasionally that they had birds from Ireland, or from Iceland, and so on. The difference in the fauna of birds might give them information. In their sailing directions it is also stated that they observed the whale; thus in the Landnámabók (Hauksbók) we read that when sailing from Norway to Greenland one should keep far enough to the south of Iceland to have birds and whales from thence. This is more difficult to understand, as the whale is not confined to the land, and the same whales are found in various parts of the northern seas. But drift-ice or icebergs, if they met them, might serve to show their direction, as might occasionally driftwood or floating seaweed. The colour of the sea may certainly have been of importance to such keen observers, even though we hear nothing of it; it cannot have escaped them, for instance, that the water of the Gulf Stream was of a purer blue than the rather greenish-brown water of the coastal current near Norway and in the North Sea, or in the East Iceland Polar Current; the difference between the water of the East Greenland Polar Current and in the Atlantic is also striking. It may likewise be supposed that men who were dependent to such a degree on observing every sign may have remarked the distribution in the ocean of so striking a creature as the great red jelly-fish. If so, it may often have given them valuable information of their approximate position. They used the lead, as appears, amongst other authorities, from the "Historia Norwegiæ," where we read that Ingolf and Hjorleif found Iceland "by probing the waves with the lead."

But that it was not always easy to find their course is shown, amongst other instances, by the account of Eric the Red's settlement in Greenland, when twenty-five ships left Iceland, but only fourteen are said to have arrived. Here, as elsewhere, it was the more capable commanders who came through.

THE NORWEGIAN SETTLEMENT IN ICELAND

Oldest authorities

The island of Iceland is mentioned, as we have seen, for the first time in literature by Dicuil, in 825, who calls it Thyle and speaks of its discovery by the Irish. As he says nothing about "Nortmannic" pirates having arrived there, whereas he mentions their having expelled the Irish monks from the Faroes, we may conclude that the Norsemen had not yet reached Iceland at that time. The first certain mention of the name Iceland is in the German poem "Meregarto" (see p. 181),[1] and in Adam of Bremen, where we find the first description of the island derived from a Scandinavian source (see p. 193).

Narratives of its discovery by the Norsemen and of their first settlement there are to be found in Norse-Icelandic literature; but they were written down 250 or 300 years after the events. These narratives of the first discoverers mentioned

---

[1] Presuming that King Alfred's "Iraland" is not an error for "Isaland" and does not mean Iceland (see p. 179).

THE VOYAGES OF THE NORSEMEN

by name and their deeds, which were handed down by tradition for so long a time, can therefore scarcely be regarded as more than legendary; nevertheless they may give us a picture in broad outlines of how voyages of discovery were accomplished in those times.

CHAPTER VII

As the Norwegians visited the Scottish islands and Ireland many centuries before they discovered Iceland, it is highly probable that they had information from the Irish of this great island to the north-west; if so, it was natural that they should afterwards search for it, although according to most Norse-Icelandic accounts it is said to have been found accidentally by mariners driven out of their course.

According to the sagas a Norwegian Viking, Grim Kamban, had established himself in the Faroes (about 800 A.D.) and had expelled thence the Irish priests; but possibly there was a Celtic population, at any rate in the southern islands (cf. p. 164). After that time there was comparatively active communication between the islands and Norway, and it was on the way to the Faroes or to the Scottish islands that certain voyagers were said to have been driven northward by a storm to the great unknown island. The earliest and, without comparison, the most trustworthy authority, Are Frode,[1] gives in his "Íslendingabók" (of about 1120-1130) no information of any such discovery, and this fact does not tend to strengthen one's belief in it. Are tells us briefly and plainly:

Are Frode on the settlement of Iceland

"Iceland was first settled from Norway in the days of Harold Fairhair, the son of Halfdan the Black; it was at that time—according to Teit, Bishop Isleif's son, my foster-brother, the wisest man I have known, and Thorkel Gellisson, my uncle, whose memory was long, and Thorid, Snorre Gode's daughter, who was both exceeding wise and truthful—when Ivar, Ragnar Lodbrok's son, caused St. Edmund, the king of the Angles [i.e., the English king], to be slain. And that was 870 winters after the birth of Christ, as it is written in his saga. Ingolf hight the Norseman of whom it is truthfully related that he first fared thence [from Norway] to Iceland, when Harold Fairhair was sixteen winters old, and for the second time a few winters later; he settled south in Reykjarvik; the

---

[1] The priest Ari Thorgilsson, commonly called Ari hinn Fróði or Are Frode (i.e., the learned), lived from 1068 to 1148.

253

IN NORTHERN MISTS

CHAPTER VII

place is called Ingolfshövde; Minthakseyre, where he first came to land, but Ingolfsfell, west of Ölfossá, of which he afterwards possessed himself. At that time Iceland was clothed with forest [i.e., birch forest] from the mountains to the strand. There were Christian men here, whom the Norsemen called 'Papar'... [6] and who were Irish, as already mentioned, pp. 165 f. "And then there was great resort of men hither from Norway, until King Harold forbade it, since he thought that the land [i.e., Norway] would be deserted," etc.

We may certainly assume that this description of Are's is at least as trustworthy as the later statements on the same subject; but as Are probably also wrote a larger Íslendingabók, which is now lost, there is a possibility that he there related the discovery of Iceland in greater detail, and that the later authors have drawn from it.

The next written account of the discovery of Iceland is found in the "Historia de Antiquitate regum Norwagiensium"[1] of the Norwegian monk Tjodrik (written about 1180), where we read:

Tjodrik Monk on the discovery of Iceland

Dragon-ship with a king and warrior (from the Flateyjarbók, circa 1390)

"In Harold's ninth year—some think in his tenth—certain merchants sailed to the islands which we call 'Phariæ' ['Færeyjar' = the Faroes]; there they were attacked by tempest and wearied long and sore, until at last they were driven by the sea to a far distant land, which some think to have been the island of Thule; but I cannot either confirm or deny this, as I do not know the true state of the matter. They landed and wandered far and wide; but although they climbed mountains, they nowhere found trace of human habitation. When they returned to Norway they told of the country they had found and by their praises incited many to seek it. Among them especially a chief named Ingolf, from the district that is called Hordaland; he made ready a ship, associated with himself his brother-in-law Hjorleif and many others, and sought and found the country we speak of, and began to settle it together with his companions, about the tenth year of Harold's reign. This was the beginning of the settlement of that country which we now call Iceland—unless we take into account that certain persons, very few in number, from Ireland (that is, little Britain) are believed to have been there in older times, to judge from certain books and other articles that were found after them. Nevertheless two others preceded Ingolf in this matter;

---

[1] G. Storm, "Monumenta Historica Norvegiæ," 1880, pp. 8 f.

254

THE VOYAGES OF THE NORSEMEN

the first was named Garðar, after whom the land was at first called Garðarsholmr, the second was named Floki. But what I have related may suffice concerning this matter."

It is probable that Tjodrik Monk was acquainted with Are Frode's Íslendingabók, or at least had sources connected with it. In the "Historia Norwegiæ" by an unknown Norwegian author (written according to G. Storm about 1180–1190, but probably later, in the thirteenth century) [1] we read of the discovery of Iceland [Storm, 1880, p. 92]:

"Next, to the west, comes the great island which by the Italians is called Ultima Tile ; but now it is inhabited by a considerable multitude, while formerly it was waste land, and unknown to men, until the time of Harold Fairhair. Then certain Norsemen, namely Ingolf and Hjorleif, fled thither from their native land, being guilty of homicide, with their wives and children, and resorted to this island, which was first discovered by Gardar and afterwards by another (?), and found it at last, by probing the waves with the lead."

In Sturla's Landnámabók, called the Sturlubók, of about 1250, we find almost the same story of the first discovery as in Tjodrik Monk. It runs :

" Thus it is related that men were to go from Norway to the Faroes—some mention Naddodd the Viking among them—but were driven westward in the ocean and there found a great land. They went up a high mountain in the Eastfjords and looked around them, whether they could see smoke or any sign that the land was inhabited, and they saw nothing. They returned in the autumn to the Faroes. And as they sailed from the land, much snow fell upon the mountains, and therefore they called the land Snowland. They praised the land much. It is now called Reydarfjeld in the East-fjords, where they landed, so said the priest Sæmund the Learned. There was a man named Gardar Svavarsson, of Swedish kin, and he went forth to seek Snowland, by the advice of his mother, who had second sight. He reached land east of East Horn, where there was then a harbour. Gardar sailed around the country and proved that it was an island. He wintered in the north at Husavik in Skialfanda and there built a house. In the spring, when he was ready for sea, a man in a boat, whose name was Nattfari, was driven away from him, and a thrall and a bondwoman. He afterwards dwelt at the place called Natfaravik. Gardar then went to Norway and praised the land much. He was the father of Uni, the father of Hroar Tungugodi. After that the land was called Gardarsholm, and there was then forest between the mountains and the strand."

CHAPTER VII

"Historia Norwegiæ"

The Landnáma on the discovery of Iceland

---

[1] R. Meissner [1902, pp. 43 f.] thinks it was written between 1260 and 1264.

255

IN NORTHERN MISTS

CHAPTER VII

In Hauk's Landnámabók (of the beginning of the fourteenth century) Gardar's voyage is mentioned as the first, and Naddodd's as the second, and it is said of Gardar that he was "son of Svavar the Swede; he owned lands in Sealand, but was born in Sweden. He went to the Southern isles [Hebrides] to fetch her father's inheritance for his wife. But as he was sailing through Pettlands firth [Pentland, between Orkney and Shetland] a storm drove him back, and he drifted westward in the ocean, etc." The Sturlubók was doubtless written some fifty years before Hauk's Landnámabók, and was the authority for the latter and for the lost Landnámabók of Styrmir enn froði[1] (ob. 1245); but as the copy that has come down to us of the Sturlubók is later (about 1400), many have thought that on this point the Hauksbók is more to be relied upon, and have therefore held that according to the oldest Icelandic tradition the Swedish-born Dane Gardar was the first Scandinavian discoverer of Iceland. Support for this view has also been found in the fact that in another passage of the Sturlubók we read: "Uni, son of Gardar who first found Iceland." It has therefore been held that it was not till after 1300 that a transposition was made in the order of Gardar's and Naddodd's voyages at the beginning of the book [cf. F. Jónsson, 1900, p. xxx.]. But this assertion may be doubtful; it seems rather as though the Icelandic tradition itself was uncertain on this point. We have seen above that the Norwegian work "Historia Norwegiæ" mentions Gardar as the first; while the yet earlier Tjodrik Monk [1177-1180] has a tale of a first accidental voyage to Iceland, which is the same, in parts word for word, as the stories of both the Sturlubók and the Hauksbók of Naddodd's voyage, only that Tjodrik mentions no name in connection with it. He certainly says later that Gardar and Floki went there before Ingolf; but this must mean that all three came after the first-mentioned nameless voyage. If we compare with this the vague expression of the Sturlubók that "some mention Naddodd the Viking" in connection with that first accidental voyage, the logical conclusion must be that there was an old tradition that some one, whose identity is uncertain, had been long ago driven by weather to this Snowland, in the same way as there was a tradition in Iceland that Gunnbjörn had been driven long ago to Gunnbjörnskerries, before Greenland was discovered by Eric the Red. Some have then connected this first storm-driven mariner with a Norwegian Viking-name, Naddodd. Thus are legends formed. But the first man to circumnavigate the country and to become more closely acquainted with it was, according to the tradition, Gardar, whose name was more certainly known; for which reason he was also readily named as the first discoverer of the country (just as Eric the Red and not Gunnbjörn was named as the discoverer of Greenland). Hauk Erlendsson then, in agreement with this, amended the Landnámabók by placing Gardar's voyage first, while at the same time he made the mention of Naddodd more precise, which was necessary, since his was to be a later and

---

[1] The original Landnámabók, which was the source of both Styrmir's and Sturle's versions, must have been written at the beginning of the thirteenth century.

THE VOYAGES OF THE NORSEMEN

therefore equally well-known voyage. He also gives Naddodd's kin, which is not alluded to in the Sturlubók. This hypothesis is strengthened by the latter's vague expression, above referred to, about Naddodd, and by the fact that only Gardar's and Floki's names are mentioned by Tjodrik Monk, and only Gardar and another (Floki?) in the "Historia Norwegiæ." If Naddodd's voyage had come after Gardar's, and consequently was equally well known, it would be strange that it should not be mentioned together with his and with the third voyage that succeeded them. But the whole question is of little importance, since, as we have said, these narratives must be regarded as mere legends.

The third voyage, according to both the Hauksbók and Sturlubók, was made by a great Viking named Floki Vilgerdarson. He fitted out in Rogaland to seek Gardarsholm (or Snowland). He took with him three ravens which

"were to show him the way, since seafaring men had no 'leidarstein' [lodestone, magnetic needle] at that time in the North. . . ." "He came first to Hjaltland [Shetland] and lay in Floka-bay. There Geirhild, his daughter, was drowned in Geirhilds-lake." "Floki then sailed to the Faroes, and there gave his [other] daughter in marriage. From her is come Trond in Gata. Thence he sailed out to sea with the three ravens. . . . And when he let loose the first it flew back astern [i.e., towards the Faroes]. The second flew up into the air and back to the ship. The third flew forward over the prow, where they found the land. They came to it on the east at Horn. They then sailed along the south of the land. But when they were sailing to the west of Reykjanes and the fjord opened up, so that they saw Snæfellsnes, Faxi [a man on board] said, 'This must be a great land that we have found; here are great waterfalls.' This is since called Faxa-os. Floki and his men sailed west over Breidafjord, and took land there which is called Vatsfjord, by Bardastrond. The fjord was quite full of fish, and on account of the fishing they did not get in hay, and all their cattle died during the winter. The spring was a cold one. Then Floki went northward on the mountain and saw a fjord full of sea-ice. Therefore they called the country Iceland. . . . In the summer they sailed to Norway. Floki spoke very unfavourably of the country. But Herjolf said both good and evil of the country. But Thorolf said that butter dripped from every blade of grass in the country they had found; therefore he was called Thorolf Smor [Butter]."

These three voyages of discovery are supposed to have taken place about 860–870. A few years after that time began the permanent settlement of the country by Norwegians; according to the chronicles this was initiated by Ingolf Arnarson with his establishment at Reykjarvik (about the year 874), which is mentioned as early as Are Frode (see above, p. 253), and this establishment may be more historical.

IN NORTHERN MISTS

CHAPTER VII

Harold Fairhair's conquest of the whole of Norway, of which he made one kingdom, and his hard-handed procedure may have been partly responsible for the emigration of Norwegians to the poorer island of Iceland; many of the chiefs preferred to live a harder life there than to remain at home under Harold's dominion. A larger part of the settlers, and among them many of the best, had first emigrated from Norway to the Scottish isles and to Ireland, but on account of troubles moved once more to Iceland.[1] As has been suggested already (p. 167), there was probably, besides the Irish priests, some Celtic population before the Norwegians arrived, which gave Celtic names to various places in the country. The omission of any mention of these Celts, with the exception of the "Papar," in the Landnáma is no more surprising than the strange silence about the primitive people of Greenland, whom we now know with certainty to have been in the country when the Icelanders came thither.

THE DISCOVERY AND SETTLEMENT OF GREENLAND BY THE NORWEGIANS

Oldest authority on Greenland

The earliest mention of Greenland known in literature is that found in Adam of Bremen (see above, p. 194). It was written about a hundred years after the probable settlement of the country, and shows that at least the name had reached Denmark at that time. In another passage of his work Adam says that "emissaries from Iceland, Greenland and the Orkneys" came to Archbishop Adalbert of Bremen "with requests that he would send preachers to them."

Are Frode, circa 1120

The oldest Icelandic account of the discovery of Greenland, and of the people settling there, is found in Are Frode's Íslendingabók (c. 1130). He had it from his uncle, Thorkel Gellisson, who had been in Greenland and had conversed with a man who himself had accompanied Eric the Red

---

[1] Cf. Vigfússon, 1856, i. p. 186; P. A. Munch, 1860; J. E. Sars, 1877, i. p. 213; A. Bugge 1905, pp. 377 ff. Finnur Jónsson, 1894, ii. p. 188, is against this view.

THE VOYAGES OF THE NORSEMEN

thither. Thorkel lived in the second half of the eleventh century, and "remembered far back." Are's statements have thus a good authority, and they may be regarded as fairly trustworthy, at all events in their main outlines; for

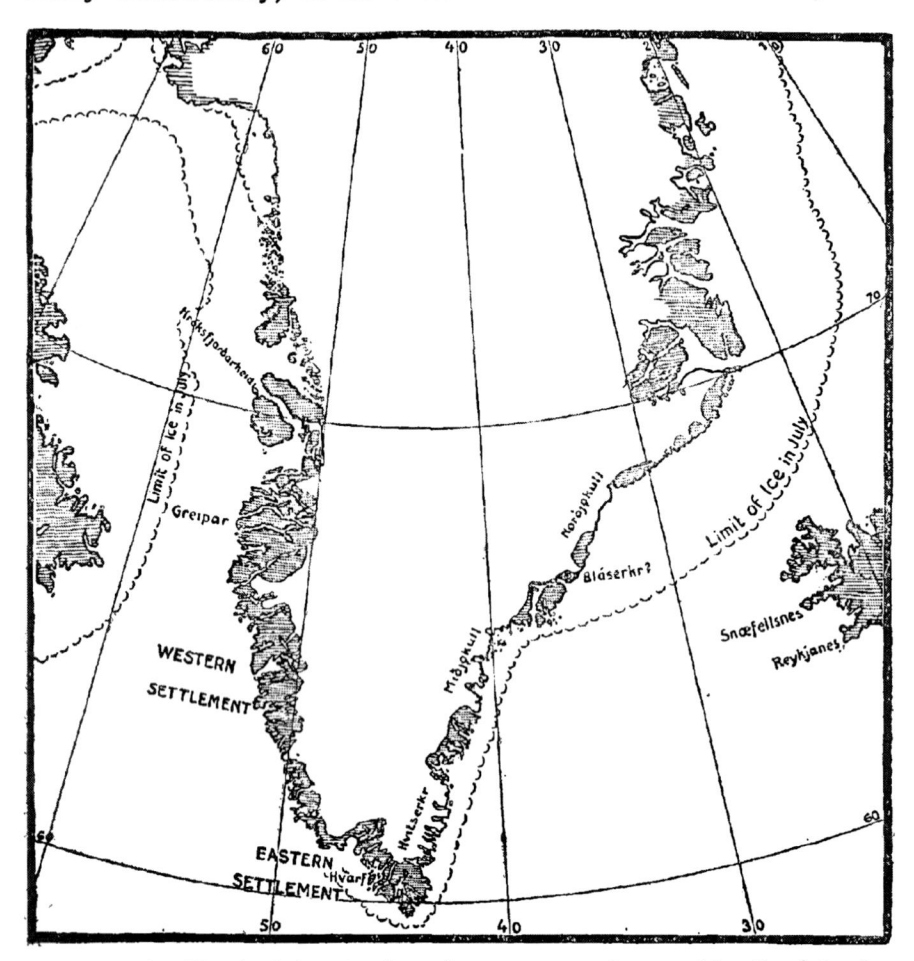

CHAPTER VII

Greenland. The shaded parts along the coast are not covered by the inland ice, which otherwise covers the whole of the interior

the events were no more remote than a couple of generations, and accounts of them may still have been extant in Iceland. Unfortunately the records that have come down to us, from the hand of Are himself, are very brief. He says:

"The land which is called Greenland was discovered and settled from Iceland.

IN NORTHERN MISTS

CHAPTER VII

Eirik Raude [Eric the Red] was the name of a man from Breidafjord, who sailed thither from hence and there took land at the place which is since called Eiriksfjord. He gave the land a name and called it Greenland, and said that having a good name would entice men to go thither. They found there dwelling-sites of men, both in the east and the west of the country, and fragments of boats ('keiplabrot') and stone implements, so that one may judge from this that the same sort of people had been there as inhabited Wineland, whom the Greenlanders [1] call Skrælings.[2] Now this, when he betook himself to settling the country, was fourteen or fifteen winters before Christianity came here to Iceland,[3] according to what Thorkel Gellisson was told in Greenland by one who himself accompanied Eric the Red thither."[1]

It is strange that we only hear of traces left by the primitive people of Greenland, the Skrælings or Eskimo. This looks as though Eric the Red did not come across the people themselves, though this seems improbable. We shall return to this later, in a special chapter on them.

It is probable that in other works, which are now lost, Are Frode wrote in greater detail of the discovery of Greenland and its first settlement by the Icelanders, and that later authors, whose works are known to us, have drawn upon him; for where they speak of other events that are mentioned in Are's Íslendingabók, the same expressions are often used, almost word for word. The oldest of the later accounts known to us, which give a more complete narrative of the discovery of Greenland, were written between 1200 and 1305. The Landnámabók may be specially mentioned; upon this is based the Saga of Eric the Red (also called Thorfinn Karlsevne's Saga), written, according to the opinion of G. Storm, between the years 1270 and 1300, while Finnur Jónsson [1901] assigns it to the first half of the thirteenth century. By collating these various accounts we can form

---

[1] Thus the Norsemen settled in Greenland are always described in the Icelandic sagas, while the Eskimo are called Skrælings.

[2] Opinions have been divided as to the origin of this name; but there can be no doubt that the word is Germanic, and is the same as the modern Norwegian word "skrælling," which denotes a poor, weak, puny creature.

[3] This took place, according to Are Frode's own statements, in the year 1000.

THE VOYAGES OF THE NORSEMEN

a picture of what took place; even though we must suppose that traditions which have been handed down orally for so long must in course of time have been considerably transformed—especially where they cannot have been based on well-known geographical conditions—and that they have received many a feature from other traditions, or from pure legend.

CHAPTER VII

Many accounts, both in Hauk's Landnámabók and in the Sturlubók, and in other sagas, mention that Greenland was first discovered by the Norwegian Gunnbjörn, son of Ulf Kråka, shortly after the settlement of Iceland. On a voyage to Iceland, presumably about the year 900, he was carried out of his course to the west, and saw there a great country, and found certain islands or skerries, which were afterwards called "Gunnbjörnskerries." These must have been off Greenland, most probably near Cape Farewell; but if it was late in the summer, in August or September, when there is little ice along the east coast, he may even have come close to the land farther north, and there found islands, at Angmagsalik, for instance. It is, however, of no great importance where it was; for when he saw that it was not Iceland that he had made, but a less hospitable country which did not look inviting for winter quarters, he probably sailed again at once, in order to reach his destination before the ice and the late season stopped him, without spending time in exploring the country. Whether Gunnbjörn established himself in Iceland we do not know; but it is recorded that his brother, Grimkell, took land at Snæfellsnes and was among the first settlers, and his sons, Gunnstein and Halldor, took land in the north-west on Isafjord.

Gunnbjörn Ulfsson

Various later writers have interpreted this to mean that Gunnbjörnskerries lay to the west of Iceland, and far from the great land that Gunnbjörn saw; but the earliest notices (in the Hauksbók and Sturlubók) do not warrant such a view. It has even been suggested as possible that Gunnbjörnskerries lay in the ocean between Iceland and Greenland, but were

IN NORTHERN MISTS

CHAPTER VII

destroyed later by a volcanic outbreak. In the Dutchman Ruysch's map of 1508 an island is marked in this ocean, with the note that: "This island was totally consumed in the year 1456 A D."[1] It is inconceivable that such an island midway in the course between Iceland and Greenland should have entirely escaped mention in the oldest accounts of the voyages of Eric the Red and later settlers in Greenland, to say nothing of the circumstance that it would certainly have been mentioned in the ancient sailing-directions (e.g., in the Hauksbók and Sturlubók) for the voyage from Iceland to Greenland. Nor are there any known banks in this part of the ocean which might indicate that such an island had existed. It is in itself not the least unlikely that Gunnbjörn reached some islands of the Greenland coast, and that these in later tradition received the name of Gunnbjornskerries.

That they were gradually transferred by tradition to a place where islands were no longer to be met with, or which in any case was unapproachable on account of ice, appears from the description of Greenland ascribed to Ivar Bárdsson (probably written in the fifteenth century), where we read:[2]

"Item from Snæfellsnes in Iceland, which is shortest to Greenland, two days' and two nights' sail, due west is the course, and there lie Gunnbjornskerries right in mid-channel between Greenland and Iceland. This was the old course, but now ice has come from the gulf of the sea to the north-east ['landnorden botnen'] so near to the said skerries, that none without danger to life can sail the old course, and be heard of again"

Later in the same statement we read:

"Item when one sails from Iceland, one must take his course from Snæfellsnes ... and then sail due west one day and one night, very slightly to the south-west[3] to avoid the before-mentioned ice which lies off Gunnbjornskerries, and

---

[1] It seems possible that this note may refer to an island which appeared in 1422 south-west of Reykjarnes, and later again disappeared [cf. Th. Thoroddsen, 1897, 1. pp. 89 f.].

[2] See "Gronlands historiske Mindesmærker," iii. p. 250; F. Jónsson, 1899, p. 322.

[3] Instead of the words "very slightly ..." some MSS. have: "but then steer south-west."

THE VOYAGES OF THE NORSEMEN

then one day and one night due north-west, and thus he will come straight on the said highland Hvarf in Greenland."

This description need not be taken to indicate that the Gunnbjörnskerries were supposed to lie in the midst of the sea between Iceland and Greenland; some place on the east coast of Greenland (e.g., at Angmagsalik) may rather be intended, which was sighted on the voyage between Iceland and the Eastern Settlement (taking " Greenland " to mean only the settled districts of the country). The direction " due west, etc.," for the voyage to the Eastern Settlement is too westerly, unless it was a course by compass, which, although possible, is hardly probable. But as we shall see later there is much that is untrustworthy in the description attributed to Ivar Bârdsson.

A later tradition of Gunnbjörn's voyage also deserves mention; it is found in the " Annals of Greenland " of the already mentioned Björn Jónsson of Skardsá (1574-1656), which he compiled from older Icelandic sources, with corrections and " improvements " of his own. He says there ("Grönl. hist. Mind.," i. p. 88) that the reason why Eric the Red

"sailed to Greenland was no other than this, that it was in the memory of old people that Gunnbjorn, Ulf Kråka's son, was thought to have seen a glacier in the western ocean ('til annars jokulsins i vestrhafnu '), but Snæfells-glacier here, when he was carried westward on the sea, after he sailed from the Gunnbjorn's islands. Iceland was then entirely unsettled, and newly discovered by Gardar, who sailed around the country from ness to ness ('nesjastefnu '), and called it Gardarsholm. But this Gunnbjorn, who came next after him, he sailed round much farther out ('djúpara '), but kept land in sight, therefore he called the islands skerries in contradistinction to the holm [i.e., Gardarsholm]; but many histories have since called these islands land, sometimes large islands."

This last statement is in any case an explanatory " improvement " by Björn Jónsson himself, and doubtless this is also true of the rest. According to this the Gunnbjörnskerries lay even within sight of Iceland. In this connection it is worth remarking that his contemporary Arngrim Jónsson imagines (" Specim. Island.," p. 34) the Gunnbjörnskerries as

CHAPTER VII

263

IN NORTHERN MISTS

CHAPTER VII

a little uninhabited island north of Iceland. This would agree best with the little Meven-klint, which lies by itself in the Polar Sea fifty-six nautical miles north of land, and perhaps it is not wholly impossible that it was rumours of this in later times that gave rise to the ideas of the Gunnbjornskerries, which however by confusion were transferred westward.

It was long before any attempt was made, according to the narratives, to search for the land discovered by Gunnbjörn. In Hauk's Landnámabók [c. 122] we read:

Snæbjorn Galti and Rolf of Raudesand

"Snæbjorn [Galti, Holmsteinsson] owned a ship in Grimså-os, and Rolf of Raudesand bought a half-share in it.[1] They had twelve men each. With Snæbjorn were Thorkel and Sumarlide, sons of Thorgeir Raud, son of Einar of Stafholt. Snæbjorn also took with him Thorodd of Thingnes, his foster-father, and his wife, and Rolf took with him Styrbjörn, who quoth thus after his dream:

> 'The bane I see
> of both of us,
> all dolefully
> north-west in the sea,
> frost and cold,
> all kinds of anguish;
> from such I foresee
> the slaying of Snæbjorn.'

"They went to seek for Gunnbjörnskerries, and found land. Snæbjorn would not let any one land at night. Styrbjörn went from the ship and found a purse of money in a grave-mound ['kuml,' a cairn over a grave], and hid it. Snæbjorn struck at him with an axe, and the purse fell. They built a house, and covered it all over with snow ['ok lagdi hann í fonn']. Thorkel Raudsson found that there was water on the fork that stuck out at the aperture of the hut. That was in the month of Goe.[2] Then they dug themselves out. Snæbjorn made ready the ship. Of his people Thorodd and his wife stayed in the house; and of Rolf's Styrbjörn and others, and the rest went hunting. Styrbjörn slew Thorodd, and both he and Rolf slew Snæbjorn. Raud's sons and all the others took oaths [i.e., oaths of fidelity] to save their lives. They came to Hálogaland, and went

---

[1] Both Snæbjorn and Rolf had to fly from Iceland for homicide. Rolf and Styrbjorn fell in blood-feud when they returned.

[2] Goe began about February 21. What is here related would thus show that it was not till after that time that mild weather began, so that the snow melted and there was water on the stick that stuck out through the aperture.

THE VOYAGES OF THE NORSEMEN

thence to Iceland, and arrived at Vadil." There both Rolf and Styrbjörn met their death.

CHAPTER VII

It is possible that this strange fragmentary tale points back to an actual attempt at settlement in Greenland, due to Snæbjörn and Rolf having to leave Iceland on account of homicide. The attempt may have been abandoned on account of dissen-

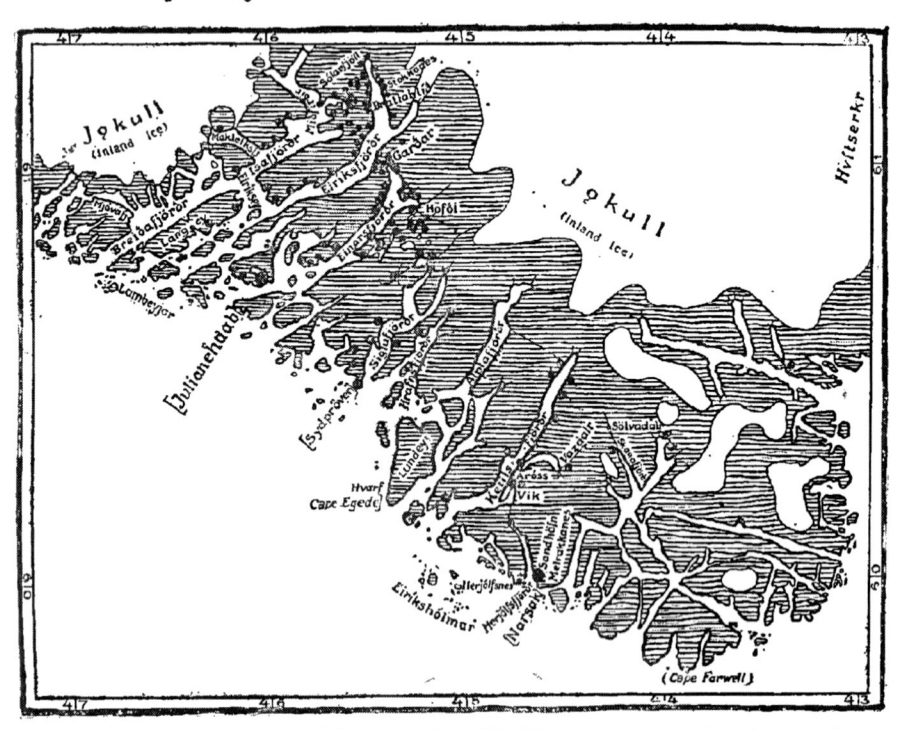

The Eastern Settlement of Greenland. The black points mark ruins of the homesteads of the ancient Greenlanders (from Finnur Jónsson, 1899)

sions, or because the country was too inhospitable. From the genealogical information the voyage may possibly be placed a little earlier than Eric the Red's first voyage to Greenland [cf. K. Maurer, 1874, p. 204]. Whereabouts in Greenland they landed and spent the winter is not stated; but the fact that the snow first began to thaw in the month of "Goe" would point to a cold climate, and this agrees best with the east coast of Greenland. But the story is so obscure that it is difficult to form any clear opinion as to its

265

CHAPTER VII

Eric the Red.

general credibility; the grave-mound and the purse of money must in any case have come from elsewhere. The circumstance that on their return they sailed first to Norway and thence to Iceland may be derived from a later time, when there was no direct communication between Greenland and Iceland, but the communication with Greenland took place by way of Norway.

The greatest and most important name connected with the discovery of Greenland is without comparison that of Eirik Raude (Erik the Red). The description of this remarkable man (in the Landnáma and in the Saga of Eric the Red) forms a good picture; warlike and hard as the fiercest Viking, but at the same time with the superior ability of the born explorer and leader to plan great enterprises, and to carry them out in spite of all difficulties. He was a leader of men. He was born in Norway (circa 950); but on account of homicide

The Western Settlement of Greenland. The black points mark ruins of the homesteads of the ancient Greenlanders (from F. Jónsson, 1899)

THE VOYAGES OF THE NORSEMEN

he and his father Thorvald left Jæderen and went to Iceland about 970. They took land on the Horn-strands, east of Horn (Cape North). There Thorvald died. Eric then married Tjodhild, whose mother, Thorbjörg Knarrar-bringa (i.e., ship's breast), lived in Haukadal. Eric therefore moved south and cleared land in Haukadal (inland of Hvamsfjord, north of Snæfellsnes) and lived at Eirikstad by Vatshorn. Eric quarrelled with his neighbours and killed several of them. He was therefore condemned to leave Haukadal. He took land on Brokó and Öksnó, islands outside Hvamsfjord; but after fresh conflicts and slaughter he and his men were declared outlaws for three years, at the Thorsnes thing, about 980. Eric then fitted out his ship, and a friend concealed him, while his enemies went all round the islands looking for him.

"He told them [i.e., his friends] that he meant to seek the land that Gunnbjorn, Ulf Kråka's son, saw when he was driven west of Iceland and found Gunnbjorn-skerries. He said he would come back for his friends, if he found the land. Eric put to sea from Snæfells-glacier;[1] he arrived off Mid-glacier, at the place called Blåserk. [Thence he went south, to see whether the land was habitable.] He sailed westward round Hvarf [west of Cape Farewell] and spent the first winter in Eiriksey near [the middle of] the Eastern Settlement. Next spring he went to Eiriksfjord [the modern Tunugdliarfik, due north of Julianehaab; see map, p. 265] and gave names to many places. The second winter he was at Eiriksholms by Hvarfsgnipa [Hvarf Point]; but the third summer he went right north to Snæfell[2] and into Ravnsfjord.[3] Then he thought he had come farther into the land than the head of Eiriksfjord. He then turned back, and was the third winter in Eiriksey off the mouth of Eiriksfjord. The following summer he went to Iceland, to Breidafjord. He passed that winter at Holmlåt with Ingolf. In the spring they fought with Thorgest [Eric's former enemy], and Eric was beaten. After

---

[1] It was, perhaps, not altogether by chance that Eric was supposed to have sailed west from this point, as Gunnbjorn's brother, Grimkell, lived on the outer side of Snæfellsnes, and it may have been on a voyage thither that Gunnbjorn was thought to have been driven westward [cf. Reeves, 1895, p. 166].

[2] Snæfell lay far north on the west coast of Greenland. A Snæfell far north is also mentioned in connection with the Nordrsetu voyages (see later); it lay north of Króksfjardarheidr; but whether it is the same as that here mentioned is uncertain.

[3] In the Eastern Settlement there was a Ravnsfjord (Hrafnsfjorðr), which is probably the same as that intended here, as it is compared with Eiriksfjord.

CHAPTER VII

IN NORTHERN MISTS

CHAPTER VII

that they were reconciled. That summer Eric went to settle the land that he had found, and he called it Greenland; because, said he, men would be more willing to go thither if it had a good name."

"[Eric settled at Brattalid in Eiriksfjord.] Then Are Thorgilsson says that that summer twenty-five ships sailed to Greenland from Borgarfjord and Breidafjord; but only fourteen came there—some were driven back, others were lost. This was sixteen winters before Christianity was made law in Iceland."[1] This would therefore be about 984.

View from the mountain Igdlerfigsalik (see map, p. 271) over Tunugdliarfik Mid-fjords) into which a glacier falls; in the right centre Korok-fjord, with ice; behind it on the right the Nunataks

Eric the Red's first voyage to Greenland is one of the most remarkable in the history of arctic expeditions, both in itself, on account of the masterly ability it shows, and for the vast consequences it was to have. With the scanty means of equipment and provisioning available at that time in the open Viking ships,[2] it was no child's play to set out

[1] The above is for the most part a translation from Hauk's Landnámabók.

[2] We know little of how the ancient Scandinavians were able to provide themselves on their long voyages with food that would keep; they used salt meat, and it is probable that when they were laid up for the winter they often died of scurvy, as indeed is indicated by the narratives. Meat and fish they could doubtless often obtain fresh by hunting and fishing; for grain products they were in a worse position; these can never have been abundant in Iceland, and

THE VOYAGES OF THE NORSEMEN

for an unknown arctic land beyond the ice, and to stay there three years. Perhaps, of course, he did it from necessity; but he not only came through it alive—he employed the three years in exploring the country, from Hvarf right up to north of Davis Strait, and from the outermost belt of skerries to the head of the long fjords. This was more than 500 years before

(Eiriksfjord and Brattalid), farther to the left Sermilik (Isafjord and the a glacier falling into it. The whole background is covered by the inland near the east coast. (After D. Bruun, 1896)

the Portuguese came to the country, and exactly 600 before John Davis thought himself the discoverer of this coast.

they certainly had no opportunity of carrying a large provision with them; but as a rule they can scarcely have got on altogether without hydro-carbons, which are considered necessary for the healthy nourishment of a European. Milk may have afforded a sufficient compensation, and in fact we see that they usually took cattle with them. In the narrative of Ravna-Floki's voyage to Iceland it is expressly said that the cattle died during the winter (see above, p. 257), and it must have been for this reason that they thought they must go home again the next summer, which shows how important it was. Probably Eric also took cattle with him on his first voyage to Greenland, and thus he was obliged before all to find a more permanent place of abode on the shores of the fjords where there was grazing for the cattle; but it is likely that he lived principally by sealing and fishing. In that case he must have been a very capable fisherman.

IN NORTHERN MISTS

CHAPTER VII

But not only does Eric seem to have been pre-eminent, first as a fighter and then as a discoverer; as the leader of the colony founded by him in Greenland he must also have had great capabilities; he got people to emigrate thither, and looked after them well; and he was regarded as a matter of course as the leading man and chief of the new free state, whom every one visited first on arrival. His successors, who resided at the chief's seat of Brattalid, were the first family of the country.

Immigration to Greenland must according to the saga have gone on rapidly; for in the year 1000 there were already so many inhabitants that Olaf Tryggvason thought it worth while to make efforts to Christianise them, and sent a priest there with Eric's son Leif. Eric's wife, Tjodhild, at once received the faith; but the old man himself did not like the new doctrine, and found it difficult to give up his own. Tjodhild built a church at some distance from the houses; "there she made her prayers, and those men who accepted Christianity, but they were the most. She would not live with Eric, after she had taken the faith; but to him this was very displeasing." In Snorre's Heimskringla we read that men called Leif "the Lucky [see Chap. ix.]; but Eric, his father, thought that one thing balanced the other, that Leif had saved the shipwrecked crew and that he had brought the hypocrite ['skæmannin'] to Greenland, that is, the priest."

Part of the interior of Eiriksfjord, at Brattalid and beyond. The mountain Igdlerfigsalik in the background (after D. Bruun, 1896)

The Norsemen established themselves in two districts of

THE VOYAGES OF THE NORSEMEN

Greenland. One of these was the "Eastern Settlement" [Öster-bygden], so called because it lay farthest to the south-east on the west coast, between the southern point, Hvarf, and about 61° N. lat. It corresponds to the modern Julianehaab District. It was the most thickly populated, and it was here that Eiriks-fjord and Brattalid lay. In the whole "Settlement" there are said to have been 190 homesteads ["Grönl. hist. Mind.," iii. p. 228]. Ruins of these have been found in at least 150 places [cf. D. Bruun, 1896; G. Holm, 1883].

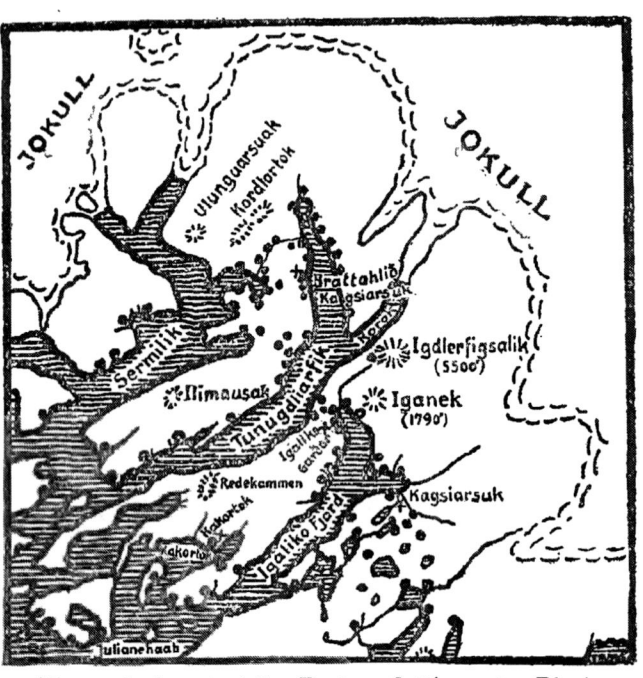

The central part of the Eastern Settlement. Black points mark ancient ruins, crosses mark churches

The other district, the "Western Settlement" [Vesterbygden], lay farther north-west between 63° and 66½° (see map, p. 266), for the most part in the modern Godthaab District, and its population was densest in Ameralik-fjord and Godthaabsfjord. There are said to have been ninety homesteads in this settlement. Many ruins of Norsemen's stone houses are still found in both districts, and they show with certainty where the settlements were and what was their extent.

On the east coast of Greenland, which is closed by drift-ice for the greater part of the year, the Norsemen had no permanent settlement, and it was only exceptionally that they were able

CHAPTER VII to land there, or they were sometimes wrecked in the drift-ice off the coast and had to take refuge ashore. Several places are, however, mentioned along the southern part of the east coast, where people from the Eastern Settlement probably went hunting in the summer.

The plain by Igaliko (Garðar) with ruins. In the background the peaks of Igdlerfigsalik, and in front of them Iganek (after N. P. Jörgensen)

Population

The population of the two settlements in Greenland can scarcely have been large at any time; perhaps at its highest a couple of thousand altogether. If we take it that there were 280 homesteads, and on an average seven persons in each, which is a high estimate, then the total will not be more than 1960. But the long distances caused the building, after the introduction of Christianity, of a comparatively large number of churches, namely, twelve in the Eastern Settlement (where the ruins of only five have been found) and four in the Western Settlement, besides which a monastery and a nunnery are mentioned in the Eastern Settlement. About 1110 Greenland became an independent bishopric, although it is said in the "King's Mirror" that

Bishops

" if it lay nearer to other lands it would be reckoned for a third part of a bishopric.

272

THE VOYAGES OF THE NORSEMEN

But now the people there have nevertheless a bishop of their own; for there is no other way, since the distance between them and other people is so great."[1]

CHAPTER VII

The chief's house Garðar in Einarsfjord (Igaliko) became the episcopal residence. There is a fairly complete record of the bishops of Greenland down to the end of the fourteenth century. During the succeeding century and even until 1530 a number of bishops of Greenland are also mentioned, who were appointed, but never went to Greenland.

Even if the conditions of life in the Greenland settlements were not luxurious, they were nevertheless not so hard as to prevent the development of an independent art of poetry. Sophus Bugge points out in " Norrœn Fornkvædi " [Christiania, 1867, p. 433] that the " Atlamál en grœnlenzku " of the Edda is, as its title shows, from Greenland, and was most probably composed there. Finnur Jónsson [1894, i. pp. 66, 68 ff.; 1897, pp. 40 ff.] would even refer four or five other Edda-lays to Greenland, namely: " Oddrúnargrátr," " Goðrúnarhvot," " Sigurðarkviða en skamma," " Helgakviða Hundingsbana," perhaps also " Helreið Brynhildar." As regards the two last-named, the assumption is certainly too doubtful, but in the case of the other three it is possible. The " Norðrsetu-drápa," to be mentioned later (p. 298), was composed in Greenland; and the so-called " Hafgerðinga-drápa " may be derived thence; in the Landnámabók, where one or two fragments of it are reproduced, it is said to have been composed by a " Christian man (monk?) from the Southern isles " (Hebrides), on the way thither. The fragments of lays on Furðustrandir and Wineland, which are given in the Saga of Eric the Red, may possibly also be from Greenland. The fact that the " Snorra-Edda " gives a particular kind of metre, called " Grönlenzkr háttr,"[1] agrees with the view that Greenland had an independent art of poetry.

Norse literature in Greenland

The Greenland lays like the Atlamál are perhaps not equal to the best Norse skald-poetry; but there runs through

[1] Edda Snorra Sturlusonar, i. pp. 686, 688, Hafniæ, 1848.

IN NORTHERN MISTS

TER them a weird, gloomy note that bears witness of the wild nature and the surroundings in which they were composed.

Within the fjords of both the ancient Greenland settlements many ruins of former habitations have been found (see maps, pp. 265, 266, 271); most of these are found in the Eastern Settlement or Julianehaab District [cf. especially D. Bruun, 1896; also G. Holm, 1883]. In a single homestead

View from the mountain Iganek, looking south over Igalikofjord (Einarsfjord) between them [after N. P.

as many as a score of scattered houses have been found; among them was a dwelling-house, and around it byres and stables for cattle, horses, sheep and goats, with adjoining hay-barns, or else open hay-fences (round stone walls within which the hay was stacked and covered with turf), besides larders, drying-houses, pens for sheep, fenced fields, etc. There were also fenced outlying hayfields with barns and with summer byres for sheep and goats, for they had even mountain pastures and hayfields. Near the shore are found sheds, possibly for gear for boats, sealing and fishing, but, on the other hand, there are no actual boathouses. Ruins of several churches (five in the Eastern Settlement) have also been found. The dwelling-houses were built of stone and

THE VOYAGES OF THE NORSEMEN

turf, like the Icelandic farmhouses; in exceptional cases clay was also used, while the outhouses were mostly built with dry stone walls. For the timber work of the roofs drift-wood must have been usually employed. The winter byres were of course made weatherproof. The size of the byres shows that the numbers of their stock were not inconsiderable, mostly sheep and goats; only where the level lands near the

and on the right Tunugdliarfik (Eiriksfjord) with the isthmus at Igaliko (Garðar Jörgensen, see D. Bruun, 1896)

fjords offered specially good pasture was there any great number of horned cattle. Everywhere in the neighbourhood of the ruins stone traps are found which show that the Greenlanders occupied themselves in trapping foxes; a few large traps have been thought to have been intended for wolves (?), which are now no longer to be found in southern Greenland. Near the main buildings are found great refuse heaps (" kitchen middens "), which give us much information as to the life they led and what they lived on. Great quantities of bones taken from five different sites in the Eastern Settlement (among them the probable sites of Brattalid and Gardar) have been examined by the Danish zoologist, Herluf Winge [cf. D. Bruun, 1896, pp. 434 ff.]. The great predominance of bones of domestic animals, especially oxen and goats, and of seals, especially the Greenland seal or saddle-back (Phoca grœnlandica), and the bladder-nose or crested seal (Cystophora cristata), show that cattle-rearing and seal-hunting were the Greenlanders' chief means of subsistence; and the latter especially must have provided the greater part of their flesh food, since as a rule the bones of seals are the most numerous. Curiously enough, few fish-bones have been found. As we know with certainty that the Greenlanders were much occupied in fishing, this absence now is accounted for by fish-bones and other offal of fish being used for fodder for cattle in winter. Various reindeer bones show that this animal was also found in ancient times in the Eastern Settlement, where it is now extinct. Besides these, bones of a single polar bear and of a few walrus have been found, which show that these animals were caught, though in small numbers; a few bones of whale have also been found. There are, strangely enough, comparatively few bones of birds. The bones of horses that have been found belong to a small race and the cattle were of small size and horned.

Remains of a sheep-pen at Kakortok. On the right the ruined church (after Th. Groth)

In the otherwise very legendary tale, in the Saga of the Foster Brothers (beginning of the thirteenth century), of Thormod Kolbrunarskald's voyage to Greenland and sojourn there, to avenge the death of his friend Thorgeir, we get here and there sidelights on the daily life of the country, which agree well with the information afforded by the remains. We hear that they often went to sea after seals, that they had

THE VOYAGES OF THE NORSEMEN

harpoons for seals ("selskutill"), that they cooked the flesh of seals, etc. From the "King's Mirror" (circa 1250) we get a good glimpse of the conditions of life in Greenland in those days :

"But in Greenland, as you probably know, everything that comes from other lands is dear there ; for the country lies so distant from other lands that men seldom visit it. And everything they require to assist the country, they must buy from elsewhere, both iron (and tar) and likewise everything for building houses. But these things are brought thence in exchange for goods : buckskin and ox-hides, and sealskin and walrus-rope and walrus-ivory." "But since you asked whether there was any raising of crops or not, I believe that country is little assisted thereby. Nevertheless there are men—and they are those who are known as the noblest and richest—who make essay to sow ; but nevertheless the great multitude in that country does not know what bread is, and never even saw bread." . . .

"Few are the people in that land, for little of it is thawed so much as to be habitable. . . . But when you ask what they live on in that country, since they have no corn, then [you must know] that men live on more things than bread alone. Thus it is said that there is good pasture and great and good homesteads in Greenland ; for people there have much cattle and sheep, and there is much making of butter and cheese. The people live much on this, and also on flesh and all kinds of game, the flesh of reindeer, whale, seal and bear ; on this they maintain themselves in that country."

We see clearly enough from this how the Greenlanders of the old settlements on the one hand were dependent on imports from Europe, and on the other subsisted largely by hunting and fishing. It appears also from a papal bull of 1282 that the Greenland tithes were paid in ox-hides, seal-skins and walrus-ivory.

It has been asserted that Greenland at that time possessed a more favourable climate, with less ice both on land and sea than at present ; but, amongst other things, the excellent description in the "King's Mirror," to be mentioned directly, shows clearly enough that such was not the case. Many will therefore ask what it was that could attract the Icelanders thither. But to one who knows both countries it will not be so surprising ; in many ways South Greenland appeals more to a Norwegian than Iceland. It lies in about the same latitude as Bergen and Christiania, and the beautiful fjords with a number of islands outside, where there are good channels for sailing and harbours everywhere, make it altogether like the coast of Norway, and different from the more exposed coasts of Iceland. Inside the fjords the summer is quite as warm and inviting as in Iceland ; it is true that there is drift-ice outside in early summer, but that brings good seal-hunting. There was, besides this, walrus-hunting and whaling, reindeer-hunting, fishing in the sea and in the rivers, fowling, etc. When we add good pasturage on the shores of the fjords, it will be understood that it was comparatively easy to support life.

The grass still grows luxuriantly around the ruins on the Greenland fjords, and might even to-day support the herds of many a homestead.

CHAPTER VIII

VOYAGES TO THE UNINHABITED PARTS OF GREENLAND IN THE MIDDLE AGES

THE EAST COAST OF GREENLAND

THE sagas give us scanty information about the east coast of Greenland—commonly called, in Iceland, the uninhabited regions (" ubygder ") of Greenland. The drift-ice renders this coast inaccessible by sea for the greater part of the year, and it was only very rarely that any one landed there, and then in most cases through an accident. As a rule sailors tried as far as possible to keep clear of the East Greenland ice, and did not come inshore until they were well past Hvarf, as appears from the ancient sailing-directions for this voyage. The "King's Mirror" (circa 1250) also shows us clearly enough that the old Norsemen had a shrewd understanding of the ice conditions off these uninhabited regions. It says:

"Now in that same sea [i.e., the Greenland sea] there are yet many more marvels, even though they cannot be accounted for witchcraft ('skrimslum'). So soon as the greater part of the sea has been traversed, there is found such a mass of ice as I know not the like of anywhere else in the world. This ice [i.e., the ice-floes] is some of it as flat as if it had frozen on the sea itself, four or five cubits thick, and lies so far from land [i.e., from the east coast of Greenland] that men

CHAPTER VIII

may have four or five days' journey across the ice [to land]. But this ice lies off the land rather to the north-east ('landnorðr') or north than to the south, south-west, or west; and therefore any one wishing to make the land should sail round it [i.e., round Cape Farewell] in a south-westerly and westerly direction, until he is past the danger of [encountering] all this ice, and then sail thence to land. But it has constantly happened that men have tried to make the land too soon, and so have been involved in these ice-floes; and some have perished in them; but others again have got out, and we have seen some of these and heard their tales and reports. But one course was adopted by all who have found themselves involved in this ice-drift ['ísavok' or 'ísaválkit'], that is, they have taken their small boats and drawn them up on to the ice with them, and have thus made for land, but their ship and all their other goods have been left behind and lost; and some of them have passed four or five days on the ice before they reached land, and some even longer. These ice-floes are strange in their nature; sometimes they lie as still as might be expected, separated by creeks or large fjords; but sometimes they move with as great rapidity as a ship with a fair wind, and when once they are under way they travel against the wind as often as with it. There are indeed some masses of ice in that sea of another shape, which the Greenlanders call 'falljökla.' Their appearance is that of a high mountain rising out of the sea, and they do not unite themselves to other masses of ice, but keep apart."

This striking description of the ice in the polar current shows that sailors were sometimes wrecked in it, and reached land on the east coast of Greenland.

The story of Snæbjörn Hólmsteinsson and his companions, who may have reached East Greenland (?), has been given above (p. 264).

Thorgils Orrabeinsfostre

An early voyage,[1] which is said to have been made along this coast, is described in the "Floamanna-saga." The Icelandic chief, Thorgils Orrabeinsfostre, is said to have left Iceland about the year 1001, with his wife, children, friends and thralls—some thirty persons in all—and his cattle, to join his friend, Eric the Red, who had invited him to Greenland. During the autumn they were wrecked on the east coast; and it was not till four years later, during which time they lived by whaling, sealing and fishing, and after

[1] If the Gunnbjörnskerries lay on the east coast, then Gunnbjorn Ulfsson was the first to reach it; but, as has been pointed out above (p. 261), they are more likely to have been near Cape Farewell, assuming the voyage to be historical.

GREENLAND VOYAGES IN THE MIDDLE AGES

adventures of many kinds, that Thorgils arrived at the Eastern Settlement. The saga is of late date, perhaps about 1400; it is full of marvels and not very credible. But the description of the country, with glaciers coming down to the sea, and ice lying off the shore for the greater part of the year, cannot have been invented without some knowledge of the east coast of Greenland; for the inhabited west coast is entirely different. The narrative of Thorgils' expedition may therefore have a historical kernel [cf. Nansen, 1890, p. 253; Engl. ed. i. 275]; and moreover it gives a graphic description of the difficulties and dangers that shipwrecked voyagers have to overcome in arctic waters; but at the same time it is gratuitously full of superstitions and dreams and the like, besides other improbabilities: such as the incident of the travellers suffering such extremities of thirst that they were ready to drink sea-water (with urine) to preserve their lives,[1] while

[1] This incident is obviously connected with Irish legends, with which that same saga shows other points of resemblance. We read in the Floamanna-saga [cf. "Grönl. hist. Mind.," ii. p. 118]: "They were then much exhausted by thirst; but water was nowhere in the neighbourhood. Then said Starkad: I have heard it said that when their lives were at stake men have mingled sea-water and urine. They then took the baler, . . . made this mixture, and asked Thorgils for leave to drink it. He said it might indeed be excused, but would not either forbid it or permit it. But as they were about to drink, Thorgils ordered them to give him the baler, saying that he wished to say a spell over their drink [or: speak over the bowl]. He received it and said: Thou most foul beast, that delayest our voyage, thou shalt not be the cause that I or others drink our own evacuation! At that moment a bird, resembling a young auk, flew away from the boat, screaming. Thorgils thereupon emptied the baler overboard. They then row on and see running water, and take of it what they want; and it was late in the day. This bird flew northwards from the boat. Thorgils said: Late has this bird left us, and I would that it may take all the devilry with it; but we must rejoice that it did not accomplish its desire."

In Brandan's first voyage, in the Irish tale, "Betha Brenainn," etc., or "Imram Brenaind" (of about the twelfth century; cf. Zimmer, 1889, pp. 137, 319], the seafarers one day suffered such thirst that they were near to death. They then saw glorious jets of water falling from a cliff. His companions asked Brandan whether they might drink of the water. He advised them first to say a blessing over it; but when this was done, the jets stopped running, and they saw the devil, who was letting the water out of himself, and killing those who drank of it. The sea closed over the devil, in order that thenceforth he might

CHAPTER VIII

rowing along a coast with ice and snow on every hand, where there cannot have been any lack of drinking water. Thorgils, or the man to whom in the first place the narrative may be due, may have been wrecked in the autumn on the east coast of Greenland, near Angmagsalik, or a little to the south of it, and may then have had a hard struggle before he reached Cape Farewell along the shore, inside the ice; but that it should have taken four years is improbable; I have myself in the same way rowed in a boat the greater part of the same distance along this coast in twelve days. It is hardly possible that the voyagers should have lost their ship much to the north of Angmagsalik, as the ice lies off the coast there usually the whole year round; nor is it credible that they should have arrived far north near Scoresby Sound, north of 70° N. lat., where the approach is easier; for they had no business to be there, if they were making for the Eastern Settlement.

In the Icelandic Annals there are frequent mentions of voyagers to Greenland being shipwrecked, and most of these cases doubtless occurred off East Greenland. In the sagas there are many narratives of such wrecks, or of people who have come to grief on this coast.

"Lik-Lodin"

In Björn Jónsson's version of the somewhat extravagant saga of Lik-Lodin we read:[1]

"Formerly most ships were always wrecked in this ice from the Northern bays,

---

do no more evil to any one. The similarities are striking: both are perishing of thirst and about to drink urine, the Icelanders their own, the Irish the devil's. They ask their leaders—the Icelanders Thorgils, the Irish Brandan—whether they may drink it. In both cases the leaders require a prayer to be said over it. Thereupon in both cases they see the devil: the Icelanders in the form of a bird that screams and finally leaves them to trouble them no more, and the Irish in the form of the devil himself, who is passing water, and disappears into the sea to do no more evil. The Icelandic tale is to some extent disconnected and incomprehensible, but is explained by being compared with the Irish; one thus sees how there may originally have been a connection between the bird (the Evil One) and the drink, which is otherwise obscure. The Icelandic account may have arisen by a distortion and adaptation, due to oral transmission, of the Irish legend.

[1] Cf. "Grönl. hist. Mind.," ii. p. 656.

GREENLAND VOYAGES IN THE MIDDLE AGES

as is related at length in the Tosta þáttr; for 'Lika-Loðinn' had his nickname from this, that in summer he often ransacked the northern uninhabited regions and brought to church the corpses of men that he found in caves, whither they had come from the ice or from shipwreck; and by them there often lay carved runes about all the circumstances of their misfortunes and sufferings."

The Northern bays here must mean "Hafsbotn," or the Polar Sea to the north of Norway and Iceland; the ice will then be that which thence drifts southward along the east coast of Greenland. According to another ancient MS. of the Tosta-þáttr,[1] Lik-Lodin had his name (which means "Corpse-Lodin") "because he had brought the bodies of Finn Fegin and his crew from Finn's booths, east of the glaciers in Greenland." This also shows that the east coast is referred to; it is said to have happened a few years before Harold Hardråda's fall in 1066.

In the Flateyjarbók's narrative of Einar Sokkason, who sailed from Greenland to Norway in 1123 to bring a bishop to the country, it is said[2] that he was accompanied on his return from Norway by a certain Arnbjörn Austman (i.e., man from the east, from Norway) and several Norwegians on another ship, who wished to settle in Greenland; but they were lost on the voyage. Some years later, about 1129, they were found dead on the east coast of Greenland, near the Hvitserk glacier, by a Greenlander, Sigurd Njálsson. "He often went seal-hunting in the autumn to the uninhabited regions [i.e., on the east coast]; he was a great seaman; they were fifteen altogether. In the summer they came to the Hvitserk glacier." They found there some human fire-places, and farther on, inside a fjord, they found a great ship, lying on and by the mouth of a stream, and a hut and a tent, and there were corpses lying in the tent, and some more lay on the ground outside. It was Arnbjörn and his men, who had stayed there.

In Gudmund Arason's Saga and in the Icelandic Annals

[1] Cf. "Gronl. hist. Mind.," ii. p. 662.
[2] Ibid. pp. 684 ff.

IN NORTHERN MISTS

CHAPTER VIII

Ingimund the priest

[Storm, 1888, pp. 22, 120, 121, 180, 181, 324, 477] it is related that in 1189 the ship "Stangarfoli," with the priest Ingimund Thorgeirsson and others on board—on the way from Bergen to Iceland—was driven westwards to the uninhabited regions of Greenland, and every man perished,

"but it was known by the finding of their ship and seven men in a cave in the uninhabited regions fourteen winters [1] later; there were Ingimund the priest, he was whole and uncorrupted, and so were his clothes; but six skeletons lay there by his side, and wax,[2] and runes telling how they lost their lives. And men thought this a great sign of how God approved of Ingimund the priest's conduct that he should have lain out so long with whole body and unhurt." [Cf. "Gronl. hist. Mind.," ii. p. 754; Biskupa Sogur, 1858, i. p. 435].

We see that the legend of the Seven Sleepers, perhaps from Paulus Warnefridi (see above, p. 156), has been borrowed; but here it is only one of the seven who is holy and unhurt. The shipwreck itself may nevertheless be historical.[3] The craft was doubtless lost on the southern east coast of Greenland, near Cape Farewell, which part was commonly frequented, and where the remains were found.

Einar Thorgeirsson

It is also related in Gudmund Arason's Saga that, some time before this, another ship was lost in the uninhabited regions of Greenland, with the priest Ingimund's brother, Einar Thorgeirsson, on board; but the crew quarrelled over the food. Einar escaped with two others and made for the settlement (i.e., the Eastern Settlement) across the glaciers (i.e., the inland ice). There they lost their lives, when only a day's journey from the settlement, and they were found one or two winters [i.e., years?] later (Einar's body was then

---

[1] According to the "Islandske Annaler" [pp. 121, 181, 477] it was in 1200, therefore eleven years later, not fourteen; it is there related merely that Ingimund the priest was found uncorrupted in the uninhabited region, but the other six are not mentioned.

[2] I.e., wax tablets to write on.

[3] The Arab Qazwini (thirteenth century) tells a story, after Omar al 'Udhri (eleventh century), of a cave in the west where lie four dead men uncorrupted [cf. G. Jacob, 1892, p. 168].

GREENLAND VOYAGES IN THE MIDDLE AGES

whole and unhurt). The shipwreck may consequently be supposed to have taken place on the southernmost part of the east coast.

CHAPTER VIII

In the Icelandic Annals it is mentioned (in various MSS.) that a new land was discovered west of Iceland in 1285. A MS. of annals, of about 1306 (written, that is, about twenty years after the event), says that in 1285: " fandz land vestr undan Islande " (a land was found to the west of Iceland). A later MS. (of about 1360) says of the same discovery : " Funduz Duneyiar " (the Down Islands were found). In another old MS. of annals there is an addition by a later hand : " fundu Helga synir nyia land Adalbrandr ok Þorvalldr " (Helge's sons Adalbrand and Thorvald found the new land). Finally we read in a late copy of an old MS. of annals : " Helga synir sigldu i Grœnlandz obygðir "[1] (Helge's sons sailed to the uninhabited regions of Greenland). According to this last statement, this would refer to the discovery of land on the east coast of Greenland, west of Iceland.[2] It may have been at Angmagsalik or farther south on the east coast that Helge's sons—two Icelandic priests—landed.[3] In the late summer this part is usually free from ice. From other Icelandic notices it may be concluded that they returned to Iceland the same autumn. We see that some years later the Norwegian king Eric attempted to get together an expedition to this new land under the so-called Landa-Rolf, who was sent to Iceland for the purpose in 1289. In 1290 Rolf went about

New Land

[1] Cf. "Islandske Annaler," edited by G. Storm, 1888, pp. 50, 70, 142, 196, 337, 383.

[2] Cf. G. Storm's arguments to this effect, 1888a, pp. 263 ff. ; 1887, pp. 71 f.

[3] It is true that in Bishop Gissur Einarsson's (bishop from 1541 to 1548) copy-book there is an addition to the ancient sailing directions for Greenland that " experienced men have said that one must sail south-west to New Land (Nyaland) from the Krysuvik mountains " (on the Reykjanes peninsula) [see " Grønl. hist. Mind.," III. p. 215 ; and G. Storm, " Hist. Tidskr.," 1888, p. 264] ; but it is impossible to attach much weight to a statement of direction in a tradition 260 years old ; it may easily have been altered or " improved " by later misconceptions.

IN NORTHERN MISTS

CHAPTER VIII

Iceland, inviting people to join the Newland expedition; but it is uncertain whether it ever came to anything, and in 1295 Landa-Rolf died. All this points to the east coast of Greenland having been little known at that time, otherwise a landing there could not be spoken of as the discovery of a new land; and it is not easy to see why the king should send Rolf to Iceland to get up an expedition to a country which, as they must have been aware, was closed by ice for the greater part of the year. As to the situation on this coast of islands to which the name of Down Islands might be appropriate, I shall not venture to offer an opinion.

The northern east coast

In the introduction to Hauk's Landnámabók we read: "en dœgr sigling er til vbygda a Grœnalandi or Kolbeins ey

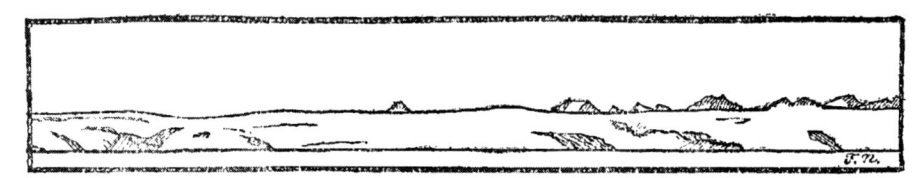

The southern glacier (Hvitserk) in 62° 10′ N. lat.; seen from the drift-ice in July 1888

i norðr" (it is a day's sail to the uninhabited regions of Greenland northward from Kolbein's island). Kolbein's island is the little Mevenklint, out at sea to the north of Grim's island and 56 nautical miles (100 kilometres) north of Iceland. The uninhabited regions here referred to are most probably East Greenland at about 69° N. lat. (Egede Land), which lies to the north-west (to the north there is no land, unless the magnetic north is meant). But it is scarcely credible that the Icelanders ever reached land on this part of the coast, which is nearly always closed by ice. It may be supposed that they often sailed along the edge of the ice when seal-hunting, as the bladder-nose is abundant there in summer; they may then have seen the land inside, and so knew of it, without having reached it. In this way the statement as to the distance

GREENLAND VOYAGES IN THE MIDDLE AGES

may have originated, and the day's sail may mean to the edge of the ice, whence the land is visible.

> According to statements in the fourth part of the "Rymbegla" [1780, p. 482], a "dœgr's" sail (dœgr = half a day of twenty-four hours) was equivalent to a distance of two degrees of latitude. But even if we accept this large estimate, it will not suffice for the distance between Mevenklint and the coast of Greenland to the north-west of it, which is about equal to three degrees of latitude (180 geographical miles).

It has been assumed that the Icelanders and Norwegians were acquainted with the east coast of Greenland north of 70° N. lat., and visited it for hunting seals, etc. But in order to reach it, it is nearly always necessary to sail through ice, and during the greater part of the summer one has to go as far north as Jan Mayen, or farther, to find the ice sufficiently open to allow one to reach the land. It is a somewhat tricky piece of sailing, which requires an intimate knowledge of the ice conditions; and it is not to be expected that any one should have acquired it without having frequently been among the ice with a definite purpose. That storm-driven vessels should have been accidentally cast ashore on this coast is unlikely; as a rule they would be stopped by the ice before they came so far. We may doubtless believe that the Norwegians and Icelanders sailed over the whole Arctic Ocean, along the edge of the ice, when hunting seals and the valuable walrus; but that on their sealing expeditions they should have made a practice of penetrating far into the ice is not credible, since their clinker-built craft were not adapted to sailing among ice; nor have we any information that would point to this. It is nevertheless not entirely impossible that they should have reached the northern east coast, since it may be comparatively free from ice in late summer and autumn. There would be plenty of seals, and especially of walrus, and on land there were reindeer and musk ox, which latter, however, is nowhere mentioned in Norse literature.

The old sea-route, the so-called "Eiriks-stefna," from

IN NORTHERN MISTS

CHAPTER VIII
Glaciers on the east coast

Iceland to Greenland (i.e., the Greenland Settlements) went westward from Snæfellsnes until one sighted the glaciers of Greenland, when one steered south-west along the drift-ice until well past Hvarf, etc. This is the route that Eric followed, according to the oldest accounts in the Landnáma, when he sailed to Greenland, and the glacier he first sighted in Greenland is there called "Miðjǫkull" (see above, p. 267). This name (the middle glacier) shows that two other glaciers must have been known, one to the north and one to the south, as indeed is explained in a far later work, the so-called "Gripla" (date uncertain, copied in the seventeenth century by Björn Jónsson), where we read : [1]

The mountains from Tingmiarmiut Fjord northward

"From Bjarmeland [i.e., northern Russia] uninhabited regions lie northward as far as that which is called Greenland. But there are bays (botnar gánga þar fyrir) and the land turns towards the south-west ; there are glaciers and fjords, and islands lying off the glaciers ; as far as [or rather, beyond] the first glacier they have not explored ; to the second is a journey of half a month, to the third a week's ; it is nearest the settlement ; it is called Hvitserk ; there the land turns to the north ; but he who would not miss the settlement, let him steer to the south-west" [that is, to get round and clear of the drift-ice that lies off Cape Farewell].

Not taking the distances into account, a sail of half a month and of a week, this is an admirable description of East Greenland from about 69° N. lat. southwards. By "glaciers" is obviously meant parts of the inland ice, which is the most noticeable feature of this coast, and which could not easily be omitted in a description of it. When we read that there are glaciers and fjords, and that islands lie off the glaciers, then every one who is familiar with this part of

[1] "Grönl. hist. Mind.," iii. pp. 222–224.

GREENLAND VOYAGES IN THE MIDDLE AGES

Greenland must be reminded of what catches the eye at the first sight of this coast from the sea: the dark stretches of land, not covered by snow, and the islands, lying in front of the vast white sheath of the inland ice, which is indented by bays and fjords. The three glaciers mentioned cannot, in my opinion, be three separate mountain summits covered with snow or ice, as has frequently been supposed. There is such a number of high summits in this country that, although I have sailed along the greater part of it, I am unable to name three as specially prominent. If one has seen from the sea the white snow-sheet of Vatnajökel in Iceland (compare also, on a smaller scale, the Hardangerjökel

in 62° 35′ N. lat. Seen from the drift-ice in July 1888

and others in Norway), then perhaps it will be easier to understand what the ancient Icelanders meant by their three glaciers on the east coast of Greenland, where the mass of glacier has a still mightier and more striking effect. Now, on that part of it which they and the Greenlanders knew, or had seen from the sea—and which extends towards the south-west (as we read) from about 70° N. lat.—there are precisely three tracts where the inland ice covers the whole country and reaches to the very shore, so that the glacier surface is visible from the sea, and forms the one conspicuous feature that must strike every one who sails along the outer edge of the ice (or drifts in the ice, as I have twice done). The northernmost tract is to the north of 67° N. lat. (see map, p. 259); there the inland ice covers the coast down to the sea itself. This was the "northern glacier," which no

[1] As we have said, they can scarcely have known anything of the coast to the north of this, which runs in a more northerly direction.

one was able to approach on account of the drift-ice, but which was only seen from a great distance. It was not until a few years ago that Captain Amdrup succeeded in travelling along this part of the country in boats, inshore of the ice.

The second tract is the coast by Pikiutdlek and Umivik, south of Angmagsalik, between Sermilik-fjord (65° 36′ N. lat.) and Cape Mösting (63° 40′ N. lat.), where the inland ice covers the whole coast land, and only a few mountain summits, or "Nunataks," rise up, and bare, scattered islands and tongues of land lie in front. This was the "Miðjǫkull" (middle glacier), which was the first land made

The northern part of the "Miðjǫkull (to the left) and the country to the west of Sermilik-fjord, in 65° 40′ N. lat. Seen from the drift-ice in July 1888

in sailing west from Snæfellsnes, and which was a good and unmistakable sea-mark. In some MSS. it is called "hinn mikla Jǫkull" (the great glacier). There the sea is often comparatively free of ice in August and September, but we may be sure that the voyagers to Greenland did not as a rule try to land there; in the words of Ivar Bárdsson's directions, they were to "take their course from Snæfellsnes and sail due west for a day and a night, but then to steer to the south-west, in order to avoid the above-mentioned ice" (cf. above, p. 262).

The third tract is the coast south of Tingmiarmiut and Mogens Heinesen's Fjord (62° 20′ N. lat.), where again the inland ice is predominant, and the only conspicuous feature that is first seen from the sea. This was the third or "southern glacier"; it lay nearest to Hvarf and was the sure sea-mark before rounding the southern end of the country. It appears to me that in this way we have a

GREENLAND VOYAGES IN THE MIDDLE AGES

natural explanation of what these disputed glaciers were. Between them lay long stretches of mountainous coast. Northward from Cape Farewell to the "southern glacier" are high mountains, so that one does not see the even expanse of the inland ice from the sea. North of the "southern glacier" is the fjord-indented mountainous country about Tingmiarmiut, Umanak and Skjoldungen, and so northward as far as Cape Mösting; there the mighty white line of the inland ice is wholly concealed behind a wall of lofty peaks. On the north side of the "Miðjǫkull" again is the mountain country about Angmagsalik, from Sermilik-fjord north-eastwards, with a high range of mountains, so that neither is the inland

The mountains near Angmagsalik, east of Sermilik-fjord. Seen from the drift-ice in July 1888

ice seen from the sea there. The most conspicuous summit of this range is Ingolf's Fjeld.

Thus, according to my view, the statements as to the glaciers on the east coast of Greenland are easily explained. It is a different matter when we come to the two names "Bláserkr" and "Hvítserkr," which, in later times especially, were those most frequently used. They have often been confused and interchanged, and while "Bláserkr" is found in the oldest authorities, the name "Hvítserkr" becomes more and more common in later writers. More recent authors have frequently regarded them as standing in a certain opposition to each other, one meaning a dark glacier or summit, and the other a white one, which may indeed seem natural. But it is striking that, while "Bláserkr" alone is mentioned in the oldest authorities, such as the Landnáma (and the Saga of Eric the Red, in the Hauksbók), it soon disappears almost entirely from literature,

CHAPTER VIII and is replaced by "Hvítserkr," which is first mentioned in MSS. of the fourteenth century and later; and in the fifteenth century MS. (A.M. 557, qv.) of the Saga of Eric the Red (as in other late extracts from the same saga) we find "Hvítserkr" instead of "Bláserkr."[1] I have not found the two names used contemporaneously in any Icelandic MS.; it is either one or the other, and nowhere are both names found as designating two separate places on the coast of Greenland. It may therefore be somewhat rash to assume, as has been done hitherto, that they were two "mountains," one of them lying a certain distance to the north on the east coast of Greenland, and the other near

The inland ice at "Miðjøkull." In the centre the mountain Kiatak, 64° 20′ N. lat. Seen from the drift-ice in July 1888

Cape Farewell. The view that they were mountains is not a new one. In Ivar Bárdsson's description Hvítserk is called "a high mountain" near Hvarf; while Björn Jónsson of Skardsá says that it is a "fuglabiarg i landnordurhafi" (i.e., a fowling cliff in the Polar Sea).

From the meaning of the names—the dark ("blá") sark and the white sark—we should be inclined to think that they were applied to snow-fields, or glaciers, like, for instance, such names as Snehætta and Lodalskåpa in Norway. But another possibility is that it was the *form* of the sark that was thought of, and that the names were applied to mountain summits; in a similar way "stakk" (stack, or gown) is used for peaks in Norway (cf. Lövstakken near Bergen); and in Shetland corresponding names are known for high cliffs on the sea: Blostakk (= Blástakkr), Grostakk

[1] Cf. G. Storm, 1891, p. 7; "Grönl. hist. Mind.," i. p. 361.

GREENLAND VOYAGES IN THE MIDDLE AGES

(= Grástakkr), Kwitastakk (= Hvíti stakkr), Gronastakk and Gronistakk (= Grœni stakkr, cliffs with grass-grown tops), etc. [cf. J. Jakobsen, 1901, p. 151].

CHAPTER VIII

In the Landnámabók (both Hauksbók and Sturlubók) we read: "Eirekr sigldi vndan Snæfells nese. En hann kom utan at Midiokli þar sem Bláserkr heitir." (Eric sailed from Snæfellsnes, and made the Mid-Glacier at a place called Blue-Sark.) In Eric the Red's Saga this has been altered to "hann kom utan at jǫkli þeim er Bláserkr heitir." (He made the glacier that is called Blue-Sark.) It is obvious that the Landnáma text is the more original, and thus two explanations are possible: either Bláserkr

The mountains about Ingolf's Fjeld, seen from a distance in June 1888

is a part of the glacier, or it is a dark mountain seen on this part of the coast. I cannot remember any place where the inland ice of this district, seen at a distance from the drift-ice, had a perceptibly darker colour; its effect is everywhere a brilliant white. On approaching an ice-glacier, as, for instance, the Colberger Heide (64° N. lat., cf. Nansen, 1890, p. 370; Engl. ed., i. 423), it may appear somewhat darker and of a bluish tinge; but this can never have been a recognisable landmark at any distance. One is therefore tempted to believe that Bláserkr was a black, bare mountain-peak. But the peaks that show up along the edge of the "Miðjǫkull" (between Sermilik and Cape Mösting) are all comparatively low; the mountain-summit Kiatak, near Umivik [see Nansen, 1890, pp. 370, 374, 444; Engl. ed., i. 423, 429, ii. 13], answers best as regards shape, and is conspicuous enough, but it is only 2450 feet high. It is possible that Bláserkr did not lie in

IN NORTHERN MISTS

CHAPTER VIII

Miðjǫkull itself, but was the lofty Ingolf's Fjeld (7300 feet high), which is the first mountain one sees far out at sea, on approaching East Greenland from Iceland; and it is seen to the north in sailing past Cape Dan and in towards Miðjǫkull. It may then have been confused with the latter in later times. But this supposition is doubtful. The most natural way for the Icelanders when making for Greenland must in any case have been first to make the edge of the ice, west-north-west from Snæfellsnes, when they sighted Ingolf's Fjeld (or Bláserkr?); then they followed the ice west or west-south-west, and came straight in to Miðjǫkull, at about 65° N. lat., or the same latitude as Snæfellsnes. Here the edge of the ice turns southward, following the land, and the course has to be altered in order to sail past the southern glacier and round Hvarf. This agrees well with most descriptions of the voyage, and among them the most trustworthy. But the names have often been confused; Hvítserk and Bláserk especially have been interchanged;[1] and this is not surprising, since the men who wrote in Iceland in the fourteenth and fifteenth centuries were themselves unacquainted with these waters.

Hvítserkr

The name "Hvítserkr" would appear most appropriate to a glacier, and in reviewing the various contexts in which it is mentioned in the narratives, my impression is rather that in later times it was often used as a name for the inland ice itself on the east and south coasts of Greenland; and as, on the voyage to the Eastern Settlement, the inland ice was most seen on the southern part of the east coast, which was also resorted to for seal-hunting, the name Hvítserk became especially applied to the southern glacier, as in the tale of Einar Sokkason (see above, p. 283); but it might also be the mid-glacier. This view is supported by, for instance,

---

[1] The mathematician and cosmographer Jacob Ziegler (ob. 1549) in his work "Scondia" (printed at Strasburg, 1536) placed the promontory of Hvítserk ("Hvetsarg promontorium") in 67° N. lat. [cf. "Gronl. hist. Mind.," iii. pp. 500, 503]. This may be the usual confusion with Bláserk. It happens to be by no means ill suited to Ingolf's Fjeld, which lies in 66° 25′ N lat.

294

GREENLAND VOYAGES IN THE MIDDLE AGES

the so-called Walkendorff addition to Ivar Bárdsson's description, where the following passage occurs about the voyage from Iceland to Greenland ["Grönl. hist. Mind.," iii. p. 491]:

"Item when one is south of Breedefjord in Iceland, then he must steer westward until he sees Hvidserch in Greenland, and then steer south-west, until the above mentioned Hvidserch is to the north of him; thus may one with God's help freely seek Greenland, without much danger from ice, and with God's help find Eric's fjord."

It is clearly enough the inland ice itself, the most prominent feature on the east coast, that is here called Hvidserch. It is first seen at Miðjǫkull, in coming westwards from Iceland; and one has the inland ice (ice-blink) on the north when about to round Cape Farewell. No single mountain can possibly fit this description; but this does not exclude the possibility of others having erroneously connected the name with such a mountain, in the same way as Danish sailors of recent times have applied it to a lofty island, "Dadloodit," in the southernmost part of Greenland ["Grönl. hist. Mind.," i. p. 453]. The fact that Hvítserk in Ivar Bárdsson's description is called "a high mountain," which is seen one day before reaching Hvarf, must be due to a similar misunderstanding. As Bláserk, although originally it may have been a mountain, was confounded with the Mid-Glacier, it is comprehensible that the name Bláserk should be gradually superseded by Hvítserk.

In one or two passages of the old narratives it is related that when one was half-way between Iceland and Greenland one could see at the same time, in clear weather, Snæfells glacier in Iceland and Bláserk (or Hvítserk)[1] in Greenland.

[1] In the Walkendorff additions to Ivar Bárdsson's description of Greenland it is called Hvítserk, which may be a confusion with Bláserk; the passage continues: "And it is credibly reported that it is not thirty sea-leagues to land, in whichever direction one would go, whether to Greenland or to Iceland" [see "Gronl. hist. Mind.," iii. p. 491]. The distance here given is remarkably correct. In Björn Jónsson's "Grönlands Annaler" (written before 1646) it is related that "Sira Einar Snorrason," priest of Stadarstad, near Snæfellsnes (he became

CHAPTER VIII

According to my experience this is not possible, even if we call in the aid of a powerful refraction, or even mirage; but, on the other hand, one can see the reflections of the land or the ice on the sky, and when sailing (along the edge of the ice) eastwards or westwards, one can very well see the top of the Snæfells glacier and the top of Ingolf's Fjeld on the same day.

Place-names on the east coast

The Icelandic accounts mention several places in East Greenland, such as "Kross-eyjar," "Finnsbuðir," "Berufjord" ("bera" = she-bear), and the fjord "Öllum-Lengri." Frequent expeditions for seal-hunting were made to these places from the Eastern Settlement, and they must have lain near it, just north of Cape Farewell.

VOYAGES TO THE NORTHERN WEST COAST OF GREENLAND, NORÐRSETUR, AND BAFFIN'S BAY IN THE MIDDLE AGES

To the north of the northernmost inhabited fjords of the Western Settlement lay the uninhabited regions. Thither the Greenlanders resorted every summer for seal-hunting; there lay what they called the "Norðrsetur" ("seta" = place of residence; the northern stations or fishing-places), and it is doubtless partly to these districts that reference is made in Eric the Red's Saga, where it is said of Thorhall the Hunter that "he had long been with Eric hunting in summer," and that "he had a wide acquaintance with the uninhabited regions." We have no information as to how far north the longest expeditions of the Greenlanders extended, but we know that they reached the neighbourhood of the modern Upernivik; for, twenty-eight miles to the north-west of it—

priest there in 1502), owned a large twelve-oared boat, which, with a cargo of dried cod, was carried away from Öndverdarnes (the western point of Snæfellsnes) "and drifted out to sea, so that they saw both the glaciers, as Gunnbjorn had done formerly, both Snæfells glacier and Blåserk in Greenland; they had thus come near to Eric's course ('Eiriksstefnu')" ["Grønl. hist. Mind.," 1. p. 123]. Here, then, we have the same idea that both glaciers can be seen simultaneously, as is also found in Bjorn's work with reference to Gunnbjorn Ulfsson's voyage (see above, p. 263).

GREENLAND VOYAGES IN THE MIDDLE AGES

on a little island called Kingigtorsuak, in 72° 55′ N. lat.— three cairns are said to have been found early in the nineteenth century (before 1824); and in one of them a small runic stone, with the inscription: "Erling Sigvathsson, Bjarne Thordarson, and Endride Oddson on the Sunday before 'gagndag' [i.e., April 25] erected these cairns and cleared . . ."[1] Then follow six secret runes, which it was formerly sought to interpret, erroneously, as a date, 1135. Professor L. F. Läffler has explained them as meaning ice;[2] it would then read "and cleared away ice." Judging from the language, the inscription would be of the fourteenth century;[3] Professor Magnus Olsen (in a letter to me) thinks it might date from about 1300, or perhaps a little later. Why the cairns were built seems mysterious. It is possible that they were sea-marks for fishing-grounds; but it is not likely that the Greenlanders were in the habit of going so far north. One would be more inclined to think they were set up as a monument of a remarkable expedition, which had penetrated to regions previously unknown; but why build more than one cairn? Was there one for each man? The most remarkable thing is that the cairns are stated to have been set up in April, when the sea in that locality is covered with ice. The three men must either have wintered there in the north, which seems the more probable alternative;

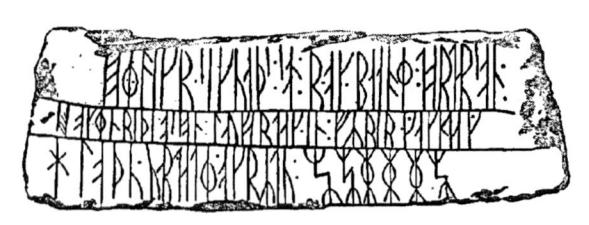

CHAPTER VIII
Runic stone from 72° 55′ N. lat.

Runic stone from Kingigtorsuak
(after A. A. Björnbo)

---

[1] Cf. "Grönl. hist. Mind.," iii. p. 843. Captain Graah brought the stone to Denmark in 1824.

[2] In a paper read before the Archæological Society at Stockholm, March 13, 1905. Cf. "Svenska Dagbladet," March 14, 1905. I owe this reference to Professor Magnus Olsen.

[3] Cf. A. Bugge, 1898, p. 506. By a printer's error, seventeenth century is given instead of fourteenth.

they may then have been starving, and the object of the cairns was to call the attention of possible future travellers to their bodies—or they may have come the same spring over the ice from the south, and in that case they most probably travelled with Eskimo dog-sledges, and were on a hunting expedition, perhaps for bears. But they cannot have travelled northwards from the Eastern or Western Settlement the same spring. In any case they may have been in company with Eskimo, whom we know to have lived on Disco Bay, and probably also farther south at that time. From them the Norsemen may have learnt to hunt on the ice, by which they were able to support themselves in the north during the winter.

The earliest mention of hunting expeditions to the northern west coast of Greenland is found in the "Historia Norwegiæ" (thirteenth century), where it is said that hunters "to the north" (of the Greenlanders) come across "certain small people whom they call Skrælings" (see later, chapter x.).

Ŏrsetur

There are few references to the "Norðrsetur" in the literature that has been preserved. A lay on the subject, "Norðrsetudrápa," was known in the Middle Ages, written by an otherwise unknown skald, Sveinn. Only a few short fragments of it are known from "Skálda," Snorra-Edda [cf. "Gronl. hist. Mind.," iii. pp. 235 ff.]. It is wild and gloomy, and speaks of the ugly sons of Fornjót [the storms] who were the first to drift [i.e., with snow], and of Ægi's storm-loving daughters [the waves], who wove and drew tight the hard sea-spray, fed by the frost from the mountains.

Reference is also made to these hunting expeditions to the north in "Skáld-Helga Rimur," where we read ["Grönl. hist. Mind.," ii. p. 492]:

"Gumnar fóru i Greipar norðr	Men went north to Greipar,
Gronlands var þar bygðar sporðr.	There was the end of Greenland's habitations.
virðar áttu viða hvar	Men might there far and wide
veiðiskapar at leita þar.	Seek for hunting.

GREENLAND VOYAGES IN THE MIDDLE AGES

Skeggi enn prúði skip sitt bjó,	Skegge the Stately fitted out his ship,	CHAPTER
skútunni rendi norðr um sjó,	With his vessel he sailed north in the sea,	VIII
holdum ekki hafit vannst,	By the men the sea was not conquered,	
hvarf í burtu, en aldri fannst." [1]	They were lost, and never found.	

It appears from Håkon Håkonsson's Saga that the Norðrsetur were a well-known part of Greenland; for we read of the submission of the Greenlanders to the Norwegian Crown that they promised

"to pay the king fines for all manslaughter, whether of Norsemen or Greenlanders, and whether they were killed in the settlements or in Norðrsetur, and in all the district to the north under the star [i.e., the pole-star] the king should have his weregild" ["Grønl. hist. Mind.," ii. p. 779].

In Björn Jónsson's "Grönlands Annaler" (cf. above, p. 263) these expeditions to the Norðrsetur are mentioned in more detail, as well as a remarkable voyage to the north in 1267 ["Grönl. hist. Mind.," iii. pp. 238 ff.]. We there read:

"All the great franklins of Greenland had large ships and vessels built to send to the 'Norðrsetur' for seal-hunting, with all kinds of sealing gear ('veiðiskap') and cut-up wood ('telgðum viðum'), and sometimes they themselves accompanied the expeditions—as is related at length in the tales, both in the Skáld-Helga saga and in that of Thordis; there most of what they took was seal-oil, for all seal-hunting was better there than at home in the settlements; melted seal-fat was poured into sacks of hide [literally boats of hide], and hung up against the wind on boards, till it thickened, then it was prepared as it should be The Norðrsetu-men had their booths or houses ('skála') both in Greipar and in Króksfjarðarheiðr [Kroksfjords-heath]. Driftwood is found there, but no growing trees. This northern end of Greenland is most liable to take up all the wood and other drift that comes from the bays of Markland...."

In an extract which follows: "On the voyage northward to the uninhabited regions" (probably from a different and later source) we read:

"The Greenlanders are constantly obliged to make voyages to the uninhabited regions in the northern land's end or point, both for the sake of wood [i.e., driftwood] and sealing; it is called Greipar and Króksfjarðarheiðr; it is a

---

[1] See also the 5th and 6th cantos of the same poem, "Grønl. hist. Mind.," ii. pp. 522 ff., for the voyage to Greipar and its being the resort of outlaws.

IN NORTHERN MISTS

CHAPTER VIII

great and long sea voyage thither;[1] as the Skáld-Helga saga clearly bears witness, where it is said of it:

"'Garpar kvomu i Greypar norðr. The men came to Greipar in the north,
Gronlands er þar bryggju sporðr.'[2] There is the bridge-spur (end) of Greenland.

"Sometimes this sealing season ('vertið') of theirs in Greipar or Króksfjardarheidr is called Norðrseta."

Greipar and Króksfjardarheidr. Their situation

According to this description we must look for Nordrsetur, with Greipar and Króksfjardarheidr, to the north of the northern extremity of the Western Settlement, which from other descriptions must have been at Straumsfjord, about $66\frac{1}{2}°$ N. lat. (see map, p. 266). There in the north, then, there was said to be driftwood, and plenty of seals. The latter circumstance is especially suited to the districts about Holstensborg and northward to Egedes Minde (i.e., between 66° and $68\frac{1}{2}°$ N. lat.), and further to Disco Bay and Vaigat (see map, p. 259). Besides abundance of seals there was also good walrus-hunting, and this was valuable on account of the tusks and hide, which were Greenland's chief articles of export [cf. for instance, "The King's Mirror," above, p. 277]. There was also narwhale, the tusk or spear of which was even more valuable than walrus tusks. "Greipar"[3] may have been near Holstensborg, about 67° N. lat. "Króks-

[1] Captain Isachsen [1907] has attached much weight to this expression (which he translates from "Gronl. hist. Mind" by "long and dangerous sea-route"; but the original is "mikit og lángt sjóleiði") in order to prove that the Nordrsetur must lie far north. But it is seen from the text itself that this idea of a long sea voyage is taken from the Skáld-Helga lay (where also similar expressions are used), which is of late origin, and consequently an untrustworthy base for such conclusions. Moreover, according to the lay itself, Skald-Helge belonged probably to the Eastern Settlement, and thence to Holstensborg, 67° N. lat., was a long voyage.

[2] This is obviously an error for "bygðar sporðr" (end of the inhabited country), as in the "Skáld-Helga Rimur" (see above, p. 298).

[3] "Greipar," plural of "Greip," would mean literally the grip or interval between the fingers, but it may also be used of mountain ravines. The name seems to point to a particularly rugged or fjord-indented coast, and would be appropriate to the whole country north of Straumsfjord, for instance about Holstensborg, in about 67°.

GREENLAND VOYAGES IN THE MIDDLE AGES

fjarðarheiðr" may have been at Disco Bay or Vaigat.[1] It also agrees with this that the northern point of Greenland ("þessi norðskagi Grœnlands") was in Norðrsetur, and that "Greipar" was at the land's end ("bygðar sporðr") of Greenland. For what the Greenlanders generally understood by Greenland was the Eastern and Western Settlements, and the broad extent of coast lying to the north of them, which was not covered by the inland ice, and which reached to Disco Bay. It was the part where human habitation was possible, and where there was no inland ice; it was therefore natural for them to call Greipar the northern end of the country.

In an old chorography, copied by Bjorn Jónsson under the name of "Gronlandiæ vetus chorographia"[2] (in his "Gronlands Annaler"), there is mention of the Western Settlement and of the districts to the north of it. After naming the fjords in the Eastern Settlement it proceeds: "Then it is six days' rowing, six men in a six-oared boat, to the Western Settlement (then the fjords are enumerated),[3] then from this Western Settlement to Lysefjord it is six days' rowing, thence six days' rowing to Karlsbuða [Karl's booths], then three days' rowing to Bjarneyjar [Bear-islands or island], twelve days' rowing around ... ey,[4] Eisunes, Ædanes in the north. Thus it is reckoned that there are 190 dwellings [estates] in the Eastern Settlement, and 90 in the Western." This description is obscure on many points. From other ancient authorities it appears that Lysefjord was the southernmost fjord in the Western Settlement [now Fiskerfjord, cf. G. Storm, 1887, p. 35; F. Jónsson, 1899, p. 315], but how in that case there could be six days' rowing from this Western Settlement to Lysefjord seems incomprehensible. It might be supposed that it is the distance from the southern extremity of the Western Settlement that is intended, and thus the passage has been translated in "Gronl. hist. Mind.," iii. p. 229; but then it is strange that in the original MS.

---

[1] "Króksfjarðar-heiðr" would literally mean the flat, waste mountain tract ("heiðr") by the crooked fjord, Kroksfjord. The latter name would be very appropriate to Disco Bay and Vaigat. The flat plateaux of basalt, which form Disco on one side, and the Nugsuak Peninsula on the other side of Vaigat, might be called "heiðr."

[2] Cf. "Gronl. hist. Mind.," iii. p. 226; F. Jónsson, 1899, p. 319.

[3] Perhaps these names of fjords were so indistinct in the original MS. that Bjorn Jónsson could not read them, and therefore inserted these words (cf. "Gronl. hist. Mind.," iii. p 233).

[4] The name of this island is left blank, and was doubtless illegible in the original.

CHAPTER VIII

the fjords of the settlement should have been enumerated before the distance to the first fjord was given. If this, however, be correct, it would then have been twelve days' rowing from the northernmost fjord in the Eastern Settlement to Lysefjord in the Western. This might perhaps agree with Ivar Bárdsson's description of Greenland, where it is stated that "from the Eastern Settlement to the Western Settlement is twelve sea-leagues, and all uninhabited." These twelve sea-leagues may be the above-mentioned twelve days' rowing, repeated in this form. It was a good two hundred nautical miles (forty ancient sea-leagues) from the northernmost fjord of the Eastern Settlement to the interior of Lysefjord. With twelve days' rowing, this would be at the rate of eighteen miles a day; but if we allow for their keeping the winding course inside the islands, it will be considerably longer. If we put a day's rowing from Lysefjord northward at, say, twenty nautical miles, then "Karlsbuðir" would lie in about 65°, and "Biarneyiar" in about 66°; but there is then a difficulty about this island, together with Eisunes and Ædanes, which it is said to have taken twelve days to row round. On the other hand, it is a good two hundred miles round Disco Island, so that this might correspond to twelve days' rowing at eighteen miles a day. And if this island is intended, then either the number of days' rowing northward along the coast must be increased, or the starting-point was not the Lysefjord (Fiskerfjord) that lay on the extreme south of the Western Settlement. But the description is altogether too uncertain to admit of any definite conclusion. It is not mentioned whether the northern localities, Karlsbuðir and farther north, were included in Nordrsetur, but it seems probable that they were.

In this connection the statement in Ivar Bárdsson's description must also be borne in mind:

Himinrað and Hunenrioth

"Item there lies in the north, farther from the Western Settlement, a great mountain that is called Himinraðzfjall,[1] and farther than to this mountain must no man sail, if he would preserve his life from the many whirlpools which there lie round all the ocean."

It is true that Ivar's description as a whole does not seem to be very trustworthy as regards details, nor do the whirlpools here spoken of tend to inspire confidence,

[1] So the mountain is called in an Icelandic translation, and this form may be nearest to the name in the original Norwegian text. In the various Danish MSS. the mountain is called "Hemeuell Radszfielt" (oldest MS.), "Hammelrads Fjeld," "Himmelradsfjeld," etc. In a MS. which is otherwise considered trustworthy, it is called "Hemelrachs Fjeld," and this has been frequently supposed to mean the heaven-reaching mountain [cf. "Gronl. hist. Mind.," iii. p. 259]. As will be mentioned later, the real name of the mountain was possibly "Himinroð" (flushing of the sky), or perhaps "Himinrǫð" (wall of heaven, i.e., wall reaching towards heaven).

GREENLAND VOYAGES IN THE MIDDLE AGES

suggesting as they do that it was near the earth's limit, where the ocean ends in one or more vast abysses ; but it is nevertheless possible that the mountain in question may have been an actual landmark in the extreme north, on that part of the west coast of Greenland to which voyages were habitually made, and in that case it must have been situated in " Nordrsetur."

Mention may also be made of a puzzling scholium to Adam of Bremen's work [cf. Lappenberg, 1838, pp 851 f.] ; it was added at a late period, ostensibly from " Danish fragments," but the form of the names betrays a Norse origin, and we must suppose that it is derived from ancient Norwegian or Icelandic sources The following is a translation of the Latin text :

"From Norway to Iceland is fourteen dozen leagues ('duodene leucarum ') across the sea (or XIII. dozen sea-leagues, that is, 168 leagues).[1] From Iceland as far as the green land (' terram viridem '] Gronlandt is about fourteen dozen (' duodenæ '). There is a promontory and it is called ' Huerff ' [i.e., Hvarf], and there snow lies continually and it is called ' Hwideserck.' From ' Hwideserck ' as far as ' Sunderbondt ' is ten dozen leagues (' duodenæ leucarum ') ; from ' Sunderbondt ' as far as ' Norderbondt ' is eleven dozen leagues (d. l). From ' Nordbundt ' to ' Hunenrioth ' is seventeen dozen leagues, and here men resort in order to kill white bears and ' Tauwallen ' " [" tandhvaler " (?)—" tusk-whales "—i e , walrus and narwhale (?)].[2]

This passage is difficult to understand. " Sunderbondt " and " Norderbondt " are probably to be regarded as translations of the Norwegian " Syd-botten " and " Nord-botten." The latter might be the Polar Sea, or " Hafsbotn," north of Iceland and Norway , on Claudius Clavus's map this is called " Nordhindh Bondh " (Nancy map) and " Nordenbodhn " (Vienna text).[3] But in that case we should have to suppose that the distances referred to a voyage from Norway to Iceland, from thence to Hvarf and Hvitserk, and then back again northward along the east coast of Greenland. It seems more probable that the direction of the voyage was supposed to be continued round Hvarf and up along the west coast ; but where " Sunderbondt " and " Norderbondt " are to be looked for on that coast

CHAPTER VIII

---

[1] The words in parenthesis are in German, and are certainly an explanation added later. XIII. is evidently an error for XIIII.

[2] It is also possible that it means whales from which " tauer " or ropes are obtained, i.e., the walrus ; the ropes of walrus-hide being so very valuable.

[3] One might then suppose that " Hunenrioth " was connected with the Norwegian word " hun " for a giant (sometimes used in our day for the Evil One). The name might then be applied to the mythical Risaland or Jotunheim, in the Polar Sea, north-east of Greenland ; but it would then be difficult to explain the meaning of the latter part of the name, -rioth.

IN NORTHERN MISTS

CHAPTER VIII

is difficult to say, the names would most naturally apply to two fjords or bays, and in some way or other these might be connected with the Eastern and Western Settlements, "Norderbondt" might, for instance, have come to mean the largest fjord, Godthaabs-fjord, in the Western Settlement. Since "hún" in Old Norse means a bear-cub or young bear, one might be inclined to connect "Hunenrioth" with Bjarn-eyar, where perhaps bears were hunted; but in that case "-rioth" must be taken to be the Old Norse "hrjotr" (growl, roar), which would be an unlikely name for islands or lands. It is more reasonable to suppose that it means the same as the above-mentioned mountain "Himinrað," from Ivar Bardsson's description. It might then be probable that this was called "Himinroð" (i.e., flushing of the sky, sun-gold, from the root-form "rioða") a natural name for a high mountain;[1] by an error in writing or reading this might easily become "Hunenrioth," as it might also become "Himinrað." Thus it is possibly a mountain in Nordrsetur (see above). But in any case the distances are impossible as they stand, and until more light has been thrown upon this scholium, we cannot attach much importance to it.

Nordrsetur not beyond Baffin's Bay

For many reasons it is unreasonable to look for "Greipar" and "Króksfjardarheidr" so far north as Smith Sound or Jones Sound (or Lancaster Sound), as, amongst others in recent times, Professor A. Bugge [1898] and Captain G. Isachsen [1907] have done:[2]

---

[1] Professor Moltke Moe has suggested to me this explanation of the name. One might also suppose it to mean the western land of sunset, that is, America, but it would be unlike the Scandinavians to use such a name for a country. There is a possibility that it was connected with "roð" (gen. "raðar," a ridge of land) and meant the ridge or wall of heaven, i.e., reaching toward heaven. It is, perhaps, less probable that "-rioth" or "-rað" came from a word of two syllables like "roða" (a rod, later a cross, Anglo-Saxon "rod," modern English "rood") or the poetical word "róði" (wind, storm). In O. Rygh: "Norske Gaardnavne," xvi. Nordlands Amt [ed. K. Rygh, 1905, p. 334], there is the name of an estate "Himmelstein" (in Busknes), which in 1567 was written "Himmelstand," "Himmelstaa" [from 1610 on = "sten"]. K. Rygh remarks of this: "Himmel occurs occasionally in names of mountains: thus, a little farther north we have the lofty Himmeltinder on the border of Busknes and Borge. One is disposed to regard this name as similar to the Danish Himmelbjerg, meaning a very high mountain. . ." Professor Torp has mentioned to me the similarity of name with the giant Hymer's ox "Himinhrjotr" in the Snorra-Edda; but it is difficult to think that a mountain should have been called after the proper name of an animal.

[2] Rafn, in "Grönl. hist. Mind.," iii. pp. 881-885, commits the absurdity of separating these two places by the whole of Baffin's Bay, in spite of their being mentioned together in the old accounts under the common designation of "Nordrsetur." He puts "Greipar" in about 67° N. lat., but makes Króksfjardarheidr

GREENLAND VOYAGES IN THE MIDDLE AGES

(1) In the first place this would assume that he Greenlanders on their Nordrsetu expeditions sailed right across the ice-blocked and difficult Baffin's Bay and Melville Bay every summer, and back again in the autumn, in their small clinker-built vessels, which were not suited for sailing among the ice. We are told indeed (see above, p. 299) that the franklins had large ships and vessels for this voyage; but this was written in Iceland by men who were not themselves acquainted with the conditions in Greenland, and the statement doubtless means no more than that these vessels, or rather boats, were large in comparison to the small boats (perhaps for the most part boats of hides) which they usually employed in their home fisheries. Timber for shipbuilding was not easy to obtain in Greenland. Drift-wood would not go very far in building boats, to say nothing of larger vessels, and they must have depended on an occasional cargo of timber from Norway, or perhaps what they could themselves fetch from Markland. They could hardly have got the material for building vessels suited for sailing through the ice of Baffin's Bay in this way. Moreover, we know from several sources that there was great scarcity of rivets and iron nails in Greenland; so that vessels were largely built with wooden nails. In 1189 a Greenlander, Asmund Kastanrasti, came with twelve others from Kross-eyjar in Greenland to Iceland "in a ship that was fastened together with wooden nails alone, save that it was also bound with thongs. . . . He had also been in Finnsbuðir." He did not sail from Iceland till the following year, and was then shipwrecked.[1] This ship must have been one of the largest and best they had in Greenland. It is therefore impossible that

CHAPTER VIII

into Lancaster Sound, 74° N. lat., on the other side of the ice-blocked Baffin's Bay.

[1] Cf. "Islandske Annaler," ed. Storm, p. 120, etc.; "Gronl. hist. Mind.," ii. pp. 754, 762. As is pointed out by Finnur Jónsson [1893, p. 539], most of the coffins found in graves in Greenland are fastened together with wooden nails. We are also told how all the iron spikes and nails were carefully taken out of a stranded Norwegian ship (about 1129).

IN NORTHERN MISTS

CHAPTER VIII

they should have been able to keep up any constant communication with the countries on the north side of Baffin's Bay.

(2) Then comes the question: what reason would they have had for exposing themselves to the many dangers involved in the long northward voyage through the ice? Their purpose may have been chiefly to kill seals and collect driftwood. But where there is much ice for the greater part of the year, the driftwood is prevented from being thrown up on shore; and it is the fact that in Baffin's Bay there is unusually little of it, so that the Eskimo of Cape York and Smith Sound are barely able to get enough wood for making weapons and implements. In addition to the ice the reason for this is that no current of importance bearing driftwood reaches the north of Baffin's Bay. Consequently, this again is conclusive proof that the Nordrsetur of the descriptions is not to be looked for there, nor was sealing particularly good; they had better sealing-grounds in the districts about Holstensborg, Egedes Minde and Disco Bay.[1]

Nordrsetur at and south of Disco Bay

Everything points to the Nordrsetur having been situated in the districts either in or to the south of Disco Bay,[2] which

[1] Since this chapter was written a few years ago, an excellent treatise by O. Solberg on the Greenland Eskimo in prehistoric times has appeared [1907]. The author has here reached conclusions similar to the above as regards the northward extension of the Nordrsetu voyages; but he proposes to place Kroksfjord south of Disco Bay, since he does not think the Greenlanders came across the Eskimo who lived there. I do not consider this view justified; on the contrary, it seems to me probable (as will be mentioned later) that the Greenlanders had intercourse with the Eskimo

[2] Otto Sverdrup found on two small islands in Jones Sound several groups of three stones, evidently set up by human hands as shelters for sitting eider-ducks, similar to those with which he was acquainted in the north of Norway. Whether these stone shelters were very ancient could not be determined. Captain Isachsen [1907] thinks they may be due to the ancient Scandinavians of the Greenland settlements, and sees in them possible evidence of Jones Sound having been Kroksfjord. But too much importance must not be attached to this: no other sign of Europeans having stayed in Jones Sound was discovered, whereas there were many signs of Eskimo. Unless we are to believe that the latter set up the stones for some purpose or other, it is just as likely that they may have been

GREENLAND VOYAGES IN THE MIDDLE AGES

must have been a natural hunting-ground for the Greenlanders, just as the Norwegians sail long distances to Lofoten for fishing. Moreover, one of the objects of the voyages to Nordrsetur was to collect driftwood; now the driftwood comes with the Polar Current round Cape Farewell and is thrown up on shore along the whole of the west coast northward as far as this current washes the land—that is to say, about as far north as Disco Bay. In the south of Greenland, the ancient Eastern Settlement, there is drift-ice for part of the year, and not so much driftwood comes ashore as farther north, in the ancient Western Settlement (especially the Godthaab district) and to the north of it. Besides, in the settlements there were many to find it and utilise it, while in the uninhabited regions there were only the Eskimo, of whom perhaps there were as yet few south of 68° N. lat. On their way to and from the Nordrsetur, therefore, the Greenlanders travelled along the shore and collected driftwood wherever they found it. In Iceland this was misunderstood in the sense that driftwood was supposed to be washed ashore chiefly in Nordrsetur; and they believed it to come from Markland, perhaps because the Greenlanders sometimes went there for timber, and it was thus regarded by them as a country rich in trees. It is, however, also possible that the name Markland, i.e., woodland, itself may have created this conception. In reality most of the driftwood comes from Siberia, which was unknown to them, and it is brought with the drift-ice over the Polar Sea and southward along the east coast of Greenland.

The following is the account of the voyage of about 1267,

Driftwood. From an Icelandic MS., fifteenth century

placed there by chance hunters in recent times as that they were due to the ancient Norsemen.

IN NORTHERN MISTS

CHAPTER VIII
Voyage to Baffin's Bay in 1267

given by Björn Jónsson (taken, according to his statement, from the Hauksbók, where it is no longer to be found):

"That summer [i.e., 1266] when Arnold the priest went from Greenland, and they were stranded in Iceland at Hitarnes, pieces of wood were found out at sea, which had been cut with hatchets and adzes ('þexlum'), and among them one in which wedges of tusk and bone were imbedded.[1] The same summer men came from Nordrsetur, who had gone farther north than had been heard of before. They saw no dwelling-places of Skrælings, except in Króksfjardarheidr, and therefore it is thought that they [i.e., the Skrælings] must there have the shortest way to travel, wherever they come from. . . . After this [the following year ?] the priests sent a ship northward to find out what the country was like to the north of the farthest point they had previously reached; and they sailed out from Króksfjardarheidr, until the land sank below the horizon ('lægði'). After this they met with a southerly gale and thick weather ('myrkri'), and they had to stand off [i.e., to the north]. But when the storm passed over ('í rauf') and it cleared ('lysti'), they saw many islands and all kinds of game, both seals and whales [i.e., walrus ?], and a great number of bears. They came right into the gulf [i.e., Baffin's Bay] and all the land [i.e., all the land not covered by ice] then sank below the horizon, the land on the south and the glaciers ('jokla'), but there was also glacier ('jokull') to the south of them as far as they could see;[2] they found there some ancient dwelling-places of Skrælings ('Skrælingja vistir fornligar'), but they could not land on account of the bears. Then they went back for three 'dœgr,' and they found there some dwelling-places of Skrælings ('nokkra Skrælingja vistir') when they landed on some islands south of Snæfell. Then they went south to Króksfjardarheidr, one long day's rowing, on St. James's day [July 25], it was then freezing there at night, but the

---

[1] As these pieces of driftwood must have been carried by the East Greenland Polar Current, this seems to show that there were already Eskimo on the east coast of Greenland at that time. As they are spoken of as something remarkable, the pieces, with wedges of tusk and bone, cannot have been due to Norsemen, either in Greenland or Iceland. Their being shaped with "hatchets" or "adzes" (i.e., Eskimo tools) was looked upon as strange.

[2] This passage seems obscure, and there may be some error or misunderstanding on the part of the various copyists. But as it now stands, it may be best taken to mean that all known land and all the known glaciers had disappeared beneath the horizon; but that the "jokull" (i.e., snow-field or inland ice) which they saw to landward extended southward along the coast as far as they could see. The expression "to the south of them" is not, of course, to be interpreted as meaning due south of the spot where they were, but rather as southward along the coast, from the part off which they lay; this is confirmed by the addition "as far as they could see," which can only refer to a coast along which they were looking southward.

GREENLAND VOYAGES IN THE MIDDLE AGES

sun shone both night and day, and, when it was in the south, was only so high that if a man lay athwartships in a six-oared boat, the shadow of the gunwale nearest the sun fell upon his face; but at midnight it was as high as it is at home in the settlement when it is in the north-west. Then they returned home to Gardar" [in the Eastern Settlement].

CHAPTER VIII

Björn Jónsson says that this account of the voyage was written by Halldor, a priest of Greenland (who did not himself take part in the expedition, but had only heard of it), to Arnold, the priest of Greenland who was stranded in Iceland in 1266. It was then rewritten in Iceland (or Norway?), perhaps by one of the copyists of the Hauksbók, who was unacquainted with the conditions in Greenland; and afterwards it was again copied, and perhaps "improved," at least once (by Björn Jónsson himself). Unfortunately, the leaves of the Hauksbók which must have contained this narrative have been lost. There is therefore a possibility that errors and misunderstandings may have crept in, and such an absurdity as that "they could not land on account of the bears" (though they nevertheless saw ancient Eskimo dwellings!) shows clearly enough that the narrative is not to be regarded as trustworthy in its details; but there is no reason to doubt that the voyage was really made, and it must have extended far north in Baffin's Bay. It cannot have taken place in the same year (1266) in which the men spoken of came from Norðrsetur, but at the earliest in the following year (1267).

We may probably regard as one of the objects of the expedition the investigation of the northward extension of the Eskimo. The voyagers sailed out through Vaigat (Króksfjord), in about $70\frac{1}{2}°$ N. lat.; they met with a southerly gale and thick weather, and were obliged to keep along the coast; the south wind, which follows the line of the coast, also swept the ice northwards, and in open sea they came far north in the Polar Sea; but, if the statements are exact, they cannot have gone farther than a point from which they were able to return to Króksfjardarheidr in four days' sailing

309

CHAPTER VIII

and rowing.[1] If we allow at the outside that in the three days they sailed on an average one degree, or sixty nautical miles, a day, which is a good deal along a coast, and if we put a good day's rowing at forty miles, we shall get a total of 220 miles; or, if they started from the northern end of Vaigat in $70\frac{1}{2}°$, they may have been as far north as 74° N. lat., or about Melville Bay. In any case there can be no question of their having been much farther north. Here the land is low, and the inland ice ("jökull") comes right down to the sea, with bare islands outside (see map, p. 259). Here they found old traces of Eskimo. Then they returned south to Vaigat, but on the way thither they found Eskimo dwellings (that is, in this case tents) on some islands at which they put in.[2] It may be objected to this explanation that it does not agree with the statement as to the sun's altitude. But here there must be a misunderstanding or obscurity in the transmission of the text. Króksfjardarheidr is always mentioned elsewhere as a particularly well-known place in Nordrsetur, to which the Greenlanders resorted every summer for seal-hunting, and it is far from likely that the statements as to the midnight sun being visible, as to the frosts at night, and the detailed information as to the sun's altitude (in a description otherwise so concise), referred to so generally familiar a part of the country. It is obvious that it must refer to the unknown regions, where they were farthest north; but we thus lose the information as to the date on which the sun's altitude was observed; it must in any case have been four days before St. James's day, and it may have

---

[1] The text has three "dœgr" (and one long day's rowing), that is, three times twelve hours; but in this case it seems most natural to suppose that days are meant, and that they put in to shore at night.

[2] The text says that these islands were to the south of "Snæfell"; but where this was we do not know. In the Saga of Eric the Red we read that in the third summer Eric (see above, p. 267) "went as far north as 'Snæfell' and into 'Hrafns-fjord.'" Whether this was the same Snæfell is uncertain, but quite possible; while Hrafns-fjord (Ravnsfjord) is most probably to be regarded as the Hrafnsfjord that lay in the Eastern Settlement, near Hvarf.

GREENLAND VOYAGES IN THE MIDDLE AGES

been more. Moreover, the information given is of no use for working out the latitude. The measurement of the shadow on a man lying athwartships does not help us much, as the height of the gunwale above the man's position is not given. The statement as to the sun's altitude at midnight might be of more value; but whether " at home in the settlement " means the Western Settlement, or whether it does not rather mean Gardar (in the Eastern Settlement) to which they " returned home," we do not now know for certain, nor do we know on what day it was that the sun was at an equal altitude in the north-west. If St. James's day (July 25) is meant, then it is unfortunate that the sun would not be visible above the horizon at Gardar when it was in the north-west. According to the Julian Calendar, which was then in use, July 25 fell seven or eight days later than now. If Midsummer Day is intended, of which, however, there is no mention in the text, then the sun would be about 3° 41′ above the horizon in the north-west at Gardar. If it is meant that on July 20 the sun was at this altitude, then the latitude would be 74° 34′ N. [cf. H. Geelmuyden, 1883a, p. 178]. But all this is uncertain. We only know that the travellers saw the sun above the horizon at midnight. If we suppose that at least the whole of the sun's disc was above the horizon, and that it was St. James's day, then they must at any rate have been north of 71° 48′ N. lat. (as the sun's declination was about 17° 54′ on July 25 in the thirteenth century).[1] If the date was earlier, then they may have been farther south.

[1] Cf. "Grønl. hist. Mind.," III. p. 885.

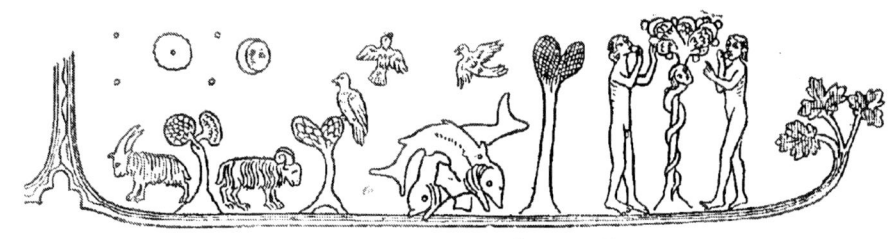

From an Icelandic MS., fourteenth century

CHAPTER IX

WINELAND THE GOOD, THE FORTUNATE ISLES, AND THE DISCOVERY OF AMERICA

CHAPTER IX
The oldest authorities on Wineland

ICELANDIC literature contains many remarkable statements about countries to the south-west or south of the Greenland settlements. They are called: "Helluland" (i.e., slate- or stone-land), "Markland" (i.e., wood-land), "Furðustrandir" (i.e., marvel-strands), and "Vínland" (also written "Vindland" or "Vinland"). Yet another, which lay to the west of Ireland, was called "Hvítramanna-land" (i.e., the white men's land). Even if certain of these countries are legendary, as will presently be shown, it must be regarded as a fact that in any case the Greenlanders and Icelanders reached some of them, which lay on the north-eastern coast of America; and they thus discovered the continent of North America, besides Greenland, about five hundred years before Cabot (and Columbus).

While Helluland, Markland and Furðustrandir are first mentioned in authorities of the thirteenth century, "Vinland" occurs already in Adam of Bremen, about 1070 (see above, pp. 195 ff.). Afterwards the name occurs in Icelandic literature: first in Are Frode's "Islendingabók," about 1130, where we are only told that in Greenland traces were found of the same kind of people as "inhabited Wineland" ("Vínland hefer bygt"; see above, p. 260); it is next mentioned together with Hvítramanna-land in the

WINELAND THE GOOD

"Landnámabók," where it may have been taken from Are Frode, as the latter's uncle, Thorkel Gellisson, is given as the authority. It has been thought that the original statement was contained in a lost work of Are's; in any case it must belong to the period before his death in 1148. We are only told that Hvítramanna-land lay to the west in the ocean near Vin(d)land; but the passage is important, because, as will be discussed later, it clearly shows that the statements about Wineland in the oldest Icelandic authorities were derived from Ireland. The next mention of Wineland is in "Kristni-saga" (before 1245) and "Heimskringla," where it is only said that Leif the Lucky found Wineland the Good. It should be remarked that while thus in the oldest authorities Wineland is only mentioned casually and in passing, it is not until we come to the Saga of Eric the Red, of the thirteenth century, and the Flateyjarbók's "Grönlendinga-þáttr," of the fourteenth, that we find any description of the country, and of voyages to it and to Helluland and Markland. But two verses, reproduced in the first of these sagas, are certainly considerably older than the saga itself; and they speak of the country where there was wine to drink instead of water, and of Furðustrandir where they boil whales' flesh.

CHAPTER IX

It may be added that in the "Eyrbyggja-saga" (of about 1250) it is said that "Snorre went with Karlsevne to Wineland the Good, and when they fought with the Skrælings there in Wineland, Snorre's son Thorbrand fell in the fight." In the "Grettis-saga" (about 1290), Thorhall Gamlason, one of those who took part in this expedition, is called "Vindlendingr" or "Víðlendingr" (which should doubtless be "Vínlendingr" in each case). If we add to this that in the Icelandic geography which is known from various MSS. of the fourteenth and fifteenth centuries, but which is attributed in part (although hardly the section about Greenland, Wineland, etc.) to Abbot Nikulás Bergsson of Thverá (ob. 1159), Helluland, Markland and Vinland are mentioned as lying to the south of Greenland (see later), then we shall have given all the certain ancient authorities in which Wineland occurs [cf. G. Storm, 1887, pp. 10 ff.]; but possibly the runic stone from Ringerike is to be added (see later).

Before I recapitulate the most important features of these voyages, as they are described more particularly in the

The formation of the saga

313

CHAPTER IX

Saga of Eric the Red, I must premise that I look upon the narratives somewhat in the light of historical romances, founded upon legend and more or less uncertain traditions. Gustav Storm in his critical review of the Wineland voyages [1887] has separated the older authorities, which he regarded as altogether trustworthy, from the later narratives in the Flateyjarbók's "Grönlendinga-þáttr," which he thought were to be rejected. The last-named was written about 1387, while Eric the Red's Saga, which we are to regard as trustworthy, must according to Storm have been written between 1270 and 1300.[1] The accounts of the discovery of Wineland and of the voyages thither are very conflicting in these two authorities; while the latter has only two voyages (after the discovery), the former has divided them into five; while one mentions Leif Ericson as the discoverer of the country, the other gives Bjarne Herjulfsson, and so on. We are led to ask whether it is reasonable to suppose that the traditions should have been handed down by word of mouth in such a remarkably unaltered and uncorrupted state during the first 250 or 300 years, when they have been transformed and confused to such an extent scarcely a hundred years later. This must rather prove that there was no fixed tradition, but that the tales became split up into more and more varying forms. Perhaps it will be answered that the Saga of Eric the Red was composed in the golden age of saga-writing, whereas the Flateyjarbók belongs to the period of decline.[2] But it cannot be psychologically probable that human nature in Iceland should suddenly have undergone so great a change, that while the saga-tellers of the fourteenth century were disposed to invent romances, they should not have had any tendency thereto throughout the three preceding centuries.

[1] Finnur Jónsson [1901, ii. p. 648] thinks it was written about 1200.
[2] Gudbrand Vigfusson [1878, i. pp. lix. f] thinks that Eric the Red's Saga and the Flateyjarbók's "Gronlendinga-þáttr" are derived, in complete independence of one another, from oral traditions, which were different in the west, at Breidafjord, where the former was written, and in the north, from whence the latter is derived.

WINELAND THE GOOD

CHAPTER IX

It is particularly natural that many alterations and additions should be made when, as here, the narratives are concerned with distant waters which lay so far out of the ordinary course of voyages, and which for a long time had ceased to be known in Iceland when the sagas were put into writing. Features belonging to the description of other quarters of the globe were also inserted. Tales which in this way live in oral tradition and gradually develop into sagas, without any written word to support them, and to some extent even without any known localities to which they can be attached, are to be regarded as living organisms dependent on accidental influence, which absorb into themselves any suitable material as they may find it; a resemblance of name between persons may thus contribute, or a similarity of situations, or events which bear the same foreign stamp. The narratives of the Wineland voyages exhibit, as we shall see, sure traces of influences of this kind.

Leif Ericso

In the year 999, according to the saga, Leif, the son of Eric the Red, sailed from Greenland to Norway. This is the first time we hear of so long a sea-voyage being attempted,[1] and it shows in any case that this long passage was not unknown to the Icelanders and Norwegians. Formerly the passage to Greenland had been by way of Iceland, thence to the east coast of Greenland, southwards along the coast, and round Hvarf. But capable seamen like the intrepid Leif thought they could avoid so many changes of course and arrive in Norway by sailing due east from the southern point of Greenland. Thereby Leif Ericson becomes the personification of the first ocean-voyager in history, who deliberately and with a settled plan steered straight across the open Atlantic, without seeking to avail himself of harbours

---

[1] We cannot here take any account of Rolf Raudesand's having come to Norway on his return from Greenland (see p 264); for even if this were historical, which is doubtful, and even if it be referred to a date anterior to Leif's voyage, which is not certain either, he was driven there accidentally instead of to Iceland.

on the way. It also appears clearly enough from the sailing directions for navigation of northern waters, which have come down to us, that voyages were made across the ocean direct from Norway to Greenland. It must be remembered that the compass was unknown, and that all the ships of that time were without fixed decks. This was an exploit equal to the greatest in history ; it is the beginning of ocean voyages.

Leif's plan of reaching Norway direct was not wholly successful according to the saga ; he was driven out of his course to the Hebrides. They stayed there till late in the summer, waiting for a fair wind. Leif there fell in love with

From an Icelandic MS. (Jónsbók), sixteenth century

a woman of high lineage, Thorgunna. When he sailed she begged to be allowed to go with him ; but Leif answered that he would not carry off a woman of her lineage in a strange country, when he had so few men with him. It was of no avail that she told him she was with child, and the child was his. He gave her a gold ring, a Greenland mantle of frieze, and a belt of walrus ivory, and sailed away from the Hebrides with his men and arrived in Norway in the autumn (999). Leif became Olaf Tryggvason's man, and spent the winter at Nidaros. He adopted Christianity and promised the king to try to introduce the faith into Greenland. For this purpose he was given a priest when he sailed. In the spring, as soon as he was ready, he set out again to sail straight across the Atlantic to Greenland. It has undoubtedly been thought that he chose the course between the Faroes (61° 50′ N. lat.) and Shetland (60° 50′ N. lat.) to reach Cape Farewell, and afterwards this became the usual course for the voyage from

WINELAND THE GOOD

Norway to Greenland. But he was driven out of his course, and

"for a long time drifted about in the sea, and came upon countries of which before he had no suspicion. There were self-sown wheat-fields, and vines grew there; there were also the trees that are called 'masur' ('mosurr'),[1] and of all these they had some specimens (some trees so large that they were laid in houses" [i.e., used as house-beams]).

This land was "Vínland hit Góða." As it was assumed that the wild vine (Vitis vulpina) grew in America as far north as 45° N. lat. and along the east coast, the historians have thought to find in this a proof that Leif Ericson must have been on the coast of America south of this latitude; but, as we shall see later, these features—the self-sown wheat-fields, the vines and the lofty trees—are probably borrowed from elsewhere.

"On his homeward voyage Leif found some men on a wreck, and took them home with him and gave them all shelter for the winter. He showed so much nobility and goodness, he introduced Christianity into the country, and he rescued the men; he was then called 'Leifr hinn Heppni' [the Lucky]. Leif came to land in Eric's fjord, and went home to Brattalid; there they received him well." This was the same autumn [1000].

So concise is the narrative of the voyage by which the first discovery of America by Europeans is said to have been made.[2]

Curiously enough, the saga tells us nothing more of Leif as a sailor. He appears after this to have lived in peace in Greenland, and he took over Brattalid after his father's death. On the other hand, we hear that his brother Thorstein made an attempt to find Wineland, which Leif had discovered. After Leif's return home "there was much

Chapter IX

Thorstein Ericson

[1] "M surr" (properly "valbirch") was probably a veined tree, like "valbjerk," which was regarded as valuable material. "Valbjerk" is birch grown in a special way so that it becomes twisted and gnarled in structure. It is still much used in Norway, e.g., for knife-handles.

[2] I do not mention here the fourteenth-century tale, (in the Flateyjarbók) of Bjarne Herjulfsson's discovery of Wineland as early as 985, since, as G. Storm has shown, this account hardly represents the tradition which in earlier times was most current in Iceland.

CHAPTER IX

talk that they ought to seek the land that Leif had found. The leader was Thorstein Ericson, a good man, and wise, and friendly." We hear earlier in the saga, where Leif's vogage to Norway is related, that both of Eric's sons "were capable men; Thorstein was at home with his father, and there was not a man in Greenland who was thought to be so manly as he." We hear nothing about Leif's taking part in the new voyage; it looks as if it had been Thorstein's turn to go abroad. But

> "Eric was asked, and they trusted in his good fortune and foresight being greatest. He was against it, but did not say no, as his friends exhorted him so to it. They therefore fitted out the ship which Thorbjorn [Vivilsson] had brought out to Greenland; [1] and twenty men were chosen for it; they took little goods with them, but more arms and provisions. The morning that Eric left home, he took a little chest, and therein was gold and silver; he hid this property and then went on his way; but when he had gone a little distance he fell from his horse, broke his ribs and hurt his shoulder, and said, 'Ah yes!' After this accident he sent word to his wife that she should take up the property that he had hidden; he had now, said he, been punished for hiding it. Then they sailed out of Eric's fjord with gladness, and thought well of their prospects They drifted about the sea for a long time and did not arrive where they desired. They came in sight of Iceland, and they had also birds from Ireland; their ship was carried eastwards over the ocean. They came back in the autumn and were then weary and very worn. And they came in the late autumn to Eric's fjord. Then said Eric: 'In the summer we sailed from the fjords more light-hearted than we now are, and yet we now have good reason to be so' Thorstein said: 'It would be a worthy deed to take charge of the men who are homeless, and to provide them with lodging.' Eric answered 'Thy words shall be followed.' All those who had no other place of abode were now allowed to accompany Eric and Thorstein. Afterwards they took land and went home."

---

[1] Thorbjorn Vivilsson came from Iceland to Greenland in 999, the same summer that Leif sailed to Norway. His daughter was Gudrid, afterwards married to Thorstein Ericson. The exact statement as to which ship was used on this occasion, and as to those which were used later on Thorfinn Karlsevne's expedition, shows how few ships there were in Greenland (and Iceland), and in what esteem the men were held who owned them. The Saga of Eric the Red seems to assume that Leif's ship was no longer very fit for sea after his last voyage, as we hear no more about it. This may perhaps be regarded as the reason for his not going again, if indeed there be any other reason than the patchwork character of the saga. In the Flateyjarbók, on the other hand, we are told that it was Leif's ship, and not Thorbjorn Vivilsson's, that was used first by Thorvald and afterwards by Thorstein.

WINELAND THE GOOD

In the autumn (1001) Thorstein celebrated his marriage with Thorbjörn Vivilsson's daughter Gudrid, at Brattalid, and it "went off well." They afterwards went home to Thorstein's property on the Lysefjord, which was the southernmost fjord in the Western Settlement; probably that which is now called Fiskerfjord (near Fiskernes) in about 63° N. lat. There Thorstein died during the winter of an illness (scurvy?) which put an end to many on the property, and Gudrid next summer returned to Eric, who received her well. Her father died also, and she inherited all his property.

That autumn (1002) Thorfinn Karlsevne came from Iceland to Eric's fjord in Greenland, with one ship and forty men. He was on a trading voyage, and was looked upon as a skilful sailor and merchant, was of good family and rich in goods. Together with him was Snorre Thorbrandsson. Another ship, with Bjarne Grimolfsson and Thorhall Gamlason and a crew likewise of forty men, had accompanied them from Iceland.

> "Eric rode to the ships, and others of the men of the country, and there was a friendly agreement between them. The captains bade Eric take what he wished of the cargo. But Eric in return showed great generosity, in that he invited both these crews home to spend the winter at Brattalid. This the merchants accepted and went with Eric."
>
> "The merchants were well content in Eric's house that winter, but when Yule was drawing nigh, Eric began to be less cheerful than was his wont." When Karlsevne asked: "Is there anything that oppresses thee, Eric?" and tried to find out the reason of his being so dispirited, it came out that it was because he had nothing for the Yule-brew; and it would be said that his guests had never had a worse Yule than with him. Karlsevne thought there was no difficulty about that; they had malt, and meal, and corn in the ships, and thereof, said he, "thou shalt have all thou desirest, and make such a feast as thy generosity demands." Eric accepted this. "The Yule banquet was prepared, and it was so magnificent that men thought they had scarcely ever seen so fine a feast."

Even if the tale is unhistorical, it gives a glimpse of the life and the hard conditions in Greenland; they only had grain occasionally when a ship arrived; for the most part they lived on what they caught, and when that failed, as we are told was the case in 999, there was famine. But to

CHAPTER IX

be without the Yule-brew was a misfortune to an Icelander; nevertheless we learn from the Foster-brothers' Saga that "Yule-drink was rare in Greenland," and that a man might become famous by holding a feast, as did Thorkel, the grandson of Eric the Red, in 1026.

After Yule, Karlsevne was married to Eric's daughter-in-law, Gudrid.

> "The feast was then prolonged, and the marriage was celebrated. There was great merry-making at Brattalid that winter; there was much playing at draughts, and making mirth with tales and much else to divert the company."

Karlsevne's voyage to Wineland

There was a good deal of talk about going to look for Wineland the Good, and it was said that it might be a fertile country. The result was that Karlsevne and Snorre got their ship ready to search for Wineland in the summer. Bjarne and Thorhall also joined the expedition with their ship and the crew that had accompanied them. Besides these, there came on a third ship a man named Thorvard—married to Eric the Red's illegitimate daughter Freydis, who also went—and Thorhall, nicknamed Veidemand (the Hunter).

From an Icelandic MS. (Jónsbók), fifteenth century

> "He had been on hunting expeditions with Eric for many summers and was a man of many crafts. Thorhall was a big man, dark and troll-like; he was well on in years, obstinate, silent and reserved in everyday life, but crafty and slanderous, ever rejoicing in evil. He had had little to do with the faith since it came to Greenland. Thorhall had little friendship for his fellow men, yet Eric had long associated with him. He was in the same ship with Thorvald and Thorvard, because he had wide knowledge of the uninhabited regions. They had the ship that Thorbjörn [Vivilsson] had brought out to Greenland [and that Thorstein Ericson had used for his unlucky voyage two years before]. Most of those on board that ship were Greenlanders. On their ships there were altogether forty men over a hundred."[1]

---

[1] If the "great hundred" is meant, this will be 160 men.

320

WINELAND THE GOOD

Eric the Red and Leif were doubtless supposed to have assisted both actively and with advice during the fitting-out, even though they would not take part in the voyage. It is mentioned later that they gave Karlsevne two Scottish runners that Leif had received from King Olaf Tryggvason.

CHAPTER IX

The three ships sailed first "to the Western Settlement and thence to Bjarneyjar" (the Bear Islands).[1] The most natural explanation of the saga making them begin their expedition by sailing in this direction (to the north-west and north)—whereas the land they were in search of lay to the south-west or south—may be that the Icelandic saga-writer (of the thirteenth century), ignorant of the geography of Greenland, assumed that the Western Settlement must lie due west of the Eastern; and as the voyagers were to look for countries in the south-west, he has made them begin by proceeding to the farthest point he had heard of on this coast, Bjarneyjar, so that they might have a prospect of better luck than Thorstein, who had sailed out from Eric's fjord. When it is said that Thorhall the Hunter accompanied Eric's son and son-in-law because of his wide knowledge of the uninhabited regions, it must be the regions beyond the Western Settlement that are meant, and the saga-writer must have thought that these extended westward or in the direction of the new countries. It must also be remembered that in the spring and early summer there is frequently drift-ice off the Eastern Settlement, from Cape

[1] From the context it would seem probable that these islands, or this island (?), lay in the Western Settlement. If they had been near Lysefjord, Karlsevne, as Storm points out, might be supposed to go there first because his wife, Gudrid, had inherited property there from Thorstein, and there might be much to fetch thence But the name Bjarneyjar itself points rather to some place farther north, since the southern part of the Western Settlement (the Godthaab district) must have been then, as now, that part of the coast where bears were scarcest. In Bjorn Jónsson's "Gronlandiæ vetus Chorographia" a "Biarney" (or "-eyiar") is mentioned, to which it was twelve days' rowing from Lysefjord [cf. above, p. 301], and as they are the only islands (or island ?) of this name mentioned on the west coast of Greenland, there is much in favour of their being the place here alluded to.

IN NORTHERN MISTS

CHAPTER IX

Farewell for a good way north-westward along the coast. The course would then naturally lie to the north-west of this ice—that is, towards the Western Settlement. But it may also be supposed that they had to begin by going northward to get seals and provision themselves with food and oil (fuel), which might be necessary for a long and unknown voyage. This explanation is, however, less probable.

From Bjarneyjar they put to sea with a north wind. They were at sea, according to the saga, for two " dœgr." [1]

"There they found land, and rowed along it in boats, and examined the country,

---

[1] " Dœgr " was half a twenty-four hours' day [cf. Rymbegla]; but whether twelve hours or twenty-four, the distance, like those given later, is impossible. They cannot have sailed from Greenland to Labrador, or even if it was Baffin Land they made, in two days of twelve hours, and scarcely in two of twenty-four. According to the MS. in the Hauksbók " they sailed thence [i.e., from Bjarneyjar] two half-days [i.e., twenty-four hours in all] to the south. Then they sighted land." It might be supposed that this should be taken to mean that the difference in latitude between this land and their starting-point was equivalent to two half-days' sail. It is true that we read in the " Rymbegla " [1780, p. 482] there are two dozen sea-leagues, or two degrees of latitude, in a " ' dœgr's ' sailing," and two " dœgr " would therefore be four degrees; but when we see later that from this first land they found to Markland (Newfoundland?) was also only two half-days' sail, then these distances become altogether impossible [cf. G. Storm, 1888, pp. 32-34; Reeves, 1895, p. 173]. Reeves proposes that "tvau" might be an error for "siau" (i.e., seven, but in the MS. of the Hauksbók we have "two" in numerals: II). It is probable that this repetition of the same distance, two " dœgr's " sail, in the case of each of the three new countries, has nothing to do with reality; it reminds us so much of the stereotyped legendary style that we are inclined to believe it to be borrowed from this. Storm thinks that as Iceland was supposed to lie in the same latitude as the Western Settlement, and Wineland in the same latitude as Ireland, there would naturally be the same distance between the Western Settlement and Wineland as between Iceland and Ireland, and the latter was put at five (or three?) " dœgr " However, it is not five, but six " dœgr " between Bjarneyjar and Furðustrandir, according to the Saga of Eric the Red [cf. Storm's ed., 1891, p. 32]. In the copy in the Hauksbók, it is true, the distance is given as two " dœgr " between Bjarneyjar and Helluland, two " dœgr " between this and Markland, and " thence they sailed south along the coast a long way and came to a promontory . . ."; but this circumstance, that the distance is not given the third time, again inclines one to think of the fairy-tale, and here again there is no statement that the distance was five " dœgr " from the Western Settlement to Kjalarnes.

WINELAND THE GOOD

and found there [on the shore] many flat stones so large that two men might easily lie stretched upon them sole to sole. There were many white foxes there.[1] They gave the land a name and called it 'Helluland.'"

It may be the coast of Labrador that is here intended, and not Baffin Land, since the statement that they sailed thither with a north wind must doubtless imply that the coast lay more or less in a southerly and not in a westerly direction from Bjarneyjar. From Helluland

"they sailed for two 'dœgr' towards the south-east and south, and then a land lay before them, and upon it were great forests and many beasts. An island lay to the south-east off the land, and there they found a polar bear,[2] and they called the island 'Bjarney'; but the country they called 'Markland' [i.e., Wood-land] on account of the forest."

The name Markland suits Newfoundland best; it had forests down to the sea-shore when it was rediscovered about 1500, and even later.

When they had once more sailed for

"two 'dœgr' they sighted land and sailed under the land. There was a promontory where they first came. They cruised along the shore, which they kept to starboard [i.e., to the west]. It was without harbours and there were long strands and stretches of sand. They went ashore in boats, and found there on the promontory a ship's keel, and called it 'Kjalarnes' [i.e., Keel-ness]; they also gave the strands a name and called them 'Furðustrandir' [i.e., the marvel-strands or the wonderful, strange strands], because it took a long time to sail past them."[3]

---

[1] The arctic fox is common in Labrador, but also in the northern peninsula of Newfoundland.

[2] Polar bears come on the drift-ice to the north and east coasts of Newfoundland, but not farther south.

[3] The name comes from "furða" (warning, marvel, terror); "furðu" (gen. sing.) placed before adjectives and adverbs has the meaning of extremely ("furðu góðr" = extremely good). As "Furðustjarna" (the wonder-star) surpassed the others in size and brilliance, these strands may be supposed to surpass others in length, and thus to be endless, but it is doubtless more likely that it means marvel-strands, where there were marvels and wonderful things. In Orskog, Sunnmore, Norway, there is a place-name "Fürstranda" (with long, closed "u"). K. Rygh [Norske Gaardnavne, xiii., 1908, p. 155] remarks: "The first syllable must be the tree-name "fura" [fir], though the pronunciation with a long, closed 'u' is strange. . . ."

IN NORTHERN MISTS

CHAPTER IX

This may apply, as Storm points out, to the eastern side of Cape Breton Island; but in that case they must have steered west-south-west from the south-eastern promontory of Markland (Newfoundland). Kjalarnes must then be Cape Breton itself. That they should have found a ship's keel there sounds strange; if this is not an invention we must suppose that it was driven ashore from a wreck; no doubt it happened often enough that vessels were lost on the voyage to Greenland. When Eric, according to the Landnámabók, sailed with twenty-five ships, many of them were lost. Wreckage would be carried by the currents from Greenland into the Labrador current, and by this southward past Markland. But it is more probable that the origin of the name was entirely different; that, for example, the promontory had the shape of a ship's keel, and that the account of the keel found has been developed much later.[1] This is confirmed by the fact that the " Grönlendinga-þáttr " gives a wholly different explanation of the name from that in Eric's Saga.

South of Furðustrandir "the land was indented by bays ('vágskorit'), and they steered the ships into a bay." Here they landed the two Scots (the man

---

[1] In the Faroes (Kodlafjord in Straumsey) there is a "Kjal(ar)nes," the origin of which is attributed to a man's name: "Kjolur á Nesi" [J. Jakobsen, 1898, p. 147]; but it is more probable that the name of the ness is the original one, and that the legend of Kjolur is later. As to place-names ending in "-nes," O. Rygh [Norske Gaardnavne, Forord og Indledning, 1898, p. 68] says: "Frequently the first part of the name is a word signifying natural conditions on or about the promontory.... Very often the first part has reference to the form of the promontory, its outline, greater or less height, length, etc.... Personal names are not usual in these combinations." In Norway names beginning with "Kjol-" ("-nes," "-berg," "-stad," "-set," etc.) are very common; they may either come from the man's name "Þjóðolfr" (which now often has the sound of "Kjolv," "Kjol," or "Kjole"), or from the Old Norse poetical word "kjóll," m, "ship," or from "kjǫlr" (gen. "kjalar"), "keel of a vessel, and hence, mountain-ridge" [cf. O. Rygh, Norske Gaardnavne, i., 1897, p. 269; iv. 2, ed. A. Kjær, 1902, p. 57; vi. ed. A. Kjær, p. 237; xiii. ed. K. Rygh, 1908 p. 344]. Our Kjalarnes above must undoubtedly be derived from the last. In Tanen, east of Berlevåg, there is a "Kjolnes"; in Iceland, just north of Reykjavik, outside Faxafjord, there is a "Kjalarnes."

WINELAND THE GOOD

"Haki" and the woman "Hekja") whom Karlsevne had received from Leif and Eric, and who ran faster than deer. They "bade them run southward and examine the condition of the country, and return before three 'dœgr' were past. They had such garments as they called 'kiafal' [or 'biafal']; it was made so that there was a hood above, and it [i.e., the 'kiafal'] was open at the sides, and without sleeves, and caught up between the legs, fastened there with a button and a loop; otherwise they were bare. They cast anchor and lay there a while; and when three days were past they came running down from the land, and one of them had grapes in his hand, the other self-sown wheat. Karlsevne said that they seemed to have found a fertile country."

CHAPTER IX

They then sailed on until they came to a fjord, into which they steered the ships.

"There was an island outside, and round the island strong currents They called it 'Straumsey.' There were so many birds there that one could hardly put one's foot between the eggs. They held on up the fjord, and called it 'Straumsfjord,' and unloaded the ships and established themselves there. They had with them all kinds of cattle, and sought to make use of the land. There were mountains there, and fair was the prospect. They did nothing else but search out the land. There was much grass. They stayed there the winter, and it was very long; but they had not taken thought of anything, and were short of food, and their catch decreased. Then they went out to the island, expecting that there they might find some fishing or something might drift up [i.e., a whale be driven ashore?]. There was, however, little to be caught for food, but their cattle throve there. Then they made vows to God that He might send them something to eat; but no answer came so quickly as they had hoped" The heathen Thorhall the Hunter then disappeared for three "dœgr," and doubtless held secret conjurations with the red-bearded One (i.e., Thor). A little later a whale was driven ashore, and they ate of it, but were all sick. When they found out how things were with Thorhall and Thor, "they cast it out over the cliff and prayed to God for mercy. They then made a catch of fish, and there was no lack of food. In the spring [1004] they entered Straumsfjord and had catches from both lands [i.e., both sides of the fjord], hunting on the mainland, eggs on the island, and fish in the sea."

This description gives a good insight both into the Norsemen's manner of equipping themselves for voyages to unknown countries, and into their superstition.

It looks as if a dissension now arose between the wayward Thorhall the Hunter and the rest, since he wanted to look for Wineland to the north of Furðustrandir, beyond Kjalarnes.

"But Karlsevne wished to go south along the coast and eastward. He thought the land became broader the farther south it bore;[1] but it seemed to him most expedient to try both ways" [i.e., both south and north].

Thorhall then parted from them; but there were no more than nine men in his company. Perhaps they were desirous of going home; for from an old lay, which the saga attributes to Thorhall, it appears that he was discontented with the whole stay there: he abuses the country, where the warriors had promised him the best of drinks, but where wine never touched his lips, and he had to take a bucket himself and fetch water to drink. And before they hoisted sail Thorhall quoth this lay:

> "Let us go homeward,
> where we shall find fellow-countrymen:
> let us with our ship seek
> the broad ways of the sea,
> while the hopeful
> warriors (those who praise
> the land) on Furðustrandir
> stay and boil whales' flesh."

"Then they parted [from Karlsevne, who had accompanied them out] and sailed north of Furðustrandir and Kjalarnes, and then tried to beat westward. Then the westerly storm caught them and they drifted to Ireland, and there they were made slaves and ill-treated. There Thorhall lost his life, as merchants have reported."

The last statement shows that according to Icelandic geographical ideas the country round Kjalarnes lay directly opposite Ireland and in the same latitude.

Karlsevne, with Snorre, Bjarne, and the rest, left Straumsfjord and sailed southward along the coast [1004].

"They sailed a long time and until they came to a river, which flowed down from the interior into a lake and thence into the sea. There were great sandbanks before the mouth of the river, and it could only be entered at high water. Karlsevne and his people then sailed to the mouth of the river and called the country 'Hóp' [i.e., a small closed bay]. There they found self-sown wheat-fields,

---

[1] This idea, that the land became broader towards the south, and the coast there turned eastward, must be the same that we meet with again in Icelandic geographies of the fourteenth and fifteenth centuries, where Wineland is thought to be connected with Africa (see later).

WINELAND THE GOOD

where the land was low, but vines wherever they saw heights (' en vínviðr allt þar sem holta kendi '). Every beck (' lòkr ') was full of fish. They dug trenches on the shore below high-water mark, and when the tide went out there were halibuts in the trenches. In the forest there was a great quantity of beasts of all kinds. They were there half a month amusing themselves, and suspecting nothing. They had their cattle with them. But early one morning, when they looked about them, they saw nine hide-boats ('huðkeipa'), and wooden poles were being waved on the ships [i.e., the hide-boats], and they made a noise like threshing-flails and went the way of the sun. Karlsevne's men took this to be a token of peace and bore a white shield towards them. Then the strangers rowed towards them, and wondered, and came ashore. They were small [or black ?][1] men, and ugly, and they had ugly hair on their heads ; their eyes were big, and they were broad across the cheeks. And they stayed there awhile, and wondered, then rowed away and went south of the headland."

This then would be the description of the first meeting in history between Europeans and the natives of America. With all its brevity it gives an excellent picture ; but whether we can accept it is doubtful. As we shall see later, the Norsemen probably did meet with Indians ; but the description of the latter's appearance must necessarily have been coloured more and more by greater familiarity with the Skrælings of Greenland when the sagas were put into writing. The big eyes will not suit either of them, and are rather to be regarded as an attribute of trolls and underground beings ; gnomes and old fairy men have big, watery eyes. The ugly hair is also an attribute of the underground beings.

"Karlsevne and his men had built their houses above the lake, some nearer, some farther off. Now they stayed there that winter. No snow fell at all, and all the cattle were out at pasture. But when spring came they saw early one morning a number of hide-boats rowing from the south past the headland, so many that it seemed as if the sea had been sown with coal in front of the bay, and they waved wooden poles on every boat. Then they set up shields and held a market, and the people wanted most to buy red cloth ; they also wanted to buy swords and spears, but this was forbidden by Karlsevne and Snorre." The Skrælings [2] gave them untanned skins in exchange for the cloth, and trade was proceeding

---

[1] "Svart" (i.e., black-haired and black-eyed) is the reading of Hauksbók, but the other MS. has "small."

[2] The word "Skrælingar" here occurs for the first time in this saga, and seems to be used as a familiar designation for the natives, which did not require further explanation ; of this more later.

IN NORTHERN MISTS

CHAPTER IX

briskly, until " an ox, which Karlsevne had, ran out of the wood and began to bellow. The Skrælings were scared and ran to their boats (keipana) and rowed south along the shore. After that they did not see them for three weeks. But when that time was past, they saw a great multitude of Skræling boats coming from the south, as though driven on by a stream. Then all the wooden poles were waved against the sun ('rangsolis,' wither-shins), and all the Skrælings howled loudly. Then Karlsevne and his men took red shields and bore them towards them. The Skrælings leapt from their boats and then they made towards each other and fought ; there was a hot exchange of missiles. The Skrælings also had catapults ('valslongur'). Karlsevne and his men saw that the Skrælings hoisted up on a pole a great ball ('knottr') about as large as a sheep's paunch, and seeming blue [1] in colour, and slung it from the pole up on to the land over Karlsevne's people, and it made an ugly noise when it came down. At this great terror smote Karlsevne and his people, so that they had no thought but of getting away and up the river, for it seemed to them that the Skrælings were assailing them on all sides ; and they did not halt until they had reached certain crags. There they made a stout resistance. Freydis came out and saw that they were giving way. She cried out : 'Wherefore do ye run away from such wretches, ye gallant men ? I thought it likely that ye could slaughter them like cattle, and had I but arms I believe I should fight better than any of you' None heeded what she said. Freydis tried to go with them, but she fell behind, for she was with child She nevertheless followed them into the wood, but the Skrælings came after her. She found before her a dead man, Thorbrand Snorrason, and a flat stone ('hellustein') was fixed in the head of him. His sword lay unsheathed by him, and she took it up to defend herself with it. Then the Skrælings came at her. She takes her breasts out of her sark and whets the sword on them. At that the Skrælings are afraid and run away back to their boats, and go off. Karlsevne and his men meet her and praise her happy device. Two men of Karlsevne's fell, and four of the Skrælings ; but nevertheless Karlsevne had suffered defeat. They now go to their houses, bind up their wounds, and consider what swarm of people it was that came against them from the land. It seemed to them now that there could have been no more than those who came from the boats, and that the other people must have been glamour. The Skrælings also found a dead man, and an axe lay beside him ; one of them took up the axe and struck at a tree, and so one after another, and it seemed to delight them that it bit so well. Then one took and smote a stone with it ; but when the axe broke, he thought it was of no use, if it did not stand against stone, and he cast it from him "

"Karlsevne and his men now thought they could see that although the land was fertile, they would always have trouble and disquiet with the people who dwelt there before. Then they prepared to set out, and intended to go to their own country. They sailed northward and found five Skrælings sleeping in fur jerkins

---

[1] Blue (bla) perhaps means rather dark or black in colour (cf. "Blue-men" for negroes), and is often used of something uncanny or troll-like.

WINELAND THE GOOD

('skinnhjúpum'), and they had with them kegs with deer's marrow mixed with blood. They thought they could understand that they were outlaws; they killed them. Then they found a headland and a multitude of deer, and the headland looked like a crust of dried dung, from the deer lying there at night. Now they came back to Straumsfjord, and there was abundance of everything. It is reported by some that Bjarne and Gudrid remained behind there, and a hundred men with them, and did not go farther; but they say that Karlsevne and Snorre went southward with forty men and were no longer at Hóp than barely two months, and came back the same summer."

Karlsevne went with one ship to search for Thorhall the Hunter. He sailed to the north of Kjalarnes, westwards, and south along the shore (Storm thought on the eastern side of Cape Breton Island to the northern side of Nova Scotia), and they found a river running from east to west into the sea.

Here Thorvald Ericson was shot one morning from the shore with an arrow which they thought came from a Uniped [legendary creature with one foot] whom they pursued but did not catch. The arrow struck Thorvald in the small intestines. He drew it out, saying: "There is fat in the bowels; a good land have we found, but it is doubtful whether we shall enjoy it." Thorvald died of this wound a little later. "They then sailed away northward again and thought they sighted 'Einfötinga-land' [the Land of Unipeds]. They would no longer risk the lives of their men," and "they went back and stayed in Straumsfjord the third winter. Then the men became very weary [so that they fell into disagreement]; those who were wifeless quarrelled with those who had wives."[1]

From an Icelandic MS. (Jónsbók), fourteenth century

The fourth summer [1006] they sailed from Wineland with a south wind and came to Markland.

There they found five Skrælings, and caught of them two boys, while the grown-up ones, a bearded man and two women, "escaped and sank into the

---

[1] Nothing of the kind is related in the "Grönlendinga-þáttr"; where, however, we are told of the first winter of Karlsevne's voyage that the cattle pastured upon the land, "but the males ('graðfe') soon became difficult to manage and troublesome."

CHAPTER IX

CHAPTER IX

earth. The boys they took with them and taught them their language, and they were baptized They called their mother 'Vætilldi' and their father 'Vægi.' They said that kings governed in Skrælinga-land; one of them was called 'Avalldamon,' the other 'Valldidida.' They said that there were no houses, and the people lay in rock-shelters or caves. They said there was another great country over against their country, and men went about there in white clothing and cried aloud, and carried poles before them, to which strips were fastened. This is thought to be 'Hvítramanna-land' [i e., the white men's land] or Great-Ireland." Then Karlsevne and his men came to Greenland and stayed the winter with Eric the Red [1006–1007].

"But Bjarne Grimolfsson [on the other ship] was carried out into the Irish Ocean [the Atlantic between Markland and Ireland] and they came into the maggot-sea ('maðk-sjá'); they did not know of it until the ship was worm-eaten under them," and ready to sink. "They had a long-boat ('eptirbát') that was coated with seal-tar, and men say that the sea-maggot will not eat wood that is coated with seal-tar." "But when they tried it, the boat would not hold more than half the ship's company." They all wanted to go in it; but Bjarne then proposed that they should decide who should go in the boat by casting lots and not by precedence, and this was agreed to. The lots fell so that Bjarne was amongst those who were to go in the boat. "When they were in it, a young Icelander, who had accompanied Bjarne from home, said: 'Dost thou think, Bjarne, to part from me here?' Bjarne answers: 'So it must be.' He says: 'This was not thy promise when I came with thee from Iceland. . . .' Bjarne answers· 'Nor shall it be so; go thou in the boat, but I must go in the ship, since I see that thy life is so dear to thee.' Bjarne then went on board the ship, and this man in the boat, and they kept on their course until they came to Dyflinar [Dublin] in Ireland, and there told this tale. But most men believe that Bjarne and his companions lost their lives in the maggot-sea, since they were not heard of again."

Thorfinn Karlsevne returned in the following summer (1007) to Iceland with Gudrid and their son Snorre, who was born at Straumsfjord in Wineland the first winter they were there. Karlsevne afterwards lived in Iceland.

The composite and legendary character of the whole saga

If we now review critically the Saga of Eric the Red and the whole of this tale of Karlsevne's voyage, together with the other accounts of Wineland voyages, we shall find one feature after another that is legendary or that must have been borrowed from elsewhere. If we examine first of all the relation of the various authorities to the events they narrate, we must be struck by the fact that in the oldest authorities, such as the Landnáma, Eric the Red has only two sons, Leif and Thorstein, whereas in Eric's Saga and in the "Gronlendinga-þáttr," for the sake of the trilogy of legend, he has begotten three sons, besides an illegitimate daughter. In the oldest MS., Hauk's Landnámabók, Leif is only mentioned in one place, and nothing more is said of him than that he was Eric's son and inherited Brattalid from his father; he is not given the nickname " heppni " (the lucky), and it is not mentioned that he had discovered Wineland, nor that he had introduced Christianity. In the Sturlubók he is again mentioned in one place as the son of Tjodhild and Eric, and there has the nickname " en hepni "; but neither is there here any mention of the discovery of Wineland or the introduction of Christianity [cf. Landnámabók, ed. F. Jónsson, 1900, pp. 35, 156, 165]. As this passage is not found in Hauk's Landnáma, it may be an addition in the later MS., which was wanting in the original Landnámabók. In the great saga of St. Olaf[1] (chapter 70)—where King Olaf asks the Icelander Thorarinn Nevjolfsson to take the blind king Rörek to Greenland to " Leif Ericson "—the latter again is not called the Lucky, nor is Wineland or its discovery mentioned. This saga was written, according to the editors, about 1230. As neither this nickname nor the tales of Leif's discovery of Wineland are found earlier than in the Kristni-saga and Heimskringla, it looks as if these features did not appear till later. There is a similar state of things with regard to the mention of Thorfinn Karlsevne; only in one passage in Hauk's Landnáma is it mentioned that he found " Vin(d)land hit Góða "; but as this does not occur in the Sturlubók, it may be an addition due to Hauk Erlendsson, who regarded Thorfinn as his ancestor. The silence of the oldest authorities on the voyages to Wineland becomes still more striking when we compare with it the fact that the Landnámabók contains statements (with careful citation of authorities, showing that they are derived from Are Frode himself) about Are Mársson, his voyage to Hvítramanna-land, and his stay there,

---

[1] Ed. by P. Munch and C. R. Unger, Christiania, 1853, p. 75.

CHAPTER IX which have generally been regarded as far less authentic than the tales of the Wineland voyages. If Are Mársson's voyage is a myth, then one would be still more inclined to regard the latter as such. The objection that it would have been beside the plan of the brief and concise earlier works (Íslendingabók and Landnámabók) to include these things, scarcely holds good. If Are has room in the Íslendingabók for a comparatively detailed account of the discovery, naming and natives of Greenland, and further for a description of the introduction of Christianity into Iceland; if the Landnámabók also gives details, derived, as we have said, from him, of Are Mársson's voyage to Hvítramanna-land, then it is difficult to understand why neither Are Frode nor the authors of the Landnámabók, when mentioning Eric the Red and Leif, should have found room for a line about Leif's having discovered Wineland and Christianised Greenland—two not unimportant pieces of information—if they had known of it. At any rate, the Christianising of Greenland must have been of interest to the priest Are and to the priest-taught authors of Landnámabók. This silence is therefore suspicious.

The personal names in the Saga of Eric the Red are also striking. With the exception of Eric himself, his wife Tjodhild and his son Leif, and a few other names in the first part, which is taken almost in its entirety from the Landnámabók, almost all the names belonging to this saga are connected with those of heathen gods, especially Thor. Eric has got a third son, Thorvald, who is not mentioned in Landnáma, besides his daughter Freydis, and his son-in-law Thorvard. The name Freydis is only known from this one woman in the whole of Icelandic literature, and several names in Norse literature compounded of Frey- seem, according to Lind,[1] to belong to myths (e.g., Freygarðr, Freysteinn and Freybjǫrn). Other names connected with the Wineland voyages in this saga are: Thor-bjǫrn Vivilsson (his brother

[1] E. H. Lind: Norsk-Isländska dopnamn, p. 283. I owe it to Moltke Moe that my attention was drawn to this feature of the numerous heathen names.

was named Thor-geir and his daughter's foster-father Orm Thor-geirsson) came to Thor-kjell of Herjolfsnes, where the prophetess was called Thor-bjorg. Leif's woman in the Hebrides was called Thor-gunna, and their illegitimate son Thor-gils. Thor-stein Ericson had a property together with another Thor-stein in Lysefjord.[1] We have further Thor-finn Karlsevne (son of Thord and Thor-unn), Snorre Thor-brandsson, Thor-hall Gamlason, Thor-hall Veidemand (who also had dealings with the red-bearded Thor), and Thor-brand Snorrason who was killed. An exception, besides Bjarne Grimolfsson (and the runners Haki and Hekja; see below), is Thorfinn Karlsevne's wife Guðríðr,[2] daughter of Thorbjörn Vivilsson, and mother of Snorre. But perhaps one can guess why she is given this name if one reads through the description of the remarkable scene of soothsaying—at Thorkjell's house on Herjolfsnes—between the fair Gudrid, who sang with such a beautiful voice, and the heathen sorceress Thorbjörg, where the former as a Christian woman refuses to sing the heathen charms "Varðlokur," as the sorceress asks her to do. These numerous Thor-names—with the two women's names, the powerful Freydis and the fair Gudrid—which are attributed to a time when heathendom and Christianity were struggling for the mastery (cf. the tale of Thorhall the Hunter and the whale), have in themselves an air of myth and invention. To this must be added mythical descriptions like those of the prophetess of Herjolfsnes, the ghosts at Lysefjord the winter Thorstein Ericson died, and others.

The Saga of Eric the Red tells of two voyages in search of Wineland, after Leif's accidental discovery of the country. The first is Thorstein Ericson's unfortunate expedition, when

CHAPTER IX

[1] His wife is called "Sigriðr," which is thus an exception; but in the Gronlendinga-þáttr she is called "Grímhildr," so that her name is uncertain. There is also mentioned a thrall "Garði," but being a thrall perhaps he could not have the name of a god.

[2] It is very curious that in the chapter-heading in the Hauksbók she is called "Þuríðr," but in the text "Guðríðr" [cf. Storm, 1891, p. 23, "Gronl. hist. Mind.," i. p. 392].

CHAPTER IX they did not find the favoured Wineland, but were driven eastward into the ocean towards Iceland and Ireland. In the Irish tale of Brandan ("Imram Brenaind," of the eleventh century), Brandan first makes an unsuccessful voyage to find the promised land, and arrives, it seems, most probably in the east of the ocean, somewhere about Brittany (cf. Vita S. Brandani; and Machutus's voyage); but he then makes a fresh voyage in which he finally reaches the land he is in search of [cf. Zimmer, 1889, pp. 135 ff.]. This similarity with the Irish legend is doubtless not very great, but perhaps it deserves to be included with many others to be mentioned later.

If we now pass to the tale itself of Karlsevne's voyage, we have already seen (p. 321) that its beginning with the journey to the Western Settlement is doubtful; next, the feature of his sailing to three different countries in turn (Helluland, Markland and Furðustrandir), with the same number of days' sail between each, must be taken directly from the fairy tales.[1] Such a voyage is in itself improbable; in the saga the countries are evidently imagined as islands or peninsulas, but nothing corresponding to this is to be found on the coast of America. It is inconceivable that a discoverer of Labrador and of the coast to the south of it should have divided this into several countries; it was not till long after the rediscovery of Newfoundland and Labrador that the sound between them was found. If we suppose that Karlsevne was making southward and came first to Labrador (= Helluland?), with a coast extending south-eastward, it

[1] It is perhaps more than a coincidence that in the classical legends there were three groups of islands, the Gorgades, the Hesperides and the Insulæ Fortunatæ, to the west of Africa. Marcianus Capella says that it was two days' sail to the Gorgades, then came the Hesperides, and besides the Insulæ Fortunatæ. Pliny also has two days to the Gorgades; beyond them there were two Hesperides; he mentions also that it was two days' sail to the Hesperian Æthiopians, etc. In the Flateyjarbók's description of Bjarne Herjolfsson's voyage, which is still more purely fairy-tale, he sails for two days from the first land he found (= Wineland) to the second (= Markland), then three days to the third (= Helluland and finally four days to Greenland.

WINELAND THE GOOD

is against common sense that he should voluntarily have lost sight of this coast and put to sea again in an easterly direction, and then sight fresh land to the south of him two days later; on the other hand, this is the usual mode of presentment in fairy tales and myth. But let us suppose now that he did nevertheless arrive in this way at Newfoundland (= Markland?), and then again put to sea instead of following the coast, how could he know that this time instead of sailing eastward he was to take a westward course? But this he must have done, for otherwise he could not have reached Cape Breton or Nova Scotia; and he must have got there, if we are to make anything out of the story. The distances given, of two "dœgr's" sail to each of the countries, as remarked on p. 322, are also foreign to reality.[1] This part of the description has therefore an altogether artificial look.

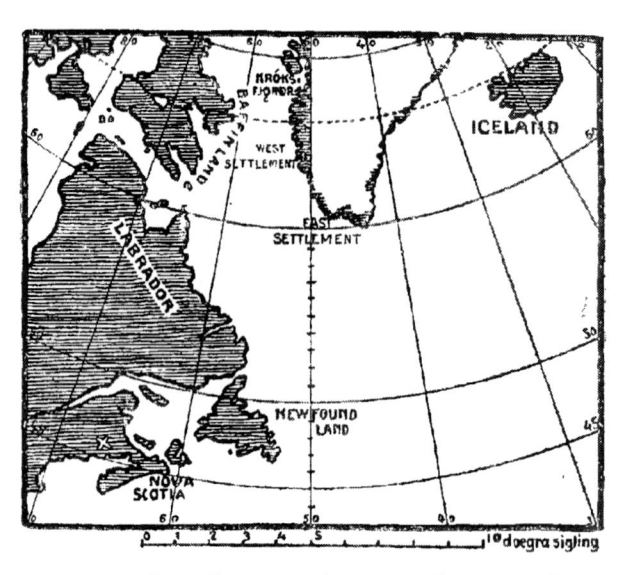

The relative distances between the countries. The scale gives "dœgr's" sailing (= 2 degrees of latitude), according to the "Rymbegla." A white cross marks the valley of the St. John

[1] If we assume that a "dœgr's" sailing is equal to two degrees of latitude or 120 nautical miles (twenty-four ancient sea-leagues), then, as shown on the map above, it will be about *four* dœgr's sail from Greenland to the nearest part of Labrador (not *two*). From Bjarneyjar to Markland should be *four* dœgr according to the saga; but the map shows that it is between *eight* and *ten* dœgr from the Western Settlement along the coast of Labrador to Newfoundland. On the other hand, between Newfoundland and Cape Breton *two* dœgr's sail will suit better.

335

IN NORTHERN MISTS

CHAPTER IX

It reminds one forcibly of many of the old Irish legendary tales of wonderful voyages ; in particular the commencement of one of the oldest and most important may be mentioned : " Imram Maelduin " (the tale of Maelduin's voyage), which is known in MSS. of the end of the eleventh century and later, but which was probably to a great extent first written down in the seventh, or at the latest in the eighth century [cf. Zimmer, 1889, p. 289].

When Maelduin and his companions put to sea from Ireland in a coracle with three hides (while Karlsevne has three ships), they came first to two small islands (while Karlsevne came to Bjarneyjar). After this for three days and three nights the Irishmen came upon no land ; " on the morning of the third day " they heard the waves breaking on a beach, but when daylight came and they approached the land, swarms of ants, as large as foals, came down to the beach and showed a desire to eat them and the boat (these are the gold-digging ants of Indo-Greek legend). This land is the parallel to Helluland, where there were a number of arctic foxes (cf. the description of the arrival there, p. 323).—After having fled thence for three days and three nights, the Irishmen heard " on the morning of the third day " the waves breaking on a beach, and when daylight came they saw a great, lofty island with terraces around it and rows of trees, on which there were many large birds ; they ate their fill of these and took some of them in the boat. This island might correspond to the wooded Markland, with its many animals, where Karlsevne and his people killed a bear.— After another three days and three nights at sea, the Irish voyagers " on the morning of the fourth day " saw a great sandy island ; on approaching the shore they saw there a fabulous beast like a horse with dog's paws and claws. For fear of the beast they rowed away without landing. This great sandy island may be compared with Furðustrandir, where there were no harbours and it was difficult to land.—The Irishmen then travelled " for a long time " before they came to a large, flat island, where two men landed to examine the island, which they found to be large and broad, and they saw marks of horses' hoofs as large as a ship's sail, and nutshells as large as " cōedi " (a measure of capacity ?), and traces of many human beings This bears a resemblance to Karlsevne's having " a long way " to sail along Furðustrandir before he came to a bay, where the two Scots went ashore to examine the country, were absent three days, and found grapes and wheat —After that the Irishmen travelled for a week, in hunger and thirst, until they came to a great, lofty island, with a great house on the beach, with two doors, " one towards the plain on the island and one towards the sea " ; and through the latter the waves of the sea threw salmon into the middle of the house. They found decorated couches and crystal goblets with good drink in the house, but no human being, and they took meat and drink and thanked God. Karlsevne proceeded from the bay and came to Straumsey, which was

WINELAND THE GOOD

thick with birds and eggs, and to Straumsfjord, where they established themselves (i.e., built houses). And there were mountains and a fair prospect and high grass; and they had catches from two sides, " hunting on the land, and eggs and fish from the sea "; and where, to begin with, they did nothing but make themselves acquainted with the land.—From the island with the house Maelduin and his men travelled about "for a long time," hungry and without food, until they found an island which was encompassed by a great cliff (" alt mor impi "). There was a very thin and tall tree there, Maelduin caught a branch of it in his hand as they passed by; for three days and three nights the branch was in his hand, while the boat was sailing past the cliff, and on the third day there were three apples at the end of the branch (cf. Karlsevne's runners who returned after three days with grapes and wheat in their hands), on which they lived for forty days Karlsevne and his men suffered great want during the winter at Straumsfjord; and from that place, where they lived on land in houses, they sailed "for a long time" before they came to the country with the self-sown wheat and vines, where there were great sandbanks off the mouth of the river, so that they had a difficulty in landing.

It is striking that in the voyage of Maelduin, the distance is only given as three days' and three nights' sail in the case of the three first passages to the three successive islands, after the first two small islands, while between the later islands we are told that they sailed " a long way," " for a week," " for a long time," etc.; just as in the Saga of Eric the Red, where, after Bjarneyjar, they sail for two " dœgr " to each of the three lands in turn, and then they had " a long way " to sail along Furðustrandir, to a bay, after which " they went on their way " to Straumsfjord, and thence they went " for a long time " to Wineland, etc. I do not venture to assert that there was a direct connection between the two productions, for that there are perhaps too many dissimilarities; but they seem in any case to have their roots in one and the same cycle of ideas, and the original legend certainly reached Iceland in the shape of oral narrative.

The number three plays an important part in Eric's Saga. Three voyages are made to or in search of Wineland, Karlsevne has three ships, three countries are visited in turn, three winters are spent away (as with Eric the Red on his first voyage to Greenland, but there this was due to his exile), they meet with the Skrælings three times, three men fall (two in the fight with the Skrælings, and afterwards Thorvald Ericson)—just as Maelduin (and also Brandan) loses three men—the expedition finally resolves itself into three separate homeward voyages,

IN NORTHERN MISTS

CHAPTER IX

Thorhall the Hunter's, Karlsevne's and Bjarne Grimolfsson's, etc. etc.[1] In the Irish legends and tales, e.g., those of Maelduin or of the Ua Corra, the repetition of the number three is even more conspicuous.

We may regard it as another feature of fairy tale that Eric the Red has three sons who set out one after another, first Leif, then Thorstein, and lastly Thorvald, who finds the land and takes part in the attempt to settle it. But th s feature is not conspicuous enough to allow of our attaching much importance to it, especially as here it is the first son who is the lucky one, while it is not so in fairy tale.

Sweet dew and manna

In Leif's voyage in the "Grönlendinga-þáttr" (which voyage partly corresponds to Karlsevne's), when they came to a country south-west of Markland, they landed on an island, to the north of the country,

"looked around them in fair weather, and found that there was dew on the grass, and it happened that they touched the grass with their hands and put them in their mouths, and they thought they had never tasted anything so sweet as it was."

This reminds one forcibly of Moses' manna in the wilderness, which appeared like dew [Exodus xvi. 14]. In the Old Norwegian free rendering of the Old Testament, called "Stjórn,"[2] of about 1300, therefore much earlier than the "Grönlendinga-þáttr," the account of this says that dew came from heaven round the whole camp, "it stuck like slime on the hands as soon as they touched it" ... "they found that it was sweet as honey in taste ..." But here again we come in contact with Irish legendary ideas. In the tale of the Navigation of the Sons of Ua Corra (of the twelfth century) the voyagers come to an island with a beautiful and wonderful plain covered with trees, full of

---

[1] One must, of course, be cautious of seeing myth in all such trilogies. As warning examples may be mentioned, that the Norwegians settled in Hjaltland (Shetland), Orkney, and the Suderoer (Hebrides); they discover the Faroes, thence Iceland, and then Greenland, in the same way as they are said from the last-named to have discovered Helluland, Markland and Wineland. On the east coast of Greenland there were three glaciers, etc. But in Eric's Saga the triads are so numerous and sometimes so peculiar, and the saga proves to be made up to such an extent of loans, that one is disposed to regard the number three as derived from mythical poetry.

[2] Cf. Unger's edition, Christiania, 1862, p. 292.

honey, and a grass-green glade in the middle with a glorious lake of agreeable taste. Later on they come to another marvellous island, with splendid green grass, and honeydew lay on the grass [cf. Zimmer, 1889, pp. 194, 195].

The name "Furðustrandir" (marvel-strands), as we shall see later (p. 357), may come from the "Tírib Ingnad" (lands of marvel) and "Trág Mór" (great strand) of Irish legend, far in the western ocean.

When Karlsevne arrived off Furðustrandir he sent out his two Scottish runners, the man "Haki" and the woman "Hekja," and told them to run southwards and examine the condition of the country and come back in three days. This is evidently another legendary trait; and equally so the circumstance that King Olaf had given these runners to Leif and told him "to make use of them if he had need of speed, for they were swifter than deer." We know of many such features in fairy tale and myth. Then, after the traditional three days, the man and woman come running from the interior of the country, one with grapes, the other with self-sown wheat in their hands. We are tempted to think of the spies Moses sent into Canaan, with orders to spy out the land, whether it was fat or lean, and who came back with a vine-branch and a cluster of grapes, which they had cut in the vale of Eshcol (i.e., the vale of grapes).[1]

But there are other remarkable points about this legend. Professor Moltke Moe has called my attention to a striking resemblance between it and the legends of the two runners or spies who accompanied Sinclair's march through Norway in 1612. They are called "wind-runners" or "bloodhounds," or again "weather-calves" or "wind-calves"; others called them "Wild Turks."

"They were ugly folk enough. Sinklar used them to run before and search out news; in the evening they came back with their reports. They were swifter

---

[1] Cf. also Joshua's two spies, who by the advice of Rahab the harlot concealed themselves in the mountains for three days, after which they descended and came to Joshua.

in running than the stag ; it is said that the flesh was cut out of their thighs and the thick of their calves. It is also said that they could follow men's tracks."[1]

We are told elsewhere that "these 'Ver-Kalvann' ('wind-calves') were more active than farm-dogs, swift as lightning, and did not look like folk. The flesh was cut out of the thick of their calves, their thighs and buttocks ; their nostrils were also slit up. People thought this was done to them to make them so much lighter to run around, and every one was more frightened of them than of the Scots themselves. They could get the scent of folk a long way off and could kill a man before he could blow his nose : they dashed up the back and broke the necks of folk."[2]

The trait that the wind-runners " did not look like folk " is expressed in another form in H. P. S. Krag's notes ; he thinks that they

"were nothing else but Sinclair's bloodhounds, which we may assume both from the description and from its being related of the one that was shot at Odegaard that it ran about the field and barked."

Something similar also occurs about the runners in Wineland in a late form of the legend of Karlsevne's voyage, where we read that

"he sailed from Greenland south-westward until the condition of the country got better and better ; he found and visited many places that have never been found since ; he found also some Skrælings ; these people are called in some books Lapps. In one place he got two creatures ('skepnur') more like apes than men, whom he called Hake and Hekja ; they ran as fast as greyhounds and had few clothes." [MS. A. M., old no. 770c, new no. 1892, 3 ; cf. Rafn : " Antiquitates Americanæ," 1837, p. 196]

It may be mentioned in addition that in the Flateyjarbók's saga of the Wineland voyages no runners appear, but on the other hand, in the tale of Leif's voyage, which has features in common with Karlsevne's, there is a " Southman " ("suðrmaðr," most frequently used of Germans)[3] of the

---

[1] Cf. Andreas Austlid : " Sinklar-soga," p. 21 (Oslo, 1899). H. P. S. Krag : " Sagn samlede i Gudbrandsdalen on slaget ved Kringlen den 26de august 1612," p. 19 (Kristiania, 1838).

[2] Ivar Kleiven : " I gamle Daagaa, Forteljingo og Bygda-Minne fraa Vaagaa," p. 63 (Kristiania, 1907).

[3] We are told that he talked in " þýrsku." Similarity of sound may here raise the question whether he was not originally supposed to be a Turk (cf the Wild Turks above), to which the name itself would point.

name of "Tyrker," who was the first to find the wild vine in the woods (like Karlsevne's runners) and intoxicated himself by eating the grapes.[1] As Moltke Moe observes, there is a remarkable resemblance between the rare name Tyrker and the fact that Sinclair's runners were called Wild Turks.

Both in the legend of Karlsevne and in that of Sinclair the two runners are connected with Scots or Scotland. One is therefore inclined to suppose that some piece of Celtic folklore is the common source of both. Now there is a Scottish mythical creature called a "water-calf"; and the unintelligible Norwegian name "weather-calf" or "wind-calf" ("veirkalv") may well be thought a corruption of this. It is true that this creature inhabits lakes, but it also goes upon dry land, and has fabulous speed and the power of scenting things far off. It can also transform itself into different shapes, but always preserves something of its animal form.

That the runners in Eric's Saga have become a man and woman may be due to a natural connection with Thor's swift-footed companions, Tjalve and Röskva. But there seems here to be another possible connection, which Moltke Moe has suggested to me. The strange garment they wore is called in one MS. "kiafal" and in another "biafal." No word completely corresponding to this is known in Celtic; but there is a modern Irish word "cabhail" (pronounced "caval" = "a body of a shirt"), which shows so much similarity both in meaning and sound that there seems undoubtedly to be a connection here. That "caval,"

---

[1] It is noteworthy that we are told of this Tyrker that he was "brattleitr" (i.e. with a flat, abrupt face); this is the only passage in Old Norse literature where this rare expression is used. The only context in which Moltke Moe has found it used in our time is in connection with the tale of the youngest son (Askeladden) in Sætersdal [cf. also H. Ross], where it is said that "Oskefis was also brasslaitte" (Ross thinks it means here "stiff in his bearing, full of self-esteem, self-sufficient"). Can it be merely a coincidence that this rare word is used of none other than the fairy-tale hero who is favoured by fortune, and of the lucky finder of the wild grapes, by eating which he intoxicates himself?

corrupted to "kiafal" (through the influence of similar-sounding names?), has been transformed into "biafal" may be due to the influence of the Norse "bjalfi" or "bjalbi" (= a fur garment without sleeves). As their costume plays such an important part in the description of the runners, and special stress is laid upon the Celtic word for it, it is probable that this word was originally used as a name for the runners themselves—in legend and epic poetry there are many examples of people being named from their dress. But gradually the Celtic word used as a name has been replaced by the corresponding Old Norse "hakull" (or "hokull" = sleeveless cloak open at the sides; cf. "messe-hagel," chasuble) and its feminine derivative "hekla" (= sleeveless cloak, with or without a hood). The use of these two words of masculine and feminine gender may be due to conceptions of them as man and woman, derived from Tjalve and Röskva. In course of time it was natural that a personal name formed from the costume, like Hakull, should easily be replaced by a real man's name of similar sound, like "Haki," specially known in legend and epic poetry as a name of sea-kings, berserkers and troll-children. Then "Hekja" was derived from "Haki," in the same way as "Hekla" from "Hakull." Hekja as a name is not met with elsewhere.[1]

That the whole of this story of the runners in the Saga of Eric the Red has been borrowed from elsewhere appears also from its being badly fitted in; for the narrative of the

[1] Professor Moltke Moe has called my attention to resemblances to these runners in the Welsh tale of "Kulhwch and Olwen." In this there occur two swift-footed knights, and Queen Gwenhwyvar's two servants (Yskyrdav and Yscudydd) "as swift as thought," and finally Arthur's wonderfully swift hound "Cavall" (in older MSS. "Cabal") [cf. Heyman, "Mabinogion," 1906, pp. 80, 82, 101, 103; J. Loth, "Les Mabinogion," i. and ii]. Of Tjalve it is related in the Snorra-Edda that he was "fóthvatastr" (the swiftest), and in Utgard he ran a race with thought (Hugi). This trait is Irish, as will be shown by Von Sydow [1910]. It resembles the two servants ("swift as thought") in the Welsh legend. The runners in the Saga of Eric the Red are also Celtic, and this in itself points to a connection.

WINELAND THE GOOD

saga continues without taking any notice of the finding of the sure tokens of Wineland: the self-sown wheat and the vine; and in the following spring there is even a dispute as to the direction in which the country is to be sought. Furthermore, after the discoveries of the runners Karlsevne continues to sail southward, at first, the same autumn, to Straumsfjord, and then still farther south the following summer, before he arrives at the country of the wheat and grapes that the runners had reached in a day and a half in a roadless land.

CHAPTER IX

The description of the stay in Straumsfjord also contains purely mythical features, such as Thorhall the Hunter's being absent for the stereotyped three days ("dœgr"), and having, when they find him, practised magic arts with the Red-Beard (Thor), as the result of which a whale is driven ashore (see p. 325). There is further a striking resemblance between the description of Thorhall's state when found and that of Tyrker after he had eaten the grapes. When, in Eric's Saga, they sought and found Thorhall on a steep mountain crag,

Mythical figures: Thorhall and Tyrker

"he lay gazing up into the air with wide-open mouth and nostrils, scratching and pinching himself and muttering something. They asked why he lay there. He answered that that did not concern anybody, and told them not to meddle with it; he had for the most part lived so, said he, that they had no need to trouble about him. They asked him to come home with them, and he did so."

In the Flateyjarbók's "Grönlendinga-þáttr" Tyrker was lost in the woods, and when Leif and his men went in search and found him again, he too behaved strangely.

"First he spoke for a long time in 'þýrsku,' and rolled his eyes many ways and twisted his mouth; but they could not make out what he said. After a while he said in Norse: I did not go much farther, and yet I have a new discovery to tell of; I have found vines and grapes ('vínvið ok vínber')."

This shows how features taken from legends originally altogether different are mingled together in these sagas, in order to fill out the description; and it shows too how the same tale may take entirely different forms. Of Tyrker we

343

IN NORTHERN MISTS

CHAPTER IX

hear further that " he was ' brattleitr ' (with a flat face and abrupt forehead), had fugitive eyes, was freckled (' smáskitligr ') in the face, small of stature and puny, but skilful in all kinds of dexterity." Thorhall, on the other hand, " was tall of stature, dark and troll-like," etc. (see p. 320), but he was also master of many crafts, was well acquainted with the uninhabited regions, and altogether had qualities different from most people. Both had long been with Eric the Red. There can scarcely be a doubt that these two legendary figures, perhaps originally derived from wholly different spheres, have been blended together.

The stranded whale

The whale that is driven ashore and that they feed on resembles the great fish that is cast ashore and that the Irish saint Brandan and his companions live on in the tale of his wonderful voyage (see below). This resemblance is confirmed by the statement in the Icelandic story that no one knew what kind of whale it was, not even Karlsevne, who had great experience of whales. There are, of course, no whales on the north-eastern coast of America that are not also found on the coasts of Greenland and Iceland; the incident therefore appears fictitious. The great whale in the legend of Brandan, on the other hand, is a fabulous monster. There is this distinction, it is true, that Karlsevne's people fall ill from eating the whale,[1] while it saves the lives of the Irish voyagers; but in both cases it is driven ashore after God, or a god, has been invoked in their need, and disappears again immediately (in the tale of Brandan it is devoured by wild beasts; in the saga it is thrown over the cliff). This difference can easily be explained by the whale in the Norse story having been sent by a heathen god, so that it was sacrilege to eat of it. In the tale of Brandan the whale is perhaps derived from Oriental legends [cf. De Goeje, 1891, p. 63]; it may, however, be a common northern feature.

[1] In the "Gronlendinga-þáttr" the whale they found was both large and good; they cut it in pieces, and "they had no lack of food."

WINELAND THE GOOD

When it is stated of Straumsfjord that there were places where eggs could be gathered, and of Straumsey that "there were so many birds that one could scarcely put one's foot down between the eggs," this is evidently an entirely northern feature, brought in to decorate the tale, and brought in so infelicitously that they are made to find all this mass of eggs there in the *autumn* (!) when they arrive. If Straumsfjord was in Nova Scotia there could not be eider-ducks nor gulls either [1] in sufficient number to form breeding-grounds of importance, and among sea-birds one would be more inclined to think of terns, as Professor R. Collett has suggested to me. As the coast is not described as one with steep cliffs, and there is mention of stepping between the eggs, auks, guillemots and similar sea-birds are out of the question, even if they occurred so far south.

CHAPTER IX
Eggs in the autumn and egg-gathering

But then comes the most important part of the saga, the description of the country itself, where grew self-sown fields of wheat, and vines on the hills, where no snow fell and the cattle were out the whole winter, where the streams and the sea teemed with fish and the woods were full of deer.

Wineland the equivalent of Fortunate Isles

Isidore says [in the "Etymologiarum," xiv. 6, 8] of the Fortunate Isles:

"The Insulæ Fortunatæ denote by their name that they produce all good things, as though fortunate ('felices') and blessed with fertility of vegetation. For of their own nature they are rich in valuable fruits ('poma,' literally tree-fruit or apples). The mountain-ridges are clothed with self-grown ('fortuites') vines, and cornfields ('messis' = that which is to be cut) and vegetables are common as grass [i.e., grow wild like grass, are self-sown]; thence comes the error of the heathen, and that profane poetry regarded them as Paradise. They lie in the ocean on the left side of Mauritania [Morocco] nearest to the setting sun, and they are divided from one another by sea that lies between." He also mentions the Gorgades, and the Hesperides.

---

[1] According to information given by Professor R. Collett, the Larus argentatus is the only species of gull that occurs in Nova Scotia in sufficiently large numbers to make it seem probable that it might breed extensively on an island. Can it be possible that these close-lying eggs are derived from the white and red "scaltæ" (?) which covered the Anchorites' Isle in the Navigatio Brandani (see below, p. 360)?

IN NORTHERN MISTS

CHAPTER IX

These ideas of the Fortunate Isles were widely current in the Middle Ages. In the English work, "Polychronicon," by Ranulph Higden, of the fourteenth century, Isidore's description took the following form:

> "A good climate have the Insulæ Fortunatæ that lie in the western ocean, which were regarded by the heathen as Paradise by reason of the fertility of the soil and of the temperate climate. For there the mountain ridges are clothed with self-grown vines, and cornfields and vegetables are common as grass [i e, grow wild]. Consequently they are called on account of the rich vegetation 'Fortunatæ,' that is to say, 'felices' [happy, fertile], for there are trees that grow as high as 140 feet. . . ."

The resemblance between this description and that of Wineland is so close that it cannot be explained away as fortuitous; the most prominent features are common to both: the self-sown cornfields, the self-grown vines on the hills, and the lofty trees (cf. Pliny, below, p. 348), which are already present in the narrative of Leif's voyage (see above, p. 317). If we go back to antiquity and examine the general ideas of the Fortunate Land or the Fortunate Isles out in the ocean in the west, we find yet more points of resemblance. Diodorus [v. 19, 20] describes a land opposite Africa, in the middle of the Atlantic Ocean, as fertile and mountainous, but also to a large extent flat. (Wineland also had hills and lowlands.) It invites to amusements and delights.[1] The mountainous country has thick forests and all kinds of fruitful trees, and many streams; there is excellent hunting with game of all sorts, big and small, and the sea is full of fish (precisely as Wineland). Moreover, the air is extremely mild (as in Wineland), and there is plenty of fruit the whole year round, etc. The land was not known in former times, but some Phœnicians on a voyage along the African coast were overtaken by a storm, were driven about the ocean for many days, until they came thither (like Leif).

It is said of Wineland, in the Saga of Eric the Red, that

---

[1] Cf. Karlsevne's people, who on arrival rested for half a month and amused themselves.

WINELAND THE GOOD

"no snow at all fell there, and the cattle were out (in winter) and fed themselves," and in the Flateyjarbók we read that "there was no frost in the winter, and the grass withered little." These, we see, are pure impossibilities. As early as the Odyssey [iv. 566] it is said of the Elysian Fields in the west on the borders of the earth :

> "There is never snow, never winter nor storm, nor streaming rain,
> But Ocean ever sends forth the light breath of the west wind
> To bring refreshment to men."

In the early civilisation of Babylon and Egypt this fortunate land seems to have been imagined as lying in the direction of the rising sun; but the ideas are always the same. An ancient Egyptian myth puts "Aalu" or "Hotep" (= place of food, land of eating), which is the abode of bliss and fortune, far in the east, where light conquers darkness.

"Both texts and pictures bear witness to the beauty which pervades this abode of life; it was a Paradise as splendid as could be imagined, 'the store-house of the great god'; where 'the corn grows seven cubits high.' It was a land of eternal life; there, according to the oldest Egyptian texts, the god of light, and with him the departed, acquire strength to renew themselves and to arise from the dead."[1]

In the same colours as these the Odyssey describes many fortunate lands and islands, such as the nymph Calypso's beautiful island Ogygia, far in the west of the ocean; and again "Scheria's delightful island" [vii. 79 ff.], where the Phæacians, "a people as happy as gods," dwell "far away amid the splashing waves of the ocean," where the mild west wind, both winter and summer, ever causes the fruit-trees and vines to blossom and bear fruit, and where all kinds of herbs grow all the year round (remark the similarity with Isidore's description). The fortunate isle of Syria, far in the western ocean, is also mentioned [xv. 402],

---

[1] W. Brede Kristensen: "Een of twe boomen in het Paradijsverhaal." Theologisch Tijdschrift, 1908, p. 218.

IN NORTHERN MISTS

CHAPTER IX

"North of Ortygia, towards the region where the sun sets;
Rich in oxen and sheep, and clothed with vines and wheat,"

where the people live free from want and sickness. These are the same ideas which were afterwards transferred to the legend of the Hyperboreans (cf. pp. 15 ff.).[1] It is natural that among the Greeks wine and the vine took a prominent place in these descriptions. In post-Homeric times the "Isles of the Blest" (Μακάρων νῆσοι) are described by Hesiod (and subsequently by Pindar) as lying in the western ocean—

"there they live free from care in the Isles of the Blest, by the deep-flowing Ocean, the fortunate heroes to whom the earth gives honey-sweet fruits three times a year."

It is these ideas—perhaps originally derived from the Orient—that have developed into the Insulæ Fortunatæ.

These islands are described by many writers of later antiquity. Pliny says [Nat. Hist., vi. 32 (37)] that according to some authors there lie to the west of Africa

"the Fortunate Isles and many others, whose number and distance are likewise given by Sebosus According to him the distance of the island of Junonia from Gades is 750,000 paces; it is an equal distance from this island westward to Pluvialia and Capraria. In Pluvialia there is said to be no water but that which the rain brings. 250,000 paces south-west of it and over against the left side of Mauritania [Morocco] lie the Fortunate Isles, of which one is called Invallis on account of its elevated form, the other Planaria on account of its flatness. Invallis has a circumference of 300,000 paces, and the trees on it are said to attain a height of 140 feet."

But as usual Pliny uncritically confuses statements from various sources, and he here adds information collected by the African king Juba about the Fortunate Isles. According to this they were six in number: Ombrios, two islands of Junonia, besides Capraria, Nivaria, and Canaria, so called from the many large dogs there, of which two were brought to Juba. Solinus mentions in one place [c. 23, 10] that

[1] Of less importance in this connection is the question how far these names of islands in the Odyssey were originally connected with islands in the Mediterranean [cf V. Bérard, 1902, i.]; in the description in the poem they have in any case become wholly mythical.

WINELAND THE GOOD

there are three Fortunatæ Insulæ, but in another place [c. 56] he gives Juba's statement from Pliny. That these islands were located to the west of Africa is certainly due to the Phœnicians' and Carthaginians' knowledge of the Canary Islands, and Ptolemy also places them here (see above, p. 117). Strabo [i. 3] thinks that the Isles of the Blest lay west of the extremity of Maurusia (Morocco), in the region where the ends of Maurusia and Iberia meet. Their name shows that they lie near to the holy region (i.e., the Elysian Fields).

In his biography of the eminent Roman general Sertorius ("imperator" in Spain for several years, died in 72 B.C.), Plutarch also mentions the Isles of the Blest. He tells us that when Sertorius landed as an exile on the south-west coast of Spain (Andalusia),

"he found there some sailors newly arrived from the Atlantic Isles. These are two in number, separated only by a narrow strait, and they are 10,000 stadia (1000 geographical miles) from the African coast. They are called the 'Isles of the Blest.' Rain seldom falls there, and when it does so, it is in moderation; but they usually have mild winds, which spread such abundance of dew that the soil is not only good for sowing and planting, but produces of itself the most excellent fruit, and in such abundance that the inhabitants have nothing else to do but to abandon themselves to the enjoyment of repose. The air is always fresh and wholesome, through the favourable temperature of the seasons and their imperceptible transition.... So that it is generally assumed, even among the barbarians, that these are the Elysian Fields and the habitations of the blest, which Homer has described with all the magic of poetry. When Sertorius heard of these marvels he had a strong desire to settle in these islands, where he might live in perfect peace and far from the evils of tyranny and war."

But this remarkable man soon had fresh warlike undertakings to think about, so that he never went there. It appears too from the fragments that have come down to us of Sallust's Histories [1] that Sertorius did not visit these islands, but only wished to do so. In fragment 102 we read:

"It is related that he undertook a voyage far out into the ocean," and Maurenbrecher adds that a scholium to Horace [Epod. 16, 42] says: "The ocean wherein

---

[1] C. Sallusti Crispi Historiarum Reliquiæ. Ed Bertoldus Maurenbrecher, Lipsiæ, 1891, pp. 43 f.

IN NORTHERN MISTS

CHAPTER IX

are the Insulæ Fortunatæ, to which Sallust in his Histories says that Sertorius wished to retire when he had been vanquished."

But in L. Annæus Florus, who lived under Hadrian (117-138 A.D.), we read [iii. 22]:[1]

"An exile and a wanderer on account of his banishment, this man [i.e., Sertorius] of the greatest but most fatal qualities filled seas and lands with his misfortunes: now in Africa, now in the Balearic Isles he sought fortune, was sent out into the ocean and reached the Fortunate Isles: finally he raised Spain to conflict."

It thus appears that by Florus's time the idea had shaped itself that Sertorius really had sought and found these islands; which, besides, in part at all events, were thought to be the same as those said to have been already discovered by the Carthaginian Hanno on the west coast of Africa about 500 B.C.

Of great interest is the description which Horace gives in his Epodes [xvi. 39 ff.] of the Fortunate Isles in the ocean, though he does not mention them by name. He exhorts the Romans, who were suffering from the civil wars, to abandon the coast of Italy (the Etruscan coast) and sail thither, away from all their miseries. Lord Lytton[2] gave the following metrical translation of the poem:

> Ye in whom manhood lives, cease woman wailings,
> Wing the sail far beyond Etruscan shores.
> Lo! where awaits an all-circumfluent ocean—
> Fields, the Blest Fields we seek, the Golden Isles
> Where teems a land that never knows the ploughshare—
> Where, never needing pruner, laughs the vine—
> Where the dusk fig adorns the stem it springs from,
> And the glad olive ne'er its pledge belies—
> There from the creviced ilex wells the honey;
> There, down the hillside bounding light, the rills
> Dance with free foot, whose fall is heard in music;
> There, without call, the she-goat yields her milk,
> And back to browse, with unexhausted udders,

---

[1] L Annæus Florus, Epitome rerum Romanum, ex editione J. Fr. Fischeri Londini, 1822. Vol. i. pp. 278 f.
[2] Lytton The Odes and Epodes of Horace. London, 1869.

WINELAND THE GOOD

Wanders the friendly flock ; no hungry bear
Growls round the sheepfold in the starry gloaming,
Nor high with rippling vipers heaves the soil.
These, and yet more of marvel, shall we witness,
We, for felicity reserved ; how ne'er
Dark Eurus sweeps the fields with flooding rain-storm,
Nor rich seeds parch within the sweltering glebe.
Either extreme the King of Heaven has tempered.
Thither ne'er rowed the oar of Argonaut,
The impure Colchian never there had footing.
There Sidon's trader brought no lust of gain ;
No weary toil there anchored with Ulysses ;
Sickness is known not ; on the tender lamb
No ray falls baneful from one star in heaven.
When Jove's decree alloyed the golden age,
He kept these shores for one pure race secreted ;
For all beside the golden age grew brass
Till the last centuries hardened to the iron,
Whence to the pure in heart a glad escape,
By favour of my prophet-strain is given.

Rendered into prose, Horace's poem will run somewhat as follows :

"Ye who have manliness, away with effeminate grief, and fly beyond the Etruscan shore. There awaits us the all-circumfluent ocean : Let us steer towards fields, happy fields and rich islands, *where the untilled earth gives corn every year, and the vine uncut* [i.e., unpruned, growing wild] *continually flourishes,* and the never-failing branch of the olive-tree blossoms forth, and the fig adorns its tree, honey flows from the hollow ilex, the light stream bounds down from the high mountain on murmuring foot," etc.

We thus find here in Horace precisely the same ideas of the Elysian Fields or the Fortunate Isles that occur later in Isidore and in the saga's description of the fortunate Wineland ; especially striking are the expressions about the corn that each year grows wild (on the unploughed earth) and the wild vine which continually yields fruit (blossoms, "floret").

These myths of the Fortunate Isles—originally derived from conceptions of the happy existence of the elect after death (in the Elysian Fields), for which reason they were called by the Greeks the Isles of the Blest—have also, of course, been blended with Indian myths of "Uttara Kuru." Among the Greeks they were sometimes the subject of humorous productions , several such of the fifth century B.C. are preserved in Athenæus. Thus Teleclides says : "Mortals live

IN NORTHERN MISTS

CHAPTER IX

there peacefully and free from fear and sickness, and all that they need offers itself spontaneously. The gutter flows with wine, wheat and barley bread fight before the mouths of the people for the favour of being swallowed, the fish come into the house, offer themselves and serve themselves up, a stream of soup bears warm pieces of meat on its waves," etc. Cf. also Lucian's description of the Isle of the Blest in Vera Historia (second century A D) : " The vines bear fruit twelve times a year . . . instead of wheat the ears put forth little loaves like sponges," etc. [Wieland, 1789, iv. p. 196].

Schlaraffenland and Fyldeholm

In the Middle Ages the tale of the land of desire was widespread : in Spain it took the name of " Tierra del Pipiripáo " or " Dorado " (the land of gold), or again " La Isla de Jauja," said to have been discovered by the ship of General Don Fernando. In it are costly foods, rich stuffs and cloths in the fields and on the trees, lakes and rivers of Malmsey and other wines, springs of brandy, pools of lemonade, a mountain of cheese, another of snow, which cools one in summer and warms in winter, etc. In the Germanic countries this took the form of the legend of Schlaraffenland.[1] This mythical country has in Norway become " Fyldeholmen " (i.e., the island of drinking),[2] which shows that to the Norwegians of later days wine or spirits were the most important feature in the description of the land of desire, as the wine was to the ancient Norsemen in the conception of Wineland.

To sum up, it appears to me clear that the saga's description of Wineland must in its essential features be derived from the myth of the Insulæ Fortunatæ. The representations of it might be taken directly from Isidore, who was much read in the Middle Ages, certainly in Iceland (where a partial translation of his work was made) and in Norway (he is often quoted in the " King's Mirror "), or orally from other old authorities, who gave still more detailed descriptions of these islands. But the difficulty is that the name of Wineland, connected with the ideas of the

---

[1] Cf. Johannes Peschel, 1878. Moltke Moe has called my attention to this essay, but, as he says, Peschel is certainly wrong in assuming that ancient notions like that of Schlaraffenland are the originals from which the ideas of the happy abodes of the departed, the Isles of the Blest (the Elysian Fields), have been developed The reverse is, of course, the case.

[2] Cf. J. N. Wilse : " Beskrivelse over Spydeberg Præstegjæld." Christiania, 1779-1780. In the appended Norwegian vocabulary, p xiii. : Fyldeholmen = Schlarafenland. I. Aasen [1873] has " Fylleholm " in the phrase " go to Fylleholm " (= go on a drinking bout), from Sogn, and other places. This may be derived from the same mythical country. H. Ross [1895] gives " Fylleholm " from Smålenene. From this it looks as if the idea was widely spread in Norway.

WINELAND THE GOOD

self-grown vine and the unsown wheat, is already found in Adam of Bremen (circa 1070, see above, pp. 195 ff). We might therefore suppose that it was his mention of the country which formed the basis of the Icelandic representation of it, although his fourth book (the description of the isles of the North) seems otherwise to have been little known in the North at that time; but here again the difficulty presents itself that the later description, that of the saga, is more developed and includes several features which agree with the classical conceptions, but which are not yet found in Adam of Bremen. I think therefore that the matter may stand thus, that "Vínland hit Góða" was the Norsemen's name for "Insulæ Fortunatæ," and was in a way a translation thereof; and oral tales about the country—based on Isidore and later on other sources as well—may have formed the foundation of the statements both in Adam and in Icelandic literature. In the latter, then, an ever-increasing number of features from the classical conceptions have crystallised upon the nucleus, when once it was formed, especially through the clerical, classically educated saga-writers.

As Norway, and still more Iceland (cf. pp. 167, 258), were closely connected in ancient days with Ireland, and as Norse literature in many ways shows traces of Irish influence, one is disposed to think that the ideas of Wineland may first have reached Iceland from that quarter. This exactly agrees with what was said at the beginning of this chapter, that the statements (in the Landnámabók) from the oldest Icelandic source, Are Frode, point directly to Ireland as the birthplace of the first reports of Wineland. We read in the Landnámabók:

CHAPTER IX

Irish happy lands and Wineland

"Hvítramanna-land, which some call 'Irland hit Mikla' [Ireland the Great], lies westward in the ocean near Wineland (Vindland) the Good. It is reckoned six 'dœgr's' sail from Ireland."

Nothing more is said about Wineland.[1] As it is added that Are Márssson's voyage to Hvítramanna-land

---

[1] In Hauk's Landnámabók Vin(d)land is mentioned in one other passage

IN NORTHERN MISTS

CHAPTER IX

"was first related by Ravn 'Hlymreks-farer,' who had long been at Limerick in Ireland,"

we see that Ravn, who was an Icelandic sailor of the beginning of the eleventh century, must have heard of both Hvítramanna-land and Wineland in Ireland, since otherwise he could not have known that one lay near the other.[1] But as Hvítramanna-land or "Great Ireland" is an Irish mythical country (see later), it becomes probable that Wineland the Good, at any rate in this connection, was one likewise. The old Irish legends mention many such fortunate islands in the western ocean, which have similar names, and which to a large extent are derived from the classical myths of the Elysian Fields and the Insulæ Fortunatæ. Voyages to them form prominent features of most of the Irish tales and legends. In the heathen tale of the Voyage of Bran ("Echtra Brain maic Febail," preserved in fifteenth and fourteenth century copies of a work of the eleventh century, but perhaps originally written down in the seventh century)[2] there are descriptions of: "Emain" or "Tír na-m-Ban" (the land of women), with thousands of amorous women and maidens, and "without care, without death, without any sickness or infirmity" (where Bran and his men live sumptuously each with his woman);[3] "Aircthech" (= the beautiful land); "Ciuin" (= the mild land), with riches and treasures of all colours, where one listens to lovely music, and drinks the most delicious wine; "Mag Mon" (= the plain of sports); "Imchiuin" (= the very mild land);

[cap. 175], in connection with Karlsevne, who is said to have discovered it, but nothing is said about this in the Sturlubok, and it may be a later addition (cf p. 331).

[1] Ravn told the story to Thorfinn, Earl of Orkney (ob. circa 1064), who in turn told it to some Icelanders, and from them it reached Thorkel Gellisson, Are Frode's uncle.

[2] Cf. Zimmer, 1889, pp. 257, 261; Kuno Meyer, 1895, i.

[3] This is evidently the land that in the Christian Breton legend of St. Machutus (ninth century) has become the paradisiacal island of "Yma," inhabited by heavenly angels.

354

WINELAND THE GOOD

"Mag Mell" (= the happy plain, the Elysium of the Irish), which is described as lying beneath the sea, where without sin, without crime, men and loving women sit under a bush at the finest sports, with the noblest wine, where there is a splendid wood with flowers and fruits and golden leaves, and the true scent of the vine; there is also "Inis Subai" (the isle of gladness), where all the people do nothing but laugh.[1] It is said in the same tale that "there are thrice fifty distant islands in the ocean to the west of us, each of them twice or thrice as large as Erin."

CHAPTER IX

That western happy lands in the Irish legends (even in the Christian "Imram Maelduin") should often be depicted as the Land of Women ("Tír na-m-Ban") or Land of Virgins ("Tír na-n-Ingen"), with amorously longing women, might be thought to have some connection with Mahomet's Paradise and the Houris; but the erotically sensuous element is everywhere so prominent in mediæval Irish literature that this feature may be a genuine Irish one.[2] It must, by the way,

[1] In the Christian Irish legend "Imram Maelduin," the voyagers arrive at two islands, that of the lamenting people with complaining voices, and that of the laughing people. The same two islands are mentioned in the Navigation of the Sons of O'Corry, "Imram Curaig Ua Corra" [cf. Zimmer, 1889, pp 160, 171, 188, 189]. They are evidently connected with Greek conceptions, as we find them in Theopompus, of the rivers Hedone and Lype in the distant land of Meropis (see above, p. 17, cf also the springs of voluptuousness and laughter in Lucian's Isle of Bliss in the Vera Historia) There may further be a connection with the island of the lamenting people in the statement of Saxo Grammaticus, in the introduction to his Danish history, that it was thought that in the noise of the drift-ice against the coast of Iceland the lamenting voices of lost souls could be heard, condemned to expiate their sins in that bitter cold.

[2] These Irish ideas of a happy land of women have, it may be remarked, many points of resemblance with our Norwegian belief in fairies ("hulder") and with the German Venusberg myth, since the "hulder," like Frau Venus, originally Frau Holle or Holda [cf. J. Grimm, 1876, ii. p. 780], kidnaps and seduces men, and keeps them with her for a long time; but the sensual element is more subdued and less prominent in the Germanic myths. It may seem probable that the Irish land of women also has some connection with the amorous, beautiful-haired nymph Calypso's island of Ogygia, far off in the sea, in the Odyssey [v. 135 ff., vii. 254 ff] Just as the men in the Irish legends neither grow older nor die when they come to the land of women, and as the queen of the country

be this "Tír na-n-Ingen" that we meet with again in the Faroese lay "Gongu-Rólv's kvæði," where the giant from Trollebotten carries Rolv to "Mòyaland" (cf. Småmöyaland); there Rolv slept three nights with the fair "Lindin mjá" (= the slender lime-tree, i.e., maid), and on the third night she lost her virginity. But the other maidens all want to see him, they all want to torment him, some want to throw him into the sea,

"Summar vildu hann á gálgan fora	Some would carry him to the gallows,
summar ríva hans hár,	some would tear his hair,
uttan frúgvin Lindin mjá,	except the damsel Lindin the slender,
hon fellir fyri hann tár."	she shed tears for him.

She sends for the bird "Skúgv," which carries him on its back for seven days and six nights across the sea to the highest mountain in Trondhjem. [Cf. Hammershaimb, 1855, pp. 138 ff.]

will not let the men go again (cf. Maelduin), so Calypso wished to keep her Odysseus, and to make him "an immortal man, ever young to eternity." In a similar way the men who come to the "hulder" in the mountain do not grow old, and they seem to have even greater difficulty in getting out again than kidnapped women. (It is a common feature that they do not grow older, or that a long time passes without their noticing it in the intoxication of pleasure. Lucian also relates that those who come to his Isle of Bliss grow no older than they are when they come.) Odysseus longs for his home, like one of Bran's men (and like Maelduin's men, the kidnapped men in the German myths, etc.), and at last receives permission to go, like Bran. Calypso means "the hidden one" (from $\kappa\alpha\lambda\acute{\upsilon}\pi\tau\omega$ = hide by enveloping) and thus answers to our "hulder" (= the hidden one, cf "hulda," something which covers, conceals, envelops), and the German Frau Holle or Holda (= "hulder"). They are precisely the same beings as the Irish "síd"-people, who are also invisible, and the women in "Tír na-m-Ban," the island in or under the sea precisely like our "hulderland" (see later).

It may further be supposed that there is some connection between the ideas which appear in certain Irish legends of the land of virgins—where there are no men, and the virgins have to go to the neighbouring land of men ("Tír na-Fer") to be married [cf. Zimmer, 1889, p 269]—and the conceptions of Sena, the Celtic island of priestesses or women, off the coast of Brittany, where according to Dionysius Periegetes there were Bacchantes who held nightly orgies, but where no men might come, and the women therefore (like the Amazons) had to visit the men on the neighbouring coast, and return after having had intercourse with them. Similar ideas of islands with women and men separated occur already in old Indian legends.

WINELAND THE GOOD

The "Promised Land" ("Tír Tairngiri") with the "Happy Plain" ("Mag Mell")[1] became in the Christian Irish legends the earthly Paradise, "Terra Repromissionis Sanctorum" (the land of promise of the saints). Other names for the happy land or happy isles in the west are: "Hy Breasail" (= the fortunate isle), "Tír na-m-Beo" (= the land of the living), "Tír na-n-Óg" (= the land of youth), "Tír na-m-Buadha" (= the land of virtues), "Hy na-Beatha" (= the isle of life). The happy isle of "Hy Breasail," which was thought to be inhabited by living people, was also frequently called the "Great Land" (which when translated into Old Norse might become "Víðland"); just as the "Land of the Living," where there were only enticing women and maidens, and neither death nor sin nor offence, was called the "Great Strand" ("Trág Mór").[2] There is also mention of "Tír n-Ingnad" (land of marvels) and "Tírib Ingnad" (lands of marvels). This Irish series of names and conceptions for the same wonderful land (or strand) may well be thought to have been the origin of the name "Furðustrandir."[3] The Irish often imagined their Promised Land, with "Mag Mell" and also the land of women, as the sunken land

CHAPTER IX

From a MS. of the thirteenth century
(Royal Library, Copenhagen)

---

[1] Cf. Zimmer, 1889, p. 287; Whitley Stokes, Revue Celtique, xv. Paris 1894, pp. 437 f.; F. Lot, Romania, xxvii. 1898, p. 559.

[2] Cf. "Lageniensis," 1870, p. 116; Zimmer, 1889, pp. 263, 279.

[3] It is stated in an Irish legend that the hero Ciaban went as an exile to "Trág in-Chairn" (the strand of cairns) [cf. Zimmer, 1889, p. 271]. This might remind us of Helluland (?).

357

CHAPTER IX

Brandan's Grape-Island

under the sea (cf. p. 355), and called it "Tír fo-Thuin" (= the land under the wave).

It is not surprising that a name like "Vínland hit Góða" should have developed from such a world of ideas as this. But Moltke Moe has drawn my attention to yet another remarkable agreement, in the Grape-Island ("Insula Uvarum"), one of the fortunate isles visited by the Irish saint Brandan. In the Latin "Navigatio Sancti Brandani" —a description of Brandan's seven years' sea voyage in search of the "Promised Land"—it is related that one day a mighty bird came flying to Brandan and the brethren who were with him in the coracle; it had a branch in its beak with a bunch of grapes of unexampled size and redness[1] [cf. Numbers xiii. 23],[2] and it dropped the branch into the lap of the man of God. The grapes were as large as apples, and they lived on them for twelve days.

"Three days afterwards they reached the island; it was covered with the thickest forests of vines, which bore grapes with such incredible fertility that all the trees were bent to the earth; all with the same fruit and the same colour; not a tree was unfruitful, and there were none found there of any other sort."

Then this man of God goes ashore and explores the island, while the brethren wait in the boat (like Karlsevne and his men waiting for the runners), until he comes back to them bringing samples of the fruits of the island (as the runners brought with them samples of the products of Wineland). He says: "Come ashore and set up the tent, and regale yourselves with the excellent fruits of this land,

---

[1] In the tale of Maelduin's voyage, which is older than the "Navigatio" (see above, p 336), there occurs a similar mighty bird bringing a branch with fruit like grapes, possessing marvellous properties; but there is no grape-island [cf. Zimmer, 1889, p. 169].

[2] In the Latin translation of the Bible in use at that time, the Vulgate [Num. xiii. 24 f.], the passage runs: "And they came to the valley of grapes, cut a branch with its cluster of grapes, and two men carried it upon a staff They also took away pomegranates and figs from this place, which is called Nehel-escol, that is, the valley of grapes, because the children of Israel brought grapes from thence."

WINELAND THE GOOD

which the Lord has shown us." For forty days they lived well on the grapes, and when they left they loaded the boat with as many of them as it would hold, exactly like Leif in the "Gronlendinga-þáttr," who loaded the ship's boat with grapes when they left Wineland; and like Thorvald at the same place, who collected grapes and vines for a cargo [cf. "Grönl. hist. Mind.," i. pp. 222, 230].

The fortunate island on which the monk Mernoc lived (at the beginning of the "Navigatio") was called "Insula Deliciosa." The great river that Brandan found in the Terra Repromissionis, and that ran through the middle of the island, may be compared to the stream that Karlsevne found at Hóp in Wineland, which fell into a lake and thence into the sea, and where they entered the mouth of the river. But the river which divided the Terra Repromissionis, and which Brandan could not cross, was evidently originally the river of death, Styx or Acheron in Greek mythology ("Gjoll" in Norse mythology). One might be tempted to suppose that, in the same way as the whole description of Wineland has been dechristianised from the Terra Repromissionis, the realistic, and therefore often rationalising, Icelanders have transformed the river in the Promised Land, the ancient river of death, into the stream at Hóp.

Other passages also of the descriptions of the Wineland voyages present similarities with Brandan's voyage; and similar resemblances are found with other Irish legends, so many, in fact, that they cannot be explained as coincidences. The "Navigatio Sancti Brandani" was written in the eleventh century, or in any case before 1100 [1] (but parts of the legend of Brandan may belong to the seventh and eighth centuries). The work was widely diffused in Europe in the twelfth century, and was also well known in Iceland; we

CHAPTER IX

The river at Hóp and the Styx

---

[1] In France a poem on Brandan of as early as 1125, founded on the "Navigatio," is known, dedicated to Queen Aélis of Louvain, cf Gaston Paris. La Littérature Française en Moyen Age, Paris, 1888, p. 214.

CHAPTER IX

still possess an Old Norse translation of parts of it in the "Heilagra Manna sǫgur" [edited by Unger, Christiania, 1877, i.]. Through oral narratives the mythical features which are included in this legend have evidently helped to form the tradition of the Wineland voyages.

In the tale of the voyage of Maelduin and his companions ("Imram Maelduin," see above, p. 336),[1] it is related that they came to an island where there were many trees, like willow or hazel, with wonderful fruit like apples, or wine-fruit, with a thick, large shell; its juice had so intoxicating an effect that Maelduin slept for a day and a night after having drunk it; and when he awoke, he told his companions to collect as much as they could of it, for the world had never produced anything so lovely. They then filled all their vessels with the juice, which they pressed out of the fruit, and left the island. They mixed the juice with water to mitigate its intoxicating and soporific effect, as it was so powerful.[2] This reminds us of Tyrker in the "Grönlendinga-þáttr," who gets drunk from eating the grapes he found.[3]

Wine-fruit and wine in Irish legend

[1] The Irish made a distinction in their tales of voyages between "Imram," which was a voluntary journey, and "Longes," which was an involuntary one, usually due to banishment. In Icelandic literature there seems to be no such distinction, but the voyages are often due to outlawry for manslaughter or some other reason; cf. Ganger-Rolf's voyage, Ingolf's and Hjorleif's voyage to Iceland, Snæbjorn Galti's and Rolf of Raudesand's voyage to the Gunnbjorn-skerries, Eric the Red's voyage with his father from Norway, and afterwards from Iceland, etc. Bjorn Breidvikingekjæmpe was also obliged to leave Iceland on account of his illicit love for Snorre Gode's sister. This agreement may, of course, be accidental, but together with the many other resemblances between Irish and Icelandic literature, it may nevertheless be worth mentioning.

[2] Cf. Zimmer, 1889, p. 168; Joyce, 1879, p. 156.

[3] To these wine-fruits in the "Imram Maelduin" correspond, perhaps, the white and purple-red "scaltæ," which in the "Navigatio Brandani" cover the low island, bare of trees, called the "Strong Men's Island" [Schroder, 1871, p. 24]. Brandan pressed one of the red ones, "as large as a ball," and got a pound of juice, on which he and his brethren lived for twelve days. It might be supposed that these white and red "scaltæ" from the flat ocean-island were connected with Lucian's water-fishes (which seem to have been white) and wine-fishes (which had the purple colour of wine) (see above) The meaning of "scaltæ"

WINELAND THE GOOD

Wine is, moreover, a prominent feature in many of the Irish legends of sea-voyages. The voyagers often find intoxicating drinks, which make them sleep for several days, and they are often tormented by burning thirst and come to islands with springs that give a marvellously quickening drink. In the tale of the voyage of the three sons of Ua Corra (twelfth century?) they arrive at an island where a stream of wine flows through a forest of oaks, which glitters enticingly with juicy fruits. They ate of the apples, drank a little of the stream of wine, and were immediately satisfied and felt neither wounds nor sickness any more. In the tale of Maelduin there is an island with soil as white as a feather and with a spring which on Wednesdays and Fridays gives whey or water, on Sundays and the days of martyrs good milk, but on the days of the Apostles, of Mary and of John the Baptist, and on the great festivals it gives ale and wine [cf. Zimmer, 1889, pp. 163, 189].

CHAPTER IX

Brandan's Grape-island, Maelduin who intoxicates himself by eating the wine-fruit, and the stream of wine flowing through the oak forest, all bear a remarkable resemblance to what the Greek sophist and satirist Lucian (second century A.D.) relates in his fables in the "Vera Historia" about the seafarers who came to a lofty wooded island. As they wandered through the woods they came to a river, which instead of water ran with wine, like Chios wine. In many places it was broad and deep enough to be navigable, and it had its source in many great vines, which hung full of grapes. In the river were fish of the colour and taste of wine. They swallowed some so greedily that they became thoroughly intoxicated. But afterwards they had the idea of mixing these wine-fish with water-fish, whereby they lost the too-powerful taste of wine and were a good dish. After wading through the river of wine they came upon some remarkable vines, the upper part of which were like well-developed women down to the belt. Their fingers ran out into twigs full of grapes, their heads were covered with vine-branches, leaves and grapes, instead of hair. "The ladies kissed us on the mouth," says Lucian, "but those who were kissed became drunk on the spot and reeled. Only their fruit they would not allow us to take, and they cried out in pain if we plucked a grape or two off them. On the other hand, some of them showed a desire to pair with us, but two of my companions who complied with them had to pay dearly for it; for . . . they grew together with them in such a way that they became one stem with common roots." After this strange experience the voyagers filled their empty barrels partly with ordinary water, partly with wine from the river, and on the following morning they left the island. In the Isle of the Blest, at which they afterwards arrived, there were, in addition to many rivers of water, of honey, of sweet-scented essences and of oil, seven rivers of milk and eight of wine. We even find a parallel in Lucian to Maelduin's white island with the springs of milk and wine, as the travellers come to a sea of milk, where there was a great island of cheese, covered with vines full of grapes; but these

Resemblances to Lucian

("scaltis") is uncertain. Schroder says "sea-snails", Professor Alf Torp thinks it may be a Celtic word, and mentions as a possibility "scalt" (= "cleft"). In that case it might be a mussel, which is "cleft" in two shells.

CHAPTER IX

yielded milk instead of wine [cf. Wieland, 1789, iv. pp. 150 ff., 188 f., 196]. A direct literary connection between Lucian and the Irish myths can hardly be probable, as he is not thought to have been known in Western Europe before the fourteenth century; but he was much read in Eastern Europe, and oral tales founded on his stories may have reached the Irish. The resemblances are so pronounced and so numerous that it does not seem very probable that they should be wholly accidental. Such an oral connection might, for instance, have been brought about by the Scandinavians, who had much intercourse with Miklagard (Byzantium), or by the Arabs, who in fact preserved a great part of Greek literature, and who were in constant communication both with Celts and with Scandinavians.

Connection of the Brandan legend with northern waters

That a mythical island like the Isle of Grapes—or perhaps others as well, such as the " Insula Deliciosa "—might be the origin of the " Vínland hit Góða " of the Icelanders, to which one sailed from Greenland (and of Adam of Bremen's Winland), appears natural also from the fact that many of the islands and tracts that are mentioned in the " Navigatio," and that for the most part are also mentioned in the older tale of Maelduin, are undoubtedly connected with northern and western waters. That this must be so is easily understood when one considers the voyages of Irish monks to the Faroes and Iceland. The Sheep Island, which was full of sheep, and where Brandan obtained his paschal lamb, must be the Faroes, where the sheep are mentioned even by Dicuil (see p. 163), just as the island with the many birds also reminds us of Dicuil's account of these islands; the island on the borders of Hell, whose steep cliffs were black as coal, where one of Brandan's monks, when he set foot ashore, was instantly seized and burnt by demons, and which at their departure they saw covered with fire and flames, may have some connection with Iceland.[1] But it also bears some

[1] D'Avezac's hypothesis [1845, p. 9] that it might be an echo of Teneriffe [cf. also De Goeje, 1891, p. 61], which in mediæval maps was called " Isola dell' Inferno," is untenable, since the Phœnicians' knowledge of the Canaries had long been forgotten at that time, and it was only after their rediscovery by the Italians, about 1300, that Teneriffe was called on the Medici map of 1351 " Isola dell' Inferno " In classical literature there is no indication that any of the Canaries was regarded as volcanic; on the contrary, Pliny's " Nivaria " (i e., the snow-island) seems to be Teneriffe with snow on the summit.

WINELAND THE GOOD

resemblance to the Hell Island that Lucian's voyagers come to, surrounded by steep cliffs, where there were stinking fumes of asphalt, sulphur, pitch, and roasted human beings. When Brandan arrives at the curdled sea ("mare quasi coagulatum"), and has to sail through darkness before he comes to the Land of Happiness, or when we hear of a thick fog like a wall about the kingdom of Manannan, we again think of the northern regions where the Liver Sea lay, and where Adam of Bremen had his dark or mist-filled sea.

While thus many features connect the legend of Brandan with northern waters, it has, on the other hand—like many other Irish myths—its roots far down in the mythical conceptions of the classics. Above all, Brandan's Paradise or "Promised Land of the Saints," Terra Repromissionis Sanctorum, is nothing but the Greeks' Isles of the Blest, blended with ideas from the Bible. As shown by Zimmer [1889, pp. 328 ff.], the Imram Maelduin (which to a large extent forms the foundation of the Navigatio St. Brandani) and other Irish tales of sea-voyages have great similarity to Virgil's Æneid, and are composed on its model. We have already said that Brandan's Grape-island may have some connection with Lucian. From him is possibly also derived Brandan's great whale, "Iasconicus," on whose back they live and celebrate Easter. But similar big fishes are known from old Indian legends, from the legends about Alexander, etc. It may also be mentioned that in the Breton legend corresponding to Brandan's, that of St. Machutus (written down by Bili, deacon at Aleth, ninth century), the latter and Brandan came to an island where they find the dead giant "Mildu," whom Machutus awakens and baptizes and who, wading through the sea, tries to draw heir ship to the Paradise-island of "Yma," which he says is surrounded by a wall of shining gold, like a mirror, without any visible entrance. But a storm raises the sea and bursts the cable by which he is towing them. Humboldt already saw in this giant the god Cronos, who, according to Plutarch, lay sleeping on an island in the Cronian Sea to the north-west of Ogygia, which lay five days' voyage to the west of Britain (see above, p. 156). It is probably the same giant who in the tale of Brandan written in Irish ("Imram Brenaind") has become a beautiful maiden, whiter than snow or sea-spray; but a hundred feet high, nine feet across between the breasts, and with a middle finger seven feet long. She is lying lifeless, killed by a spear through the shoulder; but Brandan awakens and baptizes her. She belongs to the sea-people, who are awaiting redemption. As, in answer to Brandan's question, she prefers going straight to heaven to living, she dies again immediately without a sigh after taking the sacrament [cf. Schirmer, 1888, pp. 30, 72; Zimmer, 1889, p 136, De Goeje, 1891, p. 69]. This maiden is evidently connected with the supernaturally beautiful, big, and white king's daughter from the Land of Virgins ("Tir na-n-Ingen") who seeks the protection of Finn MacCumaill, and who is also pierced by a spear [cf Zimmer, 1889, pp. 269, 325].

CHAPTER IX

Classical roots of the Brandan legend

IN NORTHERN MISTS

CHAPTER IX
The Brandan legend and Norse literature

Thus do mythical beings transform themselves till they become unrecognisable. The same woman is found again in Iceland as late as the seventeenth century.[1]

In many of its features the Brandan legend, or similar Irish legends, may be shown to have had influence on Norse literature. The theft of the neck-chain (or bridle ?) by one of the brethren, who comes to grief thereby, in the Navigatio and in other Irish tales, is found again, as Moltke Moe points out to me, in the story of Thorkel Adelfar in Saxo Grammaticus, as a theft of jewels and of a cloak, through which the thieves also come to grief. The great fish (whale) " Iasconicus," of which Brandan relates that it tries in vain to bite its own tail, is evidently the Midgardsworm of Norse literature. In the same way the little, apparently innocent, but supernatural cat in the " Imram Maelduin " which suddenly destroys the man who steals the neck-chain may be connected with the cat that Thor tries to lift in Utgard. It is doubtless the same little cat that three young priests took with them on their voyage in another Irish legend [in the Book of Leinster, of the beginning of the twelfth century]. In the " Imram Brenaind " this little cat they took with them has grown into a monkey as large as a young ox, which swims after Brandan's boat and wants to swallow it [cf. Zimmer, 1889, p. 139]. Again, quite recently Von Sydow [1910, pp. 65 ff.] has shown that the Snorra-Edda's myth of Thor's journey to Utgard is based on Irish myths and tales.

The happy land in the west known in Northern Europe

Legends of a happy land or an island far over the sea towards the sunset were evidently widely diffused in Northern Europe in those days, outside Ireland. In Anglo-Saxon literature there is a dialogue between Adrianus and Ritheus (probably of the tenth century), where we read :

" Tell me where the sun shines at night." . . . " I tell you in three places : first in the belly of the whale that is called ' Leuiathan ' ; and the second season it shines in Hell ; and the third season it shines upon the island that is called ' Glið,' and there the souls of holy men repose till doomsday." [2]

This Glið (i.e., the glittering land) is evidently the Land of the Blest, Brandan's Terra Repromissionis, that lies in dazzling sunshine, after one has passed through darkness and mist ; but whether the myth reached the Anglo-Saxons from the Irish seems doubtful.

Pseudo-Gildas's description (twelfth century) of the isle of " Avallon " (the apple-island of Welsh myth) is also of interest ; it is connected with exactly the same ideas as the Irish happy isles :

---

[1] Jens Lauritzon Wolf's Norrigia Illustrata, 1651.
[2] Cf. John M. Kemble : The Dialogue of Salomon and Saturnus, London, 1448, p 198. Moltke Moe also called my attention to this remarkable passage.

WINELAND THE GOOD

"A remarkable island is surrounded by the ocean, full of all good things; no thief, no robber, no enemy pursues one there; no violence, no winter, no summer rages immoderately; peace, concord, spring last eternally, neither flower nor lily is wanting, nor rose nor violet; the apple-tree bears flowers and fruit on the selfsame branch; there without stain youths dwell with their maidens, there is no old age and no oppressive sickness, no sorrow, all is full of joy."[1]

CHAPTER IX

It results, then, from what has here been quoted, that a Grape-island ("Insula Uvarum") makes its appearance in Irish literature in the eleventh century, at about the same time when Adam of Bremen mentions, from Danish informants, an island called "Winland." Of the same century again is the Norwegian runic stone from Honen in Ringerike, on which, as we shall see later, Wineland is possibly mentioned (?) From the form of the runes, S. Bugge ascribes it to the first half of the eleventh century, hardly older, though it may be later. "Insula Uvarum" translated into the Old Norse language could not very well become anything but Vínland (or Víney), since Vínberjarey or Vínberjarland would not sound well. We thus have the remarkable circumstance that an island with the same name and the same properties makes its appearance almost simultaneously in Ireland and in Denmark (and possibly also in Norway). That these Wine-islands or Winelands should have originated entirely independently of one another, in countries which had such close intellectual connection, would be a coincidence of the kind that one cannot very well assume, since it must be regarded as more probable that there was a connection. But Brandan's Grape-island can scarcely be derived from a Wineland discovered by the Norsemen, since, as has been mentioned, the wine and wine-fruit play such a prominent part in the older Irish legends, and the ancient tale of Bran ("Echtra Brain") describes the Irish Elysium ("Mag Mell")

The name of Wineland derived from Ireland

---

[1] W. Mannhardt: Germanische Mythen, Berlin, 1858, pp. 460 f. Cf. "Vita Merlini," the verses on the "Insula pomorum, qvæ Fortunata vocatur" (the apple-island which is called Fortunate) [San-Marte, 1853, pp. 299, 329]. "Avallon" has a remarkable resemblance in sound to Pytheas's amber-island "Abalus" (p. 70).

CHAPTER IX

as a land with magnificent woods and the true scent of the vine, etc. (see p. 355). In the next place, as has been mentioned, Brandan's Grape-island bears a resemblance to Lucian's Grape-island ; but as Lucian's descriptions seem also to have influenced, among others, the tale of the intoxicating wine-fruit in the "Imram Maelduin," it looks as though Lucian's stories had reached Ireland (e.g., by Scandinavian travellers or through Arabs ?) long before the Navigatio Brandani was written. As thus the Irish wine-island cannot well be due to a Norse discovery, it becomes probable that Adam's name Winland (as well as the possible Norwegian name) was originally derived from Ireland, and that it reached the northern countries orally. If the Danes did not get the name from the Norwegians they may have brought it themselves, as they also had direct communication with Ireland.[1] This conclusion, that the name of Wineland came from Ireland, is again strengthened from an entirely different quarter, namely, the Landnámabók, where it is said that Great-Ireland lay near Wineland. As suggested on p. 354, this shows that the Icelanders must have heard both lands spoken of in Ireland. As Ravn Hlymreks-farer is given as the original authority, and after him Thorfinn, earl of Orkney (ob. circa 1064), this may have been at the beginning of the eleventh century ; but as the statement came finally from Thorkel Gellisson (and consequently was written down by Are Frode) it may also have been in the second half of that century. In this way we seem to have

[1] Since the above was printed in the Norwegian edition of this book, Professor Moltke Moe has called my attention to the fact that, according to Icelandic sources, the Icelandic chief Gellir Thorkelsson, grandfather of Are Frode, died at Roskilde, in Denmark, in 1073, after having been prostrated there for a long time. He was then on his way home from a pilgrimage to Rome. Adam's book was written between 1072 and 1075, and he had received the statements about Wineland from Danes of rank. The coincidence here is so remarkable that there must probably be a connection. It is Gellir Thorkelsson's son, Thorkel Gellisson, who is given as the authority for the first mention of Wineland in Icelandic literature, and according to Landnámabók he seems to have got his information from Ireland through other Icelanders.

WINELAND THE GOOD

CHAPTER IX

a natural explanation of the simultaneous appearance of the name in the North.[1]

As the statement in the Landnáma is due to Thorkel Gellisson, it is doubtless most probable that the Wineland that is mentioned for the first time in Icelandic literature in a gloss in Are Frode's Íslendingabók also has Thorkel (who is mentioned immediately afterwards) for its authority

---

[1] It is not, however, quite certain that "Vínland" (with a long "í") was the original form of the name, though this is probable, as it occurs thus in the MSS. that have come down to us of the two oldest authorities: Adam of Bremen ("Winland") and Are Frode's Íslendingabók ("Vínland"). But it cannot be entirely ignored that in the oldest Icelandic MSS.—and the oldest authorities after Are and Adam—it is called · in Hauk's Landnámabók "Vindland hit goða" (in the two passages where it is mentioned), in the Sturlubók "Irland et goda," in the Kristni-saga (before 1245) probably "Vindland hit goða" [cf. F. Jónsson, Hauksbók, 1892, p. 141], and in the Grettis-saga (about 1290, but the MS. dates from the fifteenth century) Thorhall Gamlason, who sailed with Karlsevne, is called in one place a "Vindlendingr" and in another a "Víðlendingr." It is striking that the name should so often be written incorrectly; there must have been some uncertainty in its interpretation. Another thing is that in none of these oldest sources is there any mention of wine, except in Adam of Bremen, who repeats Isidore, and after him it is only when we come to the Saga of Eric the Red that "Vínland" with its wine is met with. It might therefore be supposed that the name was originally something different. The Greenlanders might, for instance, have discovered a land with trees in the west and called it "Viðland" (= tree-land). Influenced by myths of the Irish "Great Land" ("Tír Mór"), this might become "Víðland" (= the great land, p. 357): but this again through the ideas of wine (from the Fortunate Isles), as in Adam of Bremen, might become "Vínland." We have a parallel to such a change of sound in the conversion of "viðbein" (= collar-bone) into "vinbein." A form like "Vindland" may have arisen through confusion of the two forms we have given, or again with the name of Vendland A name compounded of the ancient word "vin" (= pasture) is scarcely credible, since the word went out of use before the eleventh century; besides, one would then have to expect the form "Vinjarland." In Are Frode's work, which we only know from late copies (of the seventeenth century), the original name might easily have been altered in agreement with later interpretation. But it is nevertheless most probable that "Vínland" was the original form, and that the variants are due to uncertainty. It may, however, well be supposed that there were two forms of the name, in the same way as, for instance, the "Draumkvæde" is also called the "Draug-kvæde"; or that several names may have fused to become one, similarity of sound and character being the deciding factor.

CHAPTER IX (cf. p. 258), although the sentence might be by Are himself. Thorkel may have heard of this Wineland in Greenland; but it is more likely to be the country he heard of in connection with the mythical Hvítramanna-land from Ireland, and he may have heard that there were said to dwell there wights (or trolls) that were called Skrælings. Two possibilities suggest themselves: either this Wineland with its Skrælings was nothing but the well-known mythical land with its mythical people, which required no further description. It cannot be objected that the sober, critical Are would not have mentioned a mythical country in this way; for, if he was capable of believing in a Hvítramanna-land, he could also believe in such a Wineland. Or, on the other hand, it was a land which had actually been discovered and to which the name of the mythical country had been transferred. The latter hypothesis might be strengthened by other things that point to the Greenlanders having really found land in the west. But, on the other hand, if a country actually discovered is meant, it is curious that neither Are nor the Landnáma makes any mention of the discovery, whereas the discovery of Greenland is related at some length, and also that of Hvítramanna-land. Again, when Eric the Red came to Greenland, such a land had in any case not been discovered, so that it could not have been he who named the Eskimo after the inhabitants of that land, whereas Are might readily suppose that he had taken the name of Skrælings from the people of the mythical country; thus Are's words, as they now stand, would have a clearer meaning.

It may also be worth mentioning that in the only passage of the Sturlubók where Wineland is alluded to, it is called "Irland et Goda." This has generally been regarded as a copyist's error; but that it was due to misreading of an indistinctly written "Vinland" is not likely; it might rather be due to a careless repetition, since "Irland et Mikla" is mentioned just before. This is most probable. It may, however, be supposed that it is not an error, and that just as the latter is an alternative name for Hvítramanna-land, so "Irland

WINELAND THE GOOD

et Góða " may be a corresponding alternative name for Wineland, which was situated near it. We should thus again be led to Ireland as the home of the name. In any case the uncertainty which prevails in the versions of the name of Wineland given in the oldest authorities is striking (as discussed in the last note). Nothing of the same sort occurs in the transmission of other geographical names, and a form such as Vindland in Hauk's Landnáma cannot be explained as merely a copyist's error. Again, Eric's Saga in the Hauksbók has the name correctly, although this saga as well as the Landnáma was to a great extent copied by Hauk Erlendsson himself. This may point to the form Vindland having occurred in the original from which the Landnáma was copied. This discloses uncertainty in the very reading of the name, and it seems also to point to its having been a mythical country and not the name of a known land that had been discovered.

CHAPTER IX

To any one who is familiar with Norse place-names, the addition " hit góða " to Wineland must appear foreign and unusual. It is otherwise only known in the northern countries from the name " Landegode " (originally " Landit Góða ") on the coast of Norway, for an island west of Bodö. The same name was also used (and is still used in Stad and Herö) for Svinöi, a little island off Sunnmór, and for Jomfruland (south of Langesund). It has been generally taken for a so-called tabu-name;[1] but the explanation

Landit Góða, Fairyland

---

[1] Cf. Peder Clausson Friis, Storm's edition, 1881, p. 298; A. Helland, Nordlands Amt, 1907, i. p. 59, ii. pp. 467 f. Yngvar Nielsen [1905] has remarked the resemblance between the epithet " hit Góða," applied to Wineland, and the name Landegode in Norway; but following Peder Clausson he regards this as a tabu-name. K. Rygh [Norske Gaardnavne, xvi. Nordl. Amt, 1905, p. 201] thinks that P. Clausson's explanation of the name of Jomfruland is right in all three cases, that " Norwegian seamen ' from some superstition and fear ' did not call it by the name of Jomfruland, which was already common at that time, while under sail, until they had passed it." " It is, or at any rate has been, a common superstition among sailors and fishermen that various things were not to be called by their usual names while they were at sea, presumably a relic of heathen belief in evil spirits, whose power it was hoped to avoid by not calling their attention by mentioning themselves or objects with which their evil designs were connected,

suggested to me by Moltke Moe seems more probable, that it was a designation of fairylands, which lay out in the ocean, and which were thought to sink into the sea as one approached them. The above-mentioned Norwegian islands would quite answer to such conceptions, especially when they loom up and seem larger, and all three islands were formerly fairylands ("huldrelande"). The original germ of the belief in fairies ("huldrer") is the worship of the departed. "Hulder" means "hidden" (i.e., the hidden people). Fairylands are therefore the islands of the hidden, or of the departed, and these again are the Fortunate Isles or the Isles of the Blest. A parallel to this is that "Hades" in Greek means the invisible. And, as we have seen (p. 356), the nymph Calypso (= the hidden one) answers to our "hulder." When Bran, in the Irish legend alluded to, meets on the sea Manannán mac Lir (i.e., son of the Sea), king of the sea-people, lord of the land of the dead, he tells Bran that without being able to see it he is sailing over Mag Mell (the happy plain), where happy people are sitting drinking wine, and where there is a splendid forest with vines, etc.; and the Irish happy land "Tír fo-Thuin" is, as we have said (p. 358), the land under the wave. The lands or islands of the departed in course of time became the habitations of the invisible ones (spirits), of those who possess more than human wisdom, and have a specially favourable lot; by this means the idea of a fortunate land with favoured conditions, far surpassing the ordinary lot of men, became more and more emphasised. This development may be followed both with regard to classical ideas

while it was hoped to be able to conciliate them by using flattering names instead of the proper ones. The three islands are all so situated in the fairway that they must have been unusually dangerous for coasting traffic in former times." Hans Ström in his Description of Sondmòr [Soro, 1766, ii. p. 441] thought, however, that "Landegod" in Sunnmor was so called because it was the first land one made after passing Stad; and "Svino" he thought was so called because pigs were turned out there to feed, especially in former times (see below, p. 378); he gives in addition the name Storskjær for the island.

WINELAND THE GOOD

of the Fortunate Islands and to Norse conceptions of fairylands.

That the Greeks connected the happy land with the hidden people who move upon the sea may perhaps be concluded even from the Odyssey's description of the Phæacians, who dwelt in the happy land, the glorious Scheria, far in the western ocean (see above, p. 347). That they may be compared with our fairies ("huldrefolk") appears perhaps from the name itself, which may come from φαιός (= dark) and mean "dark man," "the hidden man" [cf. Welcker, 1833, p. 231].[1] They sail at night, always shrouded in clouds and darkness, in boats as swift "as wings and the thoughts of men" [Od. vii. 35 f.]. The "huldrefolk" also travel by night (cf. p. 378). In Ireland and in Iceland the way to fairyland is through darkness and mist, or sea or water [cf. Gröndal, 1863, pp. 25, 38]; and it is the same in Nordland. A blending of the fairies ("síd"-people) and the inhabitants of the happy land or promised land is particularly observable in the Irish legends [cf. Zimmer, 1889, pp. 276 f.]. The people of the "síd" dwell partly in grave-mounds (and are thus like our "haugebonde," or mound-elf), they may also live in happy lands far west in the sea or under the sea, and are thus sea-elves, but on the whole they most resemble our "huldrefolk." The "síd"-woman entices men like our "hulder"; in the tale of "Condla Ruad" [Connla the Fair; cf. Zimmer, 1889, p. 262] she comes from the Land of the Living ("Tír na-m-Beó"), far across the sea, and entices Connla to go with her in a glass boat to the "Great Strand," where there only were women and maidens. This Irish paradise of women out in the ocean has, as we have said (p. 355), much in common with the German Venusberg, and with the invisible country of our "huldrefolk."

CHAPTER IX

---

[1] V. Bérard's explanation [1902, i. p. 579] that Phæacians (Φαίακες) means Leucadians, the white people, and comes from the Semitic "Beakim" (from "b.e.q." "to be white") does not seem convincing. Professor A. Torp finds the explanation given above more probable.

IN NORTHERN MISTS

CHAPTER IX

But the "huldrefolk" dwell now in mountains and woods, now on islands in the sea or under the sea. As will be seen, the ideas of the Fortunate Isles or of the Promised Land and those of fairyland thus often coincide. It may be added that among many peoples the souls of the dead are carried across the sea in a boat or ship to a land in the west.

This is evidently connected with the river of death, Styx, Acheron or Cocytus, of the Greeks, over which Charon ferried the souls to the lower regions in a narrow two-oared boat. Procopius [De bello Goth., iv. 20] relates that according to legends he himself heard from the natives, all the souls of the departed are carried every night at midnight from the coast of Germania to the island of Brittia (i.e., Britain) which lies over against the mouth of the Rhine between Britannia (i.e., Brittany) and Thule (Scandinavia). He whose turn it is among the dwellers on the coast to be ferryman hears at midnight a knocking at his door and a muffled voice. He goes down to the beach, sees there an empty, strange boat, into which he gets and begins to row. He then notices that the boat is filled so that the gunwale is only a finger's breadth above the water, but he sees nothing. As soon as he arrives at the opposite shore, he notices that the boat is suddenly emptied, but still he sees no one, and only hears a voice announcing the names and rank of the arrivals. The invisible souls, who always move in silence, answer to the elves.

In many ways the connection between the dead and the sea is apparent. Balder's body was laid in a ship on which a pyre was kindled, and it was abandoned to the currents of the sea. The body of the hero Scild in the lay of Beowulf was borne upon a ship, which was carried away by the sea, no one knows whither. Flosi in Njál's Saga has himself carried on board a ship and abandoned to the sea, and afterwards the ship is not heard of again, etc.[1]

That the fairylands should be called "Landit Góða" may be due to their exceeding fertility (cf. the huldreland's waving cornfields); but it may also, as Moltke Moe has pointed out, have a natural connection with the tendency the Germanic peoples in ancient times seem to have had of attaching the idea of "good" to the fairies and the dead. In Nordland the "huldrefolk" are called "godvetter" ("good wights") [cf. I. Aasen]; this among the Lapps has become "gúvitter," "gufihter," "gufittarak," etc., as a name for supernatural beings underground or in the sea;[2] the

[1] Cf. J. Grimm, D. M., ii. 1876, pp. 692 ff., iii. 1878, pp. 248 f

[2] Cf. J. A. Friis: Ordbog for det lappiske Sprog, Christiania, 1887, p. 254; J. Qvigstad, 1893, p 182; Moltke Moe's communications in A. Helland: Finmarkens Amt, 1905, vol. ii p 261.

WINELAND THE GOOD

CHAPTER IX

Swedes in North Sweden use the word "goveiter." The mound-elf ("haugebonden"), Old Norse "haugbui" (the dweller in the mound), who was the ancestor of the clan, or the representative of the departed generations, is called in Nordland "godbonden."[1]

The underground people are called in Iceland "ljúflingar," in German "die guten Leute," in English-speaking Ireland, Scotland and the Isle of Man "the good people," "good neighbours," or "the men of peace"[2] In Highland Gaelic they are called "daoine sith," in Welsh "dynion mad." In Swedish and Danish we have the designation "nisse god-dreng" ("nisse good boy"] or "goda-nisse," in Norwegian "go-granne" ("good neighbour"); (in Danish also "kære granne," "dear neighbour"]; in German "Guter (or lieber) Nachbar," or "Gutgesell" is used of a goblin; in Thuringia "Gutchen," "Gutel"; in the Netherlands "goede Kind," and in England "Robin Goodfellow."

That the epithet "good" applied to supernatural beings, especially underground ones, is so widely spread, even among the Lapps, shows it to have been common early in the Middle Ages.

It is of minor interest in this connection to inquire what the origin of the epithet may have been. We might suppose that it was the thought of the departed as the happy, blest people; but on the other hand it may have been fear; it may have been sought to conciliate them by giving them pet-names, for the same reason that thunder is called in Swedish "gobon" (godbonden), "gofar," "gogubben," "gomor," "goa" (goa går),[3] which is also Norwegian.

"Hit góða" is the altogether good, the perfect, therefore the fortunate land. When the legend of the "Insulæ Fortunatæ" and of the Irish happy lands—one of which was the sunken fairyland "Tír fo-Thuin," the land underwave—reached the North, it was quite natural that the Northerners should translate the name by one well known to them, "Landit Góða" (fairyland, the land of the unseen); indeed, the name of Insulæ Fortunatæ could not well have been translated in any other way. But as wine was so

---

[1] Cf. Moltke Moe's communications in A. Helland: Nordlands Amt, 1907, vol. ii p. 430.
[2] Cf. W. Grimm, Kleinere Schriften, i. p. 468.
[3] Rietz: Svensk Dialekt-Lexikon, 1867.

IN NORTHERN MISTS

CHAPTER IX

conspicuous a feature in the description of this southern land of myth, both in Isidore and among the Irish, and as wine more than any other feature was symbolical of the idea of happiness, it is natural, as we have seen, that the Northerners came very soon to call this country, like Brandan's Grape-island, "Vínland"; thus "Vínland hit Góða" may have arisen by a combination of "Vínland" and "Landit góða," to distinguish it from the native "Landit Góða," the fairyland of the Norwegians. A combination of "hit góða" with a proper name is otherwise unknown, and thus points to "Landit Góða" as the original form.[1]

Laudatory names for fairyland

Moltke Moe has given me an example from Gotland of a fairyland having received a laudatory name answering to Wineland, in that the popular fairyland "Sjóhaj" or "Flåjgland," out at sea, is called Smorland.[2] Sjóhaj is a mirage on the sea; and "Flåjgland" comes from "fljuga," to fly, i e, that which drifts about, floating land. It now only means looming, but it may originally have been fairyland, and it is evident that it is here described as particularly fertile. With "Smòrland" may be compared Norwegian place-names compounded with "smor": "Smortue," "Smorberg," "Smorklepp." O. Rygh includes these among "Laudatory names . . . which accentuate good qualities of the property or of the place"[3] Similarly in the place-names of Shetland: "Smerrin" (= "smjǫr-vin," fat, fertile pasture), "Smernadal" (= "smjǫr-vinjar-dalr," valley with fat pasture), "de Smerr-meadow" (= originally: "smjor-eng" or "smjor-vin"), "de Smerwel-park" (probably = "smjor-vollr"), "de Smorli" (probably = "smjor-hlið"). J. Jakobsen [1902, p. 166] says that "'smer(r)' (Old Norse 'smjǫr' or 'smœr,' Norwegian 'smor,' butter) means here fertility, good pasture, in the same way as in Norwegian names of which the first syllable is 'smor.'" With this may be compared the fact that even in early times the word "smor" was used to denote a fat land, as when Thorolf in the saga said that "it dripped butter from every blade of grass in the land they had found" (i.e, Iceland, see above, p. 257, cf. also "smjǫr-tisdagr" = "Fat Tuesday," "Mardi gras"). That the fairylands were connected with

---

[1] It may also be worth mentioning that just as there is a Bjorno (Bjorno Lighthouse) near Landegode off Bodo, so is there mention of a Bjarn-ey near Markland on the way to "Vínland hit Góða." This may, of course, be purely a coincidence; but on the other hand there may be some connection.

[2] Cf. P. A. Save: Hafvets och Fiskarens Sagor, spridda drag ur Gotlands Odlingssaga och Strandallmogens Lif. Visby, 1880.

[3] Norske Gaardnavne. Forord og Indledning 1898, p. 39

WINELAND THE GOOD

fertility appears also from a Northern legend. Nordfugloi, to the north of Karlsoi, was once a troll-island, hidden under the sea and invisible to men, thus a " huldre " island. But then certain troll-hags betook themselves to towing it to land ; a Lapp hag who happened to cast her eye through the door-opening saw them come rowing with the island, so that the spray dashed over it, and cried : " Oh, what a good ' food-land ' we have now got ! " And thereupon the island stopped at the mouth of the sea, where it now is.[1] The fertility of fairyland is doubtless also expressed in the incident of the sow that finds it (see later), usually having a litter there. Its fertility appears again, perhaps, in H. Strøm's [1766, p. 436] mention of " Buskholm " (i.e., Bush-island) in Hero (Sunnmor), which was inhabited by underground beings and protected, therefore wholly overgrown with trees and bushes The Icelandic elfland " is delightful, covered with beautiful forests and sweet smelling flowers " [cf. Gróndal, 1863, p. 25], and the Irish is the same.

CHAPTER IX

Legends of islands and countries that disappeared or moved, like the fairylands, are widely diffused. To begin with, the Delos (cf. δηλόω, become visible) of the Greeks floated about in the sea for a long time, as described by Callimachus [v.] ; now the island was found, now it was away again, until it was fixed among the Cyclades. Ireland, which also at a very early time was the holy island (cf. p. 38), floated about in the sea at the time of the Flood. Lucas Debes [1673, pp. 19 ff.] relates that " at various times a floating island is said to have been seen " among the Faroes ; but no one can reach it. " The inhabitants also tell a fable of Svinoe,[2] how that in the beginning it was a floating island : and they think that if one could come to this island, which is often seen, and throw steel upon it, it would stand still. . . . Many things are related of such floating islands, and some think that they exist in nature." Debes does not believe it. " If this was not described of the properties of various islands, I should say that it was icebergs, which come floating from Greenland : and if that be not so, then I firmly believe that it is phantoms and witchcraft of the Devil, who in himself is a thousandfold craftsman." Erich Pontoppidan [1753, ii. p. 346] defends the devil and protests against this view of Debes, that it is " phantasmata and sorcery of the devil," and says : " But as, according to the wholesome rule, we ought to give the Devil his due, I think that the devil who in haste makes floating islands is none other than that Kraken, which some seamen also call ' Soe-Draulen,' that is, the sea troll."

Floating islands

Of Svinoi in the Faroes precisely the same legend exists as of similar islands in Norway (see p. 378), that they came " up," or became visible, through a sow upon which steel had been bound [cf. Hammershaimb, 1891, p 362].

In many places there are such disappearing islands. Honorius Augustodunensis makes some remarkable statements in his work " De imagine mundi " [i. 36], of about 1125. After mentioning the Balearic Isles and the Gorgades, he says :

---

[1] O. Nicolayssen : Fra Nordlands Fortid Kristiania, 1889, pp. 30 ff.

[2] Remark that thus in the Faroes Svinoi is also a fairy island, as in Sunnmor and at Bronoi in Norway.

IN NORTHERN MISTS

CHAPTER IX

"By the side of them [lie] the Hesperides, so called from the town of Hesperia. There is abundance of sheep with white wool, which is excellent for dyeing purple. Therefore the legend says that these islands have golden apples ('mala'). For 'miclon' [error for 'malon'] means sheep in Greek.[1] To these islands belonged the great island which according to the tale of Plato sank with its inhabitants, and which exceeded Africa and Europe in extent, where the curdled sea ('Concretum Mare') now is. . . . There lies also in the Ocean an island which is called the Lost ('Perdita'); in charm and all kinds of fertility it far surpasses every other land, but it is unknown to men. Now and again it may be found by chance; but if one seeks for it, it cannot be found, and therefore it is called 'the Lost.' Men say that it was this island that Brandanus came to." It is of special interest that thus as early as that time a disappearing island occurred near the Fortunate Isles.

Columbus says in his diary that the inhabitants of Ferro and Gomera (Canary Isles) assert that every year they see land to the west. Afterwards expeditions were even sent out to search for it. The Dutchman Van Linschoten speaks in 1589 of this beautiful lost land under the name of "San Borondon" (St. Brandan), a hundred leagues to the west of the Canaries. Its inhabitants are said to be Christians, but it is not known of what nation they are, or what language they speak;[2] the Spaniards of the Canaries have made many vain attempts to find it. The same island, which sometimes shows itself near the Canaries, but withdraws when one tries to approach it, still lives in Spanish folk-lore under the name of "San Morondon."[3]

On the coast of the English Channel sailors have stories of floating islands, which many of them have seen with their own eyes. They always fly before ships, and one can never land there. They are drawn along by the devil, who compels the souls of drowned men who have deserved Hell and are damned, to stay there till the Day of Judgment. On some of them the roar of a terrible beast

---

[1] This astonishing etymological explanation of the ancient Phœnician legendary islands of the Hesperides is evidently due to a confusion of Brandan's sheep-island with Pliny's statements [Nat Hist, vi. 36] about the purple islands off Africa (near the Hesperides) which King Juba was said to have discovered, and where he learned dyeing with Gætulian purple. The idea that the sunken land Atlantis was where the "Concretum Mare" now is may be connected with the Greek myth which appears in Plutarch (see above, pp. 156 and 182) of Cronos lying imprisoned in sleep on an island in the north-west in the Cronian Sea (= "Mare Concretum"), where also the great continent was, and where the sea was heavy and thick.

[2] This is the same myth as that of Hvítramanna-land in the Eyrbyggja Saga; see later.

[3] Cf. A. Guichot y Sierra, 1884, 1. p. 296; Dumont d'Urville: Voyage autour du monde, 1. p 27. The same idea that the island withdraws when one tries to approach it appears also in Lucian's description (in the Vera Historia) of the Isle of Dreams.

WINELAND THE GOOD

is heard; and sailors look upon the meeting with such an island as a sinister warning [1]

Curiously enough, there is said to be a myth of "a floating island" among the Iroquois Indians. In their mythology the earth is due to the Indian ruler of a great island which floats in space, and where there is eternal peace. In its abundance there are no burdens to bear, in its fertility all want is for ever precluded. Death never comes to its eternal quietude—and no desire, no sorrow, no pain disturbs its peace.[2] These ideas remind one strikingly of the Isles of the Blest, and are probably derived from European influence in recent times. Again, at Boston, in America, there is found a myth of an enchanted green land out in the sea to the east; it flies when one approaches, and no white man can reach this island, which is called "the island that flies." An Indian, the last of his tribe, saw it a few times before his death, and set out in his canoe to row, as he said, to the isle of happy spirits. He disappeared in a storm the like of which had never been known, and after this the enchanted island was never seen again [cf. Sébillot, 1886, p. 349].

Even the Chinese have legends of the Isles of the Blest, which lie 700 miles from the Celestial Kingdom out in the Yellow Sea, and gleam in everlasting beauty, everlasting spring and everlasting gladness. The wizard Sun-Tshe is said once to have extorted from a good spirit the secret of their situation, and revealed the great mystery to the emperor Tshe-Huan-Ti (219 B.C.). Then the noblest youths and the most beautiful maidens of the Celestial Kingdom set out to search for Paradise, and lo! it suddenly rose above the distant horizon, wrapped in roseate glow. But a terrible storm drove the longing voyagers away with cruel violence, and since then no human eye has seen the Isles of the Blest [after Paul d'Enjoy, in "La Revue"].[3]

This is the same conception of the floating mirage that we meet with again in the Norse term "Villuland" (from "villa" = illusion, mirage, glamour), which is found, for instance, in Bjorn Jónsson of Skardsá applied to the fabulous country of Frisland (south of Iceland); it is called in one MS. "Villi-Skotland," which is probably the mythical "Irland it Mikla" (Great-Ireland), since the Irish were called Scots. Are Mársson, according to the Landnáma, reached this "Villuland" and stayed there. It is remarkable that his mother Katla, according to the Icelandic legend in the poem "Kǫtlu-draumr" (Katla's dream), was stolen by an elf-man, who kept her for four nights.[4] It may be this circumstance that led to its being Are who found the elf-country to the west of Ireland, although it is true that according to the Kǫtlu-draumr it was his one-year-older brother

CHAPTER IX

---

[1] Cf. P. Sébillot, 1886, p. 348.

[2] Cf. Harriet Maxwell Converse: Iroquois Myths and Legends. Education Department Bulletin, No. 437, Albany, N.Y., December 1908, pp. 31 f.

[3] My attention has been drawn to this by Mr. Gunnar Olsen. Similar myths are found in Japan [cf. D. Brauns, Japanische Marchen und Sagen, 1885, pp. 146 ff.].

[4] Grønl. hist. Mind., i. pp. 144 f., 157 ff.

IN NORTHERN MISTS

CHAPTER IX

Fairylands which rise and fall

Kar who was the offspring of the four nights; but the elf-man had asked that his son should be called Are.

There are many such fairylands along the coast of Norway, which used to rise up from the sea at night, but sank in the daytime.[1] If one could bring fire or steel upon them, then the spell was broken and they remained up; but the huldre-folk avenged themselves on the person who did this, and he was turned to stone; therefore it was usually accomplished by domestic animals which swam across to these islands. Many of them have come up in this way, and for this reason they frequently bear the names of animals. The most probable explanation is doubtless that they were originally given the names of animals from a similarity in shape, or some other reason; and the myth is a later interpretation of the name. It was often a pig, preferably a sow, that had acquired the habit of swimming over to the fairyland, and it frequently had litters there; the people of the farm, who noticed that it occasionally stayed away, bound steel upon it, and the island was hindered from sinking; "therefore such fairy islands are often called Svinoi." In this way Svinoi in Bronoi (in Nordland, Norway) came up, as well as Svinoi in the Faroes, and doubtless it was the same with Svinöi or Landegode in Sunnmor. It was also through a sow that Tautra, in Trondhjemsfjord, was raised, besides Jomfruland, and the north-western part of Andoi (in Vesterålen). Nay, even Oland in Limfjord (Jutland) became visible through a sow with steel bound on it, which had a litter. Other islands, like Vega and Solen, were raised by a horse or an ox, etc. Gotland was also a fairyland, but it stayed up through a man bringing fire to it.[2] Some fairy islands lie so far out at sea that no domestic animal has been able to swim over to them, and therefore they have not yet come up; such are Utröst, west of Lofoten, Sandflesa, west of Trænen, Utvega, west of Vega, Hillerei-oi, and Ytter-Sklinna, in Nordre Trondhjems Amt, and hidden fairylands off Utsire, off Lister, and to the south-west of Jomfruland.[3]

It is interesting that the notion of a sow being the cause of people coming into possession of fertile islands can also be illustrated from mediæval England. William of Malmesbury relates in his "De antiquitate Glastoniensis ecclesiæ" [cap. 1 and 2], which belongs to the twelfth century before 1143, that Glasteing ". . . went in search of his sow as far as Wellis, and followed her from Wellis by a difficult and boggy path, that is called 'Sugewege,' that is to say, 'the sow's

---

[1] This belongs to the same cycle of ideas as that of the dead rising from their graves or from the lower regions at night, but being obliged to go down again at dawn, or of trolls having to conceal themselves before the sun rises. In the same way, too, the fallen Helge Hundingsbane comes to Sigrun and sleeps with her in the mound; but when the flush of day comes he has to ride back to the west of "Vindhjelms" bridge, before Salgovne awakes. It has been pointed out above (p. 371) that the Phæacians of the Odyssey sail at night.

[2] According to the "Guta-saga" of the thirteenth century.

[3] Cf. Moltke Moe's communications in A. Helland, Nordlands Amt, 1907, ii. pp. 512 ff. In Brinck's Descriptio Loufodiæ [1676, p. 11] it is stated that the mythical land of Utrost in Nordland was called "Huldeland."

way'; at last he found her occupied in suckling her young beneath the apple-tree beside the church of which we are speaking; from this are derived the names that have come down to our time, that the apples of this tree are called 'ealdcyrcenes epple,' that is to say, 'the apples of the old church,' and the sow 'ealdcyrce suge.' While other sows have four feet, this one, strangely enough, has eight. This Glasteing, then, who came to this island and saw that it was flowing with all good things, brought all his family and established himself there and dwelt there all his life. This place is said to be populated from his offspring and the race that sprang from him. This is taken from the ancient writings of the Britons.

"Of various names for this island. This island, then, was first called by the Britons 'Ynisgwtrin'; later, when the Angles subdued the island, the name was translated into their language as 'Glastynbury' or Glasteing's town, he of whom we have been speaking The island also bears the famous name of 'Avallonia.' The origin of this word is the following: as we have related, Glasteing found his sow under an apple-tree by the old church; therefore he called ... the island in his language 'Avallonia,' that is 'The isle of apples' (for 'avalla' in British means 'poma' in Latin). ... Or else the island has its name from a certain Avalloc, who is said to have dwelt here with his daughters on account of the solitude of the place."[1]

This Somerset sow with its young and with eight legs, like Sleipner, must be Norse. The Norse myth of the sow must have found a favourable soil among the Celts, as according to the ideas of Celtic mythology the pig was a sacred animal in the religion of the Druids, specially connected with Ceridwen, the goddess of the lower world. The Celts must have heard of the pig that by the help of steel causes fairylands to remain visible; but regarded this as being connected with the animal's sacred properties. It cannot have been an originally Celtic conception, otherwise we should meet with it in other Celtic legends. Moreover the island in this case is not invisible, nor has the sow any steel upon her; these are features that have been lost in transmission. On the other hand the incident of the sow becoming pregnant in the newly found land has been preserved.

In the ocean to the west of Ireland there lay, as already mentioned (p. 354), many enchanted islands. They are in part derived from classical and oriental myths; but the native fairies (the sid-people) and fairylands have been introduced here also (p. 371). Even in the lakes of Ireland there are hidden islands, marvellously fertile with beautiful flowers[2] Giraldus Cambrensis (twelfth century) says that on clear days an island appeared to the west of Ireland, but vanished when people approached it. At last some came within bowshot, and one of the sailors shot a red-hot arrow on to it, and the island then remained fixed. The happy island "O'Brasil" ("Hy-Breasail," see p. 357) west of Ireland appears above the sea once in every seventh year—"on the edge of the azure sea . . ." and it would stay up if any one could cast fire upon it[3]

---

[1] Cf. F. Lot, "Romania," 1898, p. 530. Moltke Moe has also communicated to me this curious tale.   [2] Cf. P. Crofton Croker, 1828, ii. p. 259 f.
[3] Cf. "Lageniensis," 1870, pp 114 ff., 294; Joyce, 1879, p. 408 V Bérard

IN NORTHERN MISTS

CHAPTER IX

It is no doubt possible that myths of "villulands" or "huldrelands" far away in the sea may have arisen in various places independently of one another;[1] they may easily be suggested by mirage or other natural phenomena, and ideas about happiness are universal among men. But through many of these myths may be traced features so similar that we can discern a connection with certainty and can draw conclusions as to a common origin of the same conceptions.

The epithet "the Lucky"

That Leif of all others, the discoverer of the fortunate land, should have received the unusual surname of "hinn Heppni" (the Lucky) is also striking. There is only one other man in the sagas who is called thus: Họgni hinn Heppni, and he belongs to the period of the Iceland land-taking, but is only mentioned in a pedigree. Just as according to ancient Greek ideas and in the oldest Irish legends it was only vouchsafed to the chosen of the gods or of fortune to reach Elysium or the isle of the happy ones, so Leif, who according to tradition was the apostle of Christianity in Greenland, must have been regarded by the Christians of Iceland as the favourite of God or of destiny, to whom it was ordained to see the land of fortune. It is just this idea of the chosen of fate that lies in the words "happ" and "heppinn." That the name has such an origin is also rendered probable by the fact that the saga-tellers were evidently not clear as to the reason of Leif's being so called, and it is sometimes represented as due to his having saved the shipwrecked crew (cf. pp. 270, 317), which is meaningless, since in that case it would be the rescued and not Leif who

[1902, i. p. 286] explains the Roman name "Ispania" (Spain) as coming from a Semitic (Phœnician) root "sapan" (= hide, cover) denoting "the isle of the hidden one," which he thinks originally meant Calypso's isle; this he seeks to locate on the African coast near Gibraltar. The explanation seems very doubtful, but if there be anything in it, it is remarkable that Spain, the land rich in silver and gold, should have a name that recalls the huldre-lands (lands of the hidden ones).

[1] Cf. E. B. Tylor: Primitive Culture, 1891, ii. pp. 63 ff.

WINELAND THE GOOD

were lucky, and moreover rescue of shipwrecked sailors must have been an everyday affair. The saga-writers therefore knew that Leif had this surname, but the reason for it had in course of time been forgotten.

An interesting parallel to "Leifr hinn Heppni" has been brought to my notice by Moltke Moe in the Nordland "Lykk-Anders," the name of the lucky brother who came to the fairyland Sandflesa, off Trænen in Helgeland.[1] It is important that this epithet of Lucky is thus only known in Norway in connection with fairyland.[2] That the underground people, "huldrefolk," bring luck appears also in other superstitions.[3] He who is born with the cap of victory (Glückshaube, -helm, sigurkull, holyhow), which often seems to have the same effect as the fairy hat, is predestined to fortune and prosperity, like a Sunday child.

Another possible parallel to the lucky name is the monk "Felix" (i.e., happy, corresponding to "heppinn") who occurs in widely diffused mediæval legends. He has a foretaste of the joys of heaven through hearing a bird of paradise; he thinks that only a few hours have passed, from morning to midday, while he is listening to it in rapture, though in reality a hundred years have gone by.[4] Moltke Moe considers it probable that in this case the name Felix may be due to a Germanic conception of the lucky one.

Moltke Moe sees another parallel—a literary one, to be sure—to Leif the Lucky and Lykk-Anders in the Olaf Åsteson of the "Draumkvæde" (Dream-Lay)

---

[1] Asbjornsen: Huldre-Eventyr og Folke-Sagn, 3rd ed, pp. 343 ff.; "Tufte-folket på Sandflæsen." Cf. also Moltke Moe's note in A. Helland: Nordlands Amt, i. pp. 519 f.

[2] The name of "Lycko-Pär" in Sweden for one who "has luck" [Th. Hielmqvist, Fornamn och Familjenamn med sekundar anvandning i Nysvenskan, Lund, 1903, p. 267] has come from the Danish "Lykke-Per," which is a purely literary production, and does not concern us here.

[3] In Norway the "nisse" brings luck. "Lycko-nisse" in Småland (Sweden) is a "luck-bringing brownie. Also used occasionally of little friendly children" [Th. Hielmqvist, 1903, p. 224].

[4] Cf. Moltke Moe's communications in A. Helland: Nordlands Amt, 1907, ii. pp. 596 f.

IN NORTHERN MISTS

CHAPTER IX

which he explains as "Ástsonr" = the son of love, God's beloved son. He is so called because he is so beloved that God has given him a glimpse of the future, so that he sees behind the gate of death.[1]

All this, therefore, points in the same direction.

The oldest authority, Adam of Bremen, untrustworthy

Even Adam of Bremen's brief mention of Wineland (cf. pp. 195, 197) bears evident traces of being untrustworthy ; thus he says that the self-grown vines in Wineland "give the noblest wine." Even if wine could be produced from the small wild grapes, it would scarcely be noble, and who should have made it ? It is not very likely that the Icelanders and Greenlanders who discovered the country had any idea of making wine. If we except this fable of the wine, and the name itself, which seems to be derived from Ireland (cf. p. 366), but may have been confused with the name of Finland[2] (cf. p. 198), then Adam's statements about Wineland correspond entirely to Isidore's description of the Insulæ Fortunatæ, and contain nothing new. Adam's statement that the island was discovered by many ("multis") does not agree with the Saga of Eric the Red, which only knows of two voyages thither, but agrees better with its being a well-known mythical country, to which many mythical voyages had been made, or with its being Finmark.[2] Although it may be uncertain whether Adam thought the ice- and mist-filled sea lay beyond Wineland (cf. p. 199), this bears a remarkable resemblance to similar Arab myths of islands that lay near the "Dark Sea" in the west (cf. chapter xiii.) ; while in any case it shows how myth is introduced into his description of distant regions, and there also he places the mythical abyss of the sea. If one reads through the conclusion of his account (pp. 192 ff.), it will be seen how he takes pains to get a gradual increase of the

---

[1] Conceptions of a somewhat similar nature appear in the legends of Arthur, where only the pure, or innocent, are permitted to see the Holy Grail.

[2] The names Finmark (the land of the Finns or Lapps) and Finland were often confused in the Middle Ages (cf. Geographia Universalis, Eulogium, Polychronicon, Edrisi), and the latter again with Wineland (cf. Ordericus Vitalis, Polychronicon) It should be remarked that Adam does not know the name "Finn," but only "Finnédi" and "Scritefini."

WINELAND THE GOOD

fabulous: first Iceland with the black inflammable ice and the "simple" communistic inhabitants; then, opposite to the mountains of Svedia, Greenland, with predatory inhabitants who turn blue-green in the face from the sea-water; then Halagland, which is made into an island in the ocean, and which is called holy on account of the midnight sun, of which he gives erroneous information taken from older authors (cf. p. 194, note 2); then Wineland (the Fortunate Isles), with Isidore's self-grown vines and unsown corn; and then finally he reaches the highest pitch (unless in Harold's voyage to the abyss of the sea) in the tale of the Frisian noblemen's voyage to the North Pole, which does not contain a feature that is not borrowed from fables and myths (cf. chapter xii.); now this expedition started from Bremen, where he lived; and he mentions two archbishops as his authorities for it. When we find that all these statements about the northern islands and countries, both before and after the mention of Wineland, are more or less fables or plagiarisms; when we further see what he was capable of relating about countries that lay nearer, and about which he might easily have obtained information—for instance, his Land of Women on the Baltic, to which he transfers the Amazons and Cynocephali of the Greeks (cf. p. 187), and his Wizzi or Albanians or Alanians (sic) with battle-array of dogs (!) in Russia [iv. 19][1]—is it credible that what he says about the most distant country, Wineland, should form the only exception in this concatenation of fable and reminiscence, and suddenly be genuine and not borrowed from Isidore, to whom it bears such a striking resemblance? It must be more probable that he had heard a name, Wineland, perhaps confused with Finland, and in the belief that this meant the

CHAPTER IX

---

[1] It must be remembered that Kvænland (Woman-land), like Norway and "the island of Halagland" (!), were neighbouring countries to Sweden, where King Svein had lived for twelve years, the same who is supposed to have told Adam so much about the countries of the North; and between Sweden and Russia (Gardarike) there was also active communication at that time

IN NORTHERN MISTS

land of wine, he then, quite in harmony with what he has done in other places (cf. Kvænland), transferred thereto Isidore's description of the "Insulæ Fortunatæ."

When therefore Norsemen (like a Leif Ericson) really found new countries in the west, precisely in the quarter where the mythical "Vínland hit Góða" (or "Insulæ Fortunatæ") should be according to Irish legend, this was simply a proof that the country did exist; and the tales and ideas about it were transferred to the newly discovered land.

END OF VOL I.

PRINTED BY
BALLANTYNE & COMPANY LTD
TAVISTOCK ST COVENT GARDEN
LONDON